Substance Abuse and Dependence in Adolescence

Recent years have seen a growth in the numbers of studies of substance abuse and dependence in adolescence, focusing on prevalence, risk factors, comorbidity, course and outcome. At the same time, numerous prevention and intervention strategies have been developed. *Substance Abuse and Dependence in Adolescence* presents a comprehensive review of state-of-the-art empirical and practical information on this topic.

Cecilia A. Essau, along with an eminent group of international researchers and clinicians, summarizes the most recent empirical findings and state-of-the-art knowledge on substance abuse and dependence in adolescence and includes comprehensive information on prevention and treatment. *Substance Abuse and Dependence in Adolescence* contains:

- General issues related to substance use disorders
- Epidemiology, comorbidity, course, outcome and risk factors
- The prevention of and interventions for substance abuse and dependence
- A discussion of progress and unresolved issues in substance use disorders
- Recommendations for future studies in the field

Substance Abuse and Dependence in Adolescence will be an invaluable resource for students, researchers, and other professionals working in the fields of psychology, psychiatry, paediatrics, social work, and other mental health professions.

Cecilia A. Essau is an Associate Professor in Psychology and Head of the Unit of Developmental Psychopathology at the University of Münster, Germany. She has published extensively in the areas of anxiety, substance use and depressive disorders.

Substance Abuse and Dependence in Adolescence

Epidemiology, risk factors and treatment

Edited by Cecilia A. Essau

First published 2002
by Brunner-Routledge
27 Church Road, Hove, East Sussex BN3 2FA

Simultaneously published in the USA and Canada
by Taylor & Francis Inc
29 West 35th Street, New York, NY 10001

Brunner-Routledge is an imprint of the Taylor & Francis Group

© 2002 Editorial matter and selection Cecilia A. Essau; individual chapters, the contributors

Typeset in Times by M Rules
Printed and bound in Great Britain by Biddles Ltd, Guildford and King's Lynn

Cover design by Louise Page

All rights reserved. No part of this book may be reprinted or reproduced or utilized in any form or by any electronic, mechanical, or other means, now known or hereafter invented, including photocopying and recording, or in any information storage or retrieval system, without permission in writing from the publishers.

British Library Cataloguing in Publication Data
A catalogue record for this book is available from the British Library

Library of Congress Cataloging-in-Publication Data
Substance abuse and dependence in adolescence/[edited by] Cecilia A. Essau.
 p. cm.
 Includes bibliographical references and index.
 ISBN 1-58391-262-2 — ISBN 1-58391-263-0 (pbk.)
  1. Teenagers—Substance use. 2. Substance abuse—Treatment.
  3. Narcotic habit—Treatment. I. Essau, Cecilia.

RJ506.D78 S83 2002
362.29′0835—dc21   2001052716

ISBN 1-58391-262-2 (hbk)
ISBN 1-58391-263-0 (pbk)

Contents

List of illustrations		vii
List of contributors		ix
Preface		xiii

1 Substance use and adolescence 1
GERALD ADAMS, ANNE-MARIE CANTWELL, AND
SHAWN MATHEIS

2 Classification and assessment 21
TY A. RIDENOUR, PATRICIA FAZZONE,
AND LINDA B. COTTLER

3 Epidemiology and comorbidity 63
CECILIA A. ESSAU, HUBERT STIGLER, AND JOSEF SCHEIPL

4 Risk factors 87
TERRI N. SULLIVAN AND ALBERT D. FARRELL

5 Course and outcome 119
ERIC F. WAGNER AND SUSAN M. TAROLLA

6 Prevention 143
MARK R. DADDS AND JOHN MCALOON

7 Psychological intervention 183
ROBERT J. WILLIAMS

8 Family-based therapy 201
TIMOTHY J. OZECHOWSKI AND HOWARD A. LIDDLE

9 **Concluding remarks** 225
CECILIA A. ESSAU, PAULA BARRETT, AND KERRY
A. MARSH

Index 239

Illustrations

Tables

2.1	Symptoms of substance use dependence diagnoses	28
2.2	Symptoms of withdrawal diagnoses	29
2.3	Abuse versus harmful use diagnoses	31
2.4	Intoxication diagnoses	32
2.5	Characteristics of a good diagnostic interview for substance use-related disorders	37
3.1	Frequency of substance use disorders in adolescents	73
3.2	Frequency of substance use disorders based on DSM-IV criteria	76
3.3	Comorbidity of substance use disorders with other disorders	78
3.4	Comorbidity within the substance use disorders	79
6.1	Risk and protective factors in the development of SUDs	148
6.2	Developmental risk factors for externalizing disorders and associated intervention opportunities	149
6.3	Developmental risk factors for anxiety disorders and associated intervention strategies	156
9.1	Assessment of risk and protective factors in substance use disorders	229
9.2	Trends in the prevention and intervention of substance use disorders	234

Figures

2.1	Page 27 from the latest version of the SAM	41
7.1	Dimensions upon which formal treatment programmes vary	184
7.2	Percentage of adolescents with sustained abstinence as a function of time since discharge	188

Contributors

Gerald Adams
Department of Family Relations and Applied Nutrition
College of Social and Applied Human Sciences
University of Guelph
Guelph, Ontario, Canada N1G 2W1

Paula Barrett
Senior Lecturer and Clinic Director, Psychology
Griffith University, Gold Coast Campus
PMB 50 Gold Coast mail centre
Queensland 9726, Australia

Anne-Marie Cantwell
Department of Family Relations and Applied Nutrition
University of Guelph
Guelph, Ontario, Canada N1G 2W1

Linda B. Cottler
Washington University School of Medicine
Department of Psychiatry
40 N. Kingshighway, Suite 4
St Louis, MO 63108, USA

Mark R. Dadds
Griffith University
Brisbane, Queensland 4111, Australia

Cecilia A. Essau
Westfälische Wilhelms-Universität Münster
Psychologisches Institut I
Fliednerstr. 21
48149 Münster, Germany

Albert D. Farrell
Department of Psychology
Virginia Commonwealth University
PO Box 842018
Richmond, VA 23284-2018, USA

Patricia Fazzone
Washington University School of Medicine
Department of Psychiatry
40 N. Kingshighway, Suite 4
St Louis, MO 63108, USA

Howard A. Liddle
Director, Center for Treatment Research on Adolescent Drug Abuse
University of Miami School of Medicine
PO Box 019132
Miami, FL 33101, USA

Shawn Matheis
Department of Family Relations and Applied Nutrition
University of Guelph
Guelph, Ontario, Canada N1G 2W1

John McAloon
Griffith University
Brisbane, Queensland, 4111, Australia

Timothy J. Ozechowski
Caliber Associates
10530 Rosehaven Street, Suite 400
Fairfax, VA 22030, USA

Kerry A. Marsh
Griffith University, Gold Coast Campus
PMB 50 Gold Coast mail centre
Queensland 9726, Australia

Ty A. Ridenour
Washington University School of Medicine
Department of Psychiatry
40 N. Kingshighway, Suite 4
St Louis, MO 63108, USA

Josef Scheipl
Karl-Franzens-Universität Graz
Institut für Erziehungs- und Bildungswissenschaften
Merangasse 70/II
8010 Graz, Austria

Hubert Stigler
Karl-Franzens-Universität Graz
Institut für Erziehungs- und Bildungswissenschaften
Merangasse 70/II
8010 Graz, Austria

Terri N. Sullivan
Department of Psychology
PO Box 842018
Virginia Commonwealth University
Richmond, VA 23284-2018, USA

Susan M. Tarolla
College of Health and Urban Affairs
Florida International University
Biscayne Bay Campus, AC-1, Suite 200
North Miami, FL 33181-3600, USA

Eric F. Wagner
College of Health and Urban Affairs
Florida International University
Biscayne Bay Campus, AC-1, Suite 200
North Miami, FL 33181-3600, USA

Robert J. Williams
School of Health Sciences
University of Lethbridge
Lethbridge, Alberta, Canada T1K 3M4

Preface

Interest in studying substance use disorders (SUD) among adolescents has been spurred by recent findings among adults: (a) SUD has an age of onset in adolescence; (b) the presence of SUD in adolescence tends to increase a risk for developing comorbid disorders in adulthood; and (c) SUD is associated with psychosocial impairment in various life areas. As described in various chapters in this volume, heavy substance consumption or SUD is involved in traffic accidents, suicide and violence, teenage pregnancy, and sexually transmitted diseases, etc. Less dramatic but more insidious consequences of substance dependence in adolescence include its developmental, emotional, and social costs. The magnitude of these problems has led to much initiative and increased funding to examine the nature of SUD as well as to research related to the prevention of and interventions for SUD. Therefore, numerous studies have been conducted by various governmental agencies and research groups throughout the world. Consequently, literature on SUD in adolescents has been accumulating at a very fast pace. So the aim of this book is to provide a comprehensive summary of the state-of-the-art information on SUD in adolescents which is scientifically (e.g., prevalence and comorbidity rates, risk factors of SUD) and clinically relevant (e.g., choice of treatment and treatment guidelines) for mental health professionals.

Contributors to this volume have been carefully selected and are leading experts in their respective areas. The first five chapters of the book cover some basic information and serve as an introduction to the field of SUD, including the role of substance use in adolescence, classification and assessment, epidemiology and comorbidity, risk factors, and the course and outcome of SUD. The next three chapters deal with various types of prevention and intervention strategies used in adolescents. The last chapter briefly discusses some progress and unresolved issues in SUD and provides some recommendations for future studies in this field.

This volume is conceptualized as a tool for advanced students, researchers, and other professionals working in the fields of psychiatry, psychology, paediatrics, social work, and other mental health professions. Researchers, advanced students, and professionals working in clinical practice will find this book useful because of its wide coverage, ranging from epidemiology and risk factors to interventions for the subtypes of substance use and SUD. It is hoped that this volume will not only serve to illustrate our current knowledge of SUD, but will also stimulate and facilitate further progress in this field. This in turn may contribute to an improved understanding of SUD in adolescents.

As editor of this book, I wish to acknowledge the efforts of the contributors, whose expertise and dedication to the project have been outstanding. Without them, a comprehensive coverage of the various topics would not have been easily achieved. Additionally, I wish to acknowledge the support and patience of the staff at Brunner-Routledge.

Cecilia A. Essau

Chapter 1

Substance use and adolescence

Gerald Adams, Anne-Marie Cantwell, and Shawn Matheis

Adolescence is defined as the life stage between childhood and adulthood; in a hurried society the media pushes images of teenage behaviour at an early age. At the opposite end many adolescents are not sure when they become adults. Gullotta and colleagues (2000) indicate the three essential elements associated with adulthood by many life span theorists are financial independence, gainful employment and marriage. The end of adolescence may require occasional modification of emerging ideas of the age range associated with this period of life. Though this period is often described as including the time from the onset of puberty to the late teen years, Arnett (1992) describes adolescence as puberty to the early 20s because in American culture, adolescence is viewed as the "time from the beginning of puberty until adult responsibilities are taken on" (p. 340). The emphasis of education in our society has resulted in many more youth remaining financially dependent and unemployed while pursuing post-secondary school experiences thus remaining in the stage of adolescence for extended periods (Côté and Allahar, 1994).

Compared to other life stages, adolescence is a period characterized by an amplified capability for behaviours that have potentially dangerous outcomes (Arnett, 1992; Gullone *et al.*, 2000). Bingham and colleagues (1994) have described the period between 14 and 22 as the greatest window of vulnerability for risk consequences across the life span. Such risk-taking, thrill-seeking, and reckless behaviours have received a great deal of attention in research particularly in the last decade (Arnett, 1992, 1996; Gonzalez *et al.*, 1994; Lavery *et al.*, 1993; Levitt *et al.*, 1991). Included in this phenomenon of increased risk-taking are behaviours such as minor criminal activity, sexual activity, reckless driving, problem gambling, alcohol consumption, and drug use. The dramatic outcomes include incarceration, disease, and possibly death. For the purposes of this chapter we will focus on the last two, alcohol consumption and drug use. However, it is important to acknowledge that alcohol and drug use often accompanies the additional behaviours noted above. It is rare that adolescents will engage in only a single risk behaviour; rather adolescents are likely to participate in a variety or composite of such behaviours (Jessor *et al.*, 1991; Jessor and Jessor, 1977).

RELATED DEFINITIONS

The definitions of adolescent substance use and misuse have been the subject of active debate among scholars and clinicians alike, as well as in the media, between various political interests, and in the homes of ordinary families (Bukstein and Kaminer, 1994). As with many definitional concerns, the complexity of defining substance use and abuse in relation to adolescence stems from a variety of sources. Differing beliefs surrounding adolescent use of drugs and alcohol in western cultures is one of the major factors confusing this issue (Gilvarry, 2000). The definition and subsequent diagnosis of substance use disorders is further complicated by the differing effects of various substances on the user (Giancola and Tarter, 1999) and the frequent comorbidity of substance misuse with other mental health disorders (Costello *et al.*, 1999). Accentuating this confusion is the fact that illegal alcohol use is extremely common in adolescence, and in the majority of cases tapers off in early adulthood without the need for intervention (Cole and Weissberg, 1995), a pattern which some have suggested is a normative developmental trend (Baumrind, 1991; Bukstein and Kaminer, 1994; Newcomb and Bentler, 1989).

The complexities in the debate over defining substance use and misuse are belied by the seriousness of the issue. Substance use disorders in adolescence are associated with many problems, including poor academic performance, increased rates of school dropouts, juvenile delinquency, sexual promiscuity, early pregnancy, impaired driving, family difficulties, and mental health concerns including depression and suicide (Gilvarry, 2000). In 1999, emergency rooms in the United States were filled with an estimated 52,783 youths between the ages of 12 and 17, and an estimated 10,580 young adults between the ages of 18 and 25 for medical emergencies related to drug use, marking a steep rise from the same estimates in 1992 (Substance Abuse and Mental Health Services Administration, 2000b). Some authors claim that the problems in defining substance use and misuse have hampered efforts to effectively measure these concepts, and to recommend preventative or treatment strategies concerning substance use based on such outcomes (Bukstein and Kaminer, 1994).

THE TWO TAXONOMIES: DSM-IV AND ICD-10

The definitions of substance use disorders that are currently the most widely accepted are those identified in the *Diagnostic and Statistic Manual of Mental Disorders—IV* (DSM-IV) and the *International Statistical Classification of Diseases and Related Health Problems*, tenth edition (ICD-10). These two classification systems are similar in many respects (see also Chapter 2 in this volume). Both systems classify substance abuse into two separate categories, dependence and either abuse (DSM-IV) or harmful use (ICD-10). In both cases, dependence includes a component indicating the presence of tolerance and/or withdrawal, as well as an indication that the user cannot control the use of the substance and that the use of the substance is having a negative and tangible effect on the user's life. Finally, of particular importance to our discussion is that both systems also adopt the same criteria for diagnosis regardless of the user's age (Rounsaville *et al.*, 1993).

The most important difference between the DSM-IV and the ICD-10 is in the diagnoses of abuse and harmful use. A diagnosis of substance abuse can be made in the DSM-IV if any of the following criteria are present to a clinically significant degree due to substance use: the user is unable to fulfil major role obligations, encounters legal or interpersonal problems, gives up important activities, or uses substances in situations where they are physically hazardous. By contrast, diagnosis of harmful use in the ICD-10 requires evidence that substance use is causing psychological or physical harm to the user (Rounsaville *et al.*, 1993). Not surprisingly, diagnoses can vary based on which classification system is used. Rounsaville *et al.* (1993) studied the cross-system agreement in diagnoses of substance use disorders between the DSM-IV, ICD-10, and DSM-III-R. The findings showed a reasonable level of concordance between the DSM-IV and the ICD-10 on dependence, but highly discordant diagnoses of substance abuse as opposed to harmful use. Overall, the sample was much more likely to be diagnosed with substance abuse rather than harmful use. This effect was particularly strong for users of alcohol and marijuana (Rounsaville *et al.*, 1993). The difference between these two definitions is of particular importance in diagnosing substance use disorders in adolescents, given that some of the criteria for substance abuse in the DSM-IV are common experiences for young people. In a recent study of undergraduate students, there was a 24.5% lifetime prevalence of substance abuse or dependence as defined by the DSM-IV, while only 4% of the sample had ever sought out substance abuse treatment (Clements, 1999).

While the DSM-IV and ICD-10 definitions of substance use disorders are the most widely used and accepted, many aspects of these definitions have been criticized, particularly as they apply to adolescents. The current definitions have been derived largely on the basis of clinical and empirical work with adults who have been diagnosed as having substance use disorders, and some researchers have questioned their validity in using such measures when diagnosing such disorders in adolescents (Gilvarry, 2000; Bukstein and Kaminer, 1994). Many studies done to validate the definition provided by the DSM-IV with adolescents were mainly designed to test whether abuse and dependence really were two separate disorders, and much of this research has produced mixed results. A wide body of research has found the DSM-IV criteria to be supported in the diagnosis of substance use disorders in adolescence (Kaminer and Bukstein, 1998). For example, a one-year longitudinal study involving 1,507 Oregon high school students found that

DSM-IV criteria were highly effective in differentiating between adolescents with normative and pathological functioning related to substance use (Lewinsohn *et al.*, 1996). However, Fulkerson and colleagues (1999) found in a study using a sample of 18,803 high school students in Minnesota that substance abuse and dependence did not provide major differences in diagnosis. Nelson and colleagues (1999) studied DSM-IV classifications of substance use and abuse on a sample of 1,272 adolescents and adults from eight regions around the world, and found that substance abuse and dependence were valid as separate diagnoses for some substances and not in relation to others.

CRITICAL ISSUES IN DEFINING ADOLESCENT SUBSTANCE USE AND MISUSE

Beyond issues regarding the utility of the DSM-IV and ICD-10 in defining and diagnosing substance use disorders in adolescence, there are also several critical issues that have been raised concerning substance use and misuse in adolescence that impact on the nature of definitions. These issues include whether features of substance use and misuse are unique to adolescence, and contrasting ideas over what constitutes substance misuse in adolescence.

There is a fairly active debate regarding whether substance use and misuse can be defined by the same criteria in adolescence and adulthood. Those who are in favour of the idea that substance use and misuse are unique in adolescence usually argue that many adolescents exhibiting characteristics of substance use disorder are going through an exploratory period during which ideas and behaviours consistent with appropriate substance use are developing (Bukstein and Kaminer, 1994). Research on general populations of adolescents has shown that the vast majority of the symptoms of substance use disorder spontaneously remit as adolescents move into adulthood (Bukstein and Kaminer, 1994; Warner *et al.*, 1995), and that of those who show evidence of problem substance use behaviour in adolescence, only a small fraction will show continued problems with substance abuse in adulthood (Gilvarry, 2000).

However, others argue that while there are developmental and contextual factors unique to adolescence that should be considered, the overall definitions of substance use disorder that apply to adults also apply to adolescents. Proponents of this point of view point out that assessments of substance misuse based on definitions in the DSM-IV, which was based on disorders in adults, have been also shown to reliably diagnose substance use disorders in adolescents as well (Lewinsohn *et al.*, 1996). Diagnoses of substance use disorders in adolescence have also been shown to be predictive of the same disorder in adulthood. For example, in the Epidemiological Catchment Area study, 35% of adults with lifetime diagnoses of alcohol abuse/dependence had shown their first symptoms between the ages of 15 and 19 years (Helzer *et al.*, 1991). Overall, the literature suggests that while many adolescents engage in substance use behaviours who do not develop disorders, there is still considerable overlap between substance misuse in adolescence and adulthood.

A second and very important issue is what criteria should be used in determining substance use and misuse in adolescence. One criterion used has been amount or frequency of the substance used, with the main distinction made being between occasional use and abuse (e.g., Hillman and Sawilowsky, 1992; Tarter *et al.*, 1997). However, concerns have been raised about both of these methods. It has been argued convincingly that while information regarding the quantity of a substance consumed is useful, it does not give reliable information regarding substance abuse since individual variation is probable both in the effects of various substances and in the adolescents' reactions to them (Giancola and Tarter, 1999).

Another criterion has been the extent to which substance use has had a harmful effect on the functioning of the adolescent (e.g., Hillman and Sawilowsky, 1992; Tarter *et al.*, 1997). Some concerns have been raised about this approach as well, even though it forms the backbone of the DSM-IV system. Bukstein and Kaminer (1994) pointed out that, because substance use disorder is usually comorbid with other disorders, it is often difficult to tell whether the substance use is indeed the source of many problems faced by the adolescent. Recent studies have suggested that effects normally attributed to substance use disorder might be more accurately viewed as part of an interconnected set of relationships involving other disorders, personal traits of the adolescent, and environmental factors (Windle *et al.*, 2000).

Recent literature has suggested looking more closely at the contexts in which substance use and misuse occur in order to clarify distinctions between them. Bukstein (1998) suggests considering substance use in the context of other psychiatric diagnoses, family and peer relationships, and the surrounding community when diagnosing substance abuse disorder. Similarly, McWhirter and colleagues (1998) suggest using the following factors in determinations of substance abuse: the frequency of use, quantity typically used, variety of substances used at the same time, social context in which substances are used, and emotional state of the adolescent when using the substances. While both are examples of considerations made during clinical diagnoses, they could also be used to inform research intended to distinguish more clearly between substance use and abuse.

PREVALENCE

In order to present a complete picture of the variation evident in substance use, the following section will describe the prevalence rates for a variety of substances that are commonly used among adolescents (see also Chapter 3 in this volume). It is necessary to remember that it has been suggested that the definitions of substance use and abuse vary depending on the substance. It will also become evident that there are some differences in usage patterns for different age groups within the stage of adolescence.

Overall trends

The Monitoring the Future Study (MFS) has been collecting a nationally representative sample of the United States grade 12 population since 1975, and grades 8, 10, and 12 since 1991 (Johnston *et al.*, 2000). In 1999, a sample of 45,000 students participated. The MFS measures the prevalence of illicit drug use in the sample, providing a wealth of data on the continuing drug problem in the United States. A startling trend had taken place during the years 1991–1997, when use of illicit drugs rose rapidly from 18.7%, 30.6%, and 44.1% to 29.4%, 47.3%, and 54.3% of grade 8, 10, and 12 students respectively. More hopeful news from the 1999 survey suggests that rates of illicit drug use overall has levelled off to 28.3%, 46.2%, and 54.7% for grades 8, 10, and 12 respectively.

Statistical patterns in the 1999 report of the National Household Study on Drug Abuse (NHSDA) were similar to those in the MFS. The NHSDA showed a similar rise in overall drug use in the United States from the early 1990s to 1996, levelling off in 1997 (Substance Abuse and Mental Health Services Administration, 2000a). However, a decrease in overall use among 12- to 17-year-olds was also shown, as was an increase in use reported by 18- to 25-year-olds. Interestingly, the trends shown in these two studies were mirrored roughly by trends in drug-related emergency room visits by adolescents in the United States during the same period. In 1992, an estimated 46,822 adolescents aged 12 to 17 went to the emergency room in drug-related incidents. This number peaked at 63,949 in 1996, and dropped to 52,783 in 1999 (Substance Abuse and Mental Health Services Administration, 2000b).

The most recently available Canadian information showed the lifetime prevalence of any one of five illicit drugs (cannabis, cocaine, LSD, speed, or heroin) in 1994 was 30.4% for ages 15 to 17, 32.9% for ages 18 to 19, and 37.7% for ages 20 to 24 (Canadian Centre on Substance Abuse, 1997). Although comparisons are difficult to make due to differences in sampling and measurement, these rates are moderately lower than those in the MFS and the NHSDA in the same year. One can speculate that the frequency of use and age trends in use may vary between countries.

Alcohol

The MFS reports high rates of alcohol use among adolescents in the United States. The lifetime prevalence in 1999 for grades 8, 10, and 12 respectively were 52.1%, 70.6%, and 80.0%. A similarly high proportion of the sample reported having been drunk on at least one occasion: 24.8%, 48.9%, and 62.3% of adolescents in grades 8, 10, and 12. Somewhat alarmingly, 72.3% of respondents in grade 8 reported easy access to alcohol (Johnston *et al.*, 2000). A somewhat different perspective on alcohol use in adolescence is provided by the NHSDA. In 1997, the 30-day prevalence of alcohol use between ages 12 and 17 was 18.6%, the prevalence of "binge" drinking (having more than five drinks on at least one occasion in the past month) was 10.9%, and the prevalence of "heavy" drinking (having more than five drinks on at least five occasions in the past month) was 2.5%. A rather disturbing statistic is that the rate of initiation into alcohol use by adolescents between the ages of 12 and 17 has been increasing steadily since 1965, and has shown a very rapid increase in the mid- to late-1990s (Substance Abuse and Mental Health Services Administration, 2000a). This is particularly unnerving given that research has consistently shown that alcohol use at an early age is a strong predictor of future substance use disorders (Gilvarry, 2000).

Canadian statistics from 1993 include an interesting portrait of some problems associated with drinking experienced by adolescents. Of respondents between the ages of 15 and 17, 43.4% reported having had problems associated with their drinking. Among the more serious problems reported were family conflicts (7.1%), drinking and driving (9.8%), motor vehicle accidents (1.6%), and assault (9.3%) (Canadian Centre on Substance Abuse, 1997). Similar data were collected on a sample of 1,507 students in Oregon between the ages of 14 and 18 (Lewinsohn *et al.*, 1996). Some alcohol-related problems reported were arguments with family and friends (6.8%), having a car accident or near miss (2.5%), having missed school (4.6%), having been suspended or expelled from school (1.6%), and having had physical symptoms of withdrawal after use (2.3%).

Marijuana/hashish/cannabis

Not surprisingly, marijuana is the most frequently used illicit drug. The 1999 MFS reports lifetime prevalence of 22.0%, 40.9%, and 49.7% in grades 8, 10, and 12 respectively. Moreover, there is evidence that adolescents who do use marijuana use it often. The 30-day prevalence for daily use of marijuana is 1.4%, 3.8%, and 6.0% in grades 8, 10, and 12 respectively. The authors of the MFS suggest that perceived benefits and risks of the use of a particular drug partially determine the choice to use that drug. Perceived harmfulness of marijuana was lower than that for any other illicit drug, and the perception of harm dropped for respondents in higher grades. Another potential factor in predicting the amount of use is perceived (or actual) availability of a substance. In this sample, marijuana was reported to be the easiest illicit drug to obtain, and for those in the older grades, nearly as easy to get as cigarettes or alcohol (Johnston *et al.*, 2000). The NHSDA also reported that the estimated rates of initiation into marijuana use among 12- to 17-year-olds skyrocketed in the late 1990s, but had fallen off substantially between 1998 and 1999 (Substance Abuse and Mental Health Services Administration, 2000a).

The most recent Canadian data do not differ drastically from the other two surveys, with lifetime prevalence in 1994 at 25.4% and 23.0% for 15- to 17- and 18- to 19-year-olds, respectively. The other interesting feature in this survey is that it provides data on frequency of cannabis use. While most respondents in both age groups used cannabis once a month (67.5% and 48.7% for the 15–17 and 18–19 age groups, respectively), 23.8% of respondents aged 18–19 use more than once a week (Canadian Centre on Substance Abuse, 1997).

Inhalants

Unlike other substances, inhalant use is most prevalent among younger adolescents. The MFS reports lifetime prevalence rates in 1999 to be 19.7%, 17.0%, and 15.4%, for grades 8, 10, and 12 respectively. This reverse trend is even more pronounced when looking at the annual prevalence, which is 10.3%, 7.2%, and 5.6% for grades 8, 10, and 12 respectively, and 30-day prevalence, which is 5.0%, 2.6%, and 2.0% for grades 8, 10, and 12 respectively (Johnston *et al.*, 2000). These data are corroborated by the NHSDA, which reports that estimated rates of initiation into inhalant use were twice as high in 1998 for the 12–17 age group as they were for the 18–25 age group. It is also reported that estimated rates of initiation increased sharply throughout the 1990s for respondents aged 12–17 (Substance Abuse and Mental Health Services Administration, 2000a).

Cocaine/crack

The MFS reports that in 1999, the lifetime prevalence of cocaine use was 4.7%, 7.7%, and 9.8% of adolescents in grades 8, 10, and 12 respectively. Lifetime prevalence of crack use was 3.1%, 4.0%, and 4.6% of adolescents in grades 8, 10, and 12 respectively. A disturbing trend can be observed in adolescents' views towards the harmfulness of cocaine and crack use. For adolescents across all grades in this survey, perceptions of the harmfulness of using cocaine and crack have dropped substantially between 1991 and 1999. These trends hold true whether adolescents are asked about using only once or twice, or using occasionally. The perceived availability of crack and cocaine is also quite disturbing. Crack was described as easy to get by 25.9%, 36.5%, and 41.1% of adolescents in grades 8, 10, and 12 respectively, and the statistics for cocaine were almost identical (Johnston *et al.*, 2000). The NHSDA also yields some interesting data regarding the use of these two drugs. Unlike alcohol and marijuana, the age of initiation into the use of these drugs is more common in the 18–25 age group than ages 12–17 years. The rates of initiation have been rising in both cases since the early 1990s (Substance Abuse and Mental Health Services Administration, 2000a).

MDMA (ecstasy) and rohypnol (date rape drug)—"club drugs"

The MFS reported prevalence data on two relatively new drugs being used by adolescents: rohypnol and MDMA. Since rohypnol first appeared on the MFS reports in 1996, there has been no major increase in use, with lifetime prevalence remaining below 2% at all grade levels. However, MDMA has shown a swift increase in use among respondents in grade 12 during the same time period, with 8% reporting lifetime use in 1999. It was also reported that perceived accessibility of the drug had increased from 24.2% in 1991 to 40.1% in 1999 (Johnston *et al.*, 2000).

CAUSES AND OUTCOMES OF SUBSTANCE USE

All youth have the potential to partake in risk-taking behaviours and subsequently experience a host of problems associated with these behaviours including poor academic performance, trouble with legal authorities, depression, and strained relationships with family and friends (Côté and Allahar, 1994). However, some youth are at a higher risk than others. It has been suggested that those youth who experiment with alcohol, tobacco, and marijuana as well as those who are infrequent users of these substances are just as well-adjusted as those who abstain from substance use (Steinberg, 1996). Adolescents who are more habitual users also tend to participate more frequently in other high-risk activities and are more likely to attain lower scores on measures of psychosocial adjustment (Lavery *et al.*, 1993). In addition, according to Shedler and Block (1990), substance use during adolescence is likely to be an indication of prior psychological disturbance.

As noted above, these behaviours are commonly indicative of deeper problems in the lives of many adolescents. It has also been suggested that participation in many risk-taking activities during adolescence could stem from a host of risk factors either inherent in the adolescent's personality, evident in interpersonal relationships or apparent in the surrounding environment (e.g., Moore and Gullone, 1996; Steinberg, 1996). This area of research has exploded in recent years as the health of adolescents is in great danger as a result of participation in these and other risk-taking behaviours. In addition to health-related problems during adolescence, many of these youth carry several of these behaviours and subsequent difficulties into their adult lives (Kelly, 2000; Levitt *et al.*, 1991).

10 Substance Abuse and Dependence in Adolescence

Let us now turn to a discussion of these risk factors as they relate specifically to substance use during adolescence. Again, it is necessary to recognize the differences between substance use and abuse. This distinction is important because occasional alcohol and marijuana use has become so common among high school students that many now view such experimental use as normative (Steinberg, 1996). The risk factors discussed below are to be considered in relation to problem substance use rather than normative use.

Risk factors

"Recent research indicates that adolescents' own risk-taking behaviour is one of the greatest threats to their social, physical, and emotional development" (Levitt *et al.*, 1991, p. 349). To understand adolescent involvement in such activities, it is crucial that researchers understand the motivations or risk factors associated with participation in high-risk activities. Although parents continue to make many decisions for the adolescent, some of the biggest risks that adolescents face in today's society involve choices that they must make independently of parental authority (Levitt *et al.*, 1991). These decisions are often in relation to alcohol and drug use, sexuality and their peer groups.

Jessor and Jessor (1977) developed Problem Behaviour Theory to examine various problem behaviours associated with adolescence. They studied delinquency, drug and alcohol use and abuse, and various other forms of problem behaviours. Others (e.g., Donovan and Jessor, 1985; Jessor *et al.*, 1991) have also employed this theoretical framework to examine problem behaviours during adolescence. Findings have suggested that there is a correlation between the various behaviours in terms of risk factors. These risk factors are often placed into three broad categories: psychological, interpersonal and contextual (see also Chapter 4 in this volume). It has also been suggested that the higher the number of risk factors present, the greater the potential for problems (Steinberg, 1996).

In terms of psychological factors, individuals with specific characteristics are generally more prone to participating in risk-taking behaviours and subsequently experiencing associated health-related problems (Steinberg, 1996). Some of these characteristics include aggression, depression, impulsivity, and achievement problems, and it is likely that these traits were evident prior to adolescence (Shedler and Block, 1990). In addition to these psychological characteristics, individuals who are more tolerant of risk-taking behaviours in general are more likely to participate in such activities (Petraitis *et al.*, 1995).

In addition to psychological traits, it is vital that the individuals' interpersonal relationships be examined to gain a more in-depth understanding of the interactions between risk factors. Interpersonally, adolescents from families where a great deal of conflict is present are more likely to develop substance abuse problems (Flewelling and Bauman, 1990) and as a result participate in other risk-taking behaviours. These youth are also more likely to have permissive or authoritative parents (Baumrind, 1991) and they frequently come from homes where one or both parents use drugs and alcohol (Maguin et al., 1994).

Finally, it is important to examine contextual factors evident in the lives of adolescents in understanding their involvement in these activities. These may include the community's attitudes towards risk-taking, the degree to which laws governing such behaviours are enforced, access to drugs and alcohol, and the presentation of these behaviours in the media (Petraitis et al., 1995). It is the combination of these factors that may contribute to an increased rate of involvement of adolescents in risk-taking activities.

As previously noted, it is also important to recognize that substance use also leads to increase in other risk behaviours including sexual promiscuity, reckless driving (Donovan and Jessor, 1985; Jessor and Jessor, 1977). In addition, in more recent years, there has also been an increase in gambling behaviour among adolescents (Barnes et al., 1999; Gupta and Derevensky, 1998). As we see an increase in participation in these risky behaviours, we will see an associated increase in risk factors and subsequently problems in several aspects of adolescents' lives.

Protective factors

In addition to the risk factors noted above, many protective factors have also been identified. Protective factors have both direct and indirect effects on the adolescent's participation in risk behaviours. Directly these factors lessen the likelihood of youth engagement in risk behaviours and indirectly, they can act as defences against exposure to risk factors (Jessor, 1998). Some of the protective factors that have been identified by Jessor and colleagues include: intelligence, a cohesive family, church attendance, involvement in school and extracurricular activities, intolerance of deviance and the accessibility of neighbourhood resources.

According to Newcomb and Felix-Ortiz (1992), there are several protective factors that act to decrease the likelihood of adolescents using alcohol and drugs as well as participating in other risky behaviours. These include: positive mental health, high academic performance, close family relationships, and religious affiliation. It has been further suggested that the presence of such protective factors often supersedes many of the risk factors discussed previously.

Simantov et al. (2000) identified similar protective factors as noted above. Though positive family relationships were noted as playing a protective role, they went further to suggest that parents with high expectations regarding academic performance and those parents who had an active connection with the youth's school protected youth from a variety of risk behaviours (Wills et al., 1992).

Although we have outlined a variety of factors that appear to protect youth from participation in risky behaviours such as alcohol and drug use, it is also important to note that these factors are more salient with specific behaviours than others. For example, Simantov *et al.* (2000) found that, although participation in extracurricular activities, such as sports, was associated with decreased prevalence of smoking, it had no connection to the risk of alcohol consumption. Again, the higher the number of protective factors, the less likely the youth will be to engage in risky behaviours.

Possible outcomes

It is important to consider that there are both positive and negative outcomes resulting from adolescent substance use. As noted, increased experimental use of some substances such as alcohol, tobacco, and marijuana among youth has become commonplace and is generally accepted as an element of normative development (Newcomb and Bentler, 1989; Steinberg, 1996). However, at the other end of the spectrum there are many negative consequences related to substance use, as suggested previously. This section will highlight some of these consequences—both positive and negative.

According to Pagliaro and Pagliaro (1996), the least-researched area of substance use during adolescence is related to the consequences of alcohol and drug use. Although this area requires further research, some consequences of substance use have been identified. These consequences will be divided into three areas for the following discussion: physiological, psychosocial, and legal consequences.

Most substances have immediate physical effects and these physiological consequences vary, depending on the substance. As a result of associated physiological changes to the body, the individual is likely to experience changes in sense of reality, judgement, reaction time, and sensory perceptions; these effects may be felt for several hours to several days, depending on the substance (McWhirter *et al.*, 1998). Substance use can lead to a series of tragic events including automobile accidents and overdoses; although not often thought of in this manner, these are the result of physiological changes in the body as a result of the introduction of a substance into the system. The more common outcomes associated with physiology are those that include impaired judgement, lung cancer, respiratory problems, physiological addiction, physical pain when experiencing withdrawal from a substance, and sometimes death (McWhirter *et al.*, 1998).

Substance use during the childhood and adolescent years is often linked to more serious difficulties in early adulthood. Some of these problems include early sexual promiscuity, early marriage, failure to pursue further education, early entrance into the workplace, and early unemployment. According to Newcomb and Bentler (1989), some of the early entry into many aspects of adult life as a result of frequent drug use is beyond the level of ability of many of these youth. Because they entered these areas of life earlier than is common, they may have missed out on various developmental milestones necessary to experience a smooth transition into adulthood. In addition, heavy users of substances, particularly substances other than alcohol and/or marijuana, often report feelings of increased loneliness, depression, suicide ideation, and decreased social support (Newcomb and Bentler, 1988).

The final category of consequences related to substance use is that of legal concerns. Although laws may be different depending on the geographic location, the following are some general guidelines that may result in negative consequences for youth. As noted previously, substance use is often accompanied by other risky behaviours (Jessor and Jessor, 1977). It is participation in some of these activities that may present legal concerns such as driving under the influence, delinquent acts resulting in arrest, and the use of illicit substances. It is important for professionals working with youth to be aware of the specific laws governing their respective areas.

Though much of the research appears to focus on the negative effects of this type of behaviour among adolescents, others have suggested that there are also positive effects that require further exploration (Baumrind, 1991). It is important to note that the consequences presented above are specifically related to frequent and/or heavy substance use. It is becoming more common for researchers to note the differences related to the amount and type of substance use occurring.

PREVENTION AND TREATMENT OF PROBLEMS

Generally, efforts to thwart substance use among adolescents focus on one of the following three aspects: the availability of substances, the environment in which adolescents risk exposure to substances, and individual characteristics of the potential substance abuser (Newcomb and Bentler, 1989) (see also Chapters 6–8 in this volume). Although it is impossible to remove all substances from the community, society often focuses energy on this approach. According to Steinberg (1996), emphasis should be placed on the last two approaches noted above. These two receive little attention and it could prove more beneficial to understand the motivations surrounding substance use including the influence of their environment. In addition, if treatment and prevention programmes are to be successful, it is important to recognize that these behaviours are often associated with other negative life experiences and these should be explored with the young person and his or her environment (Simantov *et al.*, 2000).

According to Gullotta *et al.* (2000), there are six characteristics that are crucial when working with adolescents towards behaviour change. First, it is important that *trust* is developed in the relationship; otherwise the adolescent will be unlikely to share any information with the professional. To create an environment that fosters trust in this relationship, the professional must be *genuine* in his/her approach with the adolescent. The worker must show *empathy* towards the youth, indicating that he/she does feel for the young person and the situation that person is currently experiencing. Without an element of *honesty*, the relationship between these two will not be successful in changing any current problem behaviours. The fifth element to consider is the adolescent's *perception* of these qualities in the professional. It is not enough that the worker possess these characteristics, it is equally important that the young person recognizes and appreciates these qualities. Finally, the adolescent must want to succeed: *self-efficacy* must be present.

Now that the necessary ingredients of a therapeutic relationship have been identified, let us turn to the various approaches that have been employed in the treatment of adolescents. There are three basic categories of therapy in this area: individual therapy, family therapy, and group therapy. Individual therapy occurs between the therapist and the client and focuses on the client's personal feelings, thoughts, and behaviours. This form of therapy is generally the most common. A second form of therapy that may be effective with these young people is family therapy. This will include the adolescent and his/her parents, and when appropriate other family members may also be included. This method recognizes the value of examining the system surrounding the youth (Gullotta *et al.*, 2000). This may also be beneficial because it has been suggested that there is often substance use in the home that the youth has been exposed to from an earlier age (e.g., Baumrind, 1991; Brook *et al.*, 1990; Newcomb and Bentler, 1989). Finally, group therapy has been employed for many groups. This form of therapy often consists of a group of individuals experiencing similar problems. It is important to recognize that there are many varying approaches within these types of therapy (Gullotta *et al.*, 2000).

In addition to the various forms of treatment developed to address substance use and abuse during adolescence, we have also seen a focus on prevention. The idea of prevention is to prevent illness and promote health (Gullotta *et al.*, 2000). Such prevention programmes often target the individual adolescent and focus on social skills training and/or educating youth regarding the hazards of substance use (Steinberg, 1996). However, according to Kelly (2000), it is vital that the individuals responsible for such prevention programmes acknowledge that the adolescents are not solely responsible for their choices regarding substance use. Others that need to be targeted by prevention programmes are family members, peers, and school officials.

According to Dielman (1994), some of the most promising results in relation to treatment and prevention programmes have been those that combine social competence training with community-wide intervention. Rather than simply targeting the adolescent, these programmes include their peers, parents, and teachers. By including all the major players in the adolescent's life, additional support can be provided as the youth progresses towards adulthood. Furthermore, efforts made to change the youth's characteristics without considering the environment surrounding the young person will be unsuccessful (Steinberg, 1996).

In addition to programmes developed without addressing the environment from which the youth comes, another problem often associated with treatment programmes in particular is failure to distinguish between substance use and substance abuse (Newcomb and Bentler, 1989). As noted previously, it has been suggested that experimentation with substances is likely to be associated with normative development (Baumrind, 1991; Parsons *et al.*, 1997; Shedler and Block, 1990). It has further been suggested that there is some concern that adolescents who are enrolled in treatment programmes inappropriately may experience increased alienation and distress (Dielman, 1994). This finding provides additional support for the importance of accurately identifying the differences between substance use and substance abuse.

FUTURE DIRECTIONS

An in-depth discussion of any area of research is not complete without providing some information regarding what must happen in order to fill the gaps identified by such a review. The literature presented regarding definitions, prevalence of substance use among adolescents, causes and outcomes of substance use, and prevention and treatment possibilities is informative; however, there are alternatives that may prove to be beneficial to the field of adolescence.

Much of the work that has been completed in this area of research falls within the positivist paradigm. It is essential to consider and study this phenomenon from an interpretive paradigm as well. Though there are definite benefits from having this kind of information, many of the measures that are employed have been developed by adults and as the literature suggests, there are differences between adult and adolescent perceptions regarding risk perception and, as a result, decision making. Qualitative measures may be useful in uncovering some of the meaning of risk-taking from the perspective of the adolescent. In addition, peer-led interviews, focus groups (Moore and Parsons, 2000) as well as Experience Sampling Method (ESM) data (Csikszentmihalyi, 1997) may decrease the social desirability bias sometimes evident in this area of research.

As noted, much of what we know about this area is from adult-imposed definitions of substance use and abuse. It is vital that in order to better understand this phenomenon, we go directly to the youth involved. Much research is conducted with the hope of providing recommendations for education/prevention tools and treatment protocols. It is impossible to determine levels of effectiveness and applicability if we do not return to the immediate source for these responses. In addition to determining the usefulness of such tools from the adolescent's perspective, this type of research can be used as an educational tool to increase adolescent awareness of our concerns related to substance use and abuse among adolescents.

In addition to considering the implementation of multiple methods to increase our understanding of this phenomenon, it may also be beneficial to incorporate longitudinal designs. This would enable us to consider and better understand the developmental pathways for the progression from substance use to abuse and dependency. In addition, we know that there is some carryover from adolescence into adulthood. With longitudinal designs, we can better comprehend the detrimental consequences for the individual as well as society by following such youth into their adult lives. Furthermore, this design has implications for education and treatment protocols. Currently these recommendations are based on our understanding of health-compromising behaviours in adolescents; with longitudinal data we could make recommendations based on the reflections of adults who participated in such activities as adolescents. The contributions of longitudinal data in this area could be extremely valuable and, although some researchers have conducted such studies, these studies are often conducted focusing on a variety of risk problems rather than just focusing on substance use (i.e., Jessor and Jessor, 1977).

It is important that additional work be completed that emphasizes youth involvement in multiple behaviours. As noted, many adolescents who participate in one risk-taking activity are more likely to participate in other similar activities (see Arnett, 1992, 1996). It is important to begin to recognize this and incorporate multiple assessments when conducting research in this area in order to gain a better understanding of the comorbidity of these behaviours. Though Problem Behaviour Theory has been utilized in several examinations addressing the existence of multiple behaviours, the application of this theory has been rather limited to specific behaviours, including the use of alcohol and other substances and general deviant behaviour (i.e. shoplifting, lying, and aggression) (Jessor et al., 1991).

Finally, as noted above, there is a definite link between risk behaviours, including substance use, reckless driving and early sexual promiscuity; it has also been noted that there is a lack of recognition that risk-taking may act as a positive force in the development of, for example, a sense of adventure, creativity, and the desire to accept challenges (Moore and Parsons, 2000). It is important that further research in the area of moderate risk-taking be conducted to increase the understanding of the real risks related to "problem" risk-taking activities. What about studying adults who were resilient to risk factors in their youth? They may have a great deal of information to contribute in relation to our understanding of adolescence and possible treatment that may be effective with these youth.

CONCLUSION

Substance use and abuse is a growing concern in today's society as more and more youth are progressing from an experimental phase to a more addicted phase (Newcomb and Bentler, 1988). The purpose of this chapter has been to introduce to the reader a broad overview of our current state of knowledge regarding adolescence and substance use. The subsequent chapters will describe many of the ideas presented here in further detail. Topics to be addressed in more detail include: classification and assessment, issues of comorbidity and risk factors, preventative measures, and potential treatment suggestions.

REFERENCES

Arnett, J. (1992). Reckless behavior in adolescence: A developmental perspective. *Developmental Review, 12*, 339–373.

Arnett, J. J. (1996). Sensation seeking, aggressiveness, and adolescent reckless behavior. *Personality and Individual Differences, 20*, 693–702.

Barnes, G. M., Welte, J. W., Hoffman, J. H., & Dintcheff, B. A. (1999). Gambling and alcohol use among youth: Influences of demographic, socialization, and individual factors. *Addictive Behaviors, 24*, 749–767.

Baumrind, D. (1991). The influence of parenting style on adolescent competence and substance use. *Journal of Early Adolescence, 11*, 56–95.

Bingham, C. R., Bennion, L., Openshaw, D. K., & Adams, G. R. (1994). An analysis of age, gender and racial differences in recent national trends of youth suicide. *Journal of Adolescence, 17*, 53–71.

Brook, J. S., Brook, D. W., Gordon, A. S., Whiteman, M., & Cohen, P. (1990). The psychosocial etiology of adolescent drug use: A family interactional approach. *Genetic, Social and General Psychology Monographs, 116*, 111–267.

Bukstein, O. (1998). Summary of the practice parameters for the assessment and treatment of children and adolescents with substance use disorder. *Journal of the Academy of Child and Adolescent Psychiatry, 37*, 127–134.

Bukstein, O. & Kaminer, Y. (1994). The nosology of adolescent substance abuse. *The American Journal on Addictions, 3*, 1–13.

Canadian Centre on Substance Abuse; Addiction Research Foundation (1997). *Canadian profile: Alcohol, tobacco, and other drugs.* Ottawa, Ontario: ARF/CAMH.

Clements, R. (1999). Prevalence of alcohol-use disorders and alcohol-related problems in a college student sample. *Journal of American College Health, 48*, 111–118.

Cole, P. S. & Weissberg, R. P. (1995). Substance use and abuse among urban adolescents. In T. P. Gullotta, G. R. Adams, & R. Montemayor (Eds.), *Substance misuse in adolescence.* Thousand Oaks, CA: Sage.

Costello, J. E., Erkanli, A., Federman, E., & Angold, A. (1999). Development of psychiatric comorbidity with substance abuse in adolescents: Effects of timing and sex. *Journal of Clinical Child Psychology, 28*, 298–311.

Côté, J. E. & Allahar, A. L. (1994). *Generation on hold: Coming of age in the late twentieth century*. Toronto, Ontario: Stoddart.

Csikszentmihalyi, M. (1997). *Finding flow: The psychology of engagement with everyday life*. New York, NY: Basic Books.

Dielman, T. (1994). School-based research on the prevention of adolescent alcohol use and misuses: Methodological issues and advances. *Journal of Research on Adolescence, 4*, 271–293.

Donovan, J. E. & Jessor, R. (1985). Structure of problem behavior in adolescence and young adulthood. *Journal of Consulting and Clinical Psychology, 53*, 890–904.

Flewelling, R. & Bauman, K. (1990). Family structure as a predictor of initial substance use and sexual intercourse in early adolescence. *Journal of Marriage and the Family, 52*, 171–181.

Fulkerson, J. A., Harrison, P. A., & Beebe, T. J. (1999). DSM-IV substance abuse and dependence: Are there really two dimensions of substance use disorders in adolescents? *Addiction, 94*, 495–506.

Giancola, P. R. & Tarter, R. E. (1999). What constitutes a drug of abuse? In R.T. Ammerman, P. J. Ott, & R. E. Tarter (Eds.), *Prevention and societal impact of drug and alcohol abuse*. Mahwah, NJ: Lawrence Erlbaum Associates.

Gilvarry, E. (2000). Substance abuse in young people. *Journal of Child Psychology and Psychiatry, 41*, 55–80.

Gonzalez, J., Field, T., Yando, R., Gonzalez, K., Lasko, D., & Bendell, D. (1994). Adolescents' perceptions of their risk-taking behavior. *Adolescence, 29*, 701–709.

Gullone, E., Moore, S., Moss, S., & Boyd, C. (2000). The adolescent risk-taking questionnaire: Development and psychometric evaluation. *Journal of Adolescent Research, 15*, 231–250.

Gullotta, T. P., Adams, G. R., & Markstrom, C. A. (2000). *The adolescent experience* (4th edn). San Diego, CA: Academic Press.

Gupta, R. & Derevensky, J. L. (1998). Adolescent gambling behavior: A prevalence study and examination of the correlated associated with problem gambling. *Journal of Gambling Studies, 14*, 319–345.

Helzer, J. E., Burnam, A., & McEvoy, L. T. (1991). Alcohol abuse and dependence. In L. N. Robins & D. A. Reiger (Eds.), *Psychiatric disorders in America: The Epidemiological Catchment Area Study*. New York, NY: The Free Press.

Hillman, S. B. & Sawilowsky, S.S. (1992). A comparison of two grouping methods in distinguishing level of substance use. *Journal of Clinical Child Psychology, 21*, 348–353.

Jessor, R. (Ed.) (1998). *New perspectives on adolescent risk behavior*. New York, NY: Cambridge University Press.

Jessor, R., Donovan, J. E., & Costa, F. M. (1991). *Beyond adolescence: Problem behavior and young adult development*. New York, NY: Cambridge University Press.

Jessor, R. & Jessor, S. L. (1977). *Problem behavior and psychosocial development: A longitudinal study of youth*. New York, NY: Academic Press.

Johnston, L. D., O'Malley, P. M., & Bachman, J. G. (2000). *The Monitoring the Future national results on adolescent drug use: Overview of key findings, 1999*. Bethesda, MA: National Institute on Drug Abuse.

Kaminer, Y. & Bukstein, O. G. (1998). Adolescent substance abuse. In R. J. Frances & S. I. Miller (Eds.), *Clinical textbook of addictive disorders* (2nd edn). New York, NY: Guilford Press.

Kelly, P. (2000). The dangerousness of youth-at-risk: The possibilities of surveillance and intervention in uncertain times. *Journal of Adolescence, 23*, 463–476.

Lavery, B., Siegel, A. W., Cousins, J. H., & Rubovits, D. S. (1993). Adolescent risk-taking: An analysis of problem behaviors in problem children. *Journal of Experimental Child Psychology, 55*, 277–294.

Levitt, M. Z., Selman, R. L., & Richmond, J. B. (1991). The psychosocial foundations of early adolescents' high-risk behavior: Implications for research and practice. *Journal of Research on Adolescence, 1*, 349–378.

Lewinsohn, P. M., Rohde, P., & Seeley, J. R. (1996). Alcohol consumption in high school adolescents: Frequency of use and dimensional structure, of associated problems. *Addiction, 91*, 375–390.

Maguin, E., Zucker, R. A., & Fitzgerald, H. E. (1994). The path to alcohol problems through conduct problems: A family-based approach to very early intervention with risk. *Journal of Research on Adolescence, 4*, 249–269.

McWhirter, J. J., McWhirter, B. T., McWhirter, A. M., & McWhirter, E. H. (1998). *At risk youth: A comprehensive response* (2nd edn). Pacific Grove, CA: Brooks/Cole.

Moore, S. & Gullone, E. (1996). Predicting adolescent risk behavior using a personalized cost–benefit analysis. *Journal of Youth and Adolescence, 25*, 343–359.

Moore, S. & Parsons, J. (2000). A research agenda for adolescent risk-taking: Where do we go from here? *Journal of Adolescence, 23*, 371–376.

Nelson, C. B., Rehm, J., Üstün, T. B., Grant, B., & Chatterji, S. (1999). Factor structures for DSM-IV substance disorder criteria endorsed by alcohol, cannabis, cocaine and opiate users: Results from the WHO reliability and validity study. *Addiction, 94*, 843–855.

Newcomb, M. D. & Bentler, P. M. (1988). *Consequences of adolescent drug use: Impact on the lives of young adults.* Newbury Park, CA: Sage.

Newcomb, M. & Bentler, P. (1989). Substance use and abuse among children and teenagers. *American Psychologist, 44*, 242–248.

Newcomb, M. & Felix-Ortiz, M. (1992). Multiple protective and risk factors for drug use and abuse: Cross-sectional and prospective findings. *Journal of Personality and Social Psychology, 63*, 280–296.

Pagliaro, A. M. & Pagliaro, L. (1996). *Substance use among children and adolescents: Its nature, extent, and effects from conception to adulthood.* Somerset, New York, NY: John Wiley.

Parsons, J. T., Seigel, A. W., & Cousins, J. H. (1997). Late adolescent risk-taking: Effects of perceived benefits and perceived risks on behavioral intentions and behavioral change. *Journal of Adolescence, 20*, 381–392.

Petraitis, J., Flay, B., & Miller, T. (1995). Reviewing theories of adolescent substance abuse: Organizing pieces in the puzzle. *Psychological Bulletin, 117*, 67–86.

Rounsaville, B. J., Bryant, K., Babor, T., Kranzler, H., & Kadden, R. (1993). Cross system agreement for substance use disorders: DSM-III-R, DSM-IV and ICD-10. *Addiction, 88*, 337–348.

Shedler, J. & Block, J. (1990). Adolescent drug use and psychological health: A longitudinal inquiry. *American Psychologist, 45*, 612–630.

Simantov, E., Schoen, C., & Klein, D. (2000). Health-compromising behaviors: Why do adolescents smoke or drink? *Archives of Pediatrics and Adolescent Medicine, 154*, 1025–1032.

Steinberg, L. (1996). *Adolescence* (4th edn). New York, NY: McGraw-Hill.

Substance Abuse and Mental Health Services Administration (2000a). *Summary of findings from the 1999 National Household Survey on Drug Abuse*. Rockville, MD: Substance Abuse and Mental Health Services Administration, Office of Applied Studies. Available online at: http://www.samhsa.gov/OAS/NHSDA/1999/Highlights.htm

Substance Abuse and Mental Health Services Administration (2000b). *Year-End 1999 Emergency Department Data from the Drug Abuse Warning Network*, Rockville, MD: Substance Abuse and Mental Health Services Administration. Available online at: http://www.samhsa.gov/oas/DAWN/DetEDTbl/1999/Text/TOC.pdf

Tarter, R. E., Kirisci, L., & Mezzich, A. (1997). Multivariate typology of adolescents with alcohol use disorder. *The American Journal on Addictions*, 6, 150–158.

Warner, L. A., Kessler, R. C., Hughes, M., Anthony, J. C., & Nelson, C.B. (1995). Prevalence and correlates of drug use and dependence in the United States: Results from the National Comorbidity Study. *Archives of General Psychiatry*, 52, 219–229.

Wills, T. A., Vaccaro, D., & McNamara, G. (1992). The role of life events, family support, and competence in adolescent substance use: A test of vulnerability and protective factors. *American Journal of Community Psychology*, 20, 349–374.

Windle, M., Miller-Tutzauer C., & Domenico, D. (2000). Alcohol use, suicidal behaviour and risky activities among adolescents. In G. Adams (Ed.), *Adolescent development: The essential readings*. Oxford, UK: Blackwell.

Chapter 2

Classification and assessment

Ty A. Ridenour, Patricia Fazzone, and Linda B. Cottler

The existence of an adequate classification scheme for substance use disorders enhances understanding of the etiology, treatment, and prevention of substance use disorders (Cottler, 1992). The ability of a nomenclature to accomplish its goal might be measured by (a) how well it distinguishes persons who are addicted from persons who are well, (b) how acceptable it is to professionals in the field, (c) its ability to detect differences in the disorders associated with ethnicity, geographical region, gender, and age, and (d) its validity being equally good for diverse populations (Cottler, 1992; Cottler and Compton, 1993). Although the primary goal of accurate identification of persons with a substance use disorder might appear simplistic, establishing an acceptable classification nomenclature has proven difficult (Cottler, 1992). Previous substance use disorder classification schemes fell short of the ideal using the aforementioned measuring sticks of nomenclature adequacy, hence, the classifications were in a state of flux (Babor, 1993). Criticisms of specific aspects of the most recent nomenclatures point to the need for further development of the currently used diagnostic systems (Hasin *et al.*, 1997c; Morgenstern *et al.*, 1994; Langenbucher *et al.*, 2000).

The existing, widely used classification systems of substance use disorders have been developed using theory about and data collected from adults but the shortcomings of these nomenclatures also pertain to adolescents. Additional uncertainties exist regarding classification of adolescents' substance use disorders because of the developmental differences between adolescents and adults (Dawes *et al.*, 2000; Deas *et al.*, 2000; Lamminpaa, 1995; Meyers *et al.*, 1999; Weinberg *et al.*, 1998). How the developmental differences impact diagnosis of substance use disorders in adolescents is not well understood. For illustration, duration of substance use and regular use of a substance (e.g., at least once per month over a six-month period) are associated with the development of diagnostic criteria (Deas *et al.*, 2000; Mikulich *et al.*, 2001). Adolescents with substance use-related diagnoses generally consumed the substance regularly over much shorter time periods than adults with the same substance use-related diagnoses (Brown *et al.*,

1990, 1992; Deas *et al.*, 2000). One might hypothesize that psychotropic substances affect adolescents differently than adults because of biological, social, or cognitive reasons (Deas *et al.*, 2000; Dunn and Goldman, 1998; Lamminpaa, 1994, 1995). However, the specific mechanisms of this difference remain unclear. Developmental differences have implications for how to classify adolescents' substance use disorders, understanding the etiology of substance use disorders, and how to best intervene with adolescents.

A review of the revisions to one of the substance use classification systems (DSM) over the past two decades will illustrate the challenges of classifying pathology associated with misuse of psychoactive substances. A brief overview of the two widely used modern classification systems—DSM-IV and ICD-10—will provide a grounding that will be referenced throughout the remainder of the book. Ways in which current classifications might not generalize to adolescents will be illustrated with examples from the relatively scant research literature regarding substance use nomenclature using adolescent samples. Assessment of current substance use classification nomenclature will be addressed by focusing on the instruments best equipped to assess the classification schemes and briefly reviewing other instruments used to assess substance use disorders.

RECENT EVOLUTION OF DSM PATHOLOGICAL SUBSTANCE USE CLASSIFICATION

Continued efforts to better epitomize substance use disorders has resulted in numerous changes to the DSM classification system of substance use disorders since the first taxonomy was presented in DSM-III (APA, 1980; Robins and Helzer, 1986). Briefly reviewing this evolution of nomenclature illustrates the difficulties inherent in classification of substance use disorders. DSM-III nomenclature for alcohol addiction included two disorders, abuse and dependence, in place of the previously defined single disorder. DSM-III nomenclature also required that for dependence diagnosis a physiological symptom (i.e., withdrawal or tolerance) and social impairment due to substance use must be experienced. The DSM-III taxonomy was criticized on several bases, including the emphasis on physiological criteria and social impairment, lack of a specific theoretical underpinning, and inclusion of two substance use disorders (Caetano, 1987; Nathan, 1994; Rounsaville, 1987; Schuckit, 1993). Within one year of the release of the DSM-III classification, a work group was designed to revise the substance use nomenclature (Cottler, Schuckit *et al.*, 1995b). Although separate abuse and dependence disorders continued to be used in the DSM-III-R, the physiological criterion and social consequences and occupational impairment criterion were not required for a dependence diagnosis and the same nine diagnostic criteria were used for all substances (APA, 1987; Rounsaville, 1987). The dependence diagnosis criteria were based on the alcohol dependence syndrome (Edwards and Gross, 1976).

The Edwards and Gross Alcohol Dependence Syndrome (1976; Edwards, 1986) was used as the theoretical basis for DSM-III-R substance use diagnoses as well as for the DSM-IV and the ICD-10. Edwards and Gross described the elements of the alcohol dependence syndrome as the narrowing of the drinking repertoire (alcohol consumption becomes more constant), continued alcohol consumption in spite of knowledge that alcohol is the source of problems, tolerance to alcohol, withdrawal symptoms, seeking relief or avoiding withdrawal symptoms by further alcohol consumption, craving alcohol when not drinking, a compulsion to drink (a difficulty to stop drinking once alcohol consumption has ensued), return to alcohol consumption after a period of abstinence. In addition to specifying these criteria for alcohol dependence, Edwards and Gross (1976; Edwards, 1986) acknowledge that the syndrome varies in levels of severity, illustrating the difficulty in specifying a critical threshold that distinguishes the ill from the well. The narrowing of the drinking repertoire criterion was not included in the DSM-III-R or subsequent classification systems. It has been reported that the drinking repertoire is unreliable in a test–retest study of substance users (Cottler *et al.*, 1995b).

Requiring three criteria to qualify for a dependence diagnosis maximized the agreement between DSM-III and DSM-III-R classification systems regarding who receives a diagnosis (Rounsaville *et al.*, 1987). Substance abuse was intended in the DSM-III-R as a residual category for persons who did not meet dependence criteria but who nevertheless had problematic substance use (Rounsaville and Kranzler, 1989).

Revisions to the DSM-III-R were based on information collected to address questions that, in part, would help the classification system's maximal performance with regard to the aforementioned measuring sticks of nomenclature adequacy (Cottler *et al.*, 1995b). The scientific, empirically driven approach to DSM revision included collecting information from over fifty experts, a literature review on research addressing specific questions regarding DSM-III-R classification, re-analysis of existing datasets, and collection of novel data to address issues that had not been sufficiently studied (Cottler *et al.*, 1995b). Moreover, an attempt was made to reduce discrepancies between DSM nomenclature and ICD-10 nomenclature to facilitate the comparability of international studies and communication (Pincus *et al.*, 1992).

Preceding alterations to the DSM-III-R nomenclature, the ICD nomenclature was altered. Following a 1992 meeting between framers of the ICD-10 and DSM-III-R classifications, the ICD-10 narrowing of substance use repertoire criterion was dropped and the two indicators of withdrawal were combined into a single criterion (Rounsaville *et al.*, 1993). Dropping the "harrowing repertoire" criterion from ICD-10 reduced the discrepancies between the DSM-III-R and ICD-10 classification systems because the narrowing of substance use repertoire was not included in the DSM system (Rounsaville et al., 1993).

DSM-IV nomenclature differed from that of DSM-III-R in several ways (APA, 1994; Cottler et al., 1995b), including: (a) the abuse diagnosis was designed to be distinct from the dependence diagnosis rather than serve as a residual category for persons who do not meet dependence criteria, (b) the abuse diagnosis criteria were expanded from two to four, (c) the "clustering" criterion was more specific (at least three dependence criteria were required to occur during a 12-month period), and (d) dependence diagnoses were further specified as either physiological (i.e., tolerance or withdrawal was experienced) or non-physiological.

Physiological dependence debate

The DSM-III requirement of at least one physiological criterion being present for a dependence diagnosis has been controversial. Perhaps the physiological criteria have been considered for greater emphasis in diagnosis because they resemble a biological marker for the disease (Cottler and Compton, 1993). Having either tolerance or withdrawal was not required for alcoholism diagnosis in the classification nomenclatures that preceded DSM-III, namely the Feighner criteria and the Research Diagnostic Criteria (Feighner et al., 1972; Spitzer et al., 1978). Physiological criteria also have not been required for substance use dependence diagnoses in classification systems subsequent to DSM-III. This issue was addressed by the DSM-IV Substance Use Disorders Work Group by investigating the associations between having withdrawal, tolerance, and the full dependence criterion (in which physiological criteria could contribute to, but were not required for diagnosis; Cottler et al., 1995b). Among substance users, tolerance and withdrawal were relatively rare. However, 86% to 99% of persons meeting criteria for dependence diagnosis for alcohol, amphetamines, cannabis, cocaine, opiates, sedatives or nicotine reported either tolerance or withdrawal, or both. Cottler and colleagues (1995b) concluded that further research should clarify whether physiological symptoms should be required for dependence diagnosis.

The emphasis and role of the withdrawal criterion for dependence diagnosis has been a more controversial issue than tolerance. Perhaps the controversy has centred on withdrawal because tolerance is hypothesized to occur earlier than withdrawal in the sequence of criteria that are experienced (e.g., Edwards and Gross (1976) argue that withdrawal cannot occur without tolerance) or that withdrawal symptoms are more salient than tolerance symptoms. Another possible reason for focusing on withdrawal is that when physiological dependence is limited to withdrawal (as opposed to using either tolerance or withdrawal) physiological dependence is more strongly associated with substance use-related problems and relapse (Langenbucher et al., 1997, 2000). Hasin and colleagues (2000) reported that, in persons recruited from the community who met DSM-IV criteria for alcohol dependence, those who had experienced alcohol withdrawal were at nearly three times the risk for meeting alcohol dependence diagnosis one year later than persons who had not experienced alcohol withdrawal. The increased risk for relapse jumped to six times when tremors were required for withdrawal diagnosis (tremors were required to meet the withdrawal criterion in DSM-III and DSM-III-R, but not DSM-IV or ICD-10). Additional studies also suggest that withdrawal is associated with severe cases of dependence (e.g., Bucholz et al., 1996; Schuckit et al., 1998, 1999). However, in studies of drinkers recruited from the community, alcohol withdrawal is not as highly associated with the full diagnosis of alcohol dependence as other alcohol dependence criteria (Hasin et al., 1994; Muthen et al., 1993) and the alcohol and drug dependence criteria appear to emulate from a single causal factor (Feingold and Rounsaville, 1995; Hasin et al., 1994; Morgenstern et al., 1994).

Langenbucher and colleagues (2000) have tested the "withdrawal-gate" alcohol diagnosis against the traditional DSM-IV diagnosis of alcohol dependence. Their classification of diagnoses consisted of alcohol withdrawal being necessary and sufficient for dependence diagnosis and two or more of any other dependence or abuse criteria qualified an individual for the abuse diagnosis. They reported greater consistency over time for a dependence diagnosis based only on the withdrawal criterion. Negligible proportions of their sample with DSM-IV abuse qualified for the withdrawal-gate dependence. Participants reporting alcohol withdrawal also reported the worst alcohol-related pathology on a number of severity measures, participants with withdrawal-gate abuse who qualified for DSM-IV dependence had the second-worst pathology on the severity measures, and persons qualifying for abuse in each classification had the least severe pathology. These results also were reported for adolescents.

Using the withdrawal criterion in place of dependence diagnoses provides the benefit of a biological marker for disease. However, such a classification nomenclature would probably fall short of two other desirable qualities of a classification scheme. The withdrawal-gate classification fails to distinguish persons who are ill from those who are well, particularly among adolescents (Langenbucher et al., 2000). Estimates of the proportion of adolescents in treatment for substance use disorders who had experienced withdrawal are generally less than 33% (Langenbucher et al., 2000; Mikulich et al., 2001; Stewart and Brown, 1995; Winters and Stinchfield, 1995). The clinical implication of using the withdrawal criterion in place of DSM-IV dependence diagnosis is this: in regions where substance abuse is not considered to be severe enough to fund treatment, treatment would be withheld from over two-thirds of the adolescents in need of treatment. Moreover, numerous studies have found that persons, including adolescents, meeting criteria for

DSM-IV abuse have less severe substance-related pathology than persons who meet dependence criteria (e.g., Hasin *et al.*, 1997c; Langenbucher *et al.*, 2000; Pollock and Martin, 1999; Sarr *et al.*, 2000). The withdrawal-gate nomenclature would classify many persons from these apparently different subtypes of persons into a single, abuse diagnosis. Hence, the withdrawal-gate classification scheme would likely be unacceptable to a majority of professionals in the field. Nevertheless, Langenbucher and colleagues' (2000) results were consistent with the withdrawal criterion serving as a proxy for severe dependence. Hence, it appears that withdrawal provides a marker of severe dependence but is not definitive of substance dependence. These studies also support the concept of using DSM-IV and ICD-10 criteria as scales for severity of dependence on a substance (Langenbucher *et al.*, 1995; Woody *et al.*, 1993), in which withdrawal is an indicator of severe dependence.

Diagnostic orphans

Researchers recently have become interested in learning more about persons at the other end of the spectrum of dependence severity, the so-called "diagnostic orphans". Diagnostic orphans meet one or two dependence criteria only and therefore do not meet criteria for dependence, abuse, or harmful use (Hasin and Paykin, 1998, 1999; Pollock and Martin, 1999; Sarr *et al.*, 2000). These subthreshold cases experienced problems associated with use of a substance but have not met enough criteria for a DSM-IV diagnosis. When compared to persons who report no criteria, diagnostic orphans experience more severe problems (e.g., extent of substance use, number of psychiatric disorders, early age of substance use onset, proportion meeting criteria for substance dependence at a one-year follow-up) related to substance use. However, they recall less severe problems due to substance use compared to persons who meet dependence criteria (Hasin and Paykin, 1998, 1999; Pollock and Martin, 1999; Sarr *et al.*, 2000). In fact, adult "diagnostic orphans" closely resemble persons meeting criteria for abuse in terms of the severity of their substance use pathology (Pollock and Martin, 1999; Sarr *et al.*, 2000). Pollock and Martin (1999) reported data on adolescents that were consistent with the diagnostic orphans findings in adults. One difference that they reported was that among adolescent regular drinkers, nearly one-third fit the "diagnostic orphan" description, whereas "diagnostic orphans" composed approximately 20% of comparable samples of adults (Hasin and Paykin, 1999; Sarr *et al.*, 2000). At the very least, persons fitting the "diagnostic orphan" description should be researched separately from other substance users (Pollock and Martin, 1999). These data also suggest considering diagnostic nomenclature that requires fewer than three dependence criteria, particularly for classification of adolescents (Pollock and Martin, 1999; Sarr *et al.*, 2000).

CURRENT SUBSTANCE USE-RELATED CLASSIFICATION SYSTEMS

Two co-existing classification systems are widely used to diagnose substance use-related disorders. The American Psychiatric Association's *Diagnostic and Statistical Manual of Mental Disorders—IV* (DSM-IV; APA, 1994) remains the current dominant taxonomy in the United States for mental health diagnoses. The *International Classification of Diseases—10 for Research* (ICD-10; WHO, 1993a), developed by the World Health Organization, is used to guide mental health diagnoses predominantly outside of the United States. The DSM-IV and ICD-10 systems serve to guide clinical practice, research, and education. The functional utility of the two systems is most often associated with reimbursement for treatment services. The APA system is also used for research purposes, however; two versions are available for ICD criteria. The ICD-10 research criteria will be referred to throughout this chapter because they have been used in the literature. The theoretical base for substance use diagnoses of the two systems is the original alcohol dependence syndrome (Edwards and Gross, 1976); however, differences exist in the manner in which the theory is operationalized. Each classification includes (a) a dependence diagnosis, (b) an abuse (DSM-IV) or harmful use (ICD-10) diagnosis, (c) substance-specific withdrawal criteria, and (d) substance-specific intoxication diagnoses. Many more diagnoses can be made, based on the patterns of symptoms and course of the disorder. For illustration, dependence diagnosis can be further specified based on the experience of physiological symptoms and remission of the disorder. This chapter focuses primarily on the dependence and abuse/harmful use diagnoses because they are the most widely used diagnoses for identification of persons with addiction. Corresponding diagnoses from the DSM-IV and ICD-10 systems will be presented side-by-side and their differences highlighted. Because DSM-IV provides a greater description the disorders, characterizations of the diagnoses are quoted from the DSM-IV.

Substance dependence

The American Psychiatric Association characterizes substance dependence as "a cluster of cognitive, behavioral, and physiological symptoms indicating that the individual continues use of the substance despite significant substance-related problems" (2000, p. 192). The dependence diagnosis applies to all psychoactive substance classes except caffeine. At least three criteria must occur within a 12-month period for an individual to qualify for either a DSM-IV or ICD-10 dependence diagnosis. Criteria that occur together over a one-month period also qualify for ICD-10 dependence diagnosis. The criteria used to define substance dependence diagnoses (Table 2.1) are physiological (tolerance or withdrawal) and non-physiological (the remaining behavioural or emotional criteria). If an

Table 2.1 Symptoms of substance use dependence diagnoses

DSM-IV criteria for substance dependence
A maladaptive pattern of substance use, leading to clinically significant impairment or distress, as manifested by three (or more) of the following, occurring at any time in the same 12-month period:

1. Tolerance, as defined by either of the following:
   a. a need for markedly increased amounts of the substance to achieve intoxication or desired effect
   b. markedly diminished effect with continued use of the same amount of the substance
2. Withdrawal, as manifested by either of the following (see Table 2.2):
   a. the characteristic withdrawal syndrome for the substance
   b. the same (or a closely related) substance is taken to relieve or avoid withdrawal symptoms
3. The substance is often taken in larger amounts or over a longer period than was intended;
4. There is a persistent desire or unsuccessful efforts to cut down or control substance use;
5. A great deal of time is spent in activities necessary to obtain the substance (e.g., visiting multiple doctors or driving long distances), use the substance (e.g., chain-smoking), or recover from its effects;
6. Important social, occupational, or recreational activities are given up or reduced because of substance use;
7. The substance use is continued despite knowledge of having a persistent or recurrent physical or psychological problem that is likely to have been caused or exacerbated by the substance (e.g., current cocaine use despite recognition of cocaine-induced depression, or continued drinking despite recognition that an ulcer was made worse by alcohol consumption).

ICD-10 criteria for dependence syndrome
Three or more of the following manifestations should have occurred together for at least 1 month or, if persisting for periods of less than 1 month, should have occurred together repeatedly within a 12-month period:
1. Strong desire or sense of compulsion to take the substance;
2. Impaired capacity to control substance-taking behaviour in terms of its onset, termination, or levels of use, as evidenced by: the substance being often taken in larger amounts or over a longer period than intended; or by a persistent desire or unsuccessful efforts to reduce or control substance use;
3. A physiological withdrawal state . . . when substance use is reduced or ceased, as evidenced by the characteristic withdrawal syndrome for the substance, or by use of the same (or closely related) substance with the intention of relieving or avoiding withdrawal symptoms;
4. Evidence of tolerance to the effects of the substance, such that there is a need for significantly increased amounts of the substance to achieve intoxication or the desired effect, or a markedly diminished effect with continued use of the same amount of the substance;
5. Preoccupation with substance use, as manifested by important alternative pleasures or interests being given up or reduced because of substance use; or a great deal of time being spent in activities necessary to obtain, take, or recover from the effects of the substance;
6. Persistent substance use despite clear evidence of harmful consequences . . . as evidenced by continued use when the individual is actually aware, or may be expected to be aware, of the nature and extent of harm.

Source: APA (2000) (reprinted with permission from the *Diagnostic and Statistical Manual of Mental Disorders, Fourth Edition, Text Revision*. Copyright 2000 American Psychiatric Association) and WHO (1993a) (reprinted with permission. Copyright 1993 by the World Health Organization).

individual has experienced either tolerance or withdrawal, their dependence diagnosis is further specified as physiological. Tolerance is defined as "the need for greatly increased amounts of the substance to achieve intoxication (or the desired effect) or a markedly diminished effect with continued use of the same amount of the substance" (p. 192).

Substance withdrawal (Table 2.2) is defined in the DSM-IV as "the development of a substance-specific maladaptive behavioral change, with physiological and cognitive concomitants, that is due to the cessation of, or reduction in, heavy or prolonged substance use" (APA, 2000, p. 201). The symptoms of withdrawal are substance-specific and are very similar between the DSM-IV and ICD-10. For example, symptoms of cocaine withdrawal include "fatigue, vivid unpleasant dreams, insomnia or hypersomnia, increased appetite, and psychomotor retardation or agitation" (APA, 1994; p. 246) whereas opioid withdrawal can be experienced as "dysphoric mood, nausea or vomiting, muscle aches, lacrimation or rhinorrhea, pupillary dilation, piloerection, sweating, diarrhea, yawning, fever, and insomnia" (APA, 1994, p. 273). DSM-IV criteria do not provide specific withdrawal symptoms for cannabis, which must be clarified in future research. Substance-specific withdrawal symptoms correspond between DSM-IV and ICD-10 classification systems. For the withdrawal diagnosis, however, the DSM-IV nomenclature additionally requires distress or impairment related to social, occupational, or other important activities (criterion B).

Table 2.2 Symptoms of withdrawal diagnoses

DSM-IV criteria for substance withdrawal
A. The development of a substance-specific syndrome due to the cessation of (or reduction in) substance use that has been heavy or prolonged.
B. The substance-specific syndrome causes clinically significant distress or impairment in social, occupational, or other important areas of functioning.
C. The symptoms are not due to a general medical condition and are not better accounted for by another mental disorder.

ICD-10 criteria for withdrawal state
G1. There must be clear evidence of recent cessation or reduction of substance use after repeated, and usually prolonged and/or high-dose, use of that substance.
G2. Symptoms and signs are compatible with the known features of a withdrawal state form the particular substance or substances (see below).
G3. Symptoms and signs are not accounted for by a medical disorder unrelated to substance use, and not better accounted for by another mental or behavioural disorder.

Source: APA (2000) (reprinted with permission from the *Diagnostic and Statistical Manual of Mental Disorders, Fourth Edition, Text Revision.* Copyright 2000 American Psychiatric Association) and WHO (1993a) (reprinted with permission. Copyright 1993 by the World Health Organization).

Subtle differences between the ICD-10 and DSM-IV dependence criteria could lead to disagreements in decisions about which individuals meet criteria for diagnosis. Two differences are noted: (a) the inclusion of a craving symptom in the ICD-10 and (b) DSM-IV criteria three and four are combined into one criterion in ICD-10 (#2) and DSM-IV criteria five and six are combined into a single criterion in ICD-10 (#5). Craving is described as "a strong desire or sense of compulsion to take the substance" (symptom #1, WHO, 1993a, p. 57, Table 1). Hence, individuals experiencing a strong desire to consume a substance in addition to having two other criteria would qualify for ICD-10 dependence but not DSM-IV dependence. Studies regarding the rates of disagreement between DSM-IV and ICD-10 diagnoses will be presented below.

DSM-IV substance abuse versus ICD-10 harmful use

The abuse and harmful use diagnoses (Table 2.3) have been described by some researchers as similar because they are both residual categories to dependence in the sense that individuals could qualify for abuse or harmful use diagnoses only if the dependence criteria are not fulfilled. However, differences exist between the abuse and harmful use criteria. DSM-IV substance abuse is characterized as "a maladaptive pattern of substance use manifested by recurrent and significant adverse consequences related to the repeated use of substances" (APA, 2000, p. 198). DSM-IV requires "impairment or distress", as defined by the repeated experience of one of four specific criteria in a 12-month period. It should be noted that nicotine abuse does not exist. The ICD-10 requirement of actual harm (criterion A) from substance use is vague compared to the substance abuse criteria. Another difference is noted in that the ICD-10 nomenclature specifies that harmful use must persist for at least one month or occur repeatedly within a 12-month period.

Substance intoxication

Intoxication (Table 2.4) is characterized in the DSM-IV as "the development of a reversible substance-specific syndrome due to the recent ingestion of (or exposure to) a substance" (APA, 2000, p. 199). As with withdrawal, intoxication signs are defined primarily in physiologic terms and vary across substances. For example, DSM-IV (2000) diagnostic criteria for cannabis intoxication include two or more of the following signs that appear within two hours of cannabis use: "(1) conjunctival injection, (2) increased appetite, (3) dry mouth, and (4) tachycardia (p. 239)" whereas signs of hallucinogen intoxication include two or more signs that develop during or shortly after the use of the hallucinogenic substance: "(1) pupillary dilation, (2) tachycardia, (3) sweating, (4) palpitations, (5) blurred vision, (6) tremors, and (7) incoordination" (p. 253). Criteria for intoxication from ingestion of each substance are consistent between the DSM-IV and the ICD-10 systems.

Table 2.3 Abuse versus harmful use diagnoses

DSM-IV criteria for substance abuse
A. A maladaptive pattern of substance use leading to clinically significant impairment or distress, as manifested by one (or more) of the following, occurring within a 12-month period:
    (1) recurrent substance use resulting in a failure to fulfil major role obligations at work, school, or home (e.g., repeated absences or poor work performance related to substance use; substance-related absences, suspensions, or expulsions from school; neglect of children or household);
    (2) recurrent substance use in situations in which it is physically hazardous (e.g., driving an automobile or operating a machine when impaired by substance use);
    (3) recurrent substance-related legal problems (e.g., arrests for substance-related disorderly conduct);
    (4) continued substance use despite having persistent or recurrent social or interpersonal problems caused or exacerbated by the effects of the substance (e.g., arguments with spouse about consequences of intoxication, physical fights);
B. The symptoms have never met the criteria for substance dependence for this class of substance.

ICD-10 criteria for harmful use
A. There must be clear evidence that the substance use was responsible for (or substantially contributed to) physical or psychological harm, including impaired judgement or dysfunctional behaviour, which may lead to disability or have adverse consequences for interpersonal relationships.
B. The nature of the harm should be clearly identifiable (and specified).
C. The pattern of use has persisted for at least 1 month or has occurred repeatedly within a 12-month period.
D. The disorder does not meet the criteria for any other mental or behavioural disorder related to the same drug in the same time period (except for acute intoxication).

Source: APA (2000) (reprinted with permission from the *Diagnostic and Statistical Manual of Mental Disorders, Fourth Edition, Text Revision.* Copyright 2000 American Psychiatric Association) and WHO (1993a) (reprinted with permission. Copyright 1993 by the World Health Organization).

Diagnostic agreement between DSM-IV and ICD-10

One of the most comprehensive investigations of the agreement between DSM-IV and ICD-10 diagnoses of substance use-related disorders in different cultures was initiated by the World Health Organization (WHO) and conducted in partnership with the U.S. National Institute on Drug Abuse (NIDA) and National Institute on Alcoholism and Alcohol Abuse (NIAAA) (Cottler *et al.*, 1997; Hasin *et al.*, 1997b; Pull *et al.*, 1997; Ustun *et al.*, 1997). The primary aims of this project were to develop culturally acceptable instruments for diagnosing alcohol and drug use disorders internationally and to investigate the reliability and validity of the instruments. The instruments that were tested were the Composite International Diagnostic Interview (CIDI; World Health Organization, 1993b), the Schedules for Clinical Assessment in Neuropsychiatry (SCAN; World Health Organization, 1993c) and the Alcohol Use Disorder and Associated Disabilities

Table 2.4 Intoxication diagnoses

DSM-IV criteria for substance intoxication

A. The development of a reversible substance-specific syndrome due to recent ingestion of (or exposure to) a substance. Note: Different substances may produce similar or identical syndromes.
B. Clinically significant maladaptive behavioural or psychological changes that are due to the effect of the substance on the central nervous system (e.g., belligerence, mood lability, cognitive impairment, impaired judgement, impaired social or occupational functioning) and development during or shortly after use of the substance.
C. The symptoms are not due to a general medical condition and are not better accounted for by another mental disorder.

ICD-10 criteria for acute intoxication

G1. There must be clear evidence of recent use of a psychoactive substance (or substances) at sufficiently high dose levels to be consistent with intoxication.
G2. There must be symptoms or signs of intoxication compatible with the known actions of the particular substance (or substances), as specified below, and of sufficient severity to produce disturbances in the level of consciousness, cognition, perception, affect, or behaviour that are of clinical importance.
G3. The symptoms or signs present cannot be accounted for by a medical disorder unrelated to substance use, and not better accounted for by another mental or behavioural disorder.

Source: APA (2000) (reprinted with permission from the *Diagnostic and Statistical Manual of Mental Disorders, Fourth Edition, Text Revision.* Copyright 2000 American Psychiatric Association) and WHO (1993a) (reprinted with permission. Copyright 1993 by the World Health Organization).

Interview Schedule—Alcohol/Drug—Revised (AUDADIS-ADR, World Health Organization, 1993d).

Diagnostic agreement between the DSM-IV and ICD-10 nomenclatures was estimated using data collected from 1,811 participants from psychiatric treatment, other medical, and community settings at twelve international sites (Hasin *et al.*, 1997b). The sites from which participants were recruited included Amsterdam (The Netherlands), Ankara (Turkey), Athens (Greece), Bangalore (India), Farmington (Connecticut, USA), Ibadan (Nigeria), Jebel (Romania), Luxembourg (Luxembourg), St Louis (Missouri, USA), San Juan (Puerto Rico) and two sites at Sydney (Australia) (Ustun, *et al.*, 1997). Data were collected using the native languages of the locations. Level of agreement for diagnoses was estimated using the kappa statistic, which ranges from −1.0 (complete disagreement) to 0.0 (chance agreement) to 1.0 (complete agreement). Kappa estimates of .75 to 1.0 are considered excellent, .60 to .75 are good, .40 to .60 are fair, and less than .40 are considered poor (Bishop *et al.*, 1975). Agreement between DSM-IV and ICD-10 diagnoses were calculated for participants who reported using the substance.

Estimates of diagnostic agreement were calculated for each instrument, thereby providing a range of kappa values of the agreement between DSM-IV and ICD-10 diagnoses for each diagnosis. Kappas were calculated using two-by-two contingency tables categorizing persons with versus persons without the dependence diagnosis. Agreements for alcohol dependence in the past year were .90 to .92 and over the lifetime were .87 to .92 (Hasin et al., 1997b). Corresponding estimates of agreement between dependence diagnoses were .84 to .88 and .89 to .90 for cannabis, .86 to 1.0 and .92 to .95 for amphetamines, .89 to .98 and .46 to .93 for sedatives, .96 to .98 and .98 (each instrument) for opiates, and .96 to .98 and .96 to 1.0 for cocaine. With a single exception (.46 for sedative dependence measured with the CIDI), agreement estimates between DSM-IV and ICD-10 dependence diagnoses were excellent and consistent across instruments.

In contrast, agreement estimates between abuse and harmful use diagnoses were poor to fair and less consistent between instruments (Hasin et al., 1997b). Kappas were calculated using two-by-two contingency tables categorizing persons with versus persons without abuse or harmful use diagnosis. One confound to this type of analysis is that participants might meet criteria for dependence in only one diagnostic system or the other and therefore only be eligible for either abuse or harmful use. This confound will lower agreement between abuse and harmful use. For alcohol, agreement estimates between abuse and harmful use diagnoses were .24 to .40 for the past year and .23 to .38 for the lifetime. Corresponding agreement estimates between abuse and harmful use were .22 to .38 and .28 to .49 for cannabis, .46 to .61 and .34 to .45 for amphetamines, .29 to .45 and .24 to .44 for sedatives, .27 to .42 and .30 to .54 for opiates, and .01 to .60 and .09 to .51 for cocaine. Poor agreement between abuse and harmful use diagnoses has been reported for different age groups, ethnicities, and genders as well as for community and treatment samples (Hasin et al., 1996; Langenbucher et al., 1994).

The poorer agreement and greater variation in instrument kappa values between abuse and harmful use could be due to poor conceptualization of abuse or harmful use, poor operationalization of abuse or harmful use, or combinations of these possibilities. Other research suggests weaknesses with the harmful use nomenclature or assessment because of the poor reliability reported for harmful use diagnoses, which was reported for each of the instruments in this sample (e.g., Ustun et al., 1997) and other samples (e.g., Regier et al., 1994). The reliabilities of abuse criteria and of abuse diagnosis (when the requirement of not meeting dependence diagnosis is ignored) were fair to excellent (Hasin et al., 1997b; Horton et al., 2000).

CLASSIFICATION CRITERIA FOR ADOLESCENTS

The basic question, "How appropriate are substance use-related diagnostic nomenclature for adolescent?" has been addressed in few studies. Social problems due to substance use were moved from dependence criteria in DSM-III-R to the abuse criteria in DSM-IV. It appears that this change has resulted in fewer adolescents being identified for dependence diagnosis but more adolescents being identified for abuse diagnoses for alcohol, cannabis, cocaine, and hallucinogens (Mikulich *et al.*, 2001; Winters *et al.*, 1999). In contrast, fewer adolescents qualify for both of the dependence and abuse diagnoses of amphetamines, opiates, and inhalants using DSM-IV criteria compared to the DSM-III-R criteria (Mikulich *et al.*, 2001).

An illustration of why social problems are so critical to diagnosis in adolescents is the following scenario. Substance use by adolescents can lead to poorer academic performance and strain adolescents' relationships with parents when the parents are notified of their drop in academic performance. Adolescents who receive substance use treatment might do so at parents' insistence before physical or psychological problems develop, as a requirement to returning to school. Social problems is not the only substance use-related criterion that adolescents experience. Simply because they are younger, on average adolescents have had shorter time periods to use substances from the time that substance use was initiated than adults. Hence, it might be hypothesized that fewer adolescents have experienced physiological symptoms. However, relatively high proportions of adolescents receiving treatment for substance misuse report having physiological symptoms (Mikulich *et al.*, 2001).

Statistically, the agreement between DSM-III-R and DSM-IV dependence diagnoses generally have been reported to be good to excellent for adolescents (Mikulich *et al.*, 2001; Winters *et al.*, 1999). Initial results suggest that no difference occurs in which adolescents meet criteria for dependence when the clustering criterion (at least three criteria must occur within a 12-month period) dropped compared to when it is required (Mikulich *et al.*, 2001). This finding may not be specific to adolescents, however, because similar results have been reported for adults (Cottler *et al.*, 1995b).

Limited research has investigated agreement between DSM-IV and ICD-10 substance use-related diagnoses in adolescents. Pollock and colleagues (2000) investigated the agreement in alcohol diagnoses based on DSM-IV criteria and ICD-10 criteria among adolescents recruited from clinical settings and the community of Pittsburgh, Pennsylvania. All of the adolescents in their sample were regular drinkers. Assessments of substance use diagnoses were conducted using the Structured Clinical Interview for the DSM. ICD-10 harmful use diagnosis was assumed to correspond approximately to the DSM-IV abuse diagnosis. Diagnoses were handled as if they represented thresholds on a severity continuum (i.e., dependence diagnosis was worst, abuse or harmful use represented a lower level of severity and no diagnosis was healthy). Only fair agreement was reported, with the greatest discrepancies occurring between ICD-10 harmful use and DSM-IV abuse diagnosis.

Moreover, agreement between the DSM-III-R and DSM-IV abuse diagnoses has been reported to be poor to fair for adolescents receiving treatment using the Substance Abuse Module (Mikulich *et al.*, 2001). In contrast to these findings of less than ideal reliability for diagnoses, the cannabis abuse diagnosis provided useful prognostic information over a 1.5-year period for German adolescents (Perkonigg et al., 1999). Of adolescents who met criteria for cannabis abuse at the baseline assessment 44% also met abuse criteria at the 1.5-year follow-up, 5% met cannabis dependence criteria, and only 18% of the cannabis abusers abstained from cannabis use. Overall, Perkonigg and colleagues (1999) found that adolescents who used cannabis in some capacity at baseline generally continued or increased their level of use at the follow-up.

At least three investigations have led researchers to suggest combining DSM-IV abuse and dependence criteria into a single category for adolescents and differentiating abuse from dependence in terms of the number of criteria experienced (Fulkerson et al., 1999; Harrison et al., 1998; Pollock and Martin, 1999). The literature regarding classification of substance use diagnoses among adolescents is scant and research is needed to better understand how well or how poorly the DSM-IV and ICD-10 substance use classification nomenclatures generalize to adolescents. Harmful use and abuse diagnoses should be interpreted with particular caution in adolescents. Harrison and colleagues (1998) reported a greater prevalence of dependence items than abuse items, and interestingly, failure to fulfil role obligations and legal issues co-occurred more often with severe dependence symptoms than other abuse symptoms. These findings are consistent with other studies among adolescents (Martin et al., 1995, 1996; White, 1987; Winters et al., 1999).

Remaining questions

In spite of these efforts to personify a substance use classification, a number of important questions have not been adequately resolved. For illustration, one question is: Should the same criteria be used to define disorders for each substance? It was found that only for certain substances, the two definitions of withdrawal (use of a drug to get relief from withdrawal symptoms and experiencing withdrawal symptoms) overlapped (Cottler et al., 1995b; Cottler et al., 1993). Hence, for some substances, using the two definitions of withdrawal will result in a greater number of persons meeting dependence diagnosis whereas for other substances, the later definition of withdrawal might suffice as the criterion. Other important questions not adequately addressed at the time of the release of DSM-IV substance use disorder criteria included: Do the same criteria for dependence generalize to all substances? In what ways does the Alcohol Dependence Syndrome not generalize to other substances? Is abuse a distinct category from dependence, is abuse a residual category of persons with a mild form of substance use-related pathology, or should these disorders be placed on a single severity continuum? Should caffeine dependence be included as a disorder? Can the "clustering" criterion be reliably and validly assessed? Addressing these questions can only be accomplished using an instrument specifically designed to assess these aspects of substance use disorders.

ASSESSMENT

An issue that is equally important to developing a substance use disorder classification nomenclature is the availability of an instrument to assess (a) criteria of the classification system as well as (b) indicators of substance misuse that might be under consideration for classification system (Cottler and Compton, 1993; Cottler *et al.*, 1995b). In certain respects, the classification system and the assessment instrument co-evolve because an assessment of substance use disorders is necessary for research on the adequacy of the classification nomenclature (Cottler and Keating, 1990; Robins, 1989). The purpose of using an instrument to assess substance use disorders is to collect the information needed to determine how an individual fits into a substance use disorder classification scheme. Simply developing an instrument to assess diagnostic classification can improve the nomenclature of the classification system. For illustration, developing questions to assess criteria or symptoms might lead to identification of ambiguities in the nomenclature. Regarding substance use disorders, vague terms such as "persisted", "few", or "longer period of time" must be operationalized; doing so can be useful for greater specification of these terms in the nomenclature (Cottler and Keating, 1990). Another example from research with the Composite International Diagnostic Interview was the finding that cultural differences must be considered when developing the instrument. In some cultures regular consumption of alcohol is normative. In certain other cultures, however, some interviewees were confused by the question, "Were there ever objections from your family about your drinking?" because any use of alcohol was objectionable (Cottler and Compton, 1993). Such cross-cultural differences can be taken into account when translating assessments into the native languages of that culture.

Characteristics of substance use other than diagnostic nomenclature ought to be included in the assessment because they can provide insight to substance use classification. Treatment outcomes can be predicted with increased accuracy using knowledge about patients' patterns of substance use and treatment planning is often shaped, at least in part, by the antecedents and consequences of substance use (Babor, 1993). Knowledge of patterns of use, antecedents, and consequences also provide insight to the etiology of substance use disorders (Babor, 1993).

Characteristics of the ideal diagnostic interview

Robins (1988), Cottler and Keating (1990), and Cottler and Compton (1993) outline characteristics of a good diagnostic interview (Table 2.5). Before an instrument can be considered useful for assessing substance use classification, it must be demonstrated that the information obtained by the instrument is

Table 2.5 Characteristics of a good diagnostic interview for substance use-related disorders

1	The nosologies of multiple diagnostic systems are accurately operationalized
2	Persons who are ill should be distinguished from those who are well
3	Interviews should be highly structured (every question is asked the same way by every interviewer)
4	Criteria or symptoms of medical origin are excluded from contributing to substance diagnoses
5	Language should be nonidiomatic
6	Language should not be culture-specific
7	Interviews should be completable in one sitting
8	Interviews should be acceptable to everyone
9	Interviews should be error-free
10	Questions should be closed-ended
11	Questions should be as brief as possible without sacrificing clarity of meaning
12	Questions should be comprehensible to persons having all educational levels
13	"Skipouts" should be used only when it is impossible that interviewees have experienced any of the criteria that are skipped, based on the response to a probe question
14	The diagnostic criterion that is operationalized by each question should be transparent
15	Information collected should not be subject to individual interpretation
16	Information collected should not require external sources
17	Impairments not resulting from the illness should not be classified as symptoms
18	Enhancements such as reference cards or pictures should be available when needed to enhance interviewees' comprehension of questions
19	Training materials and course should be available
20	Empirical evidence (e.g., sensitivity, specificity, reliability, validity) from multiple datasets collected by different researchers should be good to excellent
21	Instrument should be computerized to maximize interview simplicity and minimize errors that might occur in the interview or data entry

Source: Cottler and Compton (1993), Cottler and Keating (1990), Robins (1988).

reliable (variation in responses to the queries is due to change in substance use characteristics rather than factors such as time or person administering the instrument) and valid (the instrument truly measures the substance use characteristics that it is purported to measure). Characteristics in Table 2.5 numbered 3, 4, 5, 6, 10, 12, 14, 15, 16, and 20 augment the reliability of an assessment instrument. Structured interviews (number 3) include those designed to have questions asked and scored in an identical manner in every interview. The reliability of an instrument is generally estimated by administering the instrument to the same individuals twice, with a one-week interval between interviews, with two different interviewers (test–retest, interrater reliability). Kappas are calculated to estimate diagnostic reliability, using the consistency of participants' responses between the two interviews.

Characteristics numbered 1, 2, 4, 11, 13, 14, 15, 16, 17, and 20 augment the validity of an assessment instrument. The validity of an instrument can be evaluated in numerous ways. Face validity refers to the concept that the questions appear to assess the trait that they are intended to assess. Concurrent validity is estimated by administering more than one substance use measure to the same individuals. Persons scoring high (low) for substance use pathology on one instrument also should score high (low) on the other instrument. Ideally all of the persons with a substance use disorder would be identified as having the disorder by the instrument (high sensitivity) and all of the persons without the disorder would not be identified as having the disorder by the instrument (high specificity).

An instrument also should not be offensive to the individuals who are assessed, which is described by characteristics numbered 7, 8, 11, and 12. Another characteristic, that the interview be pilot tested to ferret out errors (number 9), ideally would be carried out in three ways. First, an interview should be administered to a pilot sample and the participants in the pilot study would be queried about their comprehension of the assessment questions. The SAM was tested in this manner by administering it to the same persons on two occasions and using the Discrepancy Interview Protocol to ask participants to explain responses to the same question that were different at the two interviews (Cottler *et al.*, 1994; Cottler and Keating, 1990). Items that were misunderstood were then rewritten for better clarity. The second type of pilot study should consist of an expert review of the interview. The third type of pilot study applies to instruments that are computerized and involves testing the accuracy of recording and scoring of individuals' responses.

Characteristics numbered 18 through 20 augment the generalizability of the instrument so that persons who did not develop the instrument are able to administer the instrument as well as the persons who developed the instrument. The generalizability of an instrument also ought to be tested in terms of its reliability and validity with samples from cultures other than the original sample. An exceptional example of international testing of substance use diagnostic instruments is the partnership between the World Health Organization (WHO), U.S. National Institute on Drug Abuse (NIDA), and National Institute on Alcoholism and Alcohol Abuse (NIAAA) (Cottler *et al.*, 1997; Hasin *et al.*, 1997b; Pull *et al.*, 1997; Ustun *et al.*, 1997). The Composite International Diagnostic Interview, Schedules for Clinical Assessment in Neuropsychiatry, and Alcohol Use Disorder and Associated Disabilities Interview Schedule—Alcohol/Drug—Revised were independently translated from English into the native languages used at each of the international research centres (Ustun *et al.*, 1997). Using the translated instruments, each was then "back-translated" into English to ferret out errors in the original translation and further refine the translated instruments (Room *et al.*, 1996; Ustun *et al.*, 1997). Each instrument was also tested for its cross-cultural acceptability (Room *et al.*, 1996).

The three instruments used in the WHO/NIDA/NIAAA international study will be presented because of their widespread use in research on classification of substance use disorders. One of these instruments, the substance use-related portion of the CIDI, will be briefly presented in the context of a discussion of the Substance Abuse Module (SAM) because the SAM was developed from the substance use section of the CIDI-SAM. The SAM was designed to thoroughly assess substance use nomenclature as well as substance use characteristics that might be useful for clarification or revision of the current nomenclatures (Cottler and Compton, 1993; Cottler and Keating, 1990). The SAM meets the twenty-one characteristics of the ideal assessment, hence, it will continue to be used to illustrate specific aspects of the ideal characteristics of a diagnostic substance use instrument.

Substance Abuse Module (SAM)

The SAM represents a continuation of a tradition of mental health classification assessments (Cottler and Keating, 1990). At the request of the U.S. National Institute on Mental Health, Lee Robins and colleagues (1981) developed the NIMH Diagnostic Interview Schedule (DIS) to assess criteria of psychiatric disorders based on the DSM-III, Research Diagnostic Criteria (Spitzer *et al.*, 1978), and the Feighner criteria (Feighner *et al.*, 1972). The DIS was used in the landmark Epidemiological Catchment Area study, which estimated the prevalence and incidence of DSM-III psychiatric disorders in five United States metropolitan areas using data collected from nearly 20,000 participants (Robins and Regier, 1991).

The size and scope of the Epidemiological Catchment Area project forced the investigators to develop an assessment that met many of the ideal characteristics (Robins *et al.*, 1985). The DIS had to be fully structured because it had to be administered by lay interviewers, each criterion for each psychiatric disorder had to be administered because the prevalences of untreated disorders were to be estimated, and the data collected had to be in a format that could be subjected to computer algorithms to determine diagnostic status. In addition to diagnoses, the use of health services and demographic characteristics were queried. Although data were only collected in the United States, questions had to be understandable by adults of varying levels of intelligence, education, and ages, and they had to be inoffensive to persons in the general community who were generally unfamiliar with psychiatric disorders at the time. The DIS had to be completed in a single setting. The DIS has been found to be reliable and valid in psychometric studies (e.g., Robins *et al.*, 1981; Karno *et al.*, 1985)

The CIDI is an expanded version of the DIS with additional items from the Present State Examination (Robins *et al.*, 1988, 1990). The Present State Examination is used to estimate the interviewee's mental health status at the time of the interview (Wing *et al.*, 1974). Development of the CIDI was requested by the WHO/ADAMHA Task Force on Psychiatric Assessment Instruments for use in international survey research on general populations.

The CIDI was designed for cross-cultural use, is highly structured, and was originally written to assess DSM and ICD psychiatric disorders. Field testing of the CIDI was conducted in Australia, Brazil, East Germany, France, Greece, India, Italy, Luxembourg, Norway, the People's Republic of China, Portugal, Puerto Rico, Sweden, the United Kingdom, the United States, and West Germany. The CIDI was deemed acceptable in the field trials and was reported to be reliable and valid, although the substance abuse and dependence questions were reported to be too long and certain substance use-related diagnoses had less than ideal reliability (Cottler *et al.*, 1991; Robins *et al.*, 1988; Wittchen *et al.*, 1991). More recent investigations of the CIDI also support its reliability and validity; however, agreement between the CIDI and other diagnostic interviews for certain drug dependence disorders and abuse/harmful use is less than optimal (Andrews and Peters, 1998; Cottler *et al.*, 1997; Hasin *et al.*, 1997b; Pull *et al.*, 1997; Wittchen *et al.*, 1998). Inquiries into why participants provided different responses to different diagnostic interviews indicated that nearly 75% of the discrepant answers were due to differences between the CIDI, AUDADIS-ADR, and SCAN, a result that was consistent across cultures (Cottler *et al.*, 1997).

The SAM is a revised and expanded version of the substance abuse section of the CIDI (Cottler and Compton, 1993; Cottler and Keating, 1990; Cottler *et al.*, 1989). The SAM assesses substance use disorder criteria that can be used for diagnoses based on the DSM-III-R, DSM-IV and ICD-10 criteria. It has been used in numerous nosological studies of substance use classification (e.g., Cottler, *et al.*, 1995a, 1995b; Langenbucher *et al.*, 1997, 2000; Morgenstern *et al.*, 1994; Woody *et al.*, 1993). Diagnoses for interviewees' lifetime or preceding 12 months can be assessed for tobacco, alcohol, prescription psychoactive medications, amphetamines, cannabis, cocaine, hallucinogens, inhalants, opiates, PCP, stimulants, sedatives and other, miscellaneous substances. Questions regarding caffeine and club drug use-related disorders were recently added to the SAM. The SAM includes questions regarding ages of onset and most recent occurrence of each symptom (and therefore criteria), individual withdrawal symptoms for each substance, specific physical, social, and psychological consequences for each substance, and quantity and frequency of use to estimate the severity and course of each disorder. The SAM also can be used to assess substance use patterns as well as the age of onset, most recent experience, duration, and course of each symptom and criterion.

Reference cards are used to aid interviewees' comprehension of questions. Use of "skipouts" in the CIDI-SAM are minimal and used only when the response to certain questions can only be "no" based on previous questions (e.g., interviewees who report never having used opiates would not be asked about criteria and symptoms of opiate use). Page 27 from the latest version of the SAM, Version 4.1, is presented in Figure 2.1 to illustrate qualities of the SAM that fit certain characteristics of the ideal assessment instruments. The SAM is a highly structured interview and all of the questions are closed-ended. Interviewers read SAM questions and follow instructions that are presented in capital letters. Questions on page 27 of the SAM tap criteria from ICD-10, DSM-III-R, and DSM-IV alcohol diagnoses. Question C7 pertains to social problems that result from alcohol consumption. This criterion was used to operationalize alcohol dependence in DSM-III-R nomenclature (see marginal notation "AD3RA6") and alcohol abuse in DSM-IV (marginal notation "AA4A4").

Figure 1

CIDI-SAM Page 27

	C.	Was it before you were 15 years old?	NO ...... GO TO E .... 1 YES 5
	D.	IF A IS <15 OR C = YES, ASK: Did you get drunk more than once before you were 15?	NO .... 1 YES 5
DSMALCAA	E.	Have you ever kept drinking for a couple of days or more without sobering up?	NO ...... (GO TO F) .... 1 YES 5
DSMALCMR DSMALCAR	REC:	When was the last time?	__/__ __/__ MONTH AGE
DSMALCAO	ONS:	How old were you the first time?	__/__ AGE
	F.	IN C2, IF TOTAL NUMBER OF DRINKS = 20 OR MORE ON AT LEAST 2 DAYS, CODE F AND G YES WITHOUT ASKING. CODE 00 IN REC MONTH AND GO TO ONS. Have you ever drunk as much as 20 drinks in one day — that would be about a fifth of liquor, or 3 bottles of wine, or as much as 3 six-packs of beer?	NO ...... GO TO C7 .... 1 YES 5
DSMALCAA	G.	Have you done this more than once?	NO .... 1 YES 5
DSMALCMR DSMALCAR	REC:	When was the last time?	__/__ __/__ MONTH AGE
DSMALCAO	ONS:	How old were you the first time you drank 20 or more drinks in one day?	__/__ AGE
	C7.	Did drinking ever cause you to have:	NO YES
DSMALCAB		1) problems with your family?	1 5
DSMALCAB		2) problems with your friends?	1 5
DSMALCAB		3) problems with people at work or school?	1 5
DSMALCAB		4) Did you ever get into physical fights while drinking?	1 5
AA4A4 AD3RA6 AA3RA3	A.	IF ALL CODED NO, GO TO C8A. IF ANY CODED YES, CONTINUE. Did you continue to drink after you realized drinking was causing you any of these problems?	NO........ GO TO C8 .... 1 YES 5
MONTH ALCA4MR ALC3RMR DSMALCMR AGE ALBA4AR ALC3RAR DSMALCAR	REC:	When was the last time you continued to drink after you realized drinking caused you to have (LIST ALL CODED YES IN 1-4)?	__/__ __/__ MONTH AGE
ALCA4AO ALC3RAO DSMALCAO	ONS:	How old were you the first time?	__/__ AGE

JAN = 01, FEB = 02, MAR = 03, APR = 04, MAY = 05, JUN = 06, JUL = 07, AUG = 08, SEP = 09, OCT = 10, NOV = 11, DEC = 12.
Refused = 97, Don't Know = 98

1/7/00   CIDI-SAM

Figure 2.1 Page 27 from the latest version of the SAM.

The SAM has been thoroughly pilot-tested (Cottler and Compton, 1993; Cottler and Keating, 1990). An extensive training course is required to administer the SAM, during which training materials are provided. The SAM is computerized, which maximizes the convenience of administration of the interview and minimizes errors that could occur during the entry of data into databases (Cottler and Compton, 1993). The SAM has been found to provide excellent reliabilities for DSM-IV substance use-related criteria, good to excellent reliabilities for substance use dependence, and fair to excellent reliabilities for ICD-10 dependence diagnoses in samples of African-Americans, Caucasians, drug users in treatment, and community substance using samples (Compton *et al.*, 1996a,b; Cottler *et al.*, 1989; Horton *et al.*, 2000). The SAM can be used alone or in conjunction with the CIDI or the DIS to obtain information about psychiatric disorders. Data are currently being collected to investigate the psychometric properties of the SAM in adolescents (Cottler *et al.*, 1988-2001).

Alcohol Use Disorder and Associated Disabilities Interview Schedule—Alcohol/Drug—Revised (AUDADIS-ADR)

The AUDADIS-ADR was developed from the Alcohol Use Disorder and Associated Disabilities Interview Schedule (AUDADIS) (Grant *et al.*, 1995; Grant and Hasin, 1992; Chatterji *et al.*, 1997). The AUDADIS-ADR is an international version of the AUDADIS that was used in the WHO/NIDA/NIAAA international study (Chatterji *et al.*, 1997). The AUDADIS format, skipout questions, and supplemental questions were used in the AUDADIS-ADR.

The AUDADIS was developed for use in the National Longitudinal Alcohol Epidemiologic Survey of the National Institute on Alcohol and Alcohol Abuse (NIAAA). The National Longitudinal Alcohol Epidemiologic Survey was a national United States survey on the comorbidity of substance use disorders and other psychiatric disorders that began in 1992. The AUDADIS is a structured interview that includes assessments of DSM-IV, DSM-III-R, and ICD-10 diagnostic classifications of substance use disorders. It includes sections to assess mood and anxiety disorders, antisocial personality, substance use-related medical conditions and family history of substance use disorders. AUDADIS questions are largely closed-ended and the substance use-related diagnostic questions are asked for individuals admitting to having drunk alcohol at least 12 times over the course of one year or used a drug at least 12 times over their lifetime. Substance use frequency and quantity questions are included. Reference cards are used to enhance participants' comprehension of questions. The reliability of the AUDADIS, DSM-IV, and ICD-10 substance use disorders has been demonstrated to be good to excellent among a sample that was randomly selected from members of households in which at least one family member was reported to have consumed three or more drinks in the preceding year (Grant *et al.*, 1995). In this study, diagnoses were handled as if they occurred on a continuum of severity such that dependence was the most severe pathology followed by abuse/harmful use followed by not having either disorder. One weakness in the analysis was that it did not assure that data were only collected from substance users. This error has been described as a serious pitfall of many studies (Cottler, 1992).

The AUDADIS reliability study was repeated with a sample of substance treatment patients and found to provide good to excellent reliability for DSM-IV dependence diagnoses but poor reliabilities for abuse diagnoses (Hasin, Carpenter *et al.*, 1997a). The poor reliabilities for the abuse diagnoses were reported when including the criterion that dependence diagnoses are met (i.e., someone with abuse diagnosis at the first assessment might still meet abuse criteria at the later assessment but also meet criteria for dependence and thereby not qualify for an abuse diagnosis). When participants who met dependence criteria were not disqualified for the abuse diagnoses, reliabilities for abuse diagnoses were good to excellent with few exceptions (Hasin, Carpenter *et al.*, 1997a).

Modifications to the AUDADIS used in the AUDADIS-ADR include better representation of ICD-10 disorders, question refinements, and format changes to facilitate cross-cultural diversity. Substances that are assessed using the AUDADIS-ADR include alcohol, amphetamines, cocaine, cannabis, hallucinogens, inhalants/solvents, opioids, PCP, and sedatives/tranquillizers. Diagnoses are assessed for the preceding year as well as during interviewees' lifetime. The reliability of the AUDADIS-ADR was investigated using data collected from an international sample of drug users recruited from the community or persons in drug treatment settings (Chatterji *et al.*, 1997). Good to excellent reliabilities were reported for ICD-10 dependence diagnoses and fair to excellent reliabilities were reported for DSM-IV dependence diagnoses over the preceding year and lifetime. Poor to good reliabilities were reported for abuse and harmful use diagnoses in the preceding year and lifetime.

Schedules for Clinical Assessment in Neuropsychiatry (SCAN)

The SCAN is based on the Present State Exam (PSE) and was developed in response to a request from the WHO Task Force on Psychiatric Assessment Instruments (Wing *et al.*, 1990). The PSE was designed for use by experienced clinicians to assist in the diagnosis of psychiatric disorders and to evaluate the level of severity of the disorders and associated criteria. The PSE is a semi-structured interview. Hence, interviewers can use the sample questions or their own wording as well as alter the order of diagnoses that are assessed in the interview. Because the PSE was designed for use by experienced clinicians, interviewers are able to phrase questions as they see as most appropriate. Follow-up questions are used to clarify interviewees' responses and to determine the level of severity of psychiatric disorder criteria.

The seventh and eighth editions of the PSE were used in two large-scale international studies on psychiatric disorders, conducted during the late 1960s and early 1970s. A PSE syndrome checklist was designed to rate previous episodes of disorders and a PSE etiology schedule was designed to better record antecedents and possible causes of disorders. A computer program (CATEGO) can be used with the PSE to determine how an individual's symptom profile fits ICD psychiatric disorder classification. The PSE has been translated into approximately forty languages.

The SCAN was first published in 1983 and used as a research instrument in England. The SCAN originally provided a format to assess ICD-10 diagnoses (Wing *et al.*, 1990). By 1987, SCAN questions had been revised to also assess DSM-III-R criteria. Like the PSE, the SCAN is a semi-structured interview and open-ended questions may be used at the discretion of the clinician/interviewer. Follow-up questions could be devised and to clarify an interviewee's response. Hence, only clinicians who have graduated from SCAN training can use the SCAN. Unlike the PSE, the SCAN includes alcohol and drug use sections for DSM-IV and ICD-10 diagnostic classifications. The SCAN was modified for cross-cultural acceptability and then the alcohol and drug use sections were tested for their reliability in two international samples (USA and Turkey) (Easton *et al.*, 1997). No early "skipouts" are specified for SCAN questions. Diagnoses for interviewees' lifetime or preceding 12 months can be assessed for tobacco, alcohol, prescription psychoactive medications, amphetamines, cannabis, cocaine, hallucinogens, inhalants, opiates, PCP, stimulants, sedatives and other, miscellaneous substances. Drug users from general community settings and general medical settings were included in the sample along with drug treatment patients. The reliabilities of DSM-IV and ICD-10 dependence diagnoses were good to excellent and the reliability of harmful use of alcohol was good when tested in alcohol users. Ustun and colleagues (1997) reported the test–retest, inter-rater reliability of the SCAN using the international sample of the WHO/NIDA/NIAAA study. Among users of specific substances, kappa reliability estimates ranged from good to excellent for DSM-IV and ICD-10 dependence diagnoses. However, they ranged from very poor to good for abuse diagnoses and were poor for harmful use diagnoses. Compton and colleagues (1996a,b) reported good diagnostic agreement for DSM-IV and ICD-10 dependence diagnoses between SCAN and CIDI-SAM diagnoses among general population drug users and drug treatment patients. Psychometric data for using the SCAN with adolescent populations are currently being collected (Cottler *et al.*, 1988–2001).

AGREEMENT BETWEEN INTERVIEWS IN INTERNATIONAL SAMPLES

ICD-10 diagnoses

Ustun and colleagues (1997) and Pull and colleagues (1997) reported kappa estimates of agreements in ICD-10 diagnoses between the CIDI, AUDADIS-ADR, and SCAN using an international sample of approximately 600 to 730 participants. Agreements for the dependence diagnoses were consistent across the pairs of instruments and ranged from .61 to .69 for alcohol, .64 to .70 for opioids, .36 to .44 for cannabis, .39 to .50 for sedatives, and .51 to .56 for cocaine. However, estimates of agreement for harmful use diagnoses were very poor (0.0 to .34). Reliability of the harmful use diagnoses were found to be poor for each of the instruments in this sample as well as others (e.g., Regier *et al.*, 1994), hence it appears that the ICD-10 harmful use diagnoses require revision to improve their reliability and validity. Slight differences were reported in the prevalences of dependence diagnoses in Pull and colleagues' (1997) sample for specific drugs. The CIDI consistently provided estimates of prevalence that were similar to at least one of the other two instruments, whereas for certain substances the prevalences estimated by either the SCAN or the AUDADIS-ADR deviated slightly from the other two instruments. The AUDADIS-ADR-based estimate of alcohol dependence prevalence was greater (76%) than the CIDI or the SCAN (69% each), and the AUDADIS-ADR-based estimate of sedative dependence prevalence was lower (36%) than either of the other instruments (43% and 47%, respectively). SCAN-based prevalence estimates of cannabis dependence (36%) and amphetamine dependence (41%) were greater than the CIDI- and AUDADIS-ADR-based prevalence estimates of cannabis dependence (24% and 21%, respectively) and amphetamine dependence (25% and 18%, respectively). Prevalence estimates of dependence on cocaine and opioids were very similar between the three instruments.

Compton and colleagues (1996a) reported estimates of agreement between the SAM and the SCAN for a sample of drug abuse patients and community-recruited drug users from St Louis, United States. Their estimates were similar to the results reported by Pull and colleagues (1997) for the CIDI. Compton and colleagues (1996a) reported kappas for alcohol dependence (.67), opioid dependence (.55), cocaine dependence (.54), and cannabis dependence (.48).

DSM-IV diagnoses

Using community and clinical samples from Athens, Luxembourg, and St Louis, United States, Cottler and colleagues (1997) investigated the agreement of DSM-IV diagnoses and criteria over individuals' lifetime between the CIDI, SCAN, and AUDADIS-ADR. Agreement between the three instruments for DSM-IV diagnoses of dependence, using kappa, was good for alcohol (.62 – .67) and opiates (.62 – .67) and fair for cocaine (.45 – .57), sedatives (.43 – .48), and amphetamines (.38 – .53). Kappa estimates of agreement for cannabis dependence were mixed (.35 – .55). Kappa agreement estimates for specific criteria of abuse and dependence were generally consistent with those reported for diagnoses, but somewhat smaller. Moreover, kappa estimates of agreement were generally consistent for each substance regardless of which pair of instruments was analysed.

In a sample of drug abuse patients and community-recruited drug users from St. Louis, Compton and colleagues (1996b) reported kappa estimates of agreement between the CIDI-SAM and the SCAN for DSM-IV dependence diagnoses for alcohol, opiates, cocaine, and cannabis, which ranged from fair to good and were only slightly smaller than test–retest kappas for the CIDI-SAM (Compton et al., 1996b). Consistent with results from Pull and colleagues' (1997) study of ICD-10 diagnoses, a lower agreement between the CIDI-SAM and SCAN was reported for cannabis dependence (.50) than for alcohol dependence (.69) and cocaine dependence (.61).

Although the SAM, CIDI, AUDADIS-ADR, and SCAN meet all or most of the twenty-one characteristics of the ideal diagnostic interview, very little data are available for use of these instruments with adolescents. Data being collected from adolescents using the SAM and SCAN will provide initial reliability estimates and validity estimates (Cottler et al., 1988–2001). These data also should be useful for investigating substance use classification nomenclature for adolescents. Other instruments have been either designed specifically for use with adolescents or preliminary data have been collected for their use with adolescents.

ADDITIONAL INSTRUMENTS FOR SUBSTANCE USE-RELATED DIAGNOSES IN ADOLESCENTS

Some long-existing instruments have recently been used to collect data from adolescents regarding classification of substance use disorders. Some novel instruments show promise for assessment of adolescents' substance use disorders and impairments associated with substance use but will be presented only briefly because of their preliminary stage in development. All of these instruments and those reviewed above assess substance use patterns, diagnoses, and/or consequences of substance use. One unique instrument is currently under development for assessing the antecedents of substance use and misuse in early adolescents and pre-adolescents. Research on this instrument will provide scoring algorithms to estimate pre-adolescents' overall risk for substance misuse and diagnoses. The design of this instrument will be discussed briefly because of its unique approach to the assessment of substance diagnosis antecedents.

Structured Clinical Interview for the DSM (SCID)

The SCID was originally designed for assessing DSM-III diagnoses for clinical as well as research purposes and it has been recently adapted for assessment of DSM-IV and ICD-10 alcohol and drug diagnoses for adolescents (Martin *et al.*, 2000; Pollock *et al.*, 2000; Spitzer *et al.*, 1987, 1992). The SCID was developed conceptually from the DIS, but is designed for clinicians using a semi-structured format (Spitzer *et al.*, 1992). Extensive training of interviewers is available for experienced clinicians. The SCID has been translated into Dutch, English, French, German, Greek, Hebrew, Italian, Portugese, Russian, Spanish, Swedish, and Turkish.

One-week, test–retest kappa estimates of the reliability of SCID DSM-III-R diagnosis using a sample of psychiatric patients from Germany and the United States were good to excellent for substance abuse or dependence (Williams *et al.*, 1992). Data from community participants in the same study generated similar kappa reliability coefficients of lifetime substance abuse or dependence, except that reliability for any cannabis disorder (kappa = .22) was much smaller. Martin and colleagues (2000) reported interrater reliabilities of SCID diagnoses related to use of alcohol, cannabis, sedatives, hallucinogens, and inhalants for a sample of adolescents ($N=79$) recruited from clinics and the general community of Pittsburgh, Pennsylvania, United States. Kappas for substance-related diagnoses were excellent. Martin and colleagues' (2000) kappa estimates may be unstable, however, because the sample size was relatively small and a small percentage of participants reported diagnoses for certain drugs.

Diagnostic Interview for Children and Adolescents (DICA)

The DICA is a diagnostic interview of childhood and adolescent DSM-IV and DSM-III-R psychiatric disorders designed for use by the layperson (Herjanic and Reich, 1982; Reich, 2000). ICD-10 diagnoses can be extracted from DICA interview information. The DICA predecessor was the DIS and the DICA was intended for use in large-scale epidemiological research. The DICA originally used a structured format, but has been revised to use a semi-structured format. Extensive training is required to use the DICA; however, interviewers are not required to have extensive clinical experience. Current and lifetime diagnoses can be assessed using the DICA. The DICA also queries psychosocial risk factors and the parent interview queries developmental milestones. A Structured Assessment Record of Alcoholic Homes (SARAH) module was developed to query youths and their parents about the youths' exposure to parental drinking. A self-administered, computerized version of the DICA is available.

A one-week test–retest study of the DICA was conducted using a small sample of adolescents (13 to 18 years old), recruited from community and clinical settings ($N=50$; Reich, personal communication, 2001). Kappa estimates of reliability of DSM-IV dependence diagnoses were .86 for alcohol, .69 for cannabis, 1.0 for stimulants, .79 for cocaine, and .66 for hallucinogens. These kappas range from good to excellent. Our understanding of the DICA assessment of adolescents' substance use disorders will benefit in the future from further investigation of the DICA's psychometrics using larger samples of substance users, a broader range of substance use diagnoses, and additional substance use characteristics.

Diagnostic Interview Survey for Children (DISC)

The DISC-1 was designed for large-scale epidemiological studies of children's psychiatric diagnoses (Costello *et al.*, 1984; Shaffer *et al.*, 2000). The DISC is a structured interview that can be administered by laypersons. The DISC 2.1 was used in the U.S. National Institute on Mental Health study: Methods for the Epidemiology of Child and Adolescent Mental Disorders (MECA) study. Reliability studies of the DISC were conducted using international samples of the MECA study; however, reliability estimates were not reported for substance use disorders.

The latest version of the DISC, the DISC-IV, was published in 1997 and was designed for diagnosis of DSM-IV and ICD-10 childhood disorders (Shaffer *et al.*, 2000). In addition to psychiatric diagnoses, the level of impairment caused by psychiatric symptoms is assessed. Substance use-related disorders that are assessed with the DISC-IV are the abuse and dependence disorders for alcohol, nicotine, and illicit substances. The DISC-IV has a child self-report version and a parent version in which parents are queried about the child's pathology. Administration time is reduced by the use of "stem" questions, which are designed to allow children who are very unlikely to have a disorder to skip out of additional queries regarding the disorder. A disadvantage of stem questions is that specific symptoms that individuals might have experienced without meeting full criteria for disorder could be missed. The DISC-IV also assesses the degree of impairment that substance use-related disorders have on individuals' distress, academic/occupational functioning, relations with parents, caretakers, teachers, and employers as well as participation in family and peer activities. The DISC-IV is available in English, French, and Spanish translations and has been computerized.

Recent studies of the reliability of DISC disorders in community samples have not reported reliability estimates for substance use-related disorders (Breton *et al.*, 1998; Jensen *et al.*, 1995; Ribera *et al.*, 1996; Shaffer *et al.*, 1996; Schwab-Stone *et al.*, 1993). Roberts and colleagues (1996) reported kappa estimates of the one-week test–retest reliability of .53 for alcohol abuse and .448 for drug abuse using the DISC 2.1. Their sample consisted of 12- to 17-year-old psychiatric patients from southeastern Texas, United States.

Adolescent Diagnostic Interview (ADI)

The ADI is a structured interview designed for use by laypersons specifically for interviewing adolescents for research and clinical settings. ADI items query DSM-III-R and DSM-IV criteria for substance use-related diagnoses using two to four questions for each abuse and dependence criterion and symptom (Winters and Henley, 1993; Winters et al., 1999). The ADI includes screeners for certain psychiatric disorders, level of functioning, and psychosocial stressors as well as memory and orientation deficits. Training is available for the ADI. The advantage of the broad range of persons who could conduct the ADI interviews is offset somewhat by the limited scope of psychometric data available regarding the diagnoses that the ADI can provide.

The reliability and validity of the ADI was estimated for alcohol and cannabis disorders among clinical patients, aged 12 to 19 years, who had reported any alcohol or cannabis use in the preceding 12 months (Winters et al., 1993). Interrater reliability was estimated for the same interview using data from 72 patients. Kappa estimates were .86 for alcohol abuse, .76 for cannabis abuse, .53 for alcohol dependence, and .68 for cannabis dependence. Interrater reliability for individual symptoms ranged from .75 to .96 for alcohol symptoms, with one exception: a .66 kappa was observed for persistent desire or unsuccessful cutting down of use. Interrater reliability of cannabis use symptoms ranged from .82 to .97. One-week test–retest, interrater reliability estimates were estimated using data from 49 participants. Test–retest, interrater reliability estimates were not presented for the abuse diagnoses because of their low base rates. Kappas for the alcohol and cannabis abuse symptoms ranged from .53 to .70. Kappa estimates were .83 for alcohol dependence and .80 for cannabis dependence diagnoses. Test–retest, interrater reliability estimates for dependence symptoms ranged from .52 to .79. Understanding of the ADI diagnosis reliability will be enhanced using test–retest data from larger samples and community samples of substance users.

Children's Interview for Psychiatric Syndromes (ChIPS)

The ChIPS was developed to provide a structured interview assessment of children's psychiatric diagnoses (Fristad et al., 1998a,b; Teare et al., 1998). Compared to more established structured interviews of child psychiatric disorders, the authors of the ChIPS attempted to create an interview that required less administration time, included less awkward administration procedures, used age-appropriate language such as fewer words per question, and used diagnostic criteria that were consistent with DSM (Teare et al., 1998). The ChIPS utilizes a skipout procedure for each diagnosis, based on interviewees' responses to several questions. The child's experience of child abuse and psychosocial stressors is also queried.

Psychometric evaluations of the ChIPS suggest the instrument identifies childhood diagnoses in a similar manner to the DICA (Fristad *et al.*, 1998b; Teare *et al.*, 1998). In a community sample of 40 children, ages 6 to 18 (half of whom were ages 13 to 18), kappas of .48, .82, and .49 were observed for symptoms of alcohol abuse, cigarette abuse, and drug abuse, respectively. ChIPS diagnoses were also compared to diagnoses made by a group of clinicians using clinical interview and DICA information. Total agreement between ChIPS and DICA interviews was reported for alcohol abuse and drug abuse, with 97.5% agreement for cigarette abuse. These estimates should be interpreted with caution, however, until data can be reported for a larger sample of substance users.

Pictorial Instrument for Children and Adolescents (PICA-III-R)

The PICA-III-R was developed to assess DSM-III-R disorders in children and adolescents using pictures to illustrate the symptoms that are queried (Ernst *et al.*, 2000). The PICA-III-R is a semi-structured interview designed for administration by clinicians. Queries regarding psychiatric symptoms are presented with cartoon illustrations of individuals who have the symptoms. Interviewees are then asked how much the person in the illustration is like the interviewee. Ernst and colleagues (2000) report that children who see the illustrations often comment about the pictures in ways that provide insight to the child's pathology: "comments such as 'This is just like me when . . .' have been noted" (p. 95). Clinicians are required for administration of the PICA-III-R to clarify confusion that a child might have regarding pictures as well as responses by interviewees. Preliminary data suggest that the PICA-III-R could be useful for diagnosing childhood and adolescent disorders. However, psychometric data were unavailable for the PICA-III-R substance use-related diagnoses, presumably because of the very low prevalence of substance use in the sample.

Assessment of Liability and EXposure to Substance Use and Antisocial Behavior (ALEXSA)

The ALEXSA is currently being developed to assess 9- to 12-year-olds' risk and protective factors for later substance misuse, abuse, and dependence. The best predictors of substance misuse and antisocial behaviour that have been reported in prospective studies will be emulated in the ALEXSA scales. Cartoon illustrations of each item will be used to enhance communication of questions. Because children and adolescents report greater frequency of substance use and other risky behaviours when computerized interviews are used compared to interviews (Reich *et al.*, 1995; Turner *et al.*, 1998), the ALEXSA will be computerized. Questions will be presented auditorily using computer speakers, and interviewees will respond to items using a touch screen response interface by touching the illustration that corresponds to their response. Hence, no minimum reading or writing levels will be required of respondents. Prospective data will be collected on participants' substance use and diagnostic criteria at a two-year follow-up. Statistical models will be developed so that individuals' overall risk for substance misuse and disorders could be estimated from their ALEXSA responses.

CONCLUSIONS

Classification of adolescents' substance abuse and dependence diagnoses has greatly improved over the last 15 years. However, large gaps remain in our understanding of these disorders for adolescents. These gaps include very basic questions regarding the generalization of existing substance use disorder classification nomenclature to adolescents. Existing data suggest that classification schemes developed from data collected from adults do not generalize to adolescents. For this reason, "skipout" formats ought to be avoided in the assessment of adolescents' substance use-related disorders because critical pieces of information might be lost.

Encouraging preliminary data have been reported for several instruments designed to assess substance use disorders in adolescents. At this time, however, an instrument designed to assist in clarification of nomenclature for adolescents' substance use disorders is most needed. Until our understanding of adolescents' substance abuse and dependence deepens, assessments of substance abuse and dependence ought to be supplemented with measures of substance use frequency, duration, age of onset, and antecedents of substance use disorders because they could provide critical insight both for research and treatment of the disorders. As the criteria and symptoms of adolescent substance abuse and dependence are clarified, the instruments designed to assess adolescents' substance use disorders can be altered to fit such criteria. Two of the drugs most widely used by adolescents are among the least well understood. A withdrawal syndrome is not specified for cannabis in either the DSM-IV or ICD-10 nosologies. No criteria are specified for ecstasy, which is a combination of amphetamine and hallucinogen.

Simpson (1993) pointed out that, in spite of significant advances in theory and assessment, basic demographic variables such as gender, age, and socioeconomic status continue to be characteristics associated with trends in substance use. For illustration, being male is associated with an increased probability of having a substance use diagnosis, although the association between gender and substance use is not entirely understood in terms of psychological or biological mechanisms. Other domains that ought to be evaluated to obtain a comprehensive assessment of individuals' substance use disorders include medical history and current health status (Barker *et al.*, 1993), comorbid psychiatric disorders and family history of psychiatric disorders (Helzer, 1993), family functioning (Olson and Tiesel, 1993), and social functioning and support (Orvaschel, 1993). Instruments designed to evaluate these specific domains typically are added to an assessment of substance use disorders, or screeners of these areas are used (Horton, 1993). Perhaps the variety of substance use characteristics associated with understanding classification and etiology is the reason for the hundreds of substance use-related questionnaires that are in existence (Cottler and Keating, 1990; Davidson, 1987; Johnston, 1985). Unfortunately, these instruments also have been largely designed for assessment of adults and therefore represent another realm of knowledge that is lacking for adolescents (Meyers *et al.*, 1999; Weinberg *et al.*, 1998; Winters, 1999). Initial data regarding instruments that have been designed for assessment of these domains in adolescents suggest that they are likely to enhance our understanding of the etiology, consequences, and subtypes of substance use disorders in adolescents (Meyers *et al.*, 1999; Weinberg *et al.*, 1998; Winters, 1999).

Another concern regarding the assessment of adolescents' substance use disorders is how adolescents and children understand and respond to questions about substance use differently from adults. Using the DISC, Breton and colleagues (1995) found that pre-adolescents' comprehension of questions about their experience of psychiatric symptoms was best if the question contained fewer than ten words. Although pre-adolescents understood questions about the duration of a symptom, their comprehension of frequency of symptom occurrence and time period during which symptoms were experienced were not well comprehended. This finding might be confounded by the complexity of questions used to ask frequency and time period. Pre-adolescents' comprehension of these questions might be enhanced by using visual tools that they use regularly (e.g., a calendar) (Breton *et al.*, 1995). Question complexity and questions about duration, frequency, and time period also were associated with attenuation (the tendency to deny having symptoms during a second interview that were reported to have occurred during a preceding interview) (Lucas *et al.*, 1999).

Clearly, a great deal of research remains to be conducted before a classification nomenclature and assessment of adolescents' substance use disorders will be completed. Progress is ongoing, however, and because of the increased effort focused on classification and assessment issues, tremendous advances in this area should occur. Better understanding of the substance use disorders should also enhance treatment for the disorders as well as our understanding of the course, etiology, and prevention of substance use disorders.

REFERENCES

Andrews, G. & Peters, L. (1998). The psychometric properties of the Composite International Diagnostic Interview. *Social Psychiatry and Psychiatric Epidemiology*, 33, 80–88.

APA (American Psychiatric Association) (1980). *Diagnostic and Statistical Manual of Mental Disorders* (3rd edn, DSM-III). Washington, DC: Author.

APA (American Psychiatric Association) (1987). *Diagnostic and Statistical Manual of Mental Disorders* (3rd edn, revised, DSM-III-R). Washington, DC: Author.

APA (American Psychiatric Association) (1994). *Diagnostic and Statistical Manual of Mental Disorders* (4th edn). Washington, DC: American Psychiatric Association.

APA (American Psychiatric Association) (2000). *American Psychiatric Association: Diagnostic and Statistical Manual of Mental Disorders* (4th edn.; text revision). Washington, DC: American Psychiatric Association.

Babor, T. F. (1993). Alcohol and drug use history, patterns, and problems. In: B. J. Rounsaville, F. M. Tims, & A. M. Horton (Eds.), *Diagnostic source book on drug abuse research and treatment* (NIDA Monograph, NIH # 96–3508), pp. 19–34. Rockville, MD: US Department of Health and Human Services.

Barker, S. B., Kerns, L. L., & Schnoll, S. H. (1993). Assessment of medical history, health status, intoxication, and withdrawal. In: B. J. Rounsaville, F. M. Tims, & A. M. Horton (Eds.), *Diagnostic Source Book on Drug Abuse Research and Treatment* (NIDA Monograph, NIH # 96–3508, pp. 35–48). Rockville, MD: US Department of Health and Human Services.

Bishop, Y. M., Fienberg, S. & Holland, P. (1975). *Discrete multivariate analyses.* Cambridge: MIT Press.

Breton, J. J., Bergeron, L., Valla, J. P., Berthiaume, C., & St. Georges, M. (1998). Diagnostic Interview Schedule for Children (DISC-2.25) in Quebec: Reliability findings in light of the MECA study. *Journal of the American Academy of Child & Adolescent Psychiatry*, 37, 1167–1174.

Breton, J. J., Bergeron, L., Valla, J. P., Lepine, S., Houde, L., & Gaudet, N. (1995). Do children aged 9 through 11 years understand the DISC Version 2.25 questions? *Journal of the American Academy of Child & Adolescent Psychiatry*, 34, 946–954.

Brown, S. A., Mott, M. A., & Myers, M.G. (1990). Adolescent alcohol and drug treatment outcome. In: R. R. Watson (Ed.), *Drug and alcohol abuse prevention, drug and alcohol abuse review*, pp. 373–403. Clifton, NJ: Humana Press.

Brown, S. A., Mott, M. A., & Stewart, M. A. (1992). Adolescent alcohol and drug abuse. In: C. E. Walker & M. C. Roberts (Eds.), *Handbook of clinical child psychology* (2nd edn). pp. 677–693. Chichester, UK: John Wiley & Sons.

Bucholz, K. K., Heath, A. C., Reich, T., Hesselbrock, V. M., Kramer, J. R., Nurnberger, J. I., & Schuckit, M. A. (1996). Can we subtype alcoholism? A latent class analysis of data from relatives of alcoholics in a multicenter family study of alcoholism. *Alcoholism: Clinical & Experimental Research*, 20, 1462–1471.

Caetano, R. (1987). A commentary on the proposed changes in DSM-III concept of alcohol dependence. *Drug and Alcohol Dependence*, 19, 345–355.

Chatterji, S., Saunders, J. B., Vrasti, R., Grant, B. F., Hasin, D., & Mager, D. (1997). Reliability of the alcohol and drug modules of the Alcohol Use Disorder and

Associated Disabilities Interview Schedule—Alcohol/Drug—Revised (AUDADIS-ADR): An international comparison. *Drug and Alcohol Dependence, 47*, 171–185.
Compton, W. M., Cottler, L. B., Dorsey, K. B., Spitznagel, E. L., & Mager, D. E. (1996a). Structured and semi-structured assessment of ICD-10 substance dependence disorders: CIDI-SAM vs. SCAN. *International Journal of Methods in Psychiatric Research, 6*, 285–293.
Compton, W. M., Cottler, L. B., Dorsey, K. B., Spitznagel, E. L., & Mager, D. E. (1996b). Comparing assessments of DSM-IV substance dependence disorders using CIDI-SAM and SCAN. *Drug and Alcohol Dependence, 41*, 179–187.
Costello, A. J., Edelbrock, C. S., Dulcan, M. D., Kalas, R., & Klaric, S. H. (1984). *Report of the NIMH Diagnostic Interview Schedule for Children (DISC)*. Washington, DC: National Institute of Mental Health.
Cottler, L. B. (1992). Commentary. *Annual Review of Addictions Research and Treatment*, 53–55.
Cottler, L. B. (1993). Comparing DSM-III and ICD-10 substance use disorders. *Addiction, 88*, 689–696.
Cottler, L. B. & Compton, W. M. (1993). Advantages of the CIDI family of instruments in epidemiological research of substance use disorders. *International Journal of Methods in Psychiatric Research, 3*, 109–119.
Cottler, L. B., Compton, W. M., Brown, L., Shell, A., Keating, S., Shillington, A., & Hummel, R. (1994). The Discrepancy Interview Protocol: A method for evaluation and interpreting discordant survey responses. *International Journal of Methods in Psychiatric Research, 4*, 98.1–98.10.
Cottler, L. B., Compton, W. M., Robins, L. N., Spitznagel, E. L., & Ben Abdallah, A. (1988–2001, DA05585). *Reliability and validity of DSM and ICD substance use disorders*. Rockville, MD: National Institute on Drug Abuse.
Cottler, L. B., Grant, B. F., Blaine, J., Mavreas, B., Pull, C., Hasin, D., Compton, W. M., Rubio-Stipec, M., & Mager, D. (1997). Concordance of DSM-IV alcohol and drug use disorder criteria and diagnoses as measured by AUDADIS-ADR, CIDI and SCAN. *Drug and Alcohol Dependence, 47*, 195–205.
Cottler, L. B. & Keating, S. K. (1990). Operationalization of alcohol and drug dependence criteria by means of a structured interview. In M. Galanter (Ed.), *Recent developments in alcoholism, Vol. 8.* New York, NY: Plenum Press.
Cottler, L. B., Phelps, D. L., & Compton, W. M. (1995a). Narrowing of the drinking repertoire criterion: Should it have been dropped from ICD-10? *Journal of Studies on Alcohol, 56*, 173–176.
Cottler, L. B., Robins, L. N., Grant, B. F., Blaine, J., Towle, L. H., Wittchen, H.-U., Sartorius, N., & participants in the WHO/ADAMHA field trial (1991). The CIDI-Core substance abuse and dependence questions: Cross-cultural and nosological issues. *British Journal of Psychiatry, 159*, 653–658.
Cottler, L. B., Robins, L. N., & Helzer, J. E. (1989). The reliability of the CIDI-SAM: A comprehensive substance abuse interview. *British Journal of Addictions, 84*, 801–814.
Cottler, L. B., Schuckit, M. A., Helzer, J. E., Crowley, T., Woody, G., Nathan, P., & Hughes, J. (1995b). The DSM-IV field trial for substance use disorders: Major results. *Drug and Alcohol Dependence, 38*, 59–69.
Cottler, L. B., Shillington, A. M., Compton, W. M., Mager, D., & Spitznagel, E. L. (1993). Subjective reports of withdrawal among cocaine users: Recommendations for DSM-IV. *Drug and Alcohol Dependence, 33*, 97–104.

Davidson, R. (1987). Assessment of the alcohol dependence syndrome: A review of self-report screening questionnaires. *British Journal of Clinical Psychology, 26*, 243–255.

Dawes, M. A., Antelman, S. M., Vanyukov, M. M., Giancola, P., Tarter, R. E., Susman, E. J., Mezzich, A., & Clark, D. B. (2000). Developmental sources of variation in liability to adolescent substance use disorders. *Drug and Alcohol Dependence, 61*, 3–14.

Deas, D., Riggs, P., Langenbucher, J., Goldman, M., & Brown, S. (2000). Adolescents are not adults: Developmental considerations in alcohol users. *Alcoholism: Clinical and Experimental Research, 24*, 232–237.

Dunn, M. E. & Goldman, M. S. (1998). Age and drinking-related differences in the memory organization of alcohol expectancies in 3rd-, 6th-, 9th-, and 12th-grade children. *Journal of Consulting and Clinical Psychology, 66*, 579–585.

Easton, C., Meza, E., Mager, D., Ulug, B., Kilic, C., Gogus, A., & Babor, T.F. (1997). Test–retest reliability of the alcohol and drug use disorder sections of the schedules for clinical assessment in neuropsychiatry (SCAN). *Drug and Alcohol Dependence, 47*, 187–194.

Edwards, G. (1986). The alcohol dependence syndrome: A concept as stimulus to enquiry. *British Journal of Addiction, 81*, 171–183.

Edwards, G. & Gross, G. G. (1976). Alcohol dependence: Provisional description of a clinical syndrome. *British Medical Journal, 1*, 1058–1061.

Ernst, M., Cookus, B. A., & Moravec, B. C. (2000). Pictorial Instrument for Children and Adolescents (PICA-III-R). *Journal of the American Academy of Child and Adolescent Psychiatry, 39*, 94–99.

Feighner, J. P., Robins, E., Guze, S. B., Woodruff, R. A., & Winokur, G. (1972). Diagnostic criteria for use in psychiatric research. *Archives of General Psychiatry, 26*, 57–63.

Feingold, A. & Rounsaville, B. (1995). Construct validity of the dependence syndrome as measured by DSM-IV for different psychoactive substances. *Addiction, 90*, 1661–1669.

Fristad, M. A., Cummins, J., Verducci, J. S., Teare, M., Weller, E. B., & Weller, R. A. (1998a). Study IV: Concurrent validity of the DSM-IV Revised Children's Interview for Psychiatric Syndromes (ChIPS). *Journal of Child and Adolescent Psychopharmacology, 8*, 227–236.

Fristad, M. A., Glickerman, A. R., Verducci, J. S., Teare, M., Weller, E. B., & Weller, R. A. (1998b). Study V: Children's Interview for Psychiatric Syndromes (ChIPS): Psychometrics in two community samples. *Journal of Child and Adolescent Psychopharmacology, 8*, 237–245.

Fulkerson, J. A., Harrison, P. A., & Beebee, T. J. (1999). DSM-IV substance abuse and dependence: Are there really two dimensions of substance use disorders in adolescents? *Addiction, 94*, 495–506.

Grant, B. F., Harford, T. C., Dawson, D. A., Chou, P. S., & Pickering, R. P. (1995). The alcohol use disorder and associated disabilities interview schedule (AUDADIS): Reliability of alcohol and drug modules in a general population sample. *Drug and Alcohol Dependence, 39*, 37–44.

Grant, B. F. & Hasin, E. (1992). *The Alcohol Use Disorder and Associated Disabilities Interview Schedule (AUDADIS)*. Rockville, MD: National Institute on Alcohol Abuse and Alcoholism.

Harrison, P. A., Fulkerson, J. A., & Beebe, T. J. (1998). DSM-IV substance use disorder criteria for adolescents: A critical examination based on a statewide school survey. *American Journal of Psychiatry, 155*, 486–492.

Hasin, D., Carpenter, K. M., McCloud, S., Smith, M., & Grant, B. F. (1997a). The alcohol use disorder and associated disabilities interview schedule (AUDADIS): Reliability of alcohol and drug modules in a clinical sample. *Drug and Alcohol Dependence, 44*, 133–141.

Hasin, D., Grant, B. F., Cottler, L., Blaine, J., Towle, L., Ustun, B., & Sartorius, N. (1997b). Nosological comparisons of alcohol and drug diagnoses: A multisite, multi-instrument international study. *Drug and Alcohol Dependence, 47*, 217–226.

Hasin, D., McCloud, S., Li, Q., & Endicott, J. (1996). Cross-system agreement among demographic subgroups: DSM-III, DSM-III-R, DSM-IV and ICD-10 diagnoses of alcohol use disorders. *Drug and Alcohol Dependence, 41*, 127–135.

Hasin, D. S., Muthen, B., Wisnicki, K. S., & Grant, B. (1994). Validity of the bi-axial dependence concept: A test in the U.S. general population. *Addiction, 89*, 573–579.

Hasin, D. & Paykin, A. (1998). Dependence symptoms but no diagnosis: Diagnostic "orphans" in a community sample. *Drug and Alcohol Dependence, 50*, 19–26.

Hasin, D. & Paykin, A. (1999). Dependence symptoms but no diagnosis: Diagnostic "orphans" in a 1992 national sample. *Drug and Alcohol Dependence, 53*, 215–222.

Hasin, D., Paykin, A., Meydan, J., & Grant, B. (2000). Withdrawal and tolerance: Prognostic significance in DSM-IV alcohol dependence. *Journal of Studies on Alcohol, 61*, 431–438.

Hasin, D. S., Van Rossem, R., McCloud, S., & Endicott, J. (1997c). Differentiating DSM-IV alcohol dependence and abuse by course: Community heavy drinkers. *Journal of Substance Abuse, 9*, 127–135.

Helzer, J. E. (1993). Psychiatric diagnosis, family psychiatric history. In B. J. Rounsaville, F. M. Tims, & A. M. Horton (Eds.), *Diagnostic Source Book on Drug Abuse Research and Treatment* (NIDA Monograph, NIH # 96–3508, pp. 49–57). Rockville, MD: US Deptartment of Health and Human Services.

Herjanic, B. & Reich, W. (1982). Development of a structured psychiatric interview for children: Agreement between child and parent on individual symptoms. *Journal of Abnormal Child Psychology, 10*, 307–324.

Horton, A. M. (1993). Future directions in the development of addiction assessment instruments. In B. J. Rounsaville, F. M. Tims, & A. M. Horton (Eds.), *Diagnostic Source Book on Drug Abuse Research and Treatment* (NIDA Monograph, NIH # 96–3508, pp. 87–92). Rockville, MD: US Department of Health and Human Services.

Horton, J., Compton, W., & Cottler, L. B. (2000). Reliability of substance use disorder diagnoses among African-Americans and Caucasians. *Drug and Alcohol Dependence, 57*, 203–209.

Jensen, P., Margaret, R., Fisher, P., Piacentini, J., Canino, G., Richters, J., Rubio-Stipec, M., Dulcan, M., Goodman, S., Davies, M., Rae, D., Shaffer, D., Bird, H., Lahey, B., & Schwab-Stone, M. (1995). Test–retest reliability of the Diagnostic Interview Schedule for Children (DISC 2.1). *Archives of General Psychiatry, 52*, 61–71.

Johnston, L. D. (1985). Techniques for reducing measurement error in surveys of drug use. In L. N. Robins (Ed.), *Studying drug abuse*, Vol. 6. New Brunswick, NJ: Rutgers University Press.

Karno, M., Burnam, A., Escobar, J. I., Hough, R. L., & Eaton, W. W. (1985). The Spanish language version of the Diagnostic Interview Schedule. In W. W. Eaton & L. G. Kessler (Eds.), *Epidemiologic field methods in psychiatry: The NIMH Epidemiologic Catchment Area Program* (pp. 171–190). Orlando, FL: Academic Press.

Lamminpaa, A. (1994). Acute alcohol intoxication among children and adolescents. *European Journal of Pediatrics, 153*, 868–872.

Lamminpaa, A. (1995). Alcohol intoxication in childhood and adolescence. *Alcohol & Alcoholism, 30*, 5–12.

Langenbucher, J. W., Chung, T., Morgenstern, J., Labouvie, E. W., Nathan, P. E., & Bavly, L. (1997). Physiological alcohol dependence as a "specifier" of risk for medical problems and relapse liability in DSM-IV. *Journal of Studies on Alcohol, 58*, 341–350.

Langenbucher, J., Martin, C. S., Labouvie, E., Sanjuan, T. M., Bavly, L., & Pollock, N.K. (2000). Toward the DSM-IV: The withdrawal-gate model versus the DSM-IV in the diagnosis of alcohol abuse and dependence. *Journal of Consulting and Clinical Psychology, 68*, 799–809.

Langenbucher, J. W., Morgenstern, J., & Miller, K. J. (1995). DSM-III, DSM-IV and ICD-10 as severity scales for drug dependence. *Drug and Alcohol Dependence, 39*, 139–150.

Langenbucher, J. W., Morgenstern, J., Labouvie, E. W., & Nathan, P. E. (1994). Diagnostic concordance of substance use disorders in DSM-III, DSM-IV, and ICD-10. *Drug and Alcohol Dependence, 36*, 193–203.

Lucas, C. P. Fisher, P., Piancentini, J., Zhang, H., Jensen, P. S., Shaffer, D., Dulcan, M., Schwab-Stone, M., Regier, D., & Canino, G. (1999). Features of interview questions associated with attenuation of symptom reports. *Journal of Abnormal Child Psychology, 27*, 429–437.

Martin, C. S., Kaczynski, N. A., Maisto, S. A., Bukstein, O. M., & Moss, H. B. (1995). Patterns of DSM-IV alcohol abuse and dependence symptoms in adolescent drinkers. *Journal of Studies on Alcohol, 56*, 672–680.

Martin, C. S., Langenbucher, J. W., Kaczynski, N., & Chung, T. (1996). Staging in the onset of DSM-IV alcohol symptoms in adolescents: Survival/hazard analysis. *Journal of Studies on Alcohol, 57*, 549–558.

Martin, C. S., Pollock, N. K., Bukstein, O. G., & Lynch, K. G. (2000). Interrater reliability of the SCID alcohol and substance use disorders sections among adolescents. *Drug and Alcohol Dependence, 59*, 173–176.

Meyers, K., Hagan, T. A., Zanis, D., Webb, A., Frantz, J., Ring-Kurt, S., Rutherford, M., & McLellan, A. T. (1999). Critical issues in adolescent substance use assessment. *Drug and Alcohol Dependence, 55*, 235–246.

Mikulich, S. K., Hall, S. K., Whitmore, E. A., & Crowley, T. J. (2001). Concordance between DSM-III-R and DSM-IV diagnoses of substance use disorders in adolescents. *Drug and Alcohol Dependence, 61*, 237–248.

Morgenstern, J., Langenbucher, J. W., & Labouvie, E. W. (1994). The generalizability of the dependence syndrome across substance: An examination of some properties of the proposed dependence criteria. *Addiction, 89*, 1105–1113.

Muthen, B. O., Grant, B., & Hasin, D. (1993). The dimensionality of alcohol abuse and dependence: Factor analysis of DSM-III-R and proposed DSM-IV criteria in the 1988 National Health Interview Survey. *Addiction, 88*, 1079–1090.

Nathan, P. E. (1994). Psychoactive substance dependence. In T. Widiger, A. Frances, H. Pincus, M. First, & W. Davis (Eds.), *The DSM-IV Source Book*, Vol. 1. Washington, DC: American Psychiatric Association Press.

Olson, D. H. & Tiesel, J. W. (1993). Assessment of family functioning. In B.J. Rounsaville, F. M. Tims, & A. M. Horton (Eds.), *Diagnostic Source Book on Drug Abuse Research and Treatment (NIDA Monograph, NIH # 96–3508, pp. 59 – 78)*. Rockville, MD: US Department of Health and Human Services.

Orvaschel, H. (1993). Social functioning and social supports: A review of measures suitable for use with substance abusers. In B.J. Rounsaville, F.M. Tims, & A.M. Horton (Eds.), *Diagnostic Source Book on Drug Abuse Research and Treatment (NIDA Monograph, NIH # 96–3508, pp. 79 – 86)*. Rockville, MD: US Department of Health and Human Services.

Perkonigg, A., Lieb, R., Hofler, M., Schuster, P., Sonntag, H., & Wittchen, H.U. (1999). Patterns of cannabis use, abuse and dependence over time: Incidence, progression and stability in a sample of 1,228 adolescents. *Addiction, 94*, 1663–1678.

Pincus, H. A., Frances, A., Davis, W. W., First, M. B., & Widiger, T. A. (1992). DSM-IV and new diagnostic categories: Holding the line on proliferation. *American Journal of Psychiatry, 149*, 112–117.

Pollock, N. K. & Martin, C. S. (1999). Diagnostic orphans: Adolescents with alcohol symptoms who do not qualify for DSM-IV abuse or dependence diagnoses. *American Journal of Psychiatry, 156*, 897–901.

Pollock, N. K., Martin, C. S., & Langenbucher, J. W. (2000). Diagnostic concordance of DSM-III, DSM-III-R, DSM-IV and ICD-10 alcohol diagnoses in adolescents. *Journal of Studies on Alcohol, 61*, 439–446.

Pull, C. B., Saunders, J. B., Mavreas, V., Cottler, L. B., Grant, B. F., Hasin, D. S., Blaine, J., Mager, D., & Ustun, B. T. (1997). Concordance between ICD-10 alcohol and drug use disorder criteria and diagnoses as measured by the AUDADIS-ADR, CIDI, and SCAN: Results of a cross-national study. *Drug and Alcohol Dependence, 47*, 207–216.

Regier, D. A., Kaelber, C. T., Roper, M. T., Rae, D. S., & Sartorius, N. (1994). The ICD-10 clinical field trial for mental and behavioral disorders: Results in Canada and the United States. *American Journal of Psychiatry, 151*, 1340–1350.

Reich, W. (2000). Diagnostic Interview for Children and Adolescents (DICA). *Journal of the American Academy of Child and Adolescent Psychiatry, 39*, 59–66.

Reich, W., Cottler, L. B., McCallum, K., Corwin, D., & VanEerdewegh, M. (1995). Computerized interviews as a method of assessing psychopathology in children. *Comprehensive Psychiatry, 36*, 40–45.

Ribera, J. C., Canino, G., Rubio-Stipec, M., Bravo, M., Bauermeister, J. J., Algeria, M., Woodbury, M., Huertas, S., Guevara, L. M., Bird, H. R., Freeman, D., & Shrout, P. E. (1996). The Diagnostic Interview Schedule for Children (DISC-2.1) in Spanish: Reliability in a Hispanic population. *Journal of Child Psychology and Psychiatry and Allied Disciplines, 37*, 195–204.

Roberts, R. E., Solovitz, B. L., Chen, Y. W., & Casat, C. (1996). Retest stability of DSM-III-R diagnoses among adolescents using the Diagnostic Interview Schedule for Children (DISC-2.1C). *Journal of Abnormal Child Psychology, 24*, 349–362.

Robins, L. N. (1988). *Composing the CIDI: A collaboration with the WHO/ADAMHA*. Presented at the Department of Psychiatry Research Seminar, St. Louis, MO.

Robins, L. N. (1989). Diagnostic grammar and assessment. Translating criteria into questions. In L. Robins & J. Barrett (Eds.), *The validity of diagnosis*. New York, NY: Raven Press.

Robins, L. N., Cottler, L. B., & Babor, T. (1990). *WHO/ADAMHA Composite International Diagnostic Interview – Substance Abuse Module (SAM)*, (1983, revised 1987, 1988, 1988, 1989). MO: WHO/ADAMHA, St. Louis.

Robins, L. N. & Helzer, J. E. (1986) Diagnosis and clinical assessment: The current state of psychiatric diagnosis. *Annual Review of Psychology*, *37*, 409–432.

Robins, L. N., Helzer, J. E., Croughan, J., & Ratcliff, K. (1981). National Institute of Mental Health Diagnostic Interview Schedule: Its history, characteristics and validity. *Archives of General Psychiatry*, *38*, 393–398.

Robins, L. N., Helzer, J. E., Orvaschel, H., Anthony, J. C., Blazer, D. G., Burnam, A., & Burke, J. D. (1985). The Diagnostic Interview Schedule. In W. W. Eaton & L. G. Kessler (Eds.), *Epidemiologic field methods in psychiatry: The NIMH Epidemiologic Catchment Area Program* (pp. 143–170). Orlando, FL: Academic Press.

Robins, L. N. & Regier, D. A. (Eds.) (1991), *Psychiatric disorders in America*. New York: The Free Press.

Robins, L. N., Wing, J., Wittchen, H. U., Helzer, J. E., Babor, T. F., Burke, J. D., Farmer, A., Jablenski, A., Pickens, R., Regier, D. A., Sartorius, N., & Towle, L. H. (1988). The Composite International Diagnostic Interview (CIDI): An epidemiologic instrument suitable for use in conjunction with different diagnostic systems and in different cultures. *Archives of General Psychiatry*, *45*, 1069–1077.

Room, R., Jounce, A., Bennett, L. A., & Schmidt, L. (1996). WHO cross-cultural applicability research on diagnosis and assessment of substance use disorders: An overview of methods and selected results. *Addiction*, *91*, 199–220.

Rounsaville, B. J. (1987). An evaluation of the DSM-III substance use disorders. In G. Tischler (Ed.), *Treatment and classification in psychiatry*. New York, NY: Cambridge University Press.

Rounsaville, B. J., Bryant, K., Babor, T., Kranzler, H., & Kadden, R. (1993). Cross system agreement for substance use disorders: DSM-III-R, DSM-IV and DSM-10. *Addiction*, *88*, 337–348.

Rounsaville, B. J., Kosten, T., Williams, J., & Spitzer, R. L. (1987). A field trial of DSM-III-R psychoactive substance dependence disorders. *American Journal of Psychiatry*, *144*, 351–355.

Rounsaville, B. J. & Kranzler, H. R. (1989). The DSM-III-R diagnosis of alcoholism. *Review of Psychiatry*, *8*, 323–340.

Sarr, M., Bucholz, K. K., & Phelps, D. L. (2000). Using cluster analysis of alcohol use disorders to investigate "diagnostic orphans": Subjects with alcohol dependence symptoms but no diagnosis. *Drug and Alcohol Dependence*, *60*, 295–302.

Schuckit, M. A. (1993). Keeping current with the DSMs and substance use disorders. In D. Dunner (Ed.), *Current psychiatric therapy* (pp. 89–91). Philadelphia, PA: W. B. Saunders.

Schuckit, M. A., Smith, T. L., Daeppen, J. B., Eng, M., Li, T. K., Hesselbrock, V. M., Nurnberger, J. I., & Bucholz, K. K. (1998). Clinical relevance of the distinction between alcohol dependence with and without a physiological component. *American Journal of Psychiatry*, *155*, 733–740.

Schuckit, M. A., Daeppen, J. B., Danko, G. P., Tripp, M. L., Smith, T. L., Li, T. K., Hesselbrock, V. M., & Bucholz, K.K. (1999). Clinical implications for four drugs of the DSM-IV: Distinction between substance dependence with and without a physiological component. *American Journal of Psychiatry, 156,* 41–49.

Schwab-Stone, M., Fisher, P., Piacentini, J., Shaffer, D., Davies, M., & Briggs, M. (1993). The Diagnostic Interview Schedule for Children—Revised Version (DISC-R): II. Test–retest reliability. *Journal of the American Academy of Child and Adolescent Psychiatry, 32,* 651–657.

Shaffer, D., Fisher, P., Dulcan, M. K., Davies, M., Piacentini, J., Schwab-Stone, M., Lahey, B. B., Bourdon, K., Jensen, P. S., Bird, H. R., Canino, G., & Regier, D. A. (1996). The NIMH Diagnostic Interview Schedule for Children Version 2.3 (DISC-2.3): Description, acceptability, prevalence rates, and performance in the MECA study. *Journal of the American Academy of Child and Adolescent Psychiatry, 35*(7)), 865–877.

Shaffer, D., Fisher, P., Lucas, C., Dulcan, M. K., & Schwab-Stone, M. E. (2000). NIMH Diagnostic Interview Schedule for Children Version IV (NIMH DISC-IV): Description, differences from previous versions, and reliability of some common diagnoses. *Journal of the American Academy of Child and Adolescent Psychiatry, 39,* 28–38.

Simpson, D. D. (1993). Demographic, socioeconomic, and criminal background data. In B. J. Rounsaville, F. M. Tims, & A. M. Horton (Eds.), *Diagnostic Source Book on Drug Abuse Research and Treatment* (NIDA Monograph, NIH # 96–3508; pp. 11–18). Rockville, MD: US Department of Health and Human Services.

Spitzer, R. L., Endicott, J., & Robins, E. (1978). Research diagnostic criteria. *Archives of General Psychiatry, 35,* 773–782.

Spitzer, R. L., Williams, J. B. W., & Gibbon, M. (1987). *Instruction manual for the structured clinical interview for DSM-III-R.* New York, NY: Biometrics Research Department, New York State Psychiatric Institute.

Spitzer, R. L., Williams, J. B. W., Gibbon, M., & First, M. B. (1992). The structured clinical interview for DSM-III-R (SCID). *Archives of General Psychiatry, 49,* 624–629.

Stewart, M. A. & Brown, S. A. (1995). Withdrawal and dependency symptoms among adolescent alcohol and drug abusers. *Addiction, 90,* 627–635.

Teare, M., Fristad, M. A., Weller, E. B., Weller, R. A., & Salmon, P. (1998). Study I: Development and criterion validity of the Children's Interview for Psychiatric Syndromes (ChIPS). *Journal of Child and Adolescent Psychopharmacology, 8,* 205–211.

Turner, C. F., Ku, L., Rogers, S. M., Lindberg, L. D., Pleck, J. H., & Sonenstein, F. L. (1998). Adolescent sexual behavior, drug use, and violence: Increased reporting with computer survey technology. *Science, 280,* 867–873.

Ustun, B., Compton, W., Mager, D., Babor, T., Baiyewu, O., Chatterji, S., Cottler, L., Gogus, A., Mavreas, V., Peters, L., Pull, C., Saunders, J., Smeets, R., Stipec, M. R., Vrasti, R., Hasin, D., Room, R., Van den Brink, W., Regier, D., Blaine, J., Grant, B. F., & Sartorius, N. (1997). WHO study on the reliability and validity of the alcohol and drug use disorder instruments: Overview of methods and results. *Drug and Alcohol Dependence, 47,* 161–169.

Weinberg, N. Z., Rahdert, E., Colliver, J. D., & Glantz, M. D. (1998). Adolescent substance abuse: A review of the past 10 years. *Journal of the American Academy of Child and Adolescent Psychiatry, 37,* 252–261.

White, H. R. (1987). Longitudinal stability of dimensional structure of problem drinking in adolescence. *Journal of Studies on Alcohol, 48*, 541–550.

Williams, J. B. W., Gibbon, M., First, M. B., Spitzer, R. L., Davies, M., Borus, J., Howes, M. J., Kane, J., Pope, H.G., Rounsaville, B., & Wittchen, H. U. (1992). The Structured Clinical Interview for DSM-III-R (SCID). *Archives of General Psychiatry, 49*, 630–636.

Wing, J. K., Babor, T., Brugha, T., Burke, J., Cooper, J. E., Giel, R., Jablensky, A., Regier, D., & Sartorius, N. (1990). SCAN: Schedules for Clinical Assessment in Neuropsychiatry. *Archives of General Psychiatry, 47*, 589–593.

Wing, J. K., Cooper, J. E., & Sartorius, N. (1974). *The Measurement and Classification of Psychiatric Symptoms*. London, UK: Cambridge University Press.

Winters, K. C. (1999). (Revisions Consensus Panel Chair). *Screening and assessing adolescents for substance use disorders*. Rockville, MD: US Department of Health and Human Services.

Winters, K. C. & Henley, G.A. (1993). *Adolescent Diagnostic Interview Schedule and Manual*. Los Angeles, CA: Western Psychological Services.

Winters, K. C., Latimer, W., & Stinchfield, R. D. (1999). The DSM-IV criteria for adolescent alcohol and cannabis use disorders. *Journal of Studies on Alcohol, 60*, 337–344.

Winters, K. C. & Stinchfield, R. D. (1995). Current issues and future needs in the assessment of adolescent drug abuse. In E. Rahdert & D. Czechowicz (Eds.), *Adolescent drug abuse: Clinical assessment and therapeutic interventions* (NIDA Research Monograph 156) (pp. 146–171). Rockville, MD: US Department of Health and Human Services.

Winters, K. C., Stinchfield, R. D., Fulkerson, J., & Henly, G. A. (1993). Measuring alcohol and cannabis use disorders in an adolescent clinical sample. *Psychology of Addictive Behavior, 7*, 185–196.

Wittchen, H. U., Lachner, G., Wunderlich, U., & Pfister, H. (1998). Test–retest reliability of the computerized DSM-IV version of the Munich-Composite International Diagnostic Interview (M-CIDI). *Social Psychiatry and Psychiatric Epidemiology, 33*, 568–578.

Wittchen, H. U., Robins, L. B., Cottler, L. B., Sartorius, N., Burke, J. D., Regier, D., & participants in the multicentre WHO/ADAMHA Field Trials (1991). *British Journal of Psychiatry, 159*, 645–653.

Woody, G. E., Cottler, L. B., & Cacciola, J. (1993). Severity of dependence: Data from the DSM-IV field trials. *Addiction, 88*, 1573–1579.

World Health Organization (1993a). *The ICD-10 Classification of mental and Behavioural Disorders: Diagnostic Criteria for Research*. World Health Organization. Geneva, Switzerland: Author.

World Health Organization (1993b). *Composite International Diagnostic Interview, version 1.1*. Geneva, Switzerland: World Health Organization.

World Health Organization (1993c). *Schedules for clinical assessment in neuropsychiatry*. Washington, DC: American Psychiatric Association Press.

World Health Organization (1993d). *Alcohol Use Disorder and Associated Disabilities Interview Schedule—Alcohol/Drug—Revised*. Geneva, Switzerland: World Health Organization.

Acknowledgement

This work was supported by the following grants from NIAAA, NIDA, and NIMH (AA12111, DA00434, DA05585, DA07313, DA11622, DA12900, MH17104).

Chapter 3

Epidemiology and comorbidity

Cecilia A. Essau, Hubert Stigler, and Josef Scheipl

Substance use and misuse represent one of the most important public health problems which has an onset in adolescence. Given the widespread use of substances (e.g., tobacco, alcohol, marijuana) and its negative health consequence, numerous epidemiological studies on the prevalences and trends of substance use and substance use disorders (SUD) have been conducted in recent years especially in industrialized countries. The major advantage of epidemiological studies using samples from the general population is the ability to produce findings of greater generalizability than from studies of clinical samples. Data from the clinical setting are generally not representative of individuals with SUD owing to bias in service attendence (e.g., restriction of access) and selection process related to help-seeking symptoms and chronicity. Trends are examined using repeat population surveys that use similar question and sampling methods. In most studies, a repeat cross-sectional design is used, where an independent sample of adolescents rather than of the same individuals is investigated.

The main aim of this chapter is to review the epidemiology of substance use and SUD, and their comorbidity with other psychiatric disorders. SUD include substance abuse and substance dependence (see Chapter 2 in this volume) and are used to refer to malaptive behaviour associated with regular use of substances including alcohol, amphetamines, caffeine, cannabis, cocaine, hallucinogens, inhalants, nicotine, opioids, phencyclidine (PCP), and sedatives, hypnotics, or anxiolytics.

PREVALENCE OF SUBSTANCE USE

United States

Within the United States, several epidemiologic surveys have been investigating trends in substance use among youth since the early 1970s. The largest is the Monitoring the Future Survey (Johnston *et al.*, 2000), conducted by the University of Michigan Institute for Social Research. It is an ongoing study

64 Substance Abuse and Dependence in Adolescence

of adolescents, based on annual surveys of nationally representative samples of about 45,000 students across the USA in the 8th, 10th, and 12th grades in public and private schools. The main aims of the survey were to identify recent trends in the use of licit and illicit drugs, as well as in the levels of perceived risk and personal disapproval related to each drug; the types of drugs included in the survey were marijuana, LSD, other hallucinogens, crack, other cocaine, or heroin, or any use of other narcotics, amphetamines, barbiturates or tranquillizers (not prescribed by a medical doctor). According to the most recent Monitoring the Future Survey (Johnston *et al.*, 2000), about 54% of the adolescents have tried an illicit drug, and over 80% have consumed alcohol by the time they finish high school. Their data also showed that 26.8%, 45.6%, and 54% of the 8th, 10th, and 12th grades, respectively, had used any illicit drugs sometime in their lives. The annual prevalence of any illicit drug were 19.5% in the 8th graders, 36.4% in the 10th, and 40.9% in the 12th graders. The most commonly used drug was marijuana, with a lifetime prevalence of 20.3%, 40.3%, and 48.8% in the 8th, 10th, and 12th grades, respectively; the annual rate for marijuana consumption was 16% among the 8th graders, 32% for the 10th graders, and 37% among the 12th graders. These rates showed a steady but gradual decline since the 1996 survey among those in grade 8, with little change found in grades 10 and 12. However, the use of certain other illicit drugs showed an increase during the recent survey, but some others a decrease. The use of ecstasy or the so-called "club drug" (so called because of its common use at night clubs and at all-night dance parties) increased significantly in all three grades. While the increased use of ecstasy in 1999 took place mostly in the northeast states, in the 2000 Survey this increase was diffused into the other regions as well. The use of steroids and heroin also increased. Other drugs such as inhalants (e.g., glue, solvents, butane, gasoline, aerosols), LSD, crystal methamphetamine and rohypnol decreased following their peak levels in the mid-1990s. As for alcohol, 51.7%, 71.4%, and 80.3% of the 8th, 10th, and 12th graders, respectively, reported having had any alcoholic beverages. Among these adolescents, 25.1% of the 8th graders had been drunk compared to the 49.3% of the 10th graders, and 62.3% of the 12th graders.

Another large-scale survey conducted within the United States is the "National Parents' Resource Institute for Drug Education" (PRIDE). Over 200,000 adolescents ages 12 to 18 who attended high schools in 34 states across the USA participated in the survey. Findings from the 1993–1994 survey showed high use of substances in the past year. Among the 15- to 18-year olds, 65.9% reported having used alcohol, 24.6% marijuana, 6.9% inhalants, 6.6% hallucinogens, and 4% cocaine. Of the 12- to 14-year-olds, 39.3% reported having drunk alcohol in the past year, 8.2% had used marijuana, 5.9% inhalants, 2.1% hallucinogens, and 1.9% cocaine.

In the Youth Risk Behavior Survey (Merrill *et al.*, 1999), 42% of high-school seniors indicated having tried marijuana, and 38% reported using this substance more than three times. Twenty-three per cent had used at least one other illicit drug and 15% reported having used one of these substances on more than one occasion. Regular use of cigarettes and alcohol significantly increased the prevalence of marijuana use. Regular smokers were 2.6 times more likely to use marijuana than were those who did not smoke or drink on a regular basis. Regular alcohol users (i.e., ten or more times) were 2.4 times more likely to use marijuana as those who had not.

In the MECA study (Methods for the Epidemiology of Child and Adolescent Mental Disorders; Kandel *et al.*, 1997), the samples (9–18 years) were recruited from four geographic areas in the USA: Connecticut, Georgia, New York, and Puerto Rico. Almost half of the children and adolescents (47.8%) reported having ever drunk any alcoholic beverages; 5% have used marijuana, and 0.5% have used cocaine at some time in their lives. However, there were geographic differences in the prevalence of substance consumed. The rate for lifetime marijuana use in Puerto Rico was the lowest, being 1.6% compared to 5.4% to 7.2% reported in the other sites.

Greece

A large-scale study of licit and illicit substance use conducted in Greece sampled over 11,000 adolescents aged 14–18 (Kokkevi and Stefanis, 1991). The prevalence of alcohol use was 94.8% for the past year and 82.4% for the past month. The past year prevalence of marijuana use was 2.7%, cocaine 1.1%, opiates 2.1%, and hallucinogens less than 1%. Lifetime prevalence of illicit drug use was reported by 6% of the sample. About half of the adolescents who used illicit substances reported having used them more than twice. The use of substances increased significantly with age. That is, lifetime drug use for illicit substances was reported by less than 1% of the 13- and 14-year-olds, 4.3% of the 15- and 16-year-olds, and 10.9% of the 17- and 18-year-olds.

Spain

The study by Castilla *et al.* (1999) was a national household survey of the Spanish population aged 18–39 years. The main aim of the study was to examine the association between substance consumption and sexual risk behaviour. Information on health status, substance use, and sexual behaviour was collected through interviews and self-report questionnaires. About 75.2% of the 18- to 39-year-olds reported having consumed alcoholic beverages; 27.4% of these subjects had experienced one or more episodes of drunkenness, and 20.5% had used psychoactive drugs in the past 12 months. The most commonly used substances were cannabis (11.8%), tranquillizers (9.5%), cocaine (3.5%), and amphetamines (2.8%). Factors related to alcohol consumption or drunkenness and psychoactive drug use were male, younger age, higher educational level, being single, and having had more than one sexual partner in the past 12 months. Tranquillizers were used more frequently by women, persons older than 35 years, and those with a lower educational level. Their finding also showed a strong association between alcohol consumption and sexual behaviour, although the pattern of this association seemed different. That is, consumption of large amounts of alcohol on weekdays was associated with less frequent use of condoms, and heavy drinking at weekends was associated with more sexual partners. The difference between these two groups was interpreted as a result of cultural differences and modes of behaviour. That is, weekday use is considered a traditional pattern in Spain, and excessive consumption at weekends is a recently introduced pattern with a strong Northern European influence.

France and Israel

One of the few examples of comparative cross-cultural epidemiologic surveys conducted on adolescent substance use is a study of substance trends in France and Israel (Kandel *et al.*, 1981). In this study, France was found to have higher lifetime and current rates of adolescent substance use than Israel. The lifetime prevalence rates in French adolescents were 80% for alcohol and 26% for any illicit substances. Similar to other studies, the illicit drug with the highest lifetime prevalence rate was marijuana, being reported by 23% of the adolescents. Although the rate of lifetime alcohol use was similar in the Israeli sample (i.e., 70%), the lifetime prevalence of an illicit drug use of 8% was far lower than that of the French sample. Marijuana was reported to have been used by only 3% of the Israeli sample, nearly eight times lower than the rate in French youth.

United Kingdom

According to the British Office of Population Census and Survey (OPCS, 1986), 79% of the 13-year-olds reported having drunk alcohol, 29% of them drank once a week, mostly at home. By the age of 17 years, 90% have consumed alcohol at least once, with most of them (62%) reporting drinking in public places. In a survey of London schoolchildren aged 11 to 16 years old (Swadi, 1988), 20% of them reported having used illegal drugs at least once, and 10.9% had drunk alcohol at least once a week. As reported in most studies, the rate of drug use increased with age. Two per cent of 11-year-olds and 16% of 16-year-olds used illicit drugs on a regular basis. A study by Measham *et al.* (1998) showed a rise in drug use among 17- to 25-year-olds in Britain in the mid-1990s. The most commonly used drugs among them were the so-called "dance drugs", consumed within the context of the dance culture and raves/house parties.

In the 1995 national survey of adolescents (Miller and Plant, 1996), almost all had drunk alcohol in the previous month, and 42.3% had ever used illicit drugs, mainly cannabis. 45% of males and 39.8% of females reported having used illicit drugs, respectively. About one in eight adolescents (Miller and Plant, 1996) used hallucinogens, and about one-fith reported inhalation of solvents (Cooney et al., 1994). The use of narcotics or anabolic steroids had been relatively low, being less than 2%.

Another set of data on the prevalence of substance use in England has been provided by the Health Survey for England (Prescott-Clarke and Primatesta, 1997). It is a series of annual surveys, with the main aim of monitoring trends in the nation's health. The survey provided a representative sample of the population of England living in private households. Unlike the previous surveys, the 1997 Health Survey for England was concentrated on children, adolescents and young adults. When concentrating on the 16- to 24-year olds, the data showed the proportion of those who had ever drunk alcohol (beer, lager, cider and alcoholic lemonades; spirits and liqueurs; wine; sherry and martini; and shandy), the lowest being among those aged 16 (85% for both males and females). Among males, this proportion increased until age 19, after which it levelled off at about 94%. Among females, the proportion increased from 85% at age 16 to 92% at age 17, and then remained fairly steady until age 21, after which there was a further small increase to about 95%. Among males aged 16, 10% drank on three or more days a week. At the age of 21 years, the proportion of those who drank with this frequency increased, but showed a decrease at the age of 24 years with 42% of them reported drinking at least three days a week. A similar pattern was found for women aged 16–24, in that the proportion drinking on three or more days a week increased from 6% at age 16 to 32% at age 21, followed by a declined to 18% at age 24. Only very few of the adolescents (men = 8%, women = 4%) drank every day. Among current drinkers, 78% of male drinkers and 66% of female drinkers had been drunk at least once in the last three months. The proportion was slightly lower among drinkers aged 16–17 years. After the age of 18 years, there was very little variation by age among men, while among women the prevalence of drunkenness was lower at the age 22–24 years than at the age 18–21 years. Their findings also showed that 37% of the current male drinkers and 21% of females had been drunk at least once a week on average in the past three months.

Austria

Data registered by the Austrian Department of Health and Consumer Protection has shown an increase in licit and illicit drug consumption (e.g., marijuana, cocaine and heroin) among adolescents since 1991. In summarizing the few studies on adolescent drug experiences, Eisenbach-Stangl (1983) reported a "new sobriety" of adolescents in the 1990s. Although adolescents seem to have easy access to drugs (50% of Viennese adolescents reported a marijuana addict among their peers), the use of illicit drugs has not changed since the 1980s. The consumption of hard and soft drugs remained at 5% and did not increase with age.

In Austria, three studies on marijuana consumption have been conducted since the early 1990s, two in Vienna and another one in Tyrol. In these three studies, between 15% and 22% (Dür, 1990; Springer and Uhl, 1993) of the adolescents reported having used marijuana at some time in their lives. The most recent and largest study to examine the prevalence of substance use was the Styrian study (Gasser-Steiner and Stigler, 1997). In the Styrian study, 12% of the adolescents reported having tried illegal drugs at least once in their life. There was a varying affinity towards different drug types. Intake of stimulants (13.3%) was most common, followed by marijuana (12.1%) and medication in combination with alcohol (8.8%). The use of ecstasy (2.6%) was less frequent. The use of drugs increased with age and reached a plateau between the ages of 18 and 20. Single use of marijuana was reported by 24.5% of the 16-year-olds and by 25% of the 18-year-olds. The pattern of stimulant use was different: 10% of the 12-year-olds, and 15.5% of the 14-year-olds reported having consumed stimulants. Female adolescents consumed these drugs more moderately compared to their male counterparts. Between the ages of 12 and 13, single use or repeated consumption is not different based on gender but the gender gap increases with age. That is, among the 18- to 20-year-olds drug consumers, male single users account for 30%, and among females it was 20%. Repeated consumption was found in 20% of males, but only 10% of females. One-third of the adolescents between the ages of 14 and 15 admitted consuming alcoholic beverages occasionally (i.e., several times per month). The percentages of the 16-year-olds and older increased to 58%, with one-third of them consuming alcohol on a regular basis (i.e., several times per week). About 40% of the adolescents reported having smoked, and about one-quarter of them smoke daily. Their finding also showed alcohol consumption and smoking as being related to adolescents' educational status, with apprentices being at the highest risk. That is, one-third consumed alcoholic beverages regularly and almost half of them smoked regularly. Forty per cent of males, compared to 10% of females, consumed alcohol regularly. The gender difference in terms of cigarette smoking was less striking.

In comparison to alcohol, first contact with smoking is not through the family but it is tried in the company of friends, with the first attempt being at the age of 14. Consumption of these substances is regarded as less problematic than that of marijuana, ecstasy, or other, hard drugs. Cigarette and alcohol consumption are socially tolerated among adults and reflect culturally accepted behaviour. For example, 60% of the 16-year-olds regarded alcohol as an integral part of their everyday life.

Germany

Until the mid-1970s, surveys of adolescents were primarily conducted in schools (Reuband, 1992). In the early 1970s, surveys on attitudes to and use of alcohol among adolescents have been conducted by the "Institute of Adolescent Research" (Institut für Jugendforschung). In the 1980s, national mail surveys were conducted by a private institute ("Infratest Institute") on behalf of the Federal Ministry of Health. It is only since 1990 that large epidemiological studies on substance use and SUD among adolescents have been conducted by several research teams (e.g., Essau *et al.*, 1998a; Wittchen *et al.*, 1998) and institutes (e.g., Institut für Therapieforschung and Infratest).

According to a representative study conducted between 1990 and 1991, 14.4% of 12- to 39-year-olds in the former East Germany and 7.9% in the former West Germany have reported daily consumption of alcohol (DFG, 1991; cited in: Perkonigg *et al.*, in press). In Nordlohne's study (1992), 50% of the 12- to 17-year-olds indicated having drunk "soft" (e.g., wine, beer) and 25% "hard" alcoholic beverages (e.g., spirits) at some time in their lives. According to Silbereisen *et al.*'s report (1995), the drinking pattern in Germany among adolescents seemed to be affected by the German reunification. As a consequence of the open market that followed unification, the East German data showed a twofold increase in alcohol consumption from 1989 to 1990. As for drug consumption, the West German adolescents showed the highest use in the early 1970s, but then it declined significantly thereafter (Reuband, 1988). Among the 12- to 25-year-olds, 5% reported current use in 1990, and at the beginning of the 1980s only half these numbers have reported using drugs.

According to the most recent Federal Study (cited in: Federal Government Drug Commissioner, 2000), 26% of the 12- to 25-year-olds drank beer, 9% drank wine once or several times per week, 7% drank mixed drinks containing alcohol, and 5% drank spirits at least once per week. These findings showed an overall reduction in the frequency of alcohol consumption, which could have been attributed to young men drinking beer much less frequently in East Germany, but a slight increase among young women in East Germany. The proportion of adolescents drinking wine and spirits had also decreased. Cannabis was the most commonly used illegal drug in Germany. That is, 20% and 7.8% of the 18- to 39-year-olds in West and East Germany, respectively, reported having had experience with cannabis. In fact, in the 1998 survey, cannabis was the third reason after alcohol and tobacco for seeking treatment. About 0.6% and 0.1% of the 18- to 39-year-olds in West and East Germany, respectively, have consumed heroin at some time in their lives. However, the highest proportion of experience with heroin was found in the 25- to 29-year-old West Germans, and in the 18- to 24-year-old East Germans. The use of ecstasy and amphetamines was less frequent, being reported by less than 2% of the adolescents. In terms of smoking, higher proportions of smokers were found in the 12- to 17- and 18- to 25-year-olds in East Germany than in West Germany. However, when comparing the number of smokers among the 12- to 17-year-olds in West Germany during the period 1993–1997, the results showed an increase of 5%. Among East Germans, a large increase was found among young women.

Additionally, two large studies have recently been conducted in Germany on the prevalence of substance use and SUD among adolescents and young adults. The Early Development Stages of Psychopathology (EDSP; Wittchen *et al.*, 1998) was conducted in southern Germany, and the Bremen Adolescent Study (Essau *et al.*, 1998a) in northern Germany. The sample for the EDSP study (Wittchen *et al.*, 1998) was drawn from the 1994 Bavarian government registry of residents in metropolitan Munich. From the total of 4,809 sampled individuals, aged 14- to 24 years, 4,263 were located and determined to be eligible for the study. Of the 4,263 individuals a total of 3,021 interviews were completed. The design of the study is prospective consisting of a baseline survey and two follow-up surveys at approximately 15 and 30 months after the baseline. Diagnostic assessments were based on the computerized version of the Munich-Composite International Diagnostic Interview to cover DSM-IV and ICD-10 criteria. The Bremen Adolescent Study is a longitudinal, large-scale, community-based study of the epidemiology of SUD and other psychiatric disorders among 12- to 17-year-olds (Essau, 2000a; Essau *et al.*, 1998a). The specific aims were to estimate the prevalence, risks, course and outcome of psychiatric disorders, to determine their age of onset and severity, to examine the comorbidity patterns of disorders, and associated psychosocial impairment, as well as service utilization patterns. The computerized version of the Munich-Composite International Diagnostic Interview was used to diagnose SUD based on DSM-IV criteria. Participants in the Bremen Adolescent Study were recruited from 36 schools in the province of Bremen. Of the 1,035 adolescents with a complete data set, 421 were males and 614 females. The average age was 14.3 years.

In the EDSP (Perkonigg *et al.*, 1997), 34.9% of the 14- to 24-year-olds reported having used at least one drug at some time in their lifetime; of these, 17.6% reported infrequent and 17.3% regular use. The most commonly used drug was cannabis, with 6.5% of the probands reporting a single use, 11% consumed cannabis 2–4 times and 15.5% more than 5 times. Stimulants such as amphetamine (5.0%), cocaine (4.0%), and hallucinogens (3.2%) were also common. Opioid use, that includes prescription drugs such as codeine and methadone, was reported by 3.4% of the subjects. In another publication of the EDSP (Holly *et al.*, 1997), almost all (94.5%) of the adolescents and young adults reported having consumed some alcoholic drink in their life. The proportions of adolescents who consumed alcohol on a regular basis increased with age, ranging from 13.2% in the youngest to 75.6% in the oldest group. Alcohol users who first consumed alcohol at the age of 14 years or younger were at higher risk for meeting a diagnosis of dependence and abuse compared to those who initiated alcohol use at 15 years of age or older (Holly *et al.*, 1997). Among alcohol users, 35.9% of males and 11.6% of females met the criteria for either alcohol abuse or dependence at some time in their life.

In the Bremen Adolescent Study (Essau *et al.*, 1998b), 77.2% of the 12–17-year-olds had consumed some alcoholic beverage at some time in their life, and 245 (23.7%) reported having consumed at least one of the illegal drugs – the most common being cannabis. While significantly more boys than girls had consumed drugs, no such gender differences could be found for alcohol consumption.

The high rates of alcohol consumption in these two German studies may be related to German law and the societal view about the use of alcohol in adolescence. That is, legal access to alcohol beverages in Germany begins at age 16 years, and is accompanied by a widespread acceptance of alcohol use in this age group. This is in contrast to many other countries where the age for legal access to alcohol is much older. For example, in the United States, the legal age for buying alcohol beverages is 21 years.

Switzerland

In the Zurich Adolescent Psychopathology Project (ZAPP; Steinhausen and Metzke, 1998), 28.5% of the 10- to 17-year-olds had consumed at least one glass of alcohol, with boys (33.3%) significantly outnumering girls (23.4%). Among those who had consumed alcoholic beverages, 2.5% of them reported drinking beer weekly, 1.4% drank wine, 0.8% drank aperitifs and 0.8% cider, and 0.7% drank liquor and brandy. About 9.5% of the youth reported having been drunk at least once in their lifetime, with significantly more boys than girls reporting having been drunk. In 68% of the adolescents, events related to alcohol consumption included getting together with friends or family members, or parties. In 9% of the alcohol users, drinking was associated with personal problems or feelings of loneliness, or was due to boredom. The frequency of drinking was also associated with parents' substance-consuming behaviour. That is, the more the parents drank and smoked, the more likely that their children also used alcohol and nicotine.

In Madianos *et al.*'s study (1995), 2.7% of male and 2.9% of female adolescents reported lifetime use of cannabis, hallucinogens, heroin or cocaine. The lifetime rate of illicit drugs, by young adults, was 15.7% in males and 4.2% in females. In the study by Konings *et al.* (1995), 3.1% of the adolescents had ever used heroin or cocaine, and only 0.3% of adolescents reported ever using non-prescribed drugs such as barbiturates, codeine, amphetamines or anticholinergic drugs.

Australia and New Zealand

In Australia, the National Drug Strategy Survey (NDS) has undertaken six surveys (1985, 1988, 1991, 1993, 1995, 1998) on licit and illicit drug use, drug-related knowledge, awareness, and attitudes related to drugs in persons aged 14 years and older. The sample was based on households, thereby excluding homeless and institutional persons. In the 1998 survey (Australian Institute of Health and Welfare, 1999), of the 14- to 19-year-olds, 50.6% of males and

51.6% of females reported having used some illicit drug at some time in their life. This finding, compared to the one obtained in the 1995 survey, showed a constant rate among males, but an increase in females (1995 = 33.5%; 1998 = 51.6%). The rate of recent use in the 1998 survey was also high, being reported by 38.3% of males and 37.1% of females. The most commonly used drug was marijuana. As for alcohol consumption, 30% of the 14- to 19-year-olds consumed alcohol on a regular basis (i.e., at least one day per week) and 40.5% occasionally (i.e., less than one day per week).

The 1996 National Secondary School Students Drug Use Survey was conducted to provide information on alcohol, tobacco, and illicit drug use in 12- to 17-year-olds (Letcher and White, 1998). In this survey, the most commonly used substances were painkillers/analgesics (e.g., paracetamol and codeine), followed by alcohol and tobacco. Except for the use of inhalants and steroids, the number of adolescents who reported ever using a substance increased with age. The lifetime use of marijuana was highest among 16- to 17-year-olds, being 33% higher than for the general population (in 16- to 17-year-old students = 52%; samples from the general population = 39%) and were significantly more common in males than females. Slightly more males than females used illicit drugs such as heroin or cocaine, whilst slightly more females used painkillers, tranquillizers and inhalants than males.

In New Zealand, 27.2% of the 15-year-olds reported drinking alcohol at least once a month (Fergusson *et al.*, 1993), and 53.1% of all respondents drank up to 30 ml (or 24 g) pure alcohol. High odds-ratios were found for a high level of use and the presence of other substance use or abuse symptoms.

PREVALENCE OF SUBSTANCE ABUSE AND DEPENDENCE

United States

At least four large-scale studies have examined the prevalence of SUD in adolescents (Table 3.1). These include the Oregon Adolescent Depression Project (OADP; Lewinsohn *et al.*, 1993), the MECA study (Kandel *et al.*, 1997), and the studies by Reinherz *et al.* (1993), and Cohen *et al.* (1993). In the OADP (Lewinsohn *et al.*, 1993), the lifetime prevalence rate of alcohol use disorders among community adolescents was 4.6% and of hard drug use disorders (i.e., cocaine, amphetamine, hallucinogen, inhalant, opioid, phencyclidine and sedative abuse/dependence) was 2.6%. In a community-based study of 386 adolescents, Reinherz and colleagues (1993) found high prevalence rates of substance-related disorders. Alcohol abuse/dependence had the highest lifetime prevalence rate at 32.4% while drug abuse/dependence were found among 9.8% of the sample. Cohen *et al.*

(1993) focused particularly on sex differences in substance-related disorders and found similar rates of alcohol abuse for 14- to 16-year-old males and females. However, among 17- to 20-year-olds, prevalence rate for males was 20%, more than twice that of females (8.9%). Marijuana abuse was relatively rare in both males (4.1%) and females (1.8%). In the MECA study (Kandel et al., 1997), 2% of the adolescents (N=26) met the criteria for DSM-III-R SUD based on DSM-III-R criteria. Twenty-one of these adolescents had one SUD, four had two different SUD, and one had three SUD. The most commonly diagnosed SUD was alcohol abuse or dependence, followed by marijuana abuse or dependence. Five met the diagnosis of illicit substance (excluding marijuana). As in most studies, the rate of SUD increased with age, ranging from 1.5% in the 14-year-olds to 8.7% in the 17-year-olds. About 30.8% of boys and 41.7% of girls who drank weekly or smoked daily in the past 6 months, or who had used any illicit substances in the past year received the diagnosis of any SUD. Frequent consumption of alcohol, cigarettes, and illicit substances was also associated with an increased risk of meeting not only SUD, but also a wide range of other psychiatric disorders, particularly anxiety, mood, and disruptive behavioural disorders.

Table 3.1 Frequency of substance use disorders in adolescents

	Country	Age	Alcohol use disorders	Drug use disorders
Giaconia et al. (1994)*	USA	18	32.4%	9.8%
Reinherz et al. (1993)***	USA	18	26.1%	4.4%
Lewinsohn et al. (1993)*	USA	12–18	4.6%	2.6%
Fergusson et al. (1993)*	New Zealand	15		
(self-report)			3.5%	—
(mother's report)			1.9%	—
Feehan et al. (1994)**	New Zealand	18	10.4%	—
Essau et al. (1998b)*	Germany	12–17	12.3%	0.1–6.4%

Note: *lifetime prevalence; **one-year prevalence; ***six-month prevalence.

New Zealand

In New Zealand, data on the prevalence of SUD in adolescents mostly come from the Dunedin Multidisciplinary Health and Developmental Study (McGee et al., 1994). The sample for this study was a cohort of children born at the city's maternity hospital between 1972 and 1973. The children have been followed from birth to age 21. At ages 5, 7, and 9 years, the children were assessed with the Rutter Child Scales (Rutter et al., 1970). At age 11, diagnostic interviews were conducted using the Diagnostic Interview Schedule for Children (DISC; Costello et al., 1982); whereas at 13 and 15 a modified DISC was used (McGee et al., 1990), and at age 18, a modified version of the adult Diagnostic Interview Schedule was employed (Feehan et al., 1994).

Another study conducted in New Zealand was the Christchurch Health and Developmental Study (Fergusson *et al.*, 1993). This longitudinal study has followed a birth cohort of 1,265 New Zealand children, born in the Christchurch urban region during mid-1977, at birth, 4 months, 1 year, and annual intervals to the age of 15 years. Data were available from various combination of informants: mother, child, and teacher. At ages 15 and 16 years, maternal reports and self-reports of different symptoms were used. Substance abuse behaviour (tobacco, alcohol, and illicit drug abuse) was assessed using survey questions, supplemented by the Rutgers Alcohol Problems Index (White and Labouvie, 1989). Children's problems with tobacco, alcohol, and illicit drugs were obtained from questions about the parents' perceptions.

Findings of the Dunedin Multidisciplinary Health and Developmental Study showed a one-year prevalence of alcohol dependence to be 10.4% and of marijuana dependence 5.2% among 18-year-olds (Feehan *et al.*, 1994). In the Christchurch Health and Development Study (Fergusson *et al.*, 1993), the rates of SUD ranged from 5.2% to 7.7%, depending on the informants. That is, the rate of alcohol abuse/dependence based on maternal report was 1.9% and on self-report was 3.5%. The differences in prevalence rates between these two studies could have been accounted for by differences in age: the sample in the Dunedin study was 18 years old, and in the Christchurch study 15 years old.

Netherlands

The study by Verhulst and colleagues (1997) provided the prevalence of SUD in the Netherlands. It was a two-phase survey to estimate the 6-month prevalence of SUD and other psychiatric disorders in adolescents. During the first phase, the parent, self-report and teacher versions of the CBCL were used to screen a sample of 13- to 18-year-olds. A subsample of these adolescents was interviewed during the second phase, using the parent and child versions of the Diagnostic Interview Schedule for Children to obtain DSM-III-R diagnoses. The 6-month prevalence of any SUD varied, based on the informant. That is, the 6-month rate according to parental report was 0.4% and according to adolescent report it was 3.3%. Significantly more boys than girls met the diagnosis of any SUD.

Spain

The prevalence of SUD in Spanish adolescents comes from the study of Canals *et al.* (1997). The main aims of their study were to estimate the prevalence and comorbidity rates of SUD and other psychiatric disorders based on DSM-III-R and ICD-10. The Spanish version of the Schedules for Clinical Assessment in Neuropsychiatry (SCAN) was used to generate current diagnoses in the 18-year-olds; these adolescents were recruited from either high schools or technical schools. Their findings showed that 0.3% of the subjects met the diagnosis of any SUD.

Germany

In the Bremen Adolescent Study (Essau *et al.*, 1998b; Essau, 2000b), 12.3% of the 12- to 17-year-olds met the lifetime diagnosis for any SUD (Table 3.2). Of the substances covered, the most commonly used was alcohol, with a rate of 9.3%. Illegal drug usage was less common, being reported by 6.9% of the adolescents. SUD were significantly higher in males than in females, with a ratio of 2 to 1. The disorders increased with age, with the lowest rate found in the youngest age group, and the highest in the oldest age group.

In the EDSP, the lifetime cumulative incidence of alcohol abuse was 15.1% for men and 4.5% for women, and for dependence it was 10.0% for men and 2.5% for women (Holly *et al.*, 1997). Age patterns of cumulative incidence differed by gender. For men, the cumulative incidence for both alcohol abuse and dependence increased consistently with age. Among women, the cumulative incidence of alcohol abuse increased up to age 22, with no new cases. For alcohol dependence, it showed a strong initial increase before age 17, with few new cases after this age. This pattern of diagnosis onset also differed across gender. That is, the higher cumulative incidence of dependence among 14- to 15-year-old women compared to males among alcohol users showed the liability for dependence among these young females. This pattern may also indicate birth cohort effects, in that 14- to 17-year-old females reported a higher incidence of SUD than the 18- to 24-year-old males. Interestingly, females with alcohol abuse and dependence consumed significantly lower amounts of alcohol than their male counterparts.

Summary

Recent studies have shown that a high number of adolescents have had some experience with alcohol and drugs, with some variations across countries. These variations could have accounted for differences of age for the legal access to alcoholic beverages across countries. For example, the age of legal access in Germany begins at 16 years. In some other countries, such as the USA, the legal age for buying alcoholic beverages has even risen from 18 to 21 years since the early 1980s. Other explanations may include cultural views about the use of certain substances (e.g., alcohol) which may determine the accessibility and the acceptance of their use. All these (i.e., societal, political differences) make it difficult to compare findings across studies. Another reason accounting for the variations of findings across studies may be related to methodological differences such as the subjects' age and gender, the sampling procedure, the assessment instruments, and the classification systems. Even in studies that used the DSM systems,

Table 3.2 Frequency of substance use disorders based on DSM-IV criteria

Substance use disorders	Male (N=421) N	(%)	Female (N=614) N	(%)	12–13 (N=380) N	(%)	14–15 (N=350) N	(%)	16–17 (N=305) N	(%)
Any substances	71	(16.9)	56	(9.1)***	3	(0.8)	40	(11.4)	84	(27.5)***
Alcohol	54	(12.8)	42	(6.8)**	3	(0.8)	31	(8.9)	62	(20.3)***
Cannabis	44	(10.5)	22	(3.6)	—	—	22	(6.3)	43	(14.1)***
Opiate	2	(0.5)	2	(0.3)	0	(0)	1	(0.3)	3	(1.0)
Amphetamine	1	(0.2)	3	(0.5)	0	(0)	—	—	3	(1.0)
Hallucinogen	3	(0.7)	3	(0.5)	0	(0)	0	(0)	6	(2.0)**
Phencyclidine	1	(0.2)	0	(0)	0	(0)	0	(0)	1	(0.3)
Other	0	(0)	1	(0.2)	0	(0)	0	(0)	1	(0.3)

*Source: Essau, 2000b. ** $p < .01$, *** $p < .001$.

some changes have taken place in the different versions of the DSM. For example, DSM-IV differs from DSM-III and DSM-III-R in the segregation of the social consequences of alcohol use from compulsive behaviour and physiological adaptation associated with use, and the syndromal conceptualization of dependence where no single criterion is necessary for a diagnosis.

THE SETTINGS OF ADOLESCENT SUBSTANCE USE

The settings in which adolescents use alcohol and drugs are less clear. In a study by Mayer *et al.* (1998), younger adolescents, regardless of gender, tended to use alcohol and drugs in their own homes rather than in the homes of others or in open fields. Among frequent alcohol users alcohol consumption was associated with drinking while driving, before participating in school events, and while walking on the streets (Donnermeyer and Park, 1995). By contrast, less frequent alcohol use was associated with drinking at home with parents or guardians.

In the study by Sussman *et al.* (1998), the most common place for drug use was in the adolescent's bedroom (26%). Other common places include a room (excluding the bedroom) at a friend's home (17%), home yard (14%), public sidewalk (12.8%), another location outside the home (12%), and outside the school (12%), the bedroom at a friend's home (11.8%), and an outside specified location within the general other location (11.8%). Fifty-eight per cent reported consuming drugs with one to four friends, 7% with a boyfriend or girlfriend, 2% with family members, and 27% with a large group of people. In 61% of the adolescents, use of drugs at home or at another location generally took place after 5:00 p.m., and among those who used drugs at school, it usually took place before 5:00 p.m.

Another relevant issue is related to the way in which adolescents obtained their first supply of a substance. In the Australian National Drug Strategy Survey (Australian Institute of Health and Welfare, 1999), relatives (51.3%) and friends or acquaintances (44.1%) were reported as the source of first supply of alcohol in adolescents under the age of 18 years. The first supplies of cigarettes were most likely friends or acquaintances (78%), followed by relatives (11.3%).

COMORBIDITY AND TEMPORAL SEQUENCE OF DISORDERS

The popularity of the comorbidity concept in psychology and psychiatry can be said to go hand-in-hand with the introduction of the third edition of the Diagnostic and Statistical Manual of Mental Disorders (DSM-III, APA, 1980).

In the DSM-III, some exclusion criteria to the diagnosis in the lower hierarchy are removed. In DSM-III-R and DSM-IV, the different conditions can be assessed on their own merits and each be diagnosed together with SUD.

Substance use disorder co-occurs frequently with other psychiatric disorders such as anxiety, depressive, and disruptive behaviour disorders (Bukstein et al., 1989; Fergusson et al., 1993; Lewinsohn et al., 1993). Comorbidity occurred not only between substance and other psychiatric disorders, but also within the SUD. In the Bremen Adolescent Study (Essau et al., 1998b; Essau, 2000b), about half (47.2%) of the adolescents who met the diagnosis of any SUD were diagnosed with only these disorders; 37.1% had one additional and 12.7 % had at least two other mental disorders (Table 3.3). The most common comorbidity pattern was that of substance and depressive disorders. Furthermore, about one-third of those with one type of SUD had at least one other type of abuse/dependence, with alcohol use disorders being the most common comorbid disorder (Table 3.4).

Table 3.3 Comorbidity of substance use disorders with other disorders

DSM-IV disorders	N	%
Anxiety disorders	22	17.3
Panic disorder	2	1.6
Agoraphobia	11	8.7
Social phobia	4	3.1
Specific phobia	3	2.4
Obsessive-compulsive disorder	3	2.4
Generalized anxiety disorder	3	2.4
Post-traumatic stress disorder	5	3.9
NNB phobia	10	7.9
Depressive disorders	35	27.6
Major depression	29	22.8
Dysthymic disorders	13	10.2
Somatoform disorders	35	27.6
Undifferentiated somatoform disorder	27	21.3
Conversion disorders	3	2.4
Pain disorder	6	4.7

Source: Essau, 2000b.

In the EDSP (Perkonigg et al., 1997), 80% of the young adults with a cannabis disorder were exclusively abusing or dependent on this substance. Eighteen per cent also used amphetamines, 11.7% cocaine and 4.1% hallucinogens. Among those with hallucinogen or amphetamine disorders, not one single case was identified as having just this disorder. About 88% of those with amphetamine use disorders also had a cannabis use disorder, 76% had hallucinogen use disorder and 20% had an opioid use disorder.

Table 3.4 Comorbidity within the substance use disorders

Substance use disorders	Male (N = 71) N	(%)	Female (N = 56) N	(%)
Alcohol	26	(37.0)	30	(54.0)
Cannabis	15	(21.0)	9	(16.0)
Opioid	1	(1.0)	2	(4.0)
Hallucinogens	0	(0)	2	(4.0)
Alcohol and cannabis	24	(34.0)	9	(16.0)
Alcohol, cannabis and amphetamine	1	(0)	2	(4.0)
Alcohol, cannabis and hallucinogens	2	(3.0)	0	(0)
Alcohol, cannabis and other	0	(0)	1	(2.0)
Alcohol, cannabis, hallucinogens and phencyclidine	1	(1.0)	0	(0)
Cannabis and opioid	1	(1.0)	0	(0)
Cannabis, amphetamine and hallucinogens	0	(0)	1	(2.0)

Source: Essau et al., 1998b. Copyright 2002 by Hogrefe Verlag, Göttingen. Translated by permission.

In the OADP, over 80% of the adolescents with an alcohol disorder had another psychiatric disorder: about 20% of the cases were of an internalizing type, 35% were of the externalizing type, and the remaining 45% consisted of both internalizing and externalizing disorders (Rohde et al., 1996). Among adolescents with alcohol use disorder who had a history of major depression, 58.1% of them reported the occurrence of depression before that of alcohol. 87.5% and 80% of the adolescents reported that anxiety and disruptive behavioural disorders, respectively, preceded alcohol disorders. Similar findings have been reported by Hovens et al. (1994), in that 53% of the adolescents with dysthymia and alcohol use disorders reported dysthymia preceding alcohol use disorders. The OADP data also indicated that among those with both alcohol and drug use disorders, in 51.5% cases drug disorder occurred before that of alcohol (Rohde et al., 1996). This finding was interpreted as failing to support alcohol as a gateway to a more serious drug use in adolescence.

Studies of adolescents with SUD in clinical settings have also reported the common presence of disruptive behaviours such as conduct disorder, with estimates of incidence ranging from 40% to 70% (Bukstein, 2000; Bukstein et al., 1989; Stowell and Estroff, 1992). Attention-Deficit/ Hyperactivity Disorder (ADHD) is also common in adolescents with SUD (Bukstein et al., 1989; Kaminer, 1992), with comorbidity rates ranging from 20% to 30% (Brown et al., 1990; Horner and Scheibe, 1997). This association is most probably accounted for by a high level of comorbidity between conduct disorder and ADHD. In a study by Lynskey and Fergusson (1995), conduct problems at age 8 preceded alcohol and drug consumption at 15 years.

Studies of clinical samples have also observed a high rate of anxiety disorder among youth with SUD (Clark *et al.*, 1995). For example, in a study by Clark and Jacob (1992), 50% of the adolescents with alcohol use disorders had at least one lifetime anxiety disorder diagnosis with PTSD as the most common anxiety diagnosis. The order of appearance of anxiety and SUD is variable, depending on the specific anxiety disorders. Social phobia and agoraphobia usually preceded alcohol abuse, while panic disorder and generalized anxiety disorder tend to follow the onset of alcohol abuse (Kushner *et al.*, 2000).

Implication of comorbidity

Although the meaning of comorbidity is not clear, comorbidity was associated with an earlier onset of SUD and with greater likelihood of mental health treatment utilization (Rohde *et al.*, 1996). The subjects with a comorbid disorder had an earlier onset of alcohol use disorder compared to subjects with just alcohol disorder; they were also more likely to have received treatment for their alcohol use disorder. Adolescents with a comorbid disorder compared to "pure" alcohol disorder had an earlier age of onset of alcohol use disorder, and were at an increased risk of developing an episode of alcohol use disorder during the study period (Rohde *et al.*, 1996). The prevalence of comorbid disorder increased the likelihood of receiving mental health treatment for their disorder. Comorbidity was not associated with the duration and severity of alcohol use disorder, number of episodes of alcohol diagnosis, or likelihood of relapse. The finding of the high comorbidity between SUD and other disorders (especially illicit drug use, delinquent-type behaviour and tobacco use) was interpreted as being consistent with problem behaviour theory as proposed by Jessor and Jessor (1977). According to their theory, this problem behaviour is a single syndrome which is associated with the underlying construct of unconventionality.

PSYCHOSOCIAL IMPAIRMENT

Substance use and SUD in adolescents are often associated with impairment in various life areas such as negative interpersonal relationships, an increase in family conflict, a decline in academic functioning, antisocial behaviours and legal problems, failing to fulfil their major role obligations, and recurrent social or interpersonal problems (see review: Myers *et al.*, 1998). In the Bremen Adolescent Study (Essau *et al.*, 1998b), 66% of those with drug and 77% of those with alcohol problems repeatedly used these substances in hazardous situations. Adolescents with substance use disorders were psychologically more distressed compared to those without these disorders. That is, as measured using the SCL-90-R, they had significantly higher scores on the subscales: somatization, obsessive-compulsive behaviour, depression, and hostility. Despite this impairment, only 25% of them received treatment for their substance problems. In the study by Perkonigg and colleagues (1997), among adolescents with cannabis disorder, symptoms related to recurrent use in dangerous situations show a fairly steep and steadily rising cumulative incidence rate, starting after the age of 14 years. After the age of 19 years the curve levels off slightly, suggesting only a few new cases with first onset of this symptom after this age. The items related to recurrent social and interpersonal problems due to cannabis use mostly occurred slightly later, being at the age of 16 to 18 years.

The diverse nature of adolescent substance use, however, makes it difficult to ascertain the direction of causality. For example, for some adolescents substance consumption may be a reaction to certain problems (e.g., stress), and an increased involvement with alcohol and other drug use may precipitate deterioration in psychosocial functioning (e.g., school problems, withdrawal and isolation). For others, substance use is embedded within the "problem behaviour" syndrome (i.e., deviant behaviours and attitudes; Jessor and Jessor, 1977).

CONCLUSION

Numerous studies have been conducted on the prevalence of substance use and the SUD in adolescents. These studies have generally shown a high prevalence of alcohol and drug use, with some variations in rates across studies, which may reflect cultural/societal and political differences with regard to alcohol and drugs.

The experimentation and involvement with substances in some adolescents may reflect "normative behaviour", but in some adolescents may lead to the development of SUD. Furthermore, heavy substance use and a high rate of SUD during adolescence is associated with psychosocial impairment in various life areas, including impaired social relationships and psychological disturbances.

REFERENCES

APA (American Psychiatric Association) (1980). *Diagnostic and statistical manual of mental disorders* (3rd edn). Washington, DC: American Psychiatric Association.

Australian Institute of Health and Welfare (1999). *1998 National Drug Strategy Household Survey.* www.aihw.gov.au.

Brown, S. A., Mott, M. A., & Myers, M. G. (1990). Adolescent drug and alcohol treatment outcome. In R. R. Watson (Ed.), *Prevention and treatment of drug and alcohol abuse* (pp. 373–403). Clifton, NJ: Humana Press.

Bukstein, O. G. (2000). Disruptive behaviour disorders and substance use disorders in adolescents. *Journal of Psychoactive Drugs, 32*, 67–79.

Bukstein, O. G., Brent, D. A., & Kaminer, Y. (1989). Comorbidity of substance abuse and other psychiatric disorders in adolescents. *American Journal of Psychiatry, 146*, 1131-1141.

Canals, J., Domenech, E., Carbajo, G., & Blade, J. (1997). Prevalence of DSM-III-R and ICD-10 psychiatric disorders in a Spanish population of 18-year-olds. *Acta Psychiatrica Scandinavica, 96*, 287–294.

Castilla, J., Barrio, G., Belza, M. J., & Fuente, L. (1999). Drug and alcohol consumption and sexual risk behaviour among young adults: Results from a national survey. *Drug and Alcohol Dependence, 56*, 47–53.

Clark, D. B., Bukstein, O. G., Smith, M. G., Kaczynski, N. A., Mezzich, A. C., & Donovan, J. E. (1995). Identifying anxiety disorders in adolescents hospitalized for alcohol abuse or dependence. *Psychiatric Services, 46*, 618–620.

Clark, D. B. & Jacob, R. G. (1992). Anxiety disorders and alcoholism in adolescents. A preliminary report. *Alcoholism, Clinical and Experimental Research, 16*, 371.

Cohen, P., Cohen, J., Kasen, S., Velez, C. N., Hartmark, C., Johnson, J., Rojas, M., Brook, J., & Streuning, E. L. (1993). An epidemiological study of disorders in late childhood and adolescence—I: Age- and gender-specific prevalence. *Journal of Child Psychology and Psychiatry, 34*, 851–866.

Cooney, A., Dobbinson, S., & Flaherty, B. (1994). *1992 Survey of drug use by NSW secondary school students.* NWS Department of Health, Sydney NSW drug and alcohol directorate. In-house report series. ISBN: 0 7310 1542 2.

Costello, E. J., Edelbrock, C., Kalas, R., Kessler, M., & Klaric, S. (1982). *The Diagnostic Interview Schedule for Children (DISC).* Bethesda, MD: National Institute of Mental Health.

Donnermeyer, J. F. & Shik Park, D. (1995). Alcohol use among rural adolescents: Predictive and situational factors. *International Journal of Addiction, 30*, 459–479.

Dür, W. (1990). *AIDS—Aufklärung bei Jugendlichen.* Vienna: Ludwig Boltzmann – Institut für Medizinsoziologie.

Eisenbach-Stangl, I. (1983). Zur Entwicklung des Alkohol- und legalen Drogengebrauchs: Epidemiologische Ergebnisse aus den letzten 10 Jahren. In R. Mader (Ed.), *Alkohol- und Drogenabhängigkeit: Neue Ergebnisse aus Theorie und Praxis* (pp. 265–286). Vienna: Hollinek.

Essau, C. A. (2000a). Angst und Depression bei Jugendlichen. *Habilitationschrift.* Bremen: University of Bremen.

Essau, C. A. (2000b). Substance use disorders in adolescents. Paper presented at the Second International Conference on Child and Adolescent Mental Health. Kuala Lumpar, Malaysia.

Essau, C. A., Karpinski, N. A., Petermann, F., & Conradt, J. (1998a). Häufigkeit und Komorbidität psychischer Störungen bei Jugendlichen: Ergebnisse der Bremer Jugendstudie. *Zeitschrift für Klinische Psychologie, Psychiatrie und Psychotheapie, 46*, 105–124.

Essau, C. A., Karpinski, N. A., Petermann, F., & Conradt, J. (1998b). Häufigkeit und Komorbidität von Störungen durch Substanzkonsum. *Zeitschrift Kindheit und Entwicklung, 7*, 199–207.

Federal Government Drug Commissioner (2000). *1999 Drug and addiction report.* Bonn/Berlin.

Feehan, M., McGee, R., Nada-Raja, S., & Williams, S. M. (1994). DSM-III-R disorders in New Zealand 18-year-olds. *Australian and New Zealand Journal of Psychiatry, 28*, 87–99.

Fergusson, D. M., Horwood, L. J., & Lynskey, M. T. (1993). Prevalence and comorbidity of DSM-III-R diagnoses in a birth cohort of 15 year olds. *Journal of the American Academy of Child and Adolescent Psychiatry, 32,* 1127–1134.

Gasser-Steiner, P. & Stigler, H. (1997). *Jugendlicher Drogenkonsum—Epidemiologische Befunde und sozialwissenschaftliche Modelle. Zur Verbreitung des Konsums legaler und illegaler Drogen in der Steiermark.* Unpublished manuscript. Karl-Franzens-Universität Graz.

Giaconia, R., Reinherz, H. Z., Silverman, A. B., Pakiz, B., Frost, A. K., & Cohen, E. (1994). Ages of onset of psychiatric disorders in a community population of older adolescents. *Journal of the American Academy of Child and Adolescent Psychiatry, 33,* 706–717.

Holly, A., Türk, D., Nelson, B., Pfister, H. & Wittchen, H.-U. (1997). Prävalenz von Alkoholkonsum, Alkoholmissbrauch und -abhängigkeit bei Jugendlichen und jungen Erwachsenen. *Zeitschrift für Klinische Psychologie, 26,* 1717–1718.

Horner, B. R. & Scheibe, K. E. (1997). Prevalence and implications of attention deficit hyperactivity disorder among adolescents in treatment for substance misuse. *Journal of the American Academy of Child and Adolescence Psychiatry, 36,* 30–36.

Hovens, J. G., Cantwell, D. P., & Kiriakos, R. (1994). Psychiatric comorbidity in hospitalised adolescent substance misusers. *Journal of the American Academy of Child and Adolescent Psychiatry, 33,* 476–483.

Jessor, R. & Jessor, S. L. (1977). *Problem behaviour and psychosocial development: A longitudinal study of youth.* New York, NY: Academic Press.

Johnston, L. D., O'Malley, P. M., & Bachman, J. G. (2000). *The monitoring the future national results on adolescent drug use: Overview of key findings, 1999.* Bethesda, MA: National Institute on Drug Abuse.

Kaminer, Y. (1992). Desipramine facilitation of cocaine abstinence in an adolescent. *Journal of the American Academy of Child and Adolescence Psychiatry, 31/2,* 312–317.

Kandel, D. B., Adler, I., & Sudit, M. S. (1981). The epidemiology of adolescent drug use in France and Israel. *American Journal of Public Health, 71,* 256–265.

Kandel, D. B., Johnson, J. G., Bird, H. R., Canino, G., Goodman, S. H., Lahey, B. B., Regier, D. A., & Schwab-Stone, M. (1997). Psychiatric disorders associated with substance use among children and adolescents. Findings from the Methods for the Epidemiology of Child and Adolescent Mental Disorders (MECA) Study. *Journal of Abnormal Child Psychology, 25,* 121–132.

Kokkevi, A. & Stefanis, C. (1991). The epidemiology of licit and illicit substance use among high school students in Greece. *American Journal of Public Health, 81,* 48–52.

Konings, E., Dubois-Arber, F., Narring, F., & Michaud, P. (1995). Identifying adolescent drug users: Results of a national survey on adolescent health in Switzerland. *Journal of Adolescence Health, 16,* 240–247.

Kushner, M. G., Abram, K., & Borchardt, C. (2000). The relationship between anxiety disorders and alcohol use disorders: A review of the major perspectives and findings. *Clinical Psychiatric Review, 20,* 149–171.

Letcher, T. & White, V. (1998). *Australian secondary students' use of over-the-counter and illicit substances in 1996.* Canberra, Australia: Australian Government Printers.

Lewinsohn, P. M., Hops, H., Roberts, R. E., Seeley, J. R., & Andrews, J. A. (1993). Adolescent psychopathology: I. Prevalence and incidence of depression and other DSM-III-R disorders in high school students. *Journal of Abnormal Psychology, 102,* 133–144.

Lynskey, M. T. & Fergusson, D. M. (1995). Childhood conduct problems, attention deficit behaviors and adolescent alcohol, tobacco, and illicit drug use. *Journal of Abnormal Child Psychology*, *23*, 281–302.

Madianos, M. G., Gefou-Madianou, D., Richardson, C., & Stefanis, C. N. (1995). Factors affecting illicit and licit drug use among adolescent and young adults in Greece. *Acta Psychiatrica Scandinavica*, *91*, 258–264.

Mayer, R. R., Forster, J. L., Murray, D. M. & Wageneer, A. C. (1998). Social settings and situations of underage drinking. *Journal of Studies on Alcohol*, *59*, 207–215.

McGee, R., Feehan, M., Williams, S., Partridge, F., Silva, A., & Kelly, J. (1990). DSM-III disorders in a large sample of adolescents. *Journal of the American Academy of Child and Adolescence Psychiatry*, *29*, 611–619.

McGee, R., Williams, S., & Feehan, M. (1994). Behaviour problems in New Zealand children. In P. R. Joyce, R. T. Mulder, M. A. Oakley-Browne, I. D. Sellman, & W. G. A. Watkins (Eds.), *Development, personality and psychopathology* (pp. 15–22). Christchurch, New Zealand: Christchurch School of Medicine.

Measham, F., Parker, H. & Aldridge, J. (1998). The teenage transition: From adolescent recreational drug use to the young adult dance culture in Britain in the mid-1990s. *Journal of Drug Issues*, 28, 9–32.

Merrill, J. C., Kleber, H. D., Shwartz, M., Liu, H., & Lewis, S. R. (1999). Cigarettes, alcohol, marijuana, other risk factors, and American youth. *Drug and Alcohol Dependence*, *56*, 205–212.

Miller, P. & Plant, M. (1996). Drinking, smoking and illicit drug use among 15 and 16 year olds in the United Kingdom. *British Medical Journal*, *313*, 394–397.

Myers, M. G., Brown, S. A., & Vik, P. W. (1998). Adolescent substance use problems. In E. J. Mash & R. A. Barkley, (Eds.), *Treatment of childhood disorders* (pp. 692–730). New York, NY: Guilford Press.

Nordlohne, E. (1992). *Die Kosten jugendlicher Problembewältigung. Alkohol, Zigaretten- und Arzneimittelkonsum im Jugendalter.* Weinheim, München: Juvenka.

Office of Population Censuses and Surveys (1986). *Adolescent Drinking*. London: Her Majesty's Stationery Office. *134*, 1–15.

Perkonigg, A., Lieb, R., & Wittchen, H.-U. (1997). Prevalence of use, abuse and dependence of illicit drugs among adolescents and young adults in a community sample. *European Addiction Research*, *134*, 1–15.

Perkonigg, A., Wittchen, H.-U., & Lachner, G. (in press). Wie häufig sind Substanzmißbrauch und -abhängigkeit? Ein methodenkritischer Überblick. *Zeitschrift für Klinische Psychologie.*

Prescott-Clarke, P. and Primatesta, P. (1997). *Health Survey for England: The health of young people '95–97.*
http://www.official-documents.co.uk/document/doh/survey97/hse95.htm

Reinherz, H. Z., Giaconia, R. M., Lefkowitz, E. S., Pakiz, B., & Frost, A. K. (1993). Prevalence of psychiatric disorders in a community population of older adolescents. *Journal of the American Academy of Child and Adolescent Psychiatry*, *32*, 369–377.

Reuband, K. H. (1988). Drogenkonsum im Wandel. *Zeitschrift für Sozialisationsforschung und Erziehungssoziologie*, *8*, 54–68.

Reuband, K. H. (1992). *Drogenkonsum und Drogenpolitik. Deutschland und die Niederlande im Vergleich.* Opladen: Leske & Buderich.

Rohde, P., Lewinsohn, P. M., & Seeley, J. R. (1996). Psychiatric comorbidity with problematic alcohol use in high school students. *Journal of the American Academy of Child and Adolescent Psychiatry, 35,* 101–109.

Rutter, M., Tizard, J., & Whitmore, K. (1970). *Education, health and behaviour.* London: Longmans.

Silbereisen, R. E., Robins, L., & Rutter, M. (1995). Secular trends in substance use: Concepts and data on the impact of social change on alcohol and drug abuse. In M. Rutter & D. J. Smith (Eds.), *Psychosocial disorders in young people: Time trends and their causes* (pp. 490–543). Chichester, UK: John Wiley.

Springer, A. & Uhl, A. (1993). *Suchtgiftprävention in der Schule.* Vienna: Ludwig Boltzmann – Institut für Suchtforschung.

Steinhausen, H.-C. & Metzke, C. W. (1998). Frequency and correlates of substance use among preadolescents and adolescents in a Swiss Epidemiological Study. *Journal of Child Psychology and Psychiatry, 39,* 387–397.

Stowell, R. J. A. & Estroff, T. W. (1992). Psychiatric disorders in substance-abusing adolescent inpatients: A pilot study. *Journal of the American Academy of Child and Adolescent Psychiatry, 31,* 1036–1040.

Sussman, S., Stacy, A. W., Ames, S. L., & Freedman, L. B. (1998). Self-reported high-risk locations of adolescent drug use. *Addictive Behaviours, 23,* 405–411.

Swadi, H. (1988). Drug and substance use among 3333 London adolescents.. *British Journal of Addiction, 83,* 935–942.

Verhulst, F. C., van der Ende, J., Ferdinand, R. F., & Kasius, M. C. (1997). The prevalence of DSM-III-R diagnoses in a national sample of Dutch adolescents. *Archives of General Psychiatry, 54,* 329–336.

White, H. L. & Labouvie, E. W. (1989). Towards the assessment of adolescent problem drinking. *Journal of Studies in Alcohol, 50,* 30–37.

Wittchen, H.-U., Nelson, C. B., & Lachner, G. (1998). Prevalence of mental disorders and psychosocial impairments in adolescents and young adults. *Psychological Medicine, 28,* 109–126.

Chapter 4

Risk factors

Terri N. Sullivan and Albert D. Farrell

Substance abuse and dependence are characterized by detrimental patterns of use that result in adverse personal consequences (e.g., repeated interpersonal problems, physical harm) and symptoms such as tolerance and withdrawal reflecting psychological and/or physiological dependence, respectively (American Psychiatric Association, 1994). Both patterns of misuse are subsumed under the category of substance use disorders. The diagnosis of these disorders typically does not occur until late adolescence or early adulthood, but risk factors for substance use disorders are identifiable in childhood and early adolescence (Chassin and Ritter, 2001). Identification of risk factors is important for several reasons. Because risk factors increase the probability of developing substance use disorders, interventions focused on decreasing exposure to risk factors or buffering their impact should be helpful in preventing this outcome. Identification of risk factors across childhood and adolescence can inform developers of prevention programmes about relevant developmental timeframes for intervention, and guide the selection of optimum approaches for prevention and intervention (e.g., school, family, or community-based approaches). Finally, risk factor indices can be used at the individual level to identify high-risk youth and families for appropriate services (Farrell et al., 1992).

The risk factor approach stems from epidemiological roots where the primary focus is to understand which individuals develop a particular disease and what factors contribute to its emergence (Feuerstein et al., 1986). Clayton defined a risk factor as "an individual attribute, individual characteristic, situational condition, or environmental context that increases the probability of drug use or abuse or a transition in level of involvement with drugs" (1992, p. 15). Clayton also described general principles regarding risk factors. An individual risk factor is defined as a dichotomous variable that is either present or absent. For instance, the risk factor "peer pressure to use drugs" was considered to be present for middle school students who reported feeling pressure from their friends to drink or use drugs at least once in the past 30 days (Farrell et al., 1992). Risk factors for substance abuse and dependence encompass a wide variety of categories spanning broad domains such as social and environmental, biological-genetic, and psychological. Examples within the social and environmental domain are peer, family, school, and community influences as well as traumatic and negative life events. Within each category, a risk factor (e.g., peer influences) can have multiple indicators (e.g., peer models, peer attitudes, and peer pressure for drug use), and these measures have independent and also may have cumulative effects on substance use outcomes (Clayton, 1992).

The study of risk factors for adolescent drug use has progressed from the identification of individual risk factors to the use of methodological approaches that integrate risk factors across domains, identify their interrelations and the processes by which they influence behaviour, and incorporate developmental contexts (e.g., Bry et al., 1982; Sullivan and Farrell, 1999; Wills et al., 2000). Because of low base rates for adolescents diagnosed with substance abuse and dependence, the majority of studies of adolescents have focused on initiation and drug use frequency with some research addressing problem drug use in late adolescence (Chassin and Ritter, 2001). Studies have also more specifically examined risk factors for substance abuse and dependence (e.g., Kilpatrick et al., 2000). More complex methodological approaches such as multiple risk factor indices, family and twin studies, and mediational models have also been utilized (e.g., Brook et al., 1992; Chassin et al., 1999; McGue et al., 2000).

This chapter summarizes the extensive work that has been conducted to identify risk factors for adolescent substance use. We begin with a description of some methodological issues that are central to understanding the research in this area. We then provide examples of individual risk factors that have been identified within each broad domain. This is followed by a discussion of efforts to aggregate individual risk factors into multiple risk factor indices. We then discuss the relation between risk and related concepts of vulnerability and protective factors. Finally, we close with some general conclusions concerning key issues in this area.

METHODOLOGICAL ISSUES

Before describing specific approaches for studying risk factors, several general methodological issues need to be addressed. The first is the type of populations that have been studied. Research examining risk factors for escalation in substance use, abuse, and dependence has been conducted using school- and community-based populations, individuals classified as "high-risk", and clinical populations of adolescents diagnosed with substance use disorders. Chassin and Ritter (2001) provided an excellent review of the advantages and disadvantages of each approach. They noted that studies of general populations such as school- and community-based samples are able to follow risk trajectories over time for large numbers of students, but may contribute less to our understanding of risk for substance use disorders. School-based samples may be further limited because they exclude dropouts and are less likely to include students with poor attendance (Farrell *et al.*, 1999). Studies of "high-risk" samples have primarily focused on children with a parental history of substance use disorders. Chassin and Ritter observed that such studies have been able to use rigorous assessment (e.g., neuropsychological, psychophysiological) techniques, but with considerably smaller samples than school-based studies. Studying "high-risk" adolescents is important because they are more likely to be exposed to risk factors less prevalent in the general population. For example, having a parent with a substance use disorder increases not only the probability of inheriting biological and psychological vulnerabilities for these disorders but also exposure to maladaptive parenting practices and environmental stressors (Chassin *et al.*, 1997). Finally, studies that include adolescents already diagnosed with substance abuse and dependence are helpful in distinguishing the probability of certain risk factors being present for these adolescents compared to others who do not meet diagnostic criteria (e.g., Kilpatrick *et al.*, 2000). Such studies cannot, however, separate factors that are precursors of these disorders from those that are consequences (Chassin and Ritter, 2001).

Another methodological issue concerns the choice between cross-sectional and longitudinal designs. Both have a place in the literature and can be used to delineate risk factors. Cross-sectional studies are initially useful for exploring the relation between hypothesized risk factors and drug use outcomes. However, these studies can only determine the covariation of risk factors with substance use disorders and not whether risk factors predict the subsequent development of this outcome or vice versa. Longitudinal studies offer the opportunity to identify risk factors that predict future escalations in substance use, abuse, and dependence and to examine risk processes across various developmental timeframes. Some longitudinal studies have tracked individuals from early childhood to adolescence using time points several years apart (e.g., Lerner and Vicary, 1984). Although risk factors present in early development have been found to influence future outcomes, the time between assessments can be so great that it is difficult to pinpoint the order of causal mechanisms and the influence of more proximal risk processes (Windle, 1999). Studies that examine risk trajectories over shorter intervals during critical junctures in adolescent development are good companions to those that explore these processes over long intervals. For example, Sullivan and Farrell (1999) examined the relation between risk factors and drug use during the transition from middle to high school. This period has been associated with increased risk for negative outcomes with concurrent stressors including decline in social standing, disruption of pre-existing peer groups, and increased focus on and competitiveness regarding academic achievement (e.g., Eccles *et al.*, 1984; Reyes *et al.*, 1994). Chassin and colleagues (1999) explored the relation between parental psychopathology, internalizing and externalizing behaviours, and substance use disorders from late adolescence to early adulthood. It is during this timeframe that these disorders are typically first diagnosed.

A third methodological issue concerns how cutoffs are established to determine the presence or absence of risk factors. Farrell *et al.* (1992) described three approaches for selecting these cutoffs: (a) *a priori* based on a review of the literature and theoretical guidelines, (b) empirically based on the relation between these factors and drug use outcomes in a criterion-derivation sample, and (c) normatively based on the distribution of risk factors in a specific sample. For example, Bry *et al.* (1982) established cutoffs for three risk factors *a priori* based on the literature, and cutoffs for the remaining risk factors were selected empirically based on their association to a composite measure of drug involvement within a derivation sample. In contrast, Newcomb and colleagues (1986) defined cutoffs normatively based on the distribution of risk factor variables within their sample (upper or lower 25%). One problem with this approach is that the resulting cutoffs depend on the distribution obtained within a specific sample. Because such distributions may vary widely across samples, cross-study comparisons can be difficult. For example, risk factor scores may be higher in a sample of children with substance-abusing parents relative to a more general school-based sample. In contrast, use of criterion-referenced cutoffs offers a mechanism for defining risk factors that is more comparable across studies.

CATEGORIES OF RISK FACTORS

Risk factors can be conceptualized within broad domains including biological, psychological, and social and environmental. The primary biological-based risk factor is a family history of substance use disorders. Psychological factors include temperament dimensions, attitudes, behaviour, and coping styles. Specific categories of social and environmental risk factors include peer, family, school, and community influences, and traumatic and negative life events. Yet another risk factor category is substance use. Because a comprehensive review of the factors that have been associated with drug use, abuse, and dependence would be beyond the scope of any single chapter, we provide examples of specific risk factors within each of the broader domains.

Substance use

Substance use itself can result in risk for continued and escalated use. Onset of substance use prior to age 15 has been identified as a risk factor for the future development of substance use disorders (e.g., Grant and Dawson, 1997; Robin and Przybeck, 1985). Some researchers suggested that early onset reflects a genetic predisposition to a particular disorder (Kumpfer *et al.*, 1998). However, genetic studies provide evidence of the importance of environmental influences in the onset of alcohol, marijuana, and other illicit drug use (e.g., Maes *et al.*, 1999; McGue *et al.*, 2000). Others have noted that early initiation of substance use leads not only to increased frequency of use but also to the progression from alcohol and cigarettes to illicit drugs such as marijuana (Kandel, 1982; Kandel and Yamaguchi, 1985; Kandel and Yamaguchi, 1993).

Adolescence and young adulthood are peak timeframes for substance use, abuse, and dependence. The earlier adolescents initiate substance use, the more time they are exposed to drugs and related risk factors during this window. Farrell (1993) demonstrated the reciprocal relationship between escalated drug use and exposure to risk factors. Utilizing a three-wave longitudinal study, the following three potential path models were tested: (a) risk factors as a cause of drug use, (b) risk factors as a consequence of drug use, and (c) risk factors as a cause and consequence of drug use. Analyses revealed that the latter model had the best fit. In this model, drug use may increase exposure to risk factors. For example, peer influences are key risk factors for substance use, and encouragement and reinforcement of this behaviour within this context may make it more pervasive. Substance use may also exacerbate other risk factors such as delinquency, poor academic achievement, and the disengagement from family, school, and community supports. This, in turn, may result in higher levels of drug involvement, including progression to other types of substances. In addition, Spooner (1999) noted that drug use serves a functional purpose for adolescents whether it is pleasure derived from physiological responses, a part of socialization with peers, or a mechanism to cope with problems. This functional aspect also may contribute to the maintenance and acceleration of drug use behaviour.

Genetic-biological factors

A pivotal risk factor for substance use disorders is a family history for these disorders. Family aggregation studies track the transmission of these disorders from one generation to the next. These studies have demonstrated a substantial intergenerational transmission of alcohol and drug use disorders in adult samples (e.g., Merikangas *et al.*, 1998). Significant relations have also been found between parental alcoholism and elevated levels of drug and alcohol use in adolescence (e.g., Chassin *et al.*, 1991, 1996). More recently, Milberger and colleagues (1999) found that adolescents who had at least one parent with a substance use disorder had significantly higher rates of drug and alcohol use disorders than controls. This evidence of familial aggregation is an indication of genetic influences on these disorders. Examples of possible genetic markers for substance abuse and dependence include variations in biochemical factors, such as proteins related to the metabolism of substances of abuse (e.g., Agarwal and Goedde, 1992), greater sensitivity to positive effects and less sensitivity to negative effects of alcohol consumption (e.g., Chassin and Ritter, 2001), and temperament factors, such as poor psychological self-regulation (e.g., Giancola and Tarter, 1999). However, this evidence may also reflect social and environmental processes. Parental alcoholism may result in family disruption, poor parenting, and increased environmental stress (Chassin et al., 1997). Adoption studies allow the evaluation of genetic influences independent of environmental influences under the assumption of non-selective placement. For example, an adoption study may evaluate genetic influence by comparing prevalence rates for substance use disorders between adopted children of substance-abusing versus non-substance-abusing biological parents. These types of studies have demonstrated that substance abuse and dependence in a biological parent directly predicted drug abuse and dependence in the adoptee (e.g., Cadoret et al., 1995).

Psychological factors

Examples of psychological factors related to substance use disorders include temperament dimensions such as difficult temperament syndrome, behavioural disinhibition, and sensation seeking (Glantz et al., 1999). Temperament refers to the core psychological characteristics present in infancy that provide the foundation for development of personality and other behavioural competencies (Kaminer, 1994). Although we discuss temperament within the context of other psychological factors, it should be noted that genetic factors may play an important role in its development. Indeed, genetic influences account for approximately 40% to 60% of the variation in a broad range of personality characteristics (e.g., Kiesler, 1999). Temperament traits are relatively stable across time and situation, but are also influenced by social and environmental factors.

Thomas and Chess (1984) described a difficult temperament syndrome that is identifiable in infancy and includes characteristics such as social withdrawal, negative affect, distractibility, and high emotional reactivity to stimuli. Compared to children without this syndrome, those identified as having a difficult temperament at age five had higher probability of more severe patterns of use for tobacco, alcohol, and marijuana in young adulthood (Lerner and Vicary, 1984). Studies of adolescents have also examined the association between temperament, substance use, and substance use disorders (e.g., Neighbors et al., 2000; Tarter et al., 1990; Tubman and Windle, 1995; Windle, 1991). Cross-sectional research indicated that adolescents diagnosed with substance use disorders had a pattern of scores more reflective of difficult temperament compared to other adolescents without this diagnosis (Tarter et al., 1990). Difficult temperament in adolescence was also related to concurrent use of cigarettes, alcohol, marijuana, and hard drugs (Windle, 1991) and associated with higher levels of alcohol and cigarette use over a one-year timeframe (Tubman and Windle, 1995). Furthermore, Neighbors and colleagues (2000) examined the relation between a composite measure of difficult temperament including dimensions such as general activity, approach/withdrawal, flexibility, rigidity, and distractibility and symptoms of alcohol use disorders in 438 12- to 18-year-olds. Cross-sectional findings indicated that difficult temperament accounted for a significant portion of the variance in symptoms of alcohol use disorders. Path analyses have also shown an indirect relation between temperament and alcohol and tobacco use mediated by self-control and its resulting effects on negative life events, academic competence, deviant peer affiliations, and motives to use substances as coping mechanisms (Wills *et al.*, 2000).

Behavioural disregulation reflects dimensions of temperament associated with the development of externalizing behaviour problems such as aggression and delinquency (Glantz *et al.*, 1999). This term has been expanded to the more general term dysregulation which refers to poor psychological self-regulation with regard to the ability to monitor and control affective, behavioural, and cognitive processes in response to environmental stimuli (e.g., Giancola and Tarter, 1999). These researchers noted that dysregulation is linked to executive cognitive functions such as attention, planning, organization, and cognitive flexibility. Initial studies have shown that children with a history of parental substance use disorders have more deficits in this area than those without this history (e.g., Giancola *et al.*, 1996). Also, low scores on executive cognitive functioning in childhood predicted substance use in early adolescence (Aytaclar *et al.*, 1999).

Several psychological disorders (attention deficit hyperactivity disorder, oppositional defiant disorder, and conduct disorder) that have a high comorbidity with adolescent substance use disorders have also been related to affective, behavioural, and cognitive dysregulation (Dawes *et al.*, 2000). Conduct problems in adolescence have been found to be a strong predictor of elevated substance use in young adulthood (e.g., Capaldi and Stoolmiller, 1999), and also mediated the relationship between ADHD in childhood and illicit drug use in adolescence (e.g., Fergusson, 1993). Moreover, prospective studies have demonstrated that externalizing disorders in adolescence predict substance use disorders in young adulthood among those adolescents with a history of parental substance use disorders (e.g., Chassin *et al.*, 1999).

Sensation seeking is a temperament dimension that refers to the tendency to seek new experiences and involves high emotional reactivity to novel stimuli (Cloninger *et al.*, 1988). Several researchers have linked this variable to increased risk for escalated substance use in adolescence (Wills *et al.*, 2000) and alcohol abuse in young adulthood (Cloninger *et al.*, 1988). Young adults who abused alcohol were 2.4 times more likely to have high levels of sensation seeking behaviour at age 11 than other adults (Cloninger *et al.*, 1988). Sensation seeking has also been labelled risk taking and found to have not only direct effects on increased substance use among adolescents but also indirect effects through motives to use drugs as a coping mechanism and peer models for drug use (e.g., Wills *et al.*, 2000). Because this behaviour can also be normative in adolescence, productive efforts could be made to channel adolescents toward positive risk-taking behaviours (Spooner, 1999).

Peer-related factors

Adolescence is characterized by increasing alliance to peers and conformity to their values and attitudes. Peer influences such as models for substance use, attitudes favouring substance use, and pressure to use substances have been found to be among the strongest direct correlates (e.g., Ary *et al.*, 1993; Farrell *et al.*, 1992; Newcomb *et al.*, 1987) and predictors (e.g., Farrell, 1993; Newcomb *et al.*, 1986) of substance use and abuse in the literature. Although numerous other risk factors impact adolescent substance use, this behaviour is generally realized through peer group associations. Peers shape attitudes toward drugs, provide reinforcement for this behaviour, and facilitate access to drugs (Oetting and Beauvais, 1986).

Several cross-sectional studies have demonstrated a positive association between affiliation with peers who use drugs and problem use in adolescence (e.g., Brook *et al.*, 1992; Dielman *et al.*, 1987; Sussman *et al.*, 1999). In a sample of adolescents and young adults aged 16 to 21, peer models for illicit drug use differentiated heavy marijuana users from moderate users (Brook *et al.*, 1992). Association with peers who used stimulants such as methamphetamines was associated with increased involvement with these drugs among adolescents aged 14 to 19 (Sussman *et al.*, 1999). Prospective studies revealed that peer drug use not only covaries with problem use in adolescence but also predicts this behaviour over time (e.g., Bahr *et al.*, 1993; Chassin *et al.*, 1996; Fergusson *et al.*, 1995; Stice *et al.*, 1998). Bahr and colleagues (1993) used a path analysis to test the influence of family and peer variables on drug abuse in a sample of 11- to 18-year-olds. They found that peer drug use had a dominant effect in determining whether adolescents progressed to drug abuse. In a prospective study that followed children from birth to age 16, affiliation with peers who used drugs predicted alcohol abuse, and this relation was stronger for males than females (Fergusson *et al.*, 1995). For males with no history of alcohol use at age 14, 24% with high affiliation with drug-using peers at age 15 reported alcohol abuse at age 16 compared to only 3% of those with low affiliation. Peer influences including models for drug use and attitudes toward use predicted problem use resulting in negative consequences over a one-year time period both directly and by promoting increased levels of consumption that resulted in problem use among adolescents (Stice *et al.*, 1998). Thus, although other risk processes may operate retrospectively and concurrently, peers provide the main pathway for substance use and abuse in adolescence. The strength of this impact makes it essential to understand the risk factors that predispose adolescents to affiliate with drug-using peers.

Family-related factors

Family factors have also been identified as risk factors for elevated levels of substance use, abuse, and dependence. Examples include parent–child attachment, parenting practices, family structure, and parent models for drug use. These variables have been shown to increase risk for substance use both directly and indirectly. Several studies examining the direct effects of peer and parent influences on substance use among adolescents revealed stronger direct effects for peer versus parent variables on drug use outcomes (e.g., Hoffman, 1993). Some researchers suggested the primary mechanism of action for parent-related variables during this timeframe is indirect (e.g., Kandel and Andrews, 1987). Specifically, family factors are associated with involvement with peers who use drugs and this involvement leads to escalated drug use.

Parent–child attachment provides a foundation for the socialization of children and for shaping future attitudes, values, beliefs, and behaviours. Four dimensions have been used to define this construct including identification, lack of conflict, warmth, and involvement (Brook et al., 1990). Strong parent–child attachment is a prerequisite for identification with parents, and this identification leads to internalization of traditional parent values and attitudes, modelling of parent behaviour, and a decreased likelihood of affiliation with peers who use drugs. In contrast, patterns of behavioural interactions between mothers and children reflecting weak attachment in early childhood predicted frequent substance use in adolescence (e.g., Shedler and Block, 1990). These maladaptive relationship patterns in early childhood often continue into adolescence (e.g., Colder and Chassin, 1999; Johnson and Pandina, 1991). Compared to adolescents with less severe use patterns, those engaging in problematic patterns of alcohol use experienced higher levels of family dysfunction marked by family conflict and disorganization (Colder and Chassin, 1999). Also, in a prospective study of adolescents aged 12, 15, and 18, parent hostility and lack of warmth was associated with increased alcohol and marijuana use (Johnson and Pandina, 1991). Among adolescents who were 15 and 18 at the initial assessment, parent hostility and lack of warmth also predicted problem alcohol use over a three-year timeframe.

Parenting practices such as inconsistent discipline and poor monitoring have also been associated with adolescent drug use. Parents who provide clear rules that are consistently reinforced and who monitor their child's activities including peer associations have children who are less likely to use drugs. For example, Colder and Chassin (1999) found that parenting behaviours including low levels of monitoring and inconsistent discipline differentiated problem drug users from adolescents with lower levels of drug use. Chassin et al. (1996) reported that adolescents with low parental monitoring were more likely to have peers who used drugs, resulting in steeper growth curves for substance use over time. A longitudinal path model also showed that association with deviant peers mediated the relation between inadequate parental monitoring and problem behaviours including drug use (Ary *et al.*, 1999).

Family structure and disruption has been related to escalated substance use in adolescence. Several researchers indicated that children in single-parent families have higher levels of problem behaviours including drug use (e.g., Brook *et al.*, 1985; Capaldi and Patterson, 1991; Steinberg, 1987). Divorce which results in single-parent households is associated with increased risk for alcohol abuse, particularly among boys (e.g., Needle *et al.*, 1990). However, these researchers found that remarriage resulting in restoration of a two-parent household was more beneficial to boys than girls in terms of subsequent drug abuse. Similarly, the presence of either a father or stepfather was found to moderate the influence of peer pressure on increased drug use among urban adolescents (Farrell and White, 1998). The relation between single-parent families and increased risk for drug use may reflect processes within the family more than the mere structural configuration of the family. For example, Hoffman (1993) found that after a divorce, parents were less involved with children, which often led to association with peers who use drugs and then to drug use. A single parent may have less coping resources and capacity (Gabel, 1992), and engage in less monitoring and discipline (e.g., Brown *et al.*, 1993). These additional stressors may account for differences in substance use behaviour among adolescents raised in single-parent and two-parent households.

Parental models for drug use have been found to have both direct and indirect influences on increased drug involvement in adolescence (e.g., Ary *et al.*, 1993; Brook *et al.*, 1990; Hops *et al.*, 1996; Wills *et al.*, 1994). For example, parents' drug use predicted increased frequency of marijuana use among adolescents both concurrently (e.g., Brook *et al.*, 1990) and over time (Hops *et al.*, 1996). This suggests that one mechanism leading to escalated drug use among adolescents is direct modelling and imitation of parents' behaviour. The strength of this finding has, however, varied with some studies finding no direct relation between parents' and adolescents' drug use (e.g., Dishion and Loeber, 1985) and others reporting only modest effects (e.g., Wills *et al.*, 1994). Parental substance use disorders may also result in maladaptive parenting practices, weak parent–child attachment, family disruption, and increased environmental stress (Chassin *et al.*, 1991) with repercussions beginning early in development. Chassin and colleagues (1996) in particular found that parental alcoholism predicted escalated levels of substance use in adolescence via two pathways: (a) decreased parental monitoring leading to involvement with peers who use drugs, and (b) increased environmental stress leading to negative affect and then association with peers who use drugs.

School- and community-related factors

Adolescents who use drugs are more likely to be alienated from conventional supports such as school as evidenced by poor academic performance, poor attendance, and high rates of suspension (e.g., Crundall, 1993; Swadi, 1992). In a longitudinal study of 15-year-olds, school absences, being placed in a class for emotional or learning disabilities, and dropping out of school predicted subsequent substance abuse (Holmberg, 1986). Dishion and colleagues (1991) described a constellation of factors including poor academic achievement and rejection by non-deviant peers in middle childhood that resulted in association with deviant peers by early adolescence. This affiliation led not only to increased drug use but also to truancy and lack of commitment to education, contributing to further academic difficulties. Finally, risk factors including poor academic achievement, low educational aspirations, low interest in school, and low bonds to teachers have also been included in composite indicators of risk that predicted increased levels of drug use (e.g., Newcomb and Felix-Ortiz, 1992; Scheier and Newcomb, 1991a,b; Scheier et al., 1994).

Two examples of community level risk factors that have been related to elevated levels of substance use include availability of drugs and perceived community support for drug use (e.g., Felix-Ortiz and Newcomb, 1992, 1999). Availability of drugs is a potent risk factor for both drug use and drug dealing among adolescents (e.g., De La Rosa et al., 1993). The availability of drugs within a particular community has been related to increased use of cigarettes, alcohol, and marijuana (Maddahian et al., 1988). Perceived community support for drug use may also function to normalize this behaviour and decrease the perception of implicit and explicit sanctions against this behaviour (Felix-Ortiz and Newcomb, 1999). These researchers included both risk factors in a composite measure of risk that was associated with higher levels of cigarette, alcohol, marijuana, cocaine, and illicit drug use among Latino adolescents.

Traumatic and negative life events

Trauma such as physical and sexual abuse has been linked to substance abuse and dependence in adolescence (e.g., Clark et al., 1997; Kilpatrick et al., 2000). Clark and colleagues (1997) recruited 256 adolescents with alcohol use disorders from various intervention programs (e.g., hospital-based treatment, residential, juvenile justice programmes). These adolescents reported significantly higher lifetime rates of physical and sexual abuse, violent victimization, and witnessing violence compared to controls. For example, 32% of females and 39% of males diagnosed with alcohol abuse had experienced physical abuse compared to 5% of females and 3% of males in the control group. In a separate study, telephone interviews were conducted with a national household sample of 4,023 adolescents aged 12 to 17 (Kilpatrick et al., 2000). After controlling for family history of alcohol and drug problems, adolescents with substance use disorders (alcohol, marijuana, and hard drugs) were 2.4 to 5.2 times more likely to have experienced physical assault and 2.2 to 3.4

times more likely to have experienced sexual assault than adolescents without this diagnosis. These researchers also examined the relation between witnessing violence and substance use disorders. Adolescents diagnosed with these disorders were 2.8 to 4.8 times more likely to have witnessed violent events such as seeing someone being shot, stabbed, robbed, or mugged. Other studies have also documented histories of physical and sexual abuse among adolescents with substance use disorders (e.g., Harrison *et al.*, 1997).

Negative life events are also associated with escalated substance use and abuse in adolescence. Adolescents diagnosed with alcohol use disorders have not only been found to have higher lifetime prevalence rates for severe trauma but also to have experienced more discrete and chronic negative life events than controls (Clark *et al.*, 1997). Examples include not being accepted by peers, school suspension, failing grade in school, and having a parent or sibling arrested or jailed. In a school-based sample of 1,289 urban adolescents aged 11 to 13, negative life events (e.g., a parent becoming unemployed, serious illness of a family member) were related to higher levels of heavy drinking and elevations in a composite measure of cigarette, alcohol, and marijuana use (Wills *et al.*, 1992). Others have also demonstrated the relation between stressors, substance use, and alcohol-related problems in adolescent samples (e.g., Baer *et al.*, 1987; Johnson and Pandina, 1993).

Drug use may serve as a mechanism both to reduce negative affect associated with stressful and traumatic events and to increase positive affect (Wills and Shiffman, 1985). Trauma and negative life events are hypothesized to be both risk factors for problem drug and alcohol use among adolescents and consequences of this behaviour. Exposure to traumatic events sometimes results in symptoms of post-traumatic stress disorder (PTSD). Retrospective studies have documented the comorbidity of PTSD and substance use disorders among adults (e.g., Glantz *et al.*, 1999). In a study of young adults, PTSD was also demonstrated to predict subsequent development of drug and alcohol disorders (Chilcoat and Breslau, 1998). Among adolescents, negative life events predicted elevations in alcohol use and smoking for junior high students from the beginning to end of the school year, and subjective feelings of stress (e.g., tension, difficulty relaxing, somatic symptoms) predicted heavy drinking over this same period (Wills, 1986). Moreover, adolescents entering seventh grade who experienced rapid escalations in substance use from seventh to ninth grade exhibited a cluster of risk factors including negative life events (Wills *et al.*, 1996). Abuse of substances may also place adolescents in risky places where physical and sexual assault is more probable (Clayton, 1992).

Multiple risk factor indices

Although a number of individual risk factors have been identified for substance abuse and dependence, no single factor appears "sufficient" to cause these disorders. Instead, it appears that multiple risk factors combine across various pathways to heighten an individual's likelihood of developing these disorders (e.g., Chassin and Ritter, 2001). This has led to attempts to develop multiple risk factor indices that incorporate risk factors across different domains. Borrowing from public health and epidemiological methodologies, Bry *et al.* (1982) first applied a risk factor model to the study of drug use. In this model, involvement in substance use is determined by an individual's total number of risk factors present (i.e., cumulative risk) with each factor weighted equally and no one factor considered essential (Scheier and Newcomb, 1991a). The more risk factors present for an individual, the higher the probability that an individual will be involved in substance use, abuse, or dependence. In other words, the critical issue in determining substance use outcomes is not the specific type of risk individuals are exposed to but rather how much risk they have to cope with during a certain timeframe.

In an initial study in this area, Bry *et al.* (1982) identified six risk factors for adolescent drug use based on a review of the literature. Specific risk factors included poor grades, no religious affiliation, early initial use of alcohol, psychological distress, low self-esteem, and low perceived parental love. For each individual, a composite substance use index was created based on recency, frequency, and extent of use for ten substances (e.g., alcohol, marijuana, amphetamines, barbiturates, inhalants, cocaine, and opiates). Results revealed a positive linear trend between the number of risk factors present and this composite index. When individuals were assigned to four drug involvement groups ranging from low use to abuse, degree of risk for substance abuse also increased as a function of the number of risk factors. Substance abuse was 1.4 times more likely among students with one risk factor and 4.5 times more likely among students with four risk factors compared to overall base rates for substance abuse in the sample. In general, this study provided preliminary support for the risk factor model as a mechanism to study risk factors for substance abuse in adolescence.

Newcomb and colleagues extended this line of research by increasing the number of risk factors examined and analysing the relation between these factors and five separate drug categories (cigarettes, alcohol, marijuana, cocaine, hard drug use) as well as a composite measure. Newcomb and colleagues (1986) employed a longitudinal design to examine the relation between risk factors and drug use in a sample of high school students. In addition to the risk factors identified by Bry *et al.* (1982), they added sensation seeking, perceived adult and peer drug use, and deviant behaviour. Results indicated that the degree of risk predicted use for each drug over a one-year period. Newcomb and colleagues (1987) revealed similar results in a cross-sectional study of seventh, ninth, and eleventh graders. Their risk factor index (RFI) comprised 12 risk factors and included several factors not included in prior studies such as perceived peer and parent approval of drug use, poor school attendance, distrust of teacher and parent knowledge about drugs, low educational aspirations, and dissatisfaction with life. These 12 risk factors accounted for 41% of the total variance in the composite drug use measure. The scales for each drug category were then dichotomized into two groups including abstainers or occasional users, and abusers. For each substance, the prevalence of abuse increased as a function of the number of risk factors. Among individuals with no risk factors, only 1% abused cigarettes. However, for individuals with seven or more risk factors, 56% abused cigarettes, 18% abused alcohol, 40% abused marijuana, 7% abused cocaine, and 18% abused one or more hard drugs.

Scheier and Newcomb (1991b) suggested that a single RFI might be too "reductionistic" to explain all patterns of drug use. A few studies using RFIs have attempted to distinguish RFIs relevant to different stages of drug use including initiation (Farrell 1993; Scheier and Newcomb 1991a,b; Scheier *et al.*, 1994), transitions to higher levels of use (Scheier *et al.*, 1997), and abuse (Newcomb, 1992). Scheier and Newcomb (1991a) extended initial studies of the risk factor model by creating separate RFIs to differentiate risk factors for drug use initiation from those associated with problem drug use in a sample of seventh graders. The RFI for problem drug use included variables such as depression, influences (e.g., perceived approval of drug use), tolerant attitude toward drug use, and high levels of delinquent behaviour. Scheier and Newcomb examined the relation between the RFI for drug use initiation, RFI for problem drug use, and polydrug use across a two-year time interval. Results supported the distinctiveness of the two RFIs in that correlations between the RFIs at both time points were modest, and the RFI for problem drug use at Time 1 predicted polydrug use (a measure reflecting heavier drug use) at Time 2, while the RFI for drug use initiation did not.

Brook and colleagues (1992) examined 18 potential risk factors across three categories (peer, family, and personality) for alcohol and marijuana use in a sample of 417 adolescents and young adults between the ages of 16 and 21. Using logistic regression, four risk factors were identified (aggression during childhood, acting out, low maternal attachment, and illegal drug use by peers) that differentiated moderate alcohol use versus abuse. Three risk factors were also identified (acting out, low paternal attachment, and illegal drug use by peers) that differentiated moderate versus heavy marijuana use. Separate risk factor indices were created for each drug, and a positive linear relation was found between the number of risk factors present and the likelihood of alcohol abuse and heavy marijuana use. For alcohol, 8% of participants with one risk factor reported alcohol abuse compared to 43% of participants with four risk factors. For marijuana, 5% with one risk factor reported heavy use compared to 40% with four risk factors.

Farrell and colleagues (1992) conducted a series of studies that supported the generalizability of the multiple risk factor model. They identified risk factors for drug use in a sample of urban, predominantly African-American adolescents. This study differed from prior research by using predetermined (i.e., criterion-referenced) cutoffs for risk factors rather than using a norm-referenced approach based on the specific sample. Chi-square tests identified 26 risk factors that were subsequently reduced to 11 primary factors through regression analyses. These included peer influences (e.g., peer approval of drug use, friends' drug use, and peer pressure), variables related to delinquency (e.g., history of trouble with the police), prior use of alcohol and cigarettes, being home alone after school, knowing adults who use drugs, low use of demanding activity as a coping strategy, and expectations to use drugs. The sum of these 11 risk factors was significantly related to elevated use across five drug categories including cigarettes, beer and wine, hard liquor, marijuana, and other illicit drugs. Furthermore, a curvilinear trend was noted between the number of risk factors and the frequency of drug use. This suggested that the impact of additional risk factors may increase the frequency of drug use more rapidly than has been suggested by linear trends documented in prior research. A subsequent longitudinal study addressed the ability of risk factors to predict drug use across three time points and examined the reciprocal nature of risk factors and drug use (Farrell, 1993). Furthermore, the relationship between many of these same risk factors and increased frequency of drug use was found to generalize to a rural sample (Farrell *et al.*, 1992).

The multiple risk factor approach has several advantages. By assuming that risk factors are varied and complex, it offers a mechanism to integrate diverse theories and research findings (Bry *et al.*, 1982). Risk factor indices provide a cumulative indication of an individual's risk (Newcomb and Felix-Ortiz, 1992). Because individuals with substance use disorders are highly heterogeneous, it is important to understand risk factors for drug abuse on this level (Glantz *et al.*, 1999). Finally, the ability to identify unique patterns of risk for adolescents offers practical implications for designing, and assigning individuals to, appropriate prevention and intervention programs (Farrell *et al.*, 1992). A drawback of this approach is that it does not clarify the pathways by which risk factors influence the prediction of substance abuse and dependence.

Risk factors and vulnerability

Although a simple definition of a risk factor might include any variable that increases the likelihood of escalated substance use, abuse, and dependence, the concept of vulnerability has been developed to differentiate factors that represent more stable, endogenous traits that may be present to some degree throughout the lifespan (Ingram and Price, 2001). Vulnerability includes both genetically influenced biological processes and psychological traits such as neurochemical and neuropsychological functioning, physiological responsiveness, and temperament. Vulnerability symbolizes an underlying predisposition to develop substance abuse and dependence. Ongoing interactions between vulnerability dimensions and environmental dimensions (e.g., family and peer influences) over the course of development determine whether an individual will develop these disorders. Certain dimensions may be relatively more important at different points in the lifespan. Peer influences provide the main conduit for drug use behaviour during adolescence but reactivity to the pharmacological properties of drugs like analgesics in the treatment of chronic pain may be more relevant for adults due to higher prevalence of these disorders among this population (Tarter *et al.*, 1997). It is thus the overall interaction between these individual and environmental dimensions that shape drug use behaviour.

The field of behaviour genetics provides some of the best evidence of the dual importance of individual and environmental factors in the development of substance use disorders (Kiesler, 1999). Approaches used in this area include family, twin and adoption studies. Twin studies examine concordance rates between monozygotic and dyzygotic twins to estimate genetic effects (i.e., "heritability"), and shared and unshared environmental effects. Shared environmental effects reflect common situations and contextual experiences (e.g., socioeconomic status, parenting practices) encountered by all siblings in a family (Kiesler, 1999). In contrast, unshared environmental effects represent experiences that are unique for each child such as different peer groups and schools (Maes *et al.*, 1999).

Twin studies have found modest to strong heritability for alcohol and drug use disorders in adulthood (see Vanyukov and Tarter (2000) for a review). Among the few studies conducted with adolescents, several initial findings have emerged. Environmental effects have been found to be relatively stronger compared to genetic effects in predicting lifetime use (e.g., Maes *et al.*, 1999) as well as abuse and dependence of illicit drugs (McGue *et al.*, 2000). In these studies, structural equation modelling is used to estimate the relative contribution of genetic and environmental factors with the total contribution adding up to 1.0. In a sample of 17-year-old twin pairs, the phenotypic variation for drug abuse and dependence was strongly determined by shared and non-shared environment (0.52 and 0.22 for males, and 0.65 and 0.30 for females, respectively) with modest to negligible heritability estimates (0.26 for males and 0.05 for females (McGue *et al.*, 2000)). These researchers suggested that environmental risk factors related to availability of illicit drugs may be particularly salient in creating pathways to abuse and dependence for these drugs. Although modest heritability estimates for illicit drugs are consistent with some adult samples (e.g., Tsuang *et al.*, 1996), others have reported much stronger heritability estimates (e.g., Kendler *et al.*, 1999). Clearly, replication of these findings in other adolescent samples is needed.

Researchers have demonstrated a decreased influence of the shared environment on the frequency of alcohol use compared to initiation among adolescents (Viken *et al.*, 1999). For 16-year-old twin pairs, shared environment accounted for 79% of variation in determining lifetime alcohol use but only 35% of the variation for frequency of use. For frequency of use, part of the decrease in shared environment was accounted for by increases in the influence of genetic effects. Similar effects were found for another drug abuse indicator, intoxication. Finally, a shift in relative importance from environmental to genetic factors was noted as adolescents develop (Rose *et al.*, 1999; Viken *et al.*, 1999). Among 16-year-old twins followed over a one-year period, both lifetime prevalence and frequency for alcohol use and having been intoxicated were increasingly determined by genetic influences (Viken *et al.*, 1999). Also, in a three-year follow-up assessment of 17-year-old male twins in the McGue *et al.* (2000) study, heritability of illicit drug dependence was 52% (Iacono *et al.*, 1999). Overall, these findings indicate the differential relevance of individual and environmental risk factors in predicting adolescent drug use and abuse both at different time points in adolescence and for different patterns of use.

In a longitudinal study, Legrand *et al.* (1999) focused on the interaction between an individual indicator of vulnerability and environmental risk factors to determine early initiation of substance use in a sample of adolescent boys from age 11 to 14. Each boy was classified as having a low, intermediate, or high familial risk based on their parental history of substance use disorders. Scores on five environmental variables including peer models for drug use, attitudes toward school, mother–son relationship, religious interests, and extracurricular activities were used to generate a composite index of risk. Individuals with high levels of vulnerability (i.e., parental history of substance use disorders) who also had high-risk environments were significantly more likely to initiate drug use by age 14 than those with low levels of environmental risk. Thus, low levels of environmental risk appeared to attenuate the effect of inherited vulnerabilities in this sample, while high levels of environmental risk augmented these effects. This study provides an example of the moderating effect of a cluster of environmental risk factors on an indicator of vulnerability.

Some researchers have limited the conceptualization of risk factors to acute, threatening life events that interact with vulnerability processes to heighten the likelihood of developing substance use disorders (e.g., Rutter, 1987; Zubin and Steinhauser, 1981). However, numerous risk factors have been identified that span individual (e.g., sensation seeking, emotional distress) and more broad environmental dimensions (e.g., school and community). Therefore, risk factors serve as indicators of both underlying vulnerability and overt environmental dimensions at a particular point in time.

RISK AND PROTECTIVE FACTORS

Any discussion of risk factors would not be complete without some consideration of protective factors. A protective factor can be defined as "an individual attribute, individual characteristic, situational condition, or environmental context that inhibits, reduces, or buffers the probability of drug use or abuse or a transition in level of involvement with drugs" (Clayton, 1992, p. 16). Like risk factors, protective factors are defined as being present or absent and can have multiple measures reflecting specific categories (e.g., family and peer factors) within broad dimensions (e.g., social and environmental factors). Also, a specific category of protective factors (i.e., school influences) can have multiple indicators (school attendance, commitment to school) that demonstrate individual and cumulative effects on risk (Clayton, 1992). Like risk factors, protective factors can produce direct effects on a targeted outcome variable. Protective factors can also have indirect effects that are mediated by risk factors. The primary mechanism of action for a protective factor, however, is its moderating effect on risk (Rutter, 1987). More specifically, protective factors decrease the likelihood of a maladaptive outcome by mitigating the impact of risk for this outcome.

Research using the multiple risk factor model has been expanded to include protective factors (e.g., DeWit et al., 1995; Felix-Ortiz and Newcomb, 1992, 1999; Jessor et al., 1995; Newcomb and Felix-Ortiz, 1992; Scheier et al., 1994, 1997; Sullivan and Farrell, 1999). A key issue in these studies and other research incorporating protective factors is the differentiation of risk and protective factors. Some variables may be bipolar in nature with the high end of the distribution acting as a protective factor while the low end functions as a risk factor (Windle, 1999). For example, parental social support is typically classified as a protective factor (Cohen and Wills, 1985). Studies have reported a significant negative relation between high levels of parental support and increased substance use over time among adolescents (e.g., Wills et al., 1996). One mechanism of action for parental social support is to buffer the relation between negative life events and increased levels of substance use (e.g., Wills et al., 1992). High levels of parental support attenuated this relation suggesting that adolescents whose parents helped them to problem solve and develop coping strategies to deal with negative events were less likely to engage in maladaptive responses such as increased drug use. However, studies examining the relation between peer and parental social support have found that adolescents with low levels of parental social support and high levels of peer social support are at particular risk for high levels of substance use (e.g., Wills and Vaughan, 1989). Overall, these findings illustrate the complex nature of variables related to substance use in that parental social support can function as both a risk and protective factor.

Several methods have been utilized to select factors for inclusion in risk and protective factor indices. One method is a purely theoretical approach where risk and protective factors are defined *a priori* based on theoretical guidelines such as Jessor and Jessor's (1977) problem behaviour theory and then respective indices are created with these factors (e.g., Jessor et al., 1995). A second method is a purely empirical approach advocated by Newcomb and Felix-Ortiz (1992). First, scores for 14 psychosocial variables were coded at one end of the continuum (upper or lower 20%) of each variable as a risk factor and scores on the other end as a protective factor. Variables were then assigned to the RFI or protective factor index (PFI) based on which of the coded variables correlated more strongly with drug use. One disadvantage of this approach is that risk and protective factors were classified post hoc based solely on empirical criteria. Cutoffs were based on sample norms, and whether or not a variable was labelled a risk or protective factor was influenced by the specific sample distribution. When correlations among risk and protective factors were close, arbitrary decisions were used to assign variables to a particular index. For example, when coding self-acceptance based on cutoffs at the upper and lower 20% did not result in differences in the average correlation with drug use, Newcomb and Felix-Ortiz (1992) assigned it to the PFI so that the PFI and RFI would both have the same number of factors.

In a second method, Scheier and colleagues (1997) attempted to address the potential bipolar nature of some variables. For each of 22 measures included, scores were coded on one end of the continuum (upper and lower 20%) of each variable as a risk factor. For a subset of 13 measures, scores were also coded on the other end as a protective factor. These 22 binary risk and 13 binary protective factors were then assigned to one of five RFIs (competence, psychological functioning, interpersonal functioning, cognitive-affective influences, social influences) and one of three PFIs (competence, psychological functioning, interpersonal functioning), respectively based on reviews of the literature for drug use and abuse etiology and prevention. Thus, three of the RFIs and PFIs represented opposite ends of the continuum for the same variables. Although this is one way to address the potential bipolar nature of some variables, this method introduces statistical dependence between these variables and represents them as merely opposite ends of a continuum (Windle, 1999). This is also contrary to the notion of risk and protective factor being independent with the role of protective factors to moderate the impact of risk.

A final method for identifying risk factors combines theoretical and empirical criteria. For example, Sullivan and Farrell (1999) used conceptual guidelines from several theories and relevant research findings to classify variables as potential risk or protective factors *a priori*. Cutoffs based on Farrell and colleagues' (1992) primarily criterion-referenced approach cutoffs were used when possible to code each factor as present or absent. The extent to which these factors were correctly classified was then examined using an approach consistent with Rutter's (1987) theory. Risk factors were expected to have a direct effect on drug use and protective factors were expected to moderate the influence of one or more risk factors. Advantages of this model include the differentiation of risk and protective factors based on theoretical and research evidence and the incorporation of empirical methods to confirm that the mechanism of action worked in the way intended for each factor.

In a study incorporating risk and protective factor indices, Newcomb and Felix-Ortiz (1992) utilized both cross-sectional and longitudinal designs to determine the relation between risk and protective factor indices and drug use in a sample of adolescents and young adults. They identified seven protective factors including high GPA, low depression, supportive family relationships, perceiving many sanctions for drug use, high religiosity, self-acceptance, and law abidance. The RFI comprised seven factors including low educational aspirations, high perceived adult and peer drug use, high levels of deviant behaviour, perceptions of community support for drug use, and easy availability of drugs. Cross-sectional analyses revealed that the RFI was associated with increases in frequency of use for cigarettes, alcohol, marijuana, cocaine, and hard drugs, and in quantity of use for cigarettes, alcohol, and marijuana. The PFI was negatively associated with elevations across all drug categories with the exception of quantity of cigarette use for men; however, few significant RFI × PFI interactions were found. Longitudinal findings indicated that a latent variable, vulnerability, created by combining the RFI, PFI, and RFI × PFI interaction, was associated with changes in drug use from late adolescence to early adulthood.

A few studies have examined the generalizability of the multiple risk and protective factor model to Latino and African-American adolescents (e.g., Felix-Ortiz and Newcomb, 1992, 1999; Sullivan and Farrell, 1999). Using the same variables as Newcomb and Felix-Ortiz (1992) for the RFI, PFI, and substance use measures, the relations between these variables were examined separately by gender for 117 Latino adolescents (Felix-Ortiz and Newcomb, 1992). The RFI was associated with elevated use across all drug categories except frequency of cigarette use among males. The PFI was negatively associated with increased use for all drug categories except frequency and quantity of cigarette use for males, and the sum of protective factors moderated risk for hard drug use for both genders and cocaine use for females only. In a follow-up study, Felix-Ortiz and Newcomb (1999) examined the relations between risk, protection, and drug use among 516 Latino youth in ninth and tenth grades. Significant main effects were found for the RFI and PFI across all drug categories, and the PFI moderated risk for increased frequency of cigarette, marijuana, and inhalant use, and increased quantity of marijuana use. In a subsequent step, a latent variable, vulnerability, created by combining the RFI, PFI, and RFI × PFI, was significantly related to higher levels of polydrug use for both boys and girls. Finally, Sullivan and Farrell (1999) conducted a longitudinal study with African-American middle school students and identified seven risk and seven protective factors with minimal overlap. Cross-sectional analyses revealed the RFI was significantly related to escalated use of cigarettes, alcohol, marijuana, and a composite measure of drug use. The PFI moderated the relation between risk and increased use of alcohol, marijuana, and the composite measure. Longitudinal analyses indicated the RFI predicted escalations across all drug use categories except the composite. The PFI predicted changes in alcohol and composite drug use over a one-year timeframe, but moderated risk for cigarette use only. These results highlight initial findings of the generalizability of the multiple risk factor model.

In a study of 400 ninth graders, DeWit and colleagues (1995) hypothesized specific drug categories would have different configurations of risk and protective factors. These researchers constructed separate RFIs and PFIs for five measures of drug use including overall involvement in drugs, alcohol use, illegal drug use, drug abuse and quantity of daily cigarette consumption. Their examination of over 60 potential risk and protective factors revealed that each measure of drug use was associated with a different configuration of risk and protective factors forming unique indices across drug type. Results indicated that the RFI was positively related to higher levels of drug use and abuse. The PFI also served to moderate the influence of risk for escalated cigarette, alcohol, and illicit drug use. Further research replicating these patterns of drug-specific risk and protective factors is needed to establish the generalizability of these effects.

In a sample of seventh, eighth, and ninth graders, Jessor and colleagues (1995) utilized problem behaviour theory to formulate a PFI which encompassed the personality system, perceived environmental system, and behaviour system domain. This index comprised positive orientation toward school and health, intolerant attitudes toward deviance, positive relations with adults, perception of strong social controls, peer models of conventional behaviour, and involvement in prosocial behaviours. Variables from the RFI included low expectations for success, low self-esteem, hopelessness, peer drug models, greater orientation toward peers than parents, and poor school achievement. The dependent variable was a multiple problem behaviour index comprised of measures including problem drinking, delinquent behaviour, marijuana use, and sexual promiscuity. Cross-sectional analyses indicated a main effect for both the RFI and PFI, with each accounting for unique variance in the problem behaviour index, and a significant RFI × PFI interaction. In addition, a four-wave longitudinal analysis revealed that the PFI had a stronger direct effect on changes in problem behaviour over a three-year period than the RFI, but did not moderate the effect of risk for problem behaviour over time.

Scheier and colleagues (1994) incorporated a developmental perspective. They theorized that the rapid cognitive, psychosocial, and biological changes during adolescence may result in differential influences of risk and protective factors as the growth process unfolds. To address this issue, separate cross-sectional structural equation models were constructed for seventh, ninth, and eleventh graders. A latent variable, vulnerability, was developed by combining the PFI and RFIs for drug use initiation and problem use. Results indicated that the vulnerability construct was directly related to polydrug use for all age groups. In addition, a number of direct relations were found between the RFIs, PFI, and individual drug measures. For example, among eleventh grade females, the PFI was negatively associated with alcohol use and being high at school.

Scheier *et al.* (1997) incorporated multiple risk and protective factor indices to understand the relation between specific clusters of variables (e.g., social influences) and transitions to more severe patterns of alcohol use between eighth and tenth grades in a study of 823 adolescents. As previously described, five RFIs were created representing poor competence, psychological functioning, interpersonal functioning, and maladaptive cognitive-affective influences and social influences. Three PFIs were created representing high levels of competence, psychological functioning, and interpersonal functioning using the same 13 variables as in the RFI but coded to represent the opposite end of the continuum. The RFIs representing maladaptive social influences and poor competence predicted transitions from lower to more problematic patterns of alcohol use. Finally, the PFI portraying adaptive psychological functioning was inversely related to escalations in the composite alcohol measure.

CONCLUSIONS

A main focus of this chapter was to review several categories of risk factors for substance abuse and dependence in adolescence within individual and environmental contexts. Specific categories of individual risk factors included biological-genetic factors and psychological characteristics (e.g., temperament, attitudes toward drug use, behaviours, and coping strategies). Specific categories of environmental and social risk factors included family, peer, school, and community-related factors; and negative life events and trauma. Examples of risk factors were provided within each of these categories. This chapter also described efforts to integrate risk factors across individual and environmental contexts and to examine the impact of cumulative risk on substance use outcomes. Studies were reviewed that have used this model to study adolescent substance use and abuse. The relation between risk factors, protective factors, and vulnerability was then addressed. Protective factors and vulnerability were defined and methodological issues related to the relation between these constructs and risk were discussed. Finally, protective factor research was reviewed within the context of the expanded risk and protective factor model.

Research on risk factors has significantly improved our understanding of substance abuse and dependence in adolescence. A number of risk factors have been identified that related to the increased probability of escalated substance use, abuse, and dependence. Attempts have been made to categorize these risk factors into domains including biological-genetic and psychological as well as environmental and social. Methodologies have been developed such as the risk factor model to integrate risk factors across domains and categories (e.g., Bry *et al.*, 1982). Also, path models have been employed to look at the interrelations of risk factors and how distal and proximal factors are related to drug use outcomes (e.g., Wills *et al.*, 2000). The field has clearly benefited from the parallel efforts to intensively study individual risk factors and their mediators and moderators, and efforts to combine these factors into aggregate indices. The importance of the relation between underlying genetic vulnerabilities and environmental factors has been highlighted by behaviour genetics research. Gene × environment studies have also demonstrated that a high risk environment augments the effect of genetic predispositions to substance use (e.g., Legrand *et al.*, 1999). Finally, protective factors have also been offered as variables that interact with risk to attenuate the risk situation.

Future research in this area should focus on several issues. First, additional gene × environment studies are needed using an adoption study approach that will better separate the effects of environment and genetic influences. It is important to begin to understand how environmental factors impact genetic influences and what the key environmental factors are in this process. Further work is also needed to identify protective factors for substance use disorders. The majority of the studies incorporating protective factors have focused on elevations in substance use but not on substance abuse and dependence. There is also a need to understand the bidirectional influence of protective factors on risk factors and subsequent drug use behaviour (Windle, 1999). For example, various risk factors may have direct and indirect effects on protective factors. Affiliation with peers who use drugs and early initiation of drug use may alienate adolescents from the influence of possible protective factors such as bonds to school and community (Windle, 1999). Thus, the consequence of risk factors and drug use on protective factors also needs to be explored. Finally, more path models need to be examined to test models explaining the interrelation of risk and protective factors in the emergence of substance use disorders. A number of these models exist for drug use behaviour in adolescence, but relatively few have developed for substance use disorders for this population.

More generally, several issues emerged in reviewing risk factors for adolescent substance abuse and dependence that have impeded progress. Some studies have identified risk factors among adolescents diagnosed with substance use disorders by comparing the prevalence of potential risk factors among these adolescents to controls (e.g., Kilpatrick *et al.*, 2000). However, fewer prospective studies have examined risk factors associated with the development of substance abuse and dependence over time (e.g., Chassin *et al.*, 1999). Another observation was that the majority of studies focused on changes in frequency of drug use or abuse, but relatively few examined transitions in stages of substance use (e.g., Scheier *et al.*, 1997). Each stage in drug use is important in understanding why adolescents abuse drugs and become dependent. The understanding of what risk factors are related to the transitions from experimentation to continued use to abuse is critical in developing effective prevention and intervention programmes to halt this progression. Thus, continued research is needed on risk factors related to substance abuse and dependence and to transitions in level of drug use.

One issue that has significantly impeded progress in this area is the general absence of consistent definitions and methodological approaches to distinguish risk, protective, and vulnerability factors across studies. Vulnerability has been defined both as a solely endogenous process (e.g., Ingram and Price, 2001) and as a construct that encompasses individual and environmental factors (e.g., Rutter, 1987). For example, in behaviour genetics, vulnerability is viewed more specifically as the genetic-based liability for substance use disorders. Thus, this area of research supports the view of vulnerability as an endogenous process that may be responsible for the major differentiation of individuals who will progress to more advanced levels of drug use and abuse. Similar confusion exists in the study of protective factors. Although there appears to be support for the notion that protective factors operate by moderating the impact of risk factors, this criterion has not been used consistently to identify them. This conceptual and methodological Tower of Babel has led to situations where a variable such as emotional distress may be represented as a risk factor in some studies (e.g., Scheier and Newcomb, 1991a,b), and as a protective factor in others (e.g., Felix-Ortiz and Newcomb, 1992, 1999; Newcomb and Felix-Ortiz, 1992). The lack of consistent criteria for establishing cutoffs for the presence or absence of a risk or protective factor has further muddled this process. To some extent it appears that whether a given construct is a risk or protective factor and whether or not specific individuals are considered to have that factor present or absent may be in part a function of the study they are in, and not solely based on their individual characteristics. The growing body of literature on variables associated with substance abuse and dependence has identified many key players. Movement toward greater conceptual and methodological consistency across studies will hopefully lead to greater clarity regarding the specific roles they play.

REFERENCES

Agarwal, D. P. & Goedde, H. W. (1992). Pharmacogenetics of alcohol metabolism and alcoholism. *Pharmacogenetics, 2*, 48–62.

American Psychiatric Association (1994). *Diagnostic and statistical manual of mental disorders* (4th edn). Washington, DC: American Psychiatric Association.

Ary, D. V., Duncan, T. E., Duncan, S. C., & Hops, H. (1999). Adolescent problem behavior: The influence of parents and peers. *Behavior Research and Therapy, 37*, 217–230.

Ary, D. V., Tildesley, E., Hops, H., & Andrews, J. (1993). The influence of parent, sibling, and peer modeling and attitudes on adolescent use of alcohol. *The International Journal of the Addictions, 28*, 853–880.

Aytaclar, S., Tarter, R. E., Kirisci, L., & Lu, S. (1999). Association between hyperactivity and executive cognitive functioning in childhood and substance use in early adolescence. *Journal of the American Academy of Child and Adolescent Psychiatry, 38,* 172–178.

Baer, P. E., Garmezy, L. B., McLaughlin, R. J., Porkorny, A. D., & Wernick, M. J. (1987). Stress, coping, family conflict, and adolescent alcohol use. *Journal of Behavioral Medicine, 10,* 449–466.

Bahr, S. J., Hawks, R. D., & Wang, G. (1993). Family and religious influences on adolescent substance abuse. *Youth and Society, 24,* 443–465.

Brook, J. S., Brook, D. W., Gordon, A. S., Whiteman, M., & Cohen, P. (1990). The psychosocial etiology of adolescent drug use: A family interactional approach. *Genetic, Social, and General Psychology Monographs* (pp. 111–267). Washington, DC: Heldref.

Brook, J. S., Cohen, P., Whiteman, M., & Gordon, A. S. (1992). Psychosocial risk factors in the transition from moderate to heavy use or abuse of drugs. In M. D. Glantz and R. Pickens (Eds.), *Vulnerability to drug abuse* (pp. 359–388). Washington, DC: American Psychological Association.

Brook, J. S., Whiteman, M., & Gordon, A. S. (1985). Father absence, perceived family characteristics, and stage of drug use in adolescence. *British Journal of Developmental Psychopathology, 3,* 87–94.

Brown, B. B., Mounts, N., Lamborn, S. D., & Steinberg, L. (1993). Parenting practices and peer group affiliation in adolescence. *Child Development, 64,* 467–482.

Bry, B. H., McKeon, P., & Pandina, R. J. (1982). Extent of drug use as a function of number of risk factors. *Journal of Abnormal Psychology, 91,* 273–279.

Cadoret, R. J., Yates, W. R., Troughton, E., Woodworth, G., & Stewart, M. A. (1995). Adoption study demonstrating two genetic pathways to drug abuse. *Archives of General Psychiatry, 52,* 42–52.

Capaldi, D. M. & Patterson, G. R. (1991). Relation of parental transitions to boys' adjustment problems: I. A linear hypothesis. II. Mothers at risk for transitions and unskilled parenting. *Developmental Psychology, 27,* 489–504.

Capaldi, D. M. & Stoolmiller, M. (1999). Co-occurrence of conduct problems and depressive symptoms in early adolescent boys: III. Prediction to young-adult adjustment. *Development and Psychopathology, 11,* 59–84.

Chassin, L., Barrera, M., & Montgomery, H. (1997). Parent alcoholism as a risk factor. In S. Wolchik & I. Sandler (Eds.), *Handbook of children's coping: Linking theory and intervention. Issues in clinical child psychology* (pp. 101–129). New York, NY: Plenum Press.

Chassin, L., Curran, P., Hussong, A., & Colder, C. (1996). The relation of parent alcoholism to adolescent substance use: A longitudinal follow-up study. *Journal of Abnormal Psychology, 105,* 70–80.

Chassin, L., Pitts, S. C., DeLucia, C., & Todd, M. (1999). A longitudinal study of children of alcoholics: Predicting young adult substance use disorders, anxiety, and depression. *Journal of Abnormal Psychology, 108,* 106–119.

Chassin, L. & Ritter, J. (2001). Vulnerability to substance use disorders in childhood and adolescence. In R. E. Ingram & J. M. Price (Eds.), *Vulnerability to psychopathology* (pp. 107–134). New York, NY: Guilford Press.

Chassin, L., Rogosch, F., & Barrera, M. (1991). Substance use and symptomatology among adolescent children of alcoholics. *Journal of Abnormal Psychology, 100,* 449–463.

Chilcoat, H. D. & Breslau, N. (1998). Posttraumatic stress disorders and drug disorders: Testing causal pathways. *Archives of General Psychiatry, 55,* 913–917.

Clark, D. B., Lesnick, L., & Hegedus, A. M. (1997). Traumas and other adverse life events in adolescents with alcohol abuse and dependence. *Journal of the American Academy of Child and Adolescent Psychiatry, 36,* 1744–1751.

Clayton, R. R. (1992). Transitions in drug use: risk and protective factors. In M. D. Glantz and R. Pickens (Eds.), *Vulnerability to drug abuse* (pp. 15–52). Washington, DC: American Psychological Association.

Cloninger, C., Sigvardsson, S., & Bohman, M. (1988). Childhood personality predicts alcohol use in young adults. *Alcoholism, 12,* 494–505.

Cohen, S. & Wills, T. A. (1985). Stress, social support, and the buffering hypothesis. *Psychological Bulletin, 98,* 310–357.

Colder, C. R. & Chassin, L. (1999). The psychosocial characteristics of alcohol users versus problem users: Data from a study of adolescents at risk. *Development and Psychopathology, 11,* 321–348.

Crundall, I. (1993). Correlates of student substance use. *Drug and Alcohol Review, 12,* 271–276.

Dawes, M. A., Antelman, S. M., Vanyukov, M. M., Giancola, P., Tarter, R. E., Sussman, E.J. et al. (2000). Developmental sources of variation in liability to adolescent substance use disorders. *Drug and Alcohol Dependence, 61,* 3–14.

De La Rosa, M. D., Recio Adrados, L., Kennedy, N., & Milburn, N. (1993). *Current gaps and new directions for studying drug use and abuse behaviour in minority youth: Methodological issues and recent research advances* (National Institute on Drug Abuse Research Monograph Series, No. 130, pp. 321–340). Rockville, MD: National Institute on Drug Abuse.

DeWit, D. J., Silverman, G., Goodstadt, M., & Stoduto, G. (1995). The construction of risk and protective factors for adolescent alcohol and other drug use. *The Journal of Drug Issues, 25,* 837–863.

Dielman, T. E., Campanelli, P. C., Shope, J. T., & Butchart, A. T. (1987). Susceptibility to peer pressure, self-esteem, and health locus of control as correlates of adolescent substance abuse. *Health Education Quarterly, 14,* 207–221.

Dishion, T. J. & Loeber, R. (1985). Adolescent marijuana and alcohol use: The role of parents and peers revisited. *American Journal of Drug and Alcohol Abuse, 11,* 11–25.

Dishion, T. J., Patterson, G. R., Stoolmiller, M., & Skinner, M. L. (1991). Family, school, and behavioral antecedents to early adolescent involvement with antisocial peers. *Developmental Psychology, 27,* 172–180.

Eccles, J., Midgley, C., & Adler, T. (1984). Grade-related changes in the school environment: Effects on academic motivation. In J. G. Nicholls (Ed), *The development of achievement motivation* (pp. 283–331). Greenwich, CT: JAI.

Farrell, A. D. (1993). Risk factors for drug use in urban adolescents: A three-wave longitudinal study. *The Journal of Drug Issues, 23,* 443–462.

Farrell, A. D., Anchors, D. M., Danish, S. J., & Howard, C. W. (1992). Risk factors for drug use in rural adolescents. *Journal of Drug Education, 22,* 313–328.

Farrell, A. D., Danish, S. J., & Howard, C. W. (1992). Risk factors for drug use in urban adolescents: Identification and cross-validation. *American Journal of Community Psychology, 20,* 263–286.

Farrell, A. D., Kung, M. E., White, K. S., & Valois, R. F. (1999). The structure of

self-reported aggression, drug use, and delinquent behaviors during early adolescence. *Journal of Clinical Child Psychology, 29*, 282–292.
Farrell, A. D. & White, K. S. (1998). Peer influences and drug use among urban adolescents: Family structure and parent–adolescent relationship as protective factors. *Journal of Consulting and Clinical Psychology, 66*, 248–258.
Felix-Ortiz, M. & Newcomb, M. D. (1992). Risk and protective factors for drug use among Latino and White adolescents. *Hispanic Journal of Behavioral Sciences, 14*, 291–309.
Felix-Ortiz, M. & Newcomb, M. D. (1999). Vulnerability for drug use among Latino adolescents. *Journal of Community Psychology, 27*, 257–280.
Fergusson, D. M. (1993). Conduct problems and attention deficit behavior in middle childhood and cannabis use by age 15. *Australian New Zealand Journal of Psychiatry, 27*, 673–682.
Fergusson, D. M., Horwood, L. J., & Lynskey, M. T. (1995). The prevalence and risk factors associated with abusive or hazardous alcohol consumption in 16-year-olds. *Addiction, 90*, 935–946.
Feuerstein, M., Labbe, E., & Kuczmierczky, A. R. (1986). *Health psychology: A psychobiological perspective*. New York, NY: Plenum Press.
Gabel, S. (1992). Behavioral problems in sons of incarcerated or otherwise absent fathers: The issue of separation. *Family Processes, 31*, 303–314.
Giancola, P. R., Martin, C., Tarter, R. E., Pelham, W., & Moss. H. (1996). Executive cognitive functioning and aggressive behavior in preadolescent boys at high risk for substance abuse/dependence. *Journal of Studies on Alcohol, 57*, 352–359.
Giancola, P. R. & Tarter, R. E. (1999). Executive cognitive functioning and risk for substance abuse. *Psychological Science, 10*, 203–205.
Glantz, M. D., Weinberg, N.Z., Miner, L. L., & Colliver, J. D. (1999). The etiology of drug abuse: Mapping the paths. In M. D. Glantz & C. R. Hartel (Eds.), *Drug abuse: Origins and intervention* (pp. 3–45). Washington, DC: American Psychological Association.
Grant, B. F. & Dawson, D. (1997). Age of onset of alcohol use and its association with DSM-IV alcohol abuse and dependence: Results from the national longitudinal alcohol epidemiological survey. *Journal of Substance Abuse, 9*, 103–110.
Harrison, P. A., Fulkerson, J. A., & Beebe, T. J. (1997). Multiple substance use among adolescent physical and sexual abuse victims. *Child Abuse and Neglect, 21*, 529–539.
Hoffman, J. P. (1993). Exploring the direct and indirect family effects on adolescent drug use. *The Journal of Drug Issues, 23*, 535–557.
Holmberg, M. B. (1986). Longitudinal studies of drug abuse in a fifteen-year-old population: V. Prognostic factors. *Acta Psychiatrica Scandinavica, 71*(3), 207–210.
Hops, H., Duncan, T. E., Duncan, S. C., & Stoolmiller, M. (1996). Parent substance use as a predictor of adolescent use: A six-year lagged analysis. *Annals of Behavioural Medicine, 18*, 157–164.
Iacono, W. G., Carlson, S. R., Taylor, J., Elkins, I. J., & McGue, M. (1999). Behavioral disinhibition and the development of substance use disorders: Findings from the Minnesota twin family study. *Developmental Psychopathology, 11*, 869–900.
Ingram, R. E. & Price, J. M. (2001). The role of vulnerability in understanding psychopathology. In R. E. Ingram & J. M. Price (Eds.), *Vulnerability to psychopathology* (pp. 3–19). New York, NY: Guilford Press.

Jessor, R. & Jessor, S. L. (1977). *Problem behavior and psychosocial development: A longitudinal study of youth.* New York, NY: Academic Press.

Jessor, R., Van Den Bos, J., Vanderryn, J., & Costa, F. M. (1995). Protective factors in adolescent problem behavior: Moderator effects and developmental change. *Developmental Psychopathology, 31,* 923–933.

Johnson, V. & Pandina, R. J. (1991). Effects of the family environment on adolescent substance use, delinquency, and coping styles. *American Journal of Drug and Alcohol Abuse, 17,* 71–88.

Johnson, V. & Pandina, R. J. (1993). A longitudinal examination of the relationships among stress, coping strategies, and problems associated with alcohol abuse. *Alcohol and Clinical Experimental Research, 17,* 696–702.

Kaminer, Y. (1994). *Adolescent substance abuse: A comprehensive guide to theory and practice.* New York, NY: Plenum Press.

Kandel, D. B. (1982). Epidemiological and psychological perspectives on adolescent drug use. *Journal of the American Academy of Child Psychiatry, 21,* 328–347.

Kandel, D. B. & Andrews, K. (1987). Processes of adolescent socialization by parents and peers. *The International Journal of the Addictions, 22,* 319–342.

Kandel, D. B. & Yamaguchi, K. (1985). Developmental patterns of the use of legal, illegal, and medically prescribed psychotropic drugs from adolescence to young adulthood. In C. L. Jones & R. J. Battjes (Eds.), *Etiology of drug abuse: Implications for prevention* (pp. 193–235). Rockville, MD: National Institute on Drug Abuse.

Kandel, D. B. & Yamaguchi, K. (1993). From beer to crack: Developmental patterns of drug involvement. *American Journal of Public Health, 83,* 851–855.

Kendler, K. S., Karkowski, L., & Prescott, C. A. (1999). Hallucinogen, opiate, sedative, and stimulant use and abuse in population-based samples of female twins. *Acta Psychiatrica Scandinavica, 99,* 368–376.

Kiesler, D. J. (1999). *Beyond the disease model of mental disorders.* Westport, CT: Greenwood.

Kilpatrick, D. G., Acierno, R., Saunders, B., Resnick, H. S., Best, C. L., & Schnurr, P. P. (2000). Risk factors for adolescent substance abuse and dependence: Data from a national sample. *Journal of Consulting and Clinical Psychology, 68,* 19–30.

Kumpfer, K. L., Olds, D. L., & Alexander, J. F. (1998). Family etiology of youth problems. In R. S. Ashery, E. B. Robertson, & K. L., Kumpfer (Eds.), *Drug abuse prevention through family interventions* (National Institute on Drug Abuse Research Monograph No. 177, pp. 42–77). Rockville, MD: National Institute on Drug Abuse.

Legrand, L. N., McGue, M., & Iacono, W. G. (1999). Searching for interactive effects in the etiology of early-onset substance use. *Behavior Genetics, 6,* 433–444.

Lerner, J. V. & Vicary, J. R. (1984). Difficult temperament and drug use: Analyses from the New York longitudinal study. *Journal of Drug Education, 14,* 1–8.

Maddahian, E., Newcomb, M. D., & Bentler, P. M. (1988). Adolescent drug use and intention to use drugs: Concurrent and longitudinal analyses of four ethnic groups. *Addictive Behaviors, 13,* 191–195.

Maes, H. H., Woodard, C. E., Murrelle, L., Meyer, J. M., Silberg, J. L., & Hewitt, J. K., et al. (1999). Tobacco, alcohol, and drug use in eight to sixteen-year-old twins: The Virginia twin study of adolescent behavioral development. *Journal of Studies on Alcohol, 60,* 293–305.

McGue, M., Elkins, I., & Iacono, W. G. (2000). Genetic and environmental influences on adolescent substance use and abuse. *American Journal of Medical Genetics, 96*, 671–677.

Merikangas, K. R., Stolar, M., Stevens, D. E., Goulet, J., Presig, M. A., & Fenton, B. *et al.* (1998). Familial transmission of substance use disorders. *Archives of General Psychiatry, 55*, 973–979.

Milberger, S., Faraone, S. V., Biederman, J., Chu, M. P., & Feighner, J. A. (1999). Substance use disorders in high-risk adolescent offspring. *American Journal on Addictions, 8*, 211–219.

Needle, R. H., Su, S., & Doherty, W. (1990). Divorce, remarriage, and adolescent substance use: A prospective longitudinal study. *Journal of Marriage and the Family, 52*, 157–169.

Neighbors, B. D., Clark, D. B., Donovan, J. E., & Brody, G. H. (2000). Difficult temperament, parental relationships, and adolescent alcohol use disorder symptoms. *Journal of Child and Adolescent Substance Abuse, 10*, 69–86.

Newcomb, M. D. (1992). Understanding the multidimensional nature of drug use and abuse: The role of consumption, risk factors, and protective factors. In M. Glantz and R. Pickens (Eds.), *Vulnerability to drug abuse* (pp. 255–298). Washington, DC: American Psychological Association.

Newcomb, M. D. & Felix-Ortiz, M. (1992). Multiple protective and risk factors for drug use and abuse: Cross-sectional and prospective findings. *Journal of Personality and Social Psychology, 63*, 280–296.

Newcomb, M. D., Maddahian, E., & Bentler, P. M. (1986). Risk factors for drug use among adolescents: Concurrent and longitudinal analyses. *American Journal of Public Health, 76*, 525–531.

Newcomb, M. D., Maddahian, E., Skager, R., & Bentler, P. M. (1987). Substance abuse and psychosocial risk factors among teenagers: Associations with sex, age, ethnicity, and type of school. *American Journal of Drug and Alcohol Abuse, 13*, 413–433.

Oetting, E. R., & Beauvais, F. (1986). Peer cluster theory: Drugs and the adolescent. *Journal of Counseling and Development, 65*, 17–22.

Reyes, O., Gillock, K., & Kobus, K. (1994). A longitudinal study of school adjustment in urban, minority adolescents: Effects of a high school transition program. *American Journal of Community Psychology, 22*, 341–369.

Robins, L. & Przybeck, T. (1985). Age of onset of drug use as a factor in drug and other disorders. In C. R. Jones & R. J. Battjes (Eds.), *Etiology of drug abuse: Implications for prevention* (National Institute on Drug Abuse Research Monograph No. 57, pp. 178–192). Rockville, MD: National Institute on Drug Abuse.

Rose, R. J., Kaprio, J., Winter, T., Koskenvuo, M., & Viken, R. J. (1999). Familial and socioregional environmental effects on abstinence from alcohol at age sixteen. *Journal of Studies on Alcohol, 13*, 63–74.

Rutter, M. (1987). Psychosocial resilience and protective mechanisms. *American Journal of Orthopsychiatry, 57*, 316–331.

Scheier, L. M. Botvin, G. J., & Baker, E. (1997). Risk and protective factors as predictors of adolescent alcohol involvement and transitions in alcohol use: A prospective analysis. *Journal of Studies on Alcohol, 58*, 652–667.

Scheier, L. M. & Newcomb, M. D. (1991a). Differentiation of early adolescent predictors of drug use versus abuse: A developmental risk factor model. *Journal of Substance Abuse, 3*, 277–299.

Scheier, L. M. & Newcomb, M. D. (1991b). Psychosocial predictors of drug use initiation and escalation: An expansion of the multiple risk factors hypothesis using longitudinal data. *Contemporary Drug Problems, 18*, 31–73.

Scheier, L. M., Newcomb, M. D., & Skager, R. (1994). Risk, protection, and vulnerability to adolescent drug use: Latent-variable models of three age groups. *Journal of Drug Education, 24*, 49–82.

Shedler, J. & Block, J. (1990). Adolescent drug use and psychological health. *American Psychologist, 45*, 612–630.

Spooner, C. (1999). Causes and correlates of adolescent drug abuse and implications for treatment. *Drug and Alcohol Review, 18*, 453–475.

Steinberg, L. (1987). Single parents, step-parents, and the susceptibility of adolescents to antisocial peer pressure. *Child Development, 58*, 269–439.

Stice, E., Barrera, M., & Chassin, L. (1998). Prospective differential prediction of adolescent alcohol use and problem use: Examining the mechanisms of effect. *Journal of Abnormal Psychology, 107*, 616–628.

Sullivan, T. N. & Farrell, A. D. (1999). Identification and impact of risk and protective factors for drug use among urban African-American adolescents. *Journal of Clinical Child Psychology, 28*, 122–136.

Sussman, S., Dent, C. W., & Stacy, A. W. (1999). The association of current stimulant use with demographic, substance use, violence-related, social and intrapersonal variables among high risk youth. *Addictive Behaviors, 24*, 741–748.

Swadi, H. (1992). Relative risk factors in detecting adolescent drug abuse. *Drug and Alcohol Dependence, 29*, 253–264.

Tarter, R. E., Laird, S. B., Kabene, M., Bukstein, O., & Kaminer, Y. (1990). Drug abuse severity in adolescents is associated with magnitude of deviation in temperament traits. *British Journal of Addiction, 85*, 1501–1504.

Tarter, R. E., Moss, H., Blackson, T., Vanyukov, M., Brigham, J., & Loeber, R. (1997). Disaggregating the liability for drug abuse. In C. L. Wetherington and J. L. Falk (Eds.), *Laboratory behavioral studies of vulnerability to drug abuse* (NIDA Research Monograph No. 169), pp. 227–243. Rockville, MD: National Institute on Drug Abuse.

Thomas, A. & Chess, S. (1984). Genesis and evolution of behavioral disorders: From infancy to early adult life. *American Journal of Psychiatry, 141*, 1–9.

Tsuang, M. T., Lyons, M. J., Eisen, S. A., Goldberg, J., True, W., Lin, N. *et al.* (1996). Genetic influences on DSM-III-R drug abuse and dependence: A study of 3,372 twin pairs. *American Journal of Medical Genetics, 67*, 473–477.

Tubman, J. G. & Windle, M. (1995). Continuity of difficult temperament in adolescence: Relations with depression, life events, family support, and substance use across a one-year period. *Journal of Youth and Adolescence, 24* (2), 133–153.

Vanyukov, M. M. & Tarter, R. E. (2000). Genetic studies of substance abuse. *Drug and Alcohol Dependence, 59*, 101–123.

Viken, R. J., Kaprio, J., Koskenvuo, M., & Rose, R. J. (1999). Longitudinal analyses of the determinants of drinking and of drinking to intoxication in adolescent twins. *Behavior Genetics, 29*, 455–461.

Wills, T. A. (1986). Stress and coping in early adolescence: Relationships to substance use in urban school samples. *Health Psychology, 5*, 503–529.

Wills, T. A., Mariani, J., & Filer, M. (1996). The role of family and peer relationships in adolescent substance use. In G. R. Pierce, B. R. Sarason, & I. G. Sarason

(Eds.), *Handbook of social support and the family* (pp. 521–549). New York, NY: Plenum Press.

Wills, T. A., McNamara, G., Vaccaro, D., & Hirky, A. E. (1996). Escalated substance use: A longitudinal grouping analysis from early to middle adolescence. *Journal of Abnormal Psychology, 105,* 166–180.

Wills, T. A., Sandy, J. M., & Yaeger, A. (2000). Temperament and adolescent substance use: An epigenetic approach to risk and protection. *Journal of Personality, 68,* 1127–1151.

Wills, T. A., Schreibman, D., Benson, G., & Vaccaro, D. (1994). Impact of parental substance use on adolescents: A test of a mediational model. *Journal of Pediatric Psychology, 19,* 537–556.

Wills, T. A. & Shiffman, S. (1985). Coping and substance use: A conceptual framework. In S. Shiffman & T. A. Wills (Eds.), *Coping and substance use* (pp. 3–24). Orlando, FL: Academic Press.

Wills, T. A., Vaccarro, D., & McNamara, G. (1992). The role of life events, family support, and competence in adolescent substance use: A test of vulnerability and protective factors. *American Journal of Community Psychology, 20,* 349–374.

Wills, T. A. & Vaughan, R. (1989). Social support and substance use in early adolescence. *Journal of Behavioural Medicine, 12,* 321–339.

Windle, M. (1991). The difficult temperament in adolescence: Associations with substance use, family support, and problem behaviors. *Journal of Clinical Psychology, 47,* 310–315.

Windle, M. (1999). Critical conceptual and measurement issues in the study of resilience. In M. D. Glantz & J. L. Johnson (Eds.), *Resilience and development: Positive life adaptations* (pp. 161–178). New York, NY: Plenum Press.

Zubin, J. & Steinhauser, S. (1981). How to break the logjam in schizophrenia: A look beyond genetics. *Journal of Nervous and Mental Disease, 169,* 477–492.

Chapter 5

Course and outcome

Eric F. Wagner and Susan M. Tarolla

This chapter is devoted to describing variations in the course and outcomes of adolescents with alcohol or other drug problems. At the outset, we should note that teens using substances are a heterogeneous group, with wide variation in the reasons for, the correlates of, and the consequences of their substance involvement. Some adolescents who try alcohol or other drugs experience few clinically significant problems. In fact, several investigations have suggested limited substance use may be positively related to psychosocial functioning and adjustment in adolescence (Labouvie, 1990; Maggs, 1997; Marlatt, 1987; Shedler and Block, 1990; Silbereisen and Noack, 1988), and others have found adolescent substance use does not reliably predict the subsequent development of alcohol or other drug use disorders (Bukstein, 1995; White, 1992). However, other adolescents who use substances experience dramatic negative consequences because of their substance use, and place themselves at long-term risk for substance use problems. For these teens, early alcohol and other drug use may lead to serious adjustment and substance use problems later in life (e.g., substance abuse and dependence) (Hill *et al.*, 2000; Kandel, 1980; Newcomb and Bentler, 1988; White, 1987). In sum, adolescents who become involved with alcohol or other drug use are far from a monolithic group, and as a result demonstrate a variety of courses and outcomes. Our goal in this chapter is to identify and discuss some of the most important determinants of what happens to adolescents who have developed drinking or drugging problems.

While adolescent substance involvement may best be conceptualized as lying on a continuum ranging from non-use to substance dependence (Steinberg and Levine, 1990), most teenagers are experimental or occasional users. Such adolescents rarely come into contact with treatment providers in the absence of some acute provoking event (e.g., an intoxication-related accident). The types of substance using teens more typically seen in clinical settings are those identified as substance abusers or substance dependent, with the abusers outnumbering the dependent simply because very few adolescents have a long enough substance use history to develop the combination of symptoms that define dependence (e.g., withdrawal symptoms, medical complications related to the use of a substance). In this chapter, our focus will be on teenagers who demonstrate substance abuse or dependence, and what happens to them over the course of time.

There are three different types of studies relevant to understanding the course and outcome for adolescents with substance use problems. The first type involves treatment samples, and asks at least one of the three following questions: (1) How do adolescents in substance abuse treatment differ from adolescents in the general population? (2) What pretreatment characteristics are associated with post-treatment outcomes?, and (3) What post-treatment characteristics are associated with post-treatment outcomes? The second type involves community samples, and focuses on characteristics that distinguish teens with and without substance use problems. The final type involves self-recovered samples; these are young people who previously demonstrated substance use problems and recovered from them without formal intervention. In separate sections below, we review each of these three literatures.

TREATMENT SAMPLES

In an attempt to address alcohol and other drug problems among adolescents, multiple treatment approaches have been developed. Knowledge about which of these approaches is most effective for which individuals remains limited. Clinical demand for treatment programmes has been overwhelming and has outpaced empirical research evaluating their effectiveness. While a small number of investigators are currently conducting controlled clinical trials of various adolescent substance abuse interventions (e.g., Wagner *et al.*, 1999; Wagner and Waldron, 2001), most available treatment programmes have not been rigorously evaluated. At present, we do know that treatment can succeed with adolescents with substance use problems, but it generally appears that no particular treatment is superior to any other (Wagner *et al.*, 1999; Williams, Chang, and Addiction Centre Adolescent Research Group, 2000). Accordingly, Kazdin (1995) has identified substance abuse among adolescents as a child problem behaviour domain in which there remains a critical need for controlled clinical trials.

Relapse rates following substance abuse treatment are comparable across both adolescents and adults with substance use problems. One in two substance abusing adolescents will relapse within 90 days following treatment, and two-thirds of substance abusing teens will relapse within the first six months following treatment (Brown *et al.*, 1990, 1989). The greatest risk for relapse is in the initial months after treatment, and the risk for relapse reduces but remains relatively stable for survivors over the next 4 to 5 months (Brown *et al.*, 1990). Findings from the adolescent psychiatric epidemiological literature underscore the high risk for relapse: the remission interval between recurrent episodes is significantly shorter for substance use disorders than for any other adolescent psychiatric problem (Orvaschel *et al.*, 1995). While relapse rates are similar among adolescents and adults who have completed substance abuse treatment, the typical precipitants for teens relapsing to substance use differ from those for adults relapsing to substance use (Brown *et al.*, 1989). For teenagers, direct and indirect social pressure appears to be more salient in initial relapse situations; Brown and colleagues (1989) found that 90% of adolescent relapses occurred in the presence of other people. For adults, negative intrapersonal states and interpersonal situations appear to be the primary precursors to relapse.

An important question that has received only limited attention in the adolescent substance abuse literature is the following: What treatments for which adolescents under what conditions are most effective for addressing adolescent substance use problems? If one assumes, based on the existing empirical literature, that (a) treatment can work, (b) no particular treatment is better than any other, and (c) half of adolescents who participate in substance abuse treatment will relapse within three months post-treatment, this question reduces to the following: Which adolescents under what conditions demonstrate the most favourable response to substance abuse treatment? However, the existing literature on the course of adolescent post-treatment functioning offers few data on pretreatment client characteristics that may be related to post-treatment outcomes (Maisto *et al.*, 2001). Moreover, the bulk of the studies that have been done involve cross-sectional designs that measure post-treatment factors and outcome at the same time, and thus preclude insights as to causal relations among variables (Latimer, Newcomb *et al.*, 2000a). Only recently have rigorous, longitudinal studies begun to appear in the literature examining pretreatment and post-treatment characteristics of adolescents (i.e., which adolescents under what conditions) that may influence clinical course and outcome. These are summarized in the following section.

Longitudinal studies of factors related to course and outcome in treatment samples

Sandra Brown and colleagues have performed some of the most extensive work to date concerning pretreatment and post-treatment characteristics associated with adolescent treatment outcomes. In order to better understand determinants of post-treatment status, Brown (1993; Brown *et al.*, 1990) compared adolescents classified as abstainers, minor relapsers, or full relapsers at 6 months post-treatment. One-third of teens had abstained, nearly one-fourth had demonstrated minor alcohol and drug use involvement, and 43% had returned to problematic levels of alcohol or drug use. While treatment goals were exclusively abstinence-oriented, only a minority of teens maintained extended abstinence throughout the first year post-treatment, though more than three-fourths of those who were abstinent at 6 months continued their abstinence through the year.

Factors that distinguished relapsers from adolescents demonstrating more positive outcomes included post-treatment exposure to alcohol and other drug use in their social environment and lack of involvement in self-help groups. Factors that distinguished continued abstainers from adolescents demonstrating less positive outcomes included post-treatment attendance in self-help groups, staying in school, and improved grades. Moreover, abstainers were more likely to acknowledge depression and anxiety, to date less, to experience and express family problems, and to report stresses related to establishing a new group of friends and changes in activities in the first 6 months following treatment. However, at one year abstainers reported significantly less depression and anxiety than teens who had reverted to heavy drug involvement. Interestingly, level of pretreatment drug use was not predictive of one-year outcome.

In sum, Brown and colleagues documented that most teens relapse to substance use within 6 months post-treatment, and adolescents who succeed in abstaining for 6 months are likely to maintain abstinence 6 months later. For teens that do relapse, exposure to alcohol and other drug use in their post-treatment social environment and lack of involvement in self-help groups are key determinants of use. Moreover, teens that do not return to alcohol and other drug use demonstrate significant improvement in major areas of functioning within one year post-treatment, while adolescents who revert to substance use demonstrate measurable deterioration of functioning in the year following treatment. Finally, teens more substance involved at pretreatment are no less likely to respond to treatment than teens less substance involved.

More recently, William Latimer and colleagues also have undertaken the study of pretreatment and post-treatment characteristics associated with adolescent treatment outcomes. Latimer, Newcomb, and colleagues (2000a) examined the role of substance abuse problem severity, psychosocial characteristics, and treatment factors in post-treatment outcome in a multiwave study of teens in Alcoholics Anonymous-based substance abuse treatment. Pretreatment substance abuse problem severity did not predict outcome; adolescents with greater substance abuse problems were just as likely to benefit from treatment as youth with fewer problems. Gender, after controlling for treatment and psychosocial factors, also did not predict outcome. However, pretreatment psychosocial risk status, which included measures of parental substance abuse, sibling substance abuse, deviant attitudes, deviant behaviour, and impulsivity, was positively associated with substance abuse problem severity at 6 months post-treatment, though 6-month post-treatment risk did not predict subsequent substance abuse problem severity. Conversely, pretreatment psychosocial protection status, which included measures of school connectedness, social connectedness, goal directedness, and peer abstinence, was not associated with substance abuse problem severity at 6 months post-treatment, but 6-month post-treatment protection predicted subsequent substance abuse problem severity. Moreover, presence of one or more protective factors at 6 months post-treatment was found to reduce subsequent substance use even in the presence of one or more psychosocial risk factors. Finally, greater participation in aftercare predicted decreased substance abuse problem severity, reduced psychosocial risk, and increased psychosocial protection at 6 months post-treatment.

Latimer, Winters, and colleagues (2000b) tested a vulnerability model that included demographic, individual, and interpersonal variables for predicting post-treatment alcohol and marijuana use among adolescents who participated in residential or nonresidential substance abuse treatment. Demographic variables included gender, age, and ethnicity; individual variables included pretreatment substance use frequency, deviant behaviour, and psychological substance dependence; and interpersonal variables include peer, parent, and sibling substance use. In addition, treatment modality, length of treatment, and aftercare sessions were examined as potential influences on treatment outcome. Pretreatment levels of sibling substance use and aftercare involvement predicted both 6-month post-treatment alcohol use and marijuana use, which also was associated with pretreatment levels of deviant behaviour. Gender, pretreatment levels of substance use, treatment length, alcohol use at 6 months post-treatment, and peer substance use at 6 months post-treatment predicted 12-month post-treatment alcohol use. Finally, pretreatment peer substance use, marijuana use at 6 months post-treatment, psychological substance dependence at 6-months post-treatment, and peer substance use at 6 months post-treatment predicted 12-month post-treatment marijuana use.

In a third study, Winters and colleagues (2000) compared the 6- and 12-month post-treatment functioning of the following three groups of adolescents treated with a Minnesota Model approach (i.e., the 12 Steps of Alcoholics Anonymous combined with basic principles of psychotherapy): (1) those who completed treatment; (2) those who did not complete treatment; and (3) those on a waiting list. Possible differences in outcome between residential and outpatient treatment settings also were compared. Similar to Brown (1993), treatment outcomes were classified in terms of abstinence, minor relapse, and relapse. Among treatment completers, 29% were abstinent at 6 months, and 19% were abstinent at 12 months. Another 25% were minor relapsers at 6 months, and 25% were minor relapsers at 12 months. Overall, a large proportion of treatment completers demonstrated positive treatment response at both 6-month (54%) and 12-month (44%) outcomes. Completers demonstrated far superior 12-month outcomes in terms of abstinence/minor relapse compared to the incompleters (15%) and those on the waiting list (27%), which did not differ significantly from one another. Moreover, no post-treatment differences were found between treatment settings, or as a function of gender or age.

In sum, the work of Latimer and colleagues indicates most teens relapse to substance use within 6 months post-treatment, and gender, age, and treatment setting have relatively little to do with predicting treatment outcomes. Pretreatment psychosocial risk (but not protection) predicts substance abuse at 6 months post-treatment, and 6-month psychosocial protection (but not risk) predicts substance abuse at 12 months post-treatment. The degree of post-treatment peer substance involvement appears to be a particularly influential predictor of treatment outcome over time, with fewer substance involved peers associated with decreased relapse risk. Latimer and colleagues (2000b) interpreted these findings as demonstrating the increasing importance of psychosocial protective factors over the course of adolescent recovery, and suggested a lack of post-treatment psychosocial protection, rather than the presence of psychosocial risk, maybe the most important predictor of relapse. Moreover, across Latimer and colleagues' studies, greater involvement and retention both in treatment and in aftercare were found to predict better treatment outcome. This finding underscores the importance of treatment retention in treatment effectiveness, and, as Winters and colleagues (2000) note, suggests the relevance of additional factors for which retention may be a barometer, such as clients' individual needs, motivation factors, social influences, the policies and practices of treatment programmes, relationships with counsellors, and levels and types of available services.

A recent study by Maisto *et al.* (2001) also investigated the course of functioning among substance-abusing adolescents. In this study, substance-abusing teens were recruited from four different inpatient and outpatient substance abuse treatment programmes, and all members of the clinical sample met diagnostic criteria for alcohol abuse or dependence. One year after treatment, 19% remained abstinent, 33% were current drinkers but did not meet diagnostic criteria for an alcohol use disorder, 16% met criteria for alcohol abuse, and 33% met criteria for alcohol dependence. In addition, over half of the clinical group no longer met diagnostic criteria for alcohol use disorders at the one-year post-treatment contact, and more than one-third had stopped drinking altogether.

An additional component of the Maisto *et al.* (2001) study involved comparing their sample of substance-abusing adolescents to a sample of community dwelling controls. In contrast to the average across the clinical groups (i.e., the abstinent, the drinkers/no diagnosis, the abusers, and the dependent), the community sample demonstrated lower alcohol consumption and other drug use at both baseline and one-year assessments, and lower substance abuse problem severity, greater situational confidence for resisting drug use urges, higher self-esteem, higher levels of behavioural coping/positive thinking at baseline. Over time, the clinical groups demonstrated a greater reduction in problem severity than the community controls, with the drinkers/no diagnosis group showing the greatest change, and the dependent group showing greater reduction than the abuser group. The clinical groups also showed greater improvement in (a) situational confidence, with the dependent group showing greater increases than the abuser group, and (b) self-esteem, with the drinkers/no diagnosis group demonstrating more improvement than the abstainers. This latter finding appeared to be the result of higher baseline self-esteem scores among the eventual abstainers than among the drinkers/no diagnosis. Also, the clinical groups demonstrated more improvement over time than the community controls in behavioural coping/positive thinking. When compared to the community controls at one year, the abstainers were the clinical group most similar on measures of situational confidence, self-esteem, and behavioural coping/positive thinking.

In sum, Maisto *et al.*'s (2001) findings parallel those of Brown (1993) and Winters *et al.* (2000), in that most teens with substance use disorders relapsed within 12 months post-treatment. However, Maisto *et al.* (2001) documented that half of adolescents diagnosed with alcohol use disorders at pretreatment will no longer meet diagnostic criteria for alcohol abuse or dependence at 12 months post-treatment. This is similar to Winters et al.'s (2000) finding concerning the number of treatment completing adolescents demonstrating favourable response to treatment (i.e., abstinence, minor relapse) at 12 months post-treatment. Moreover, Maisto *et al.* (2001) found teens with substance use problems appear to demonstrate positive changes in response to treatment programmes on factors distinguishing clinical groups from community groups (e.g., problem severity, situational confidence for resisting urges, self-esteem, behavioural coping), with those abstaining at 12 months post-treatment resembling most the community controls on these factors.

Additional studies of factors related to course and outcome in treatment samples

Several additional investigations, many of which are cross-sectional in design (i.e., putative predictors and outcome are measured at the same time), have provided insights about potential influences on adolescent substance abuse treatment outcome. Findings from these studies are briefly reviewed in the following section.

Higher levels of pretreatment motivation to change have been shown to predict greater reductions in alcohol and other drug use frequency during treatment and higher likelihood of 6-month post-treatment abstinence among substance-abusing adolescents (Cady *et al.*, 1996). Similarly, Friedman and colleagues (1994) found that post-treatment drug use was inversely related to a rating of "the degree of wanting help". Adolescents' reports of the number of non-using social supports and the degree of satisfaction with one's social supports have been found to predict 3-month, 6-month, and 1-year substance use outcomes among teens treated for substance abuse (Richter *et al.*, 1991; Vik *et al.*, 1992). Family factors also have been shown to be influential, with pretreatment exposure to parental and sibling substance use (Kennedy and Minami, 1993; Myers *et al.*, 1993) and post-treatment family pathology (DeJong and Henrich, 1980; Shoemaker and Sherry, 1991) associated with poorer outcomes.

Hawke and colleagues (2000) found a history of childhood sexual abuse predicts earlier alcohol use and earlier illicit drug use, as well as more severe drug abuse problems, greater psychopathology, a higher likelihood of post-treatment relapse, and greater treatment dropout. Pretreatment severity of drug use, legal problems, deviant behaviour and school problems, and psychiatric severity also have been found to predict greater treatment dropout (Catalano et al., 1990; Kaminer et al., 1992), as well as poorer treatment outcomes (Benson, 1985; De Leon, 1984; Friedman et al., 1986). A positive association between length of treatment and post-treatment success has been found among adolescents who receive intensive treatments such as residential or therapeutic community approaches (De Leon, 1984; Friedman et al., 1986; Rush, 1979), though this relation has not been confirmed for teens involved in outpatient treatments. Finally, Friedman and colleagues (1986) found fewer previous admissions, drug problems other than marijuana, and non-Hispanic White background were associated with better treatment outcomes, and Holsten (1985) found being female, coming from a broken home without a family history of alcoholism and experiencing no problems specifically related to alcohol, and having no legal problems prior to treatment were associated with positive treatment outcomes.

Community samples

Several studies involving community samples have focused on substance use, individual, and social/environmental characteristics that distinguish teens with and without substance use problems. Some of these studies contrast samples of teens in substance use treatment with samples of community dwelling teens, while others sample entirely from the community and distinguish teens with substance use problems for those without substance use problems using diagnostic measures. The ultimate goal of both types of studies is to identify important correlates of adolescent substance use problems.

Regarding substance use and individual characteristics, several significant differences have been found between teens with and without substance use problems. Adolescents in treatment for substance use problems use alcohol and other drugs at an earlier age, progress more rapidly in the severity of their substance use, and are more likely to use multiple substances than adolescents from the general population (Brown et al., 1992, 1989). Substance-abusing teens are more likely to demonstrate antisocial and delinquent behaviour than non-substance-abusing teens (Ellickson et al., 1997; Wagner, 1996), and they are more likely to have been physically or sexually abused (Hawke et al., 2000). Indeed, adolescents' prior experiences of abuse or maltreatment are significant risk factors for alcohol and other drug abuse (Chatlos, 1996; Clark, 1994; Dembo et al., 1988; Finkelhor, 1995; Gil, 1996; Rotheram-Borus et al., 1996), though little is currently known about how prior abuse/maltreatment may influence treatment response among teens (Clark and Neighbors, 1996).

Positive correlations have been found between negative life events and substance abuse among teens (Brown, 1989; Bruns and Geist, 1984; Newcomb and Harlow, 1986; Turner and Wheaton, 1994), and stressful life events have been found to predict substance use and mental health problems among adolescents from different ethnic/racial groups and both sexes (Biafora et al., 1994). These findings generally have been interpreted as evidence that adolescent substance abuse usefully may be conceptualized as responses to stress, albeit maladaptive ones. In addition, the long-term impact of major life events and traumas on psychiatric disorders, including substance-related disorders, and adjustment are widely recognized (e.g., Rutter, 1989; Rutter and Maughan, 1997).

Alcohol expectancies are the effects attributed to alcohol that an individual anticipates experiencing when drinking (Brown et al., 1980). In several different studies, alcohol expectancies have been shown to be highly related to adult and adolescent drinking practices, including problem drinking and alcoholism (Brown, 1985; Brown et al., 1987, 1980; Christiansen et al., 1989; Grube et al., 1995; Southwick et al., 1981). Expectancies have proven to be significant mediators of various relationships important in adolescent substance use/abuse (e.g., the relation between parental alcoholism and adolescent heavy drinking (Colder et al., 1997)), and positive social expectancies appear to be particularly strong predictors of teen drinking and drug use (Aas et al., 1998; Laurent et al., 1997). Moreover, expectancies have been shown to be significant predictors of substance use among Black and Hispanic teens (Scheier et al., 1997).

Perhaps the most dramatic individual difference between teens with and without substance use problems is the prevalence of psychiatric disorders. Compared to the general population of teens, adolescents in substance abuse treatment are much more likely to demonstrate psychiatric problems, with upwards of 90% of substance-abusing teens demonstrating comorbid psychiatric disturbance (Brown et al., 1996). Compared to substance-abusing adults, adolescents with substance use disorders are more likely to demonstrate psychiatric comorbidity, though the patterns of comorbidity are similar across age, with disruptive and antisocial behaviour disorders the most common comorbid conditions, followed closely by depressive and anxiety disorders (Kessler et al., 1996). Kandel et al. (1999) found rates of disruptive behaviour, mood, and anxiety disorders were three times higher for community-dwelling adolescents with a current substance use disorder than for those without a substance use disorder. Similarly, Lewinsohn and colleagues (1993) found lifetime rates of anxiety, mood, or disruptive behaviour disorders were more than two times higher for adolescents with a substance use disorder than for those without a substance use disorder. In addition, retrospective, longitudinal, and comparison studies suggest high behavioural activity level (i.e., Attention

Deficit Hyperactivity Disorder) appears to be a predisposing factor for adolescent substance abuse, though particularly (and perhaps exclusively) when there are comorbid conduct problems (Aytaclar *et al.*, 1999).

While the causal direction of the association between substance use and other psychiatric problems during adolescence remains debatable (e.g., substance abuse leads to comorbid problems; comorbid problems lead to substance abuse) (Zeitlin, 2000), there is little question that the association exists and that it contributes to the course and outcome of substance use problems. Although the onset of comorbid psychiatric disorders among adolescents with substance use disorders often precedes the onset of substance abuse or dependence (Boyle and Offord, 1991; Kessler *et al.*, 1996, 1997), the reverse also has been documented (Brook *et al.*, 1998; Rohde *et al.*, 1996). The order of appearance seems to depend on the specific disorder and on gender. For both genders, conduct and anxiety disorders appear to precede substance use disorders. The sequence with depressive disorders is less clear; mood disorders have been reported both to precede and follow substance use disorders (Deykin *et al.*, 1987; DiMilio, 1989; Famularo *et al.*, 1985; Greenbaum *et al.*, 1991; Hussong and Chassin, 1994; Joshi and Scott, 1988; Kashani *et al.*, 1985; Lewinsohn *et al.*, 1994; Madianos *et al.*, 1994; Millin *et al.*, 1991; Rao *et al.*, 1999, Van Hasselt *et al*, 1993). Moreover, there is evidence of gender specificity, with female substance abusers more likely to demonstrate depression than male substance abusers (Galaif *et al.*, 1998).

In terms of course and outcome, substance-abusing adolescents comorbid with other psychiatric disorders often demonstrate poor prognoses. They are more likely to demonstrate chronic psychosocial and adaptive impairments, suicidality, poor treatment compliance and response, increased utilization of services, and poor long-term outcome than substance-abusing adolescents without psychiatric comorbidity (Aseltine *et al.*, 1998; Rao *et al.*, 1999; Ravndal and Vaglum, 1994; Westmeyer *et al.*, 1998; Wolpe *et al.*, 1995). Identification and consideration of co-existing psychiatric disorders can greatly enhance the effectiveness of adolescent substance abuse interventions, which may reduce negative effects. Thorough and accurate assessment could provide direction regarding intervention suitability, and early identification and treatment of childhood psychiatric disorders may prevent a progression into substance use problems. Interventions that take into account comorbid conditions can be tailored to each individual's needs.

In course and outcome studies of adult substance abusers in substance abuse treatment, the single most notable factor associated with positive outcomes is positive family milieu or social support (Billings and Moos, 1983; Higgins *et al.*, 1994; Longabaugh *et al.*, 1993; Moos *et al.*, 1982). In regard to social/environmental characteristics distinguishing teens with and without substance use problems, family factors have received considerable attention. The family has long been recognized as a primary source of influence in the theoretical and empirical literatures concerning the development and maintenance of adolescent substance use problems (see Hawkins *et al.*, 1992; Hops *et al.*, 1990; Petraitis *et al.*, 1995). Studies of community samples have supported an association between parental alcoholism and adolescent alcohol and other drug abuse (Brook *et al.*, 1983; West and Prinz, 1987; Windle, 2000). Indeed, Pandina and Johnson (1990) found that serious alcohol-related problems, including admissions to treatment, were greater among adolescents from families with histories of alcoholism than teens from families without such histories. It appears that the presence of an alcoholic parent severely disrupts family interaction and equilibrium, which contributes to adolescent substance use problems (West and Prinz, 1987; Windle and Tubman, 1999). Regarding family interaction, adolescents reared in environments with lax supervision, excessively severe or inconsistent disciplinary practices, or lack of involvement with parents are at greater risk for substance use problems (Ary *et al.*, 1999; Baumrind, 1991; Duncan *et al.*, 1998; Foxcroft and Lowe, 1991). Moreover, family cohesion is a strong protective factor for substance use problems among general population adolescents (Gil *et al.*, 1998), and a positive family milieu has been shown to reduce the risk of teen drug use/abuse even when multiple risk factors are present (Garmenzy, 1985; Vega and Gil, 1998). Family structure also has received a great deal of research attention, but findings have been equivocal. Some studies report higher rates of substance use problems among adolescents from single-parent households (Byram and Fly, 1984; Dembo *et al.*, 1979; Free, 1991; Needle *et al.*, 1990; Paternoster, 1989; Stern *et al.*, 1984), while other studies report no differences between youth from single-parent and two-parent households (Fawzy *et al.*, 1987).

Peer influences are another social/environmental factor that has received a great deal of attention in research designed to distinguish teens with and without substance use problems. Empirical research has demonstrated that association with friends who use drugs is among the strongest predictors of adolescent substance use and abuse (Barnes and Welte, 1986; Elliott *et al.*, 1985; Kaplan *et al.*, 1982; Spooner, 1999; Vega *et al.*, 1993). Peer rejection and associations with deviant peer groups in elementary school grades is associated with substance use and abuse (Hawkins *et al.*, 1987). Moreover, de-escalation from problem drinking levels has also been reported to follow changes in peer group affiliation among high school students (Stice *et al.*, 1998). Interestingly, younger adolescents appear more likely to use family support to change their addictive lifestyle, whereas older youth rely more on peer and other influences outside the home (Brown, 1993; Chassin *et al.*, 1985).

Self-recovered samples

Studies of adult substance abusers have shown that only a small percentage (i.e., < 10%) receive formal treatment for alcohol and drug problems (Narrow *et al.*, 1993), and many people with substance use problems recover without formal intervention (Sobell *et al.*, 2000). However, clinicians and researchers in the addiction field seldom encounter people who recover on their own, primarily because their focus typically is on substance abusers seeking treatment. Some, and perhaps many, adolescents with substance use problems also may recover without formal intervention (Fillmore, 1988; Wagner *et al.*, 1999). Longitudinal studies suggest that a portion of adolescents mature out of hazardous alcohol use and resultant problems as they transition into adulthood (e.g., Bates and Labouvie, 1994; Donovan and Jessor, 1985; Newcomb and Bentler, 1988), though only recently have studies examined the process of this self-change or natural recovery from alcohol problems among youth (Smart and Stoduto, 1997; Wagner *et al.*, 1999). In a review of the past decade of adolescent substance abuse research, Weinberg and colleagues (1998) noted the relative absence of research examining the natural course of substance use disorders among non-clinical samples. Sobell and colleagues (2000) recently published an exhaustive review of the empirical literature on natural recovery that included 38 studies with data from 40 samples. The mean age of participants across studies was 40.5 years, with a range of 19 to 58.2 years, and none of the studies focused on or included adolescent samples. This speaks to the paucity of research on adolescent natural recovery processes.

Very recently, Brown has begun to study alternative (i.e., non-treatment) routes to recovery among adolescents with substance use problems (Brown, 2001; Wagner *et al.*, 1999). Her latest studies suggest that significant proportions of high school students (i.e., approximately 25% of drinkers) make purposeful attempts to cut down or stop their drinking, and a substantial proportion of high-risk youth who experience alcohol problems resolve their problems without formal treatment. Understanding the strategies that adolescents employ in their natural environment to resolve their own alcohol problems can facilitate our understanding of the process of self-change, potentially enhance the effectiveness of all intervention efforts, and allow treatment to reach portions of the adolescent population that do not currently seek treatment (Brown and D'Amico, in press; Sobell *et al.*, 1996; Watson and Sher, 1998).

Brown and colleagues, as reported in Wagner *et al.* (1999), conducted a series of alcohol and drug surveys with 1,388 students that included questions regarding self-change efforts and found 15% of the total sample (25% of current drinkers) reported that they had made personal attempts to cut down or stop their alcohol use. Of these, 69% reported one or two attempts to cut down or stop, and 15% reported five or more specific attempts. Additionally, comparable portions of the total sample (16–18%) reported efforts to reduce or stop use of nicotine and other drugs as well.

More recently, Brown (2001) replicated these findings in a second sample of over 620 high school students and found that 22% who drank in the last month reported attempts within the last year to limit or reduce their alcohol use, and 13% of the students reported a history of specific quit attempts. Similarly, efforts to limit or quit cigarette use (31%) and other drug use (27%) were reported. It is notable that rates are slightly higher among the 56% of the sample that report having been recently high from alcohol, with reduction and quit attempts reported by 26% to 16%, respectively.

In a prospective study, Brown (2001) examined whether teens that develop alcohol-related problems are able to resolve those problems without formal treatment. Over four years, 122 high-risk community adolescents with no initial history of alcohol abuse or problems were studied. Within the first four years of the study, 34.6% began drinking heavily and reported objective alcohol-related problems that were corroborated by family members. Of adolescents who progressed to problem drinking, 69% subsequently had at least a one-year period of no heavy drinking or alcohol or drug problems. Using a standard criterion for natural recovery (i.e., minimum of one-year abstinence or non-problematic use without formal treatment subsequent to problems), it appears that two-thirds of these high-risk community teens evidenced resolution of their alcohol problems without formal treatment.

To explore strategies typically employed by youth seeking to reduce or end their alcohol and drug involvement, Brown (2001) evaluated 30 adolescents in alcohol and drug treatment and 30 demographically matched high-risk youth from the community. Youth were asked what they found useful or helpful in their efforts to reduce or stop their alcohol or other drug involvement. Verbatim responses were content analysed to generate six types of personal change strategies: (1) Independent efforts; (2) Structured activities; (3) School/Work; (4) Friends; (5) Family; and (6) Twelve-Step/Support groups. Youth who developed alcohol problems then rated these strategies on a Helpfulness Scale from "not at all" to "extremely" for usefulness in their personal change efforts. The majority of respondents endorsed two or more strategies as moderately to extremely helpful. Independent efforts (i.e., will-power, self-control, forced myself) were rated as most helpful, and Twelve-Step/Support groups received the lowest rating, with 82% of the sample rating in the little or no help range. Structured activities (e.g., recreation, sports, hobbies, church, or volunteer work) obtained the second highest mean rating. The remaining categories of School/Work, Friends, and Family received moderate levels of endorsement. Intercorrelations of helpfulness ratings were examined to evaluate potential patterns of efforts. Significant correlations were obtained between Family, Friends, and Support Groups, and between Independent efforts and School/Work. Thus, the majority of adolescents with former problems found multiple strategies useful in their reduction/cessation efforts.

In another study, personal change efforts were evaluated for 167 adolescents that received inpatient treatment for alcohol and drug problems (Brown, 2001). Using the Helpfulness Ratings Scale, ratings for Old friends and New friends were separated and a write-in option was added to identify new strategies. Youth were classified as Positive Outcome (PO; 35%) if they abstained one year following treatment, or had fewer than 30 use days with no more than two consecutive days of use per episode, no binge drinking (five drinks per setting), and no identifiable problems (e.g., arrests, missed school or work) resulting from substance use during the post-treatment period. Youth using alcohol or other drugs more frequently or with problems were classified Negative Outcome (NO; 65%). Four different types of personal change efforts were found to be very helpful: Independent/Personal efforts, Family, New friends, and Structured activities. Old friends and Twelve-Step/Support groups were rated as much less helpful. Both groups evaluated Old friends (Pretreatment) as only marginally helpful. Additionally, 8% identified an additional mechanism as helpful (e.g., counsellor).

Finally, Stice and colleagues (1998) completed analyses of 600 high school students who completed two surveys spanning the academic year. Using theoretically determined predictors, groups of students who increased their alcohol use (non-use to use; moderate use to heavy use), maintained stable alcohol use patterns (non-use, moderate use, heavy use), or decreased their drinking (moderate use to abstention, heavy use to moderate use) were compared. Findings indicated that a change in peer group/peer use (e.g., activities, fostering new friendships) predicated a change from heavy use to moderate use, and parent engagement (increased parental control) predicted reductions from moderate use to abstinence.

In sum, substantial portions of adolescents in high school make personal attempts to reduce or stop their substance involvement. The majority of adolescents find multiple strategies useful in their reduction/cessation efforts, with Independent/Personal efforts, Family, New friends, and Structured activities rated as most helpful by youth. The same strategies identified by community adolescents as helpful in their efforts to make self-changes appear relevant to adolescents with severe alcohol problems who are attempting to maintain abstinence following treatment for such problems. Factors related to change in peer group/peer use and parental involvement (e.g., parent/family discussions about alcohol use) may be useful components of intervention. To the extent that these strategies are perceived as helpful by youth, secondary interventions including the diversity of strategies youth normally use may increase the likelihood of youth engagement in treatment and subsequent utilization of the strategies peers use to successfully change their drinking.

CONCLUSIONS AND FUTURE DIRECTIONS

Due to the heterogeneous nature of adolescent substance abuse, there is wide variation in course and outcome. This chapter reviewed the three main types of studies relevant to understanding course, outcome, and associated factors: treatment, community, and natural recovery studies. Individual differences, factors associated with positive outcome, social/environmental characteristics, strategies adolescents employ, and the process of self-change also were discussed. While the research base is growing, much more remains to be learned about the course and outcome of adolescents with substance use problems.

What we do know is that the majority of adolescents relapse to substance use within one year of treatment, though many demonstrate clinically significant improvement in functioning despite some occasional use. Not surprisingly, the post-treatment environment seems to play a large role in how adolescents respond to treatment, in some cases as a risk factor and in other cases as a protective factor. Generally speaking, adolescents with substance use problems demonstrate poorer functioning in a number of areas of psychosocial adjustment than adolescents without substance use problems. One area that is particularly notable is comorbid psychopathology, especially because it appears to have a significant negative impact on long-term course and outcome. Regarding self-change, it appears that many adolescents are able to reduce or end their substance use involvement on their own, using strategies including self-determined effort, positive social influences, and non-drug involved structured activities.

Currently, the clinical demand for adolescent substance abuse intervention is overwhelming and has outpaced empirical research on a variety of important issues including the course and outcome of adolescents with substance use problems. In order to enhance the effectiveness of adolescent substance abuse intervention efforts and allow programmes to reach portions of the teen population that do not currently seek treatment, more developmentally and contextually sensitive research on course and outcome is needed. First, it is particularly important to investigate the prognostic indicators of longer-term course among both treated and non-treated adolescent substance abusers, particularly as they transition into young adulthood, which is the highest risk period for alcohol and drug abuse. Second, long-term outcomes for adolescents that experience alcohol- and drug-related problems severe enough to merit treatment by age 12 or 13 need to be examined, as they may be quite different from individuals whose first alcohol- or drug-related problems appear later in adolescence. Third, individual patterns of course and outcome among adolescents with initially similar substance use problems should be investigated further. Stated differently, we know there are many paths that lead to adolescent substance abuse; there also may be many paths that lead away from adolescent substance abuse. Finally, possible racial/ethnic and gender differences in teen substance abuse course and outcome need to be explored. Epidemiological studies have indicated significant variation by race/ethnicity and by gender in the prevalence of and risk factors for alcohol and other drug use problems among adolescents (Vega and Gil, 1998); similar variation by race/ethnicity and by gender may exist in the course and outcome of substance use problems among teenagers. In conclusion, we believe strongly that intervention efforts can and will be improved as we gain additional knowledge in these and other areas related to adolescent substance abuse course and outcome.

REFERENCES

Aas, H. N., Leigh, B. C., Anderssen, N., & Jakobsen, R. (1998). Two-year longitudinal study of alcohol expectancies and drinking among Norwegian adolescents. *Addiction, 93*, 373–384.

Ary, D. V., Duncan, T. E., Duncan, S. C., & Hops, H. (1999). Adolescent problem behavior: The influence of parents and peers. *Behavior Research & Therapy, 37*, 217–230.

Aseltine, R. H., Gore, S., & Colten, M. E. (1998). The co-occurrence of depression and substance abuse in late adolescence. *Developmental Psychopathology, 10*, 549–570.

Aytaclar, S., Tarter, R. E., Kirisci, L. & Lu, S. (1999). Association between hyperactivity and executive cognitive functioning in childhood and substance use in early adolescence. *Journal of the American Academy of Child and Adolescent Psychiatry, 38*, 172–178.

Barnes, G. M. & Welte, J. W. (1986). Patterns and predictors of alcohol use among 7–12th grade students in New York State. *Journal of Studies on Alcohol, 47*, 53–62.

Bates, M. E. & Labouvie, E. W. (1994). Familial alcoholism and personality–environment fit: A developmental study in risk in adolescents. *Annals of the New York Academy of Sciences, 708*, 202–213.

Baumrind, D. (1991). The influence of parenting style on adolescent competence and substance use. *Journal of Early Adolescence, 11*, 56–95.

Benson, G. (1985). Course and outcome of drug abuse and medical and social conditions in selected young drug abusers. *Acta Psychiatrica Scandinavica, 71*, 48–66.

Biafora, F. A., Warheit, G. J., Vega, W. A., & Gil, A. G. (1994). Stressful life events and changes in substance use among a multi-racial/ethnic sample of adolescent boys. *Journal of Community Psychology, 22*, 296–311.

Billings, A. G. & Moos, R. H. (1983). Psychosocial processes of recovery among alcoholics and their families: Implications for clinicians and program evaluators. *Addictive Behaviors, 8*, 205–218.

Boyle, M. H. & Offord, D. R. (1991). Psychiatric disorder and substance use in adolescence. *Canadian Journal of Psychiatry, 36*, 699–705.

Brook, J. S., Cohen, P., & Brook, D. W. (1998). Longitudinal study of co-occurring psychiatric disorders and substance use. *Journal of the American Academy of Child and Adolescent Psychiatry, 37*, 322–330.

Brook, J. S., Whiteman, M., Gordon, A. S., & Brook, D. W. (1983). Fathers and sons: Their relationship with personality characteristics associated with the son's smoking behavior. *Journal of Genetic Psychology, 156*, 393–410.

Brown, S. A. (1985). Context of drinking and reinforcement from alcohol: Alcoholic patterns. *Addictive Behaviors, 10*, 191–195.

Brown, S. A. (1989). Life events of adolescents in relation to personal and parental substance abuse. *American Journal of Psychiatry, 146*, 484–489.

Brown, S. A. (1993). Recovery patterns in adolescent substance abuse. In J. S. Baer, G. A. Marlatt, & R. J. McMahon (Eds.), *Addictive behaviors across the life span: Prevention, treatment, and policy issues* (pp. 161–183). Newbury Park, CA: Sage.

Brown, S. A. (2001). Facilitating change for adolescent alcohol problems: A multiple options approach. In E. F. Wagner & H. B. Waldron (Eds.), *Innovations in adolescent substance abuse intervention.* Oxford, UK: Elsevier Science.

Brown, S. A., Christiansen, B. A., & Goldman, M. S. (1987). The Alcohol Expectancy Questionnaire: An instrument for the assessment of adolescent and adult alcohol expectancies. *Journal of Studies on Alcohol, 48,* 483–491.

Brown, S. A., Cleghorn, A., Schuckit, M. A., Myers, M. G., & Mott, M. A. (1996). Conduct disorder among adolescent alcohol and drug misusers. *Journal of Studies on Alcohol, 57,* 314–324.

Brown, S. A. & D'Amico, E. J. (in press). Outcomes for alcohol treatment for adolescents. In M. Gallanter (Ed.), *Recent developments in alcoholism: Services research in the era of managed care.* New York, NY: Plenum Press.

Brown, S. A., Goldman, M. S., Inn, A., & Anderson, L. R. (1980). Expectancies of reinforcement from alcohol: Their domain and relation to drinking patterns. *Journal of Consulting and Clinical Psychology, 48,* 419–426.

Brown, S. B., Mott, M. A., & Myers, M. G. (1990). Adolescent alcohol and drug treatment outcome. In R. R. Watson (Ed.), *Drug and alcohol abuse prevention* (pp. 373–403). Totowa, NJ: Humana Press.

Brown, S. A., Mott, M. A., & Stewart, M. A. (1992). Adolescent alcohol and drug abuse. In C. E. Walker & M. C. Roberts (Eds.), *Handbook of clinical child psychology,* 2nd edn (pp. 677–693). New York, NY: John Wiley.

Brown, S. B., Vik, P. W., & Creamer, V. A. (1989). Characteristics of relapse following adolescent substance treatment. *Addictive Behaviors, 14,* 291–300.

Bruns, C. & Geist, C. S. (1984). Stressful life events and drug use among adolescents. *Journal of Human Stress, 9,* 135–139.

Bukstein, O. (1995). *Adolescent Substance Abuse.* New York, NY: John Wiley.

Byram, O. & Fly, J. (1984). Family structure, race and adolescent drug use: A research note. *American Journal of Alcohol Abuse, 10,* 467–478.

Cady, M. E., Winters, K. C., Jordan, D. A., Solberg, K. B., & Stinchfield, R. D. (1996). Motivation to change as a predictor of treatment outcome for adolescent substance abusers. *Journal of Child and Adolescent Substance Abuse, 5,* 73–91.

Catalano, R. F., Hawkins, J. D., Wells, E. A., Miller, J., & Brewer, D. (1990). Evaluation of the effectiveness of adolescent drug abuse treatment, assessment of risks for relapse, and promising approaches for relapse prevention. *International Journal of the Addictions, 25,* 1085–1140.

Chassin, L. A., Presson, C. C., & Sherman, S. J. (1985). Stepping backward in order to step forward: An acquisition-oriented approach to primary prevention. *Journal of Consulting and Clinical Psychology, 53,* 612–622.

Chatlos, J. C. (1996). Recent trends and a developmental approach to substance abuse in adolescents. *Child and Adolescent Psychiatric Clinics of North America, 5,* 1–27.

Christiansen, B. A., Smith, G. T., Roehling, P. V., & Goldman, M. (1989). Using alcohol expectancies to predict adolescent drinking behaviour after one year. *Journal of Consulting and Clinical Psychology, 57,* 93–99.

Clark, D. B. (1994). Trauma and alcohol abuse in adolescents (abstract). *Alcoholism: Clinical and Experimental Research, 18,* 507.

Clark, D. B. & Neighbors, B. (1996). Adolescent substance abuse and internalizing disorders. *Child and Adolescent Psychiatric Clinics of North America, 5,* 45–57.

Colder, C. R., Chassin, L., Stice, E. M., & Curran, P. J. (1997). Alcohol expectancies as potential mediators of parent alcoholism effects on the development of adolescent heavy drinking. *Journal of Research on Adolescence, 7,* 349–374.

DeJong, R. & Henrich, G. (1980). Follow-up results of a behavior modification program for juvenile drug addicts. *Addictive Behaviors, 5,* 49–57.

De Leon, G. (1984, April). *Adolescent substance abusers in the therapeutic community: Treatment outcomes.* Paper presented at the Research Conference on Juvenile Offenders with Serious Alcohol, Drug Abuse, and Mental Health Problems.

Dembo, R., Burgos, W., Des Jarlais, D., & Schmeidler, J. (1979). Ethnicity and drug use among urban Junior High School Students. *International Journal of the Addictions, 14,* 557–568.

Dembo, R., Dertke, M., Borders, S., Washburn, M., & Schmeidler, J. (1988). The relationship between physical and sexual abuse and tobacco, alcohol, and illicit drug use among youths in a juvenile detention center. *The International Journal of the Addictions, 23,* 351–378.

Deykin, E. Y., Levy, J. C., & Wells, V. (1987). Adolescent depression, alcohol and drug abuse. *American Journal of Public Health, 77,* 178–182.

DiMilio, L. (1989). Psychiatric syndromes in adolescent substance abusers. *American Journal of Psychiatry, 146,* 1212–1214.

Donovan, J. & Jessor, R. (1985). Structure of problem behavior in adolescence and young adulthood. *Journal of Consulting and Clinical Psychology, 53,* 890–904.

Duncan, S. C., Duncan, T. E., Biglan, A., & Ary, D. (1998). Contributions of the social context to the development of adolescent substance use: A multivariate latent growth modeling approach. *Drug and Alcohol Dependence, 50,* 57–71.

Ellickson, P., Saner, H., & McGuigan, K. (1997). Profiles of violent youth: Substance use and other concurrent problems. *American Journal of Public Health, 87,* 985–991.

Elliott, D. S., Huizinga, D., & Ageton, S. S. (1985). *Explaining delinquency and drug use.* Beverly Hills, CA: Sage.

Famularo, R., Stone, K., & Popper, C. (1985). Preadolescent alcohol abuse and dependence. *Americal Journal of Psychiatry, 142,* 1212–1218.

Fawzy, F., Coombs, R., Simon, J., & Bownan-Terrell, M. (1987). Family composition, socioeconomic status, and adolescent substance use. *Addictive Behaviors, 12,* 79–83.

Fillmore, K. M. (1988). *Alcohol use across the life course: A critical review of 70 years of international longitudinal research.* Toronto, Ontario: Addiction Research Foundation.

Finkelhor, D. (1995). The victimization of children: A developmental perspective. *American Journal of Orthopsychiatry, 65,* 177–193.

Foxcroft, D. R. & Lowe, G. (1991). Adolescent drinking behavior and family socialization factors: A meta-analysis. *Journal of Adolescence, 14,* 255–273.

Free, M. D. (1991). Clarifying the relationship between the broken home and juvenile delinquency: A critique of the current literature. *Deviant Behavior, 12,* 109–167.

Friedman, A. & Glickman, N. (1986). Program characteristics for successful treatment of adolescent drug abuse. *Journal of Nervous and Mental Disease, 174,* 669–679.

Friedman, A., Glickman, N., & Morrisey, M. (1986). Prediction to successful treatment outcome by client characteristics and retention in treatment in adolescent

drug treatment programs: A large-scale cross validation study. *Journal of Drug Education, 16,* 149–165.
Freidman, A., Granick, S., & Kreisher, C. (1994). Motivation for adolescent drug abusers for help and treatment. *Journal of Child and Adolescent Substance Abuse, 3,* 69–88.
Galaif, E. R., Chou, C. P., Sussman, S., & Dent, C. W. (1998). Depression, suicidal ideation, and substance use among continuation high school students. *Journal of Youth and Adolescence, 27,* 275–299.
Garmenzy, N. (1985). Stress-resistant children: The search for protective factors. In J. E. Stevenson (Ed.), *Recent research in developmental psychopathology* (pp. 213–233). New York, NY: Pergamon Press.
Gil, A. G., Vega, W. A., & Biafora, F. (1998). Temporal influences of family structure and family risk factors on drug use initiation in a multiethnic sample of adolescent boys. *Journal of Youth and Adolescence, 27,* 373–393.
Gil, E. (1996). *Treating abused adolescents.* New York, NY: Guilford Press.
Greenbaum, P. E., Prange, M. E., Friedman, R. M., & Silver, S. E. (1991). Substance abuse prevalence and comorbidity with other psychiatric disorders among adolescents with severe emotional disorders. *Journal of the Academy of Child and Adolescent Psychiatry, 30,* 575–583.
Grube, J. W., Chen, M. J., Madden, P., & Morgan, M. (1995). Predicting adolescent drinking from alcohol expectancy values: A comparison of additive, interactive, and nonlinear models. *Journal of Applied Social Psychology, 25,* 839–857.
Hawke, J. M., Jainchill, N., & De Leon, G. (2000). The prevalence of sexual abuse and its impact on the onset of drug use among adolescents in therapeutic community drug treatment. *Journal of Child & Adolescent Substance Abuse, 9,* 35–49.
Hawkins, J. D., Catalano, R. F., & Miller, J. Y. (1992). Risk and protective factors for alcohol and other drug abuse problems in adolescence and early adulthood: Implications for substance abuse prevention. *Psychological Bulletin, 112,* 64–105.
Hawkins, J. D., Lishner, D. M., Jenson, J. M., & Catalano, R. F. (1987). Delinquents and drugs: What the evidence suggests about prevention and treatment programming. In B. S. Brown, A. R. Mills et al. (Eds.) *Youth at high risk for substance abuse* (pp. 81–131). Rockville, MD: National Institute on Drug Abuse.
Higgins, S. T., Budney, A. J., Bickel, W. K., & Badger, G. J. (1994). Participation of significant others in outpatient behavioral treatment predicts greater cocaine abstinence. *American Journal of Drug and Alcohol Abuse, 20,* 47–56.
Hill, K. G., White, H. R., Chung, I. J., Hawkins, J. D., & Catalano, R. F. (2000). Early adult outcomes of adolescent binge drinking: Person- and variable-centered analyses of binge drinking. *Alcoholism: Clinical and Experimental Research, 24,* 892–901.
Holsten, F. (1985). The female drug abuser: Has she a shorter way out? *Journal of Drug Issues, 15,* 383–392.
Hops, H., Tildesley, E., Lichtenstein, E., Ary, D., & Sherman, L. (1990). Parent–adolescent problem-solving interactions and drug use. *American Journal of Drug and Alcohol Abuse, 16,* 239–258.
Hussong, A. M. & Chassin, L. (1994). The stress-negative affect model of adolescent alcohol use: Disaggregating negative affect. *Journal of Studies on Alcohol, 55,* 707–718.
Joshi, N. P. & Scott, M. (1988). Drug use, depression and adolescents. *The Pediatric Clinics of North America, 35,* 1349–1364.

Kaminer, Y., Tarter, R. E., Bukstein, O. G., & Kabene, M. (1992). Comparison between treatment completers and noncompleters among dually-diagnosed substance-abusing adolescents. *Journal of the American Academy of Child and Adolescent Psychiatry, 31,* 1046–1049.

Kandel, D. B. (1980). Developmental stages in adolescent drug involvement. In D. J. Letteri, M. Sayers, & H. W. Pearson (Eds.), *Theories on drug abuse: Selected contemporary perspectives* (pp. 120–127). Rockville, MD: National Institute on Drug Abuse.

Kandel, D. B., Johnson, J. G., Bird, H. R., Weissman, M. M., Goodman, S. H., Lahey, B. B., Regier, D. A., & Schwab-Stone, M. E. (1999). Psychiatric comorbidity among adolescents with substance use disorders: Finding from the MECA study. *Journal of the American Academy of Child and Adolescent Psychiatry, 38,* 693–699.

Kaplan, H. B., Martin, S. S., & Robbins, C. (1982). Application of a general theory of deviant behavior: Self derogation and adolescent drug use. *Journal of Health and Social Behavior, 23,* 274–294.

Kashani, J. H., Keller, M. B., Solomon, N., Reid, J. C., & Mazzola, D. (1985). Double depression in adolescent substance abusers. *Journal of Affective Disorders, 8,* 153–157.

Kazdin, A. E. (1995). Scope of child and adolescent psychotherapy research: Limited sampling of dysfunctions, treatments, and client characteristics. *Journal of Clinical Child Psychology, 24,* 125–140.

Kennedy, B. P. & Minami, M. (1993). The Beech Hill Hospital/Outward Bound Adolescent Chemical Dependency Program. *Journal of Substance Abuse Treatment, 10,* 395–406.

Kessler, R. C., Crum, R. M., Warner, L. A., Nelson, C. B., Schulenberg, J., & Anthony, J. C. (1997). Lifetime co-occurrence of DSM-II-R abuse and dependence with other psychiatric disorders in the National Comorbidity Survey. *Archives of General Psychiatry, 54,* 313–321.

Kessler, R. C., Nelson, C. B., McGonagle, K. A., Edlund, M. J., Fraak, R. G., & Leaf, J. P. (1996). The epidemiology of co-occurring mental disorders and substance use disorders in the National Comorbidity Survey: Implications for service utilization. *American Journal of Orthopsychiatry, 66,* 17–31.

Labouvie, E. W. (1990). Personality and alcohol and marijuana use: Patterns of convergence in young adulthood. *International Journal of the Addictions, 25,* 237–252.

Latimer, W. W., Newcomb, M., Winters, K. C., & Stinchfield, R. D. (2000a). Adolescent substance abuse treatment outcome: The role of substance abuse problem severity, psychosocial and treatment factors. *Journal of Consulting and Clinical Psychology, 68,* 684–696.

Latimer, W. W., Winters, K. C., Stinchfield, R., & Traver, R. E. (2000b). Demographic, individual, and interpersonal predictors of adolescent alcohol and marijuana use following treatment. *Psychology of Addictive Behaviors, 14,* 162–173.

Laurent, J., Catanzaro, S. J., & Callan, M. K. (1997). Stress, alcohol-related expectancies and coping preferences: A replication with adolescents of the Cooper *et al.* (1992) model. *Journal of Studies on Alcohol, 58,* 644–651.

Lewinsohn, P. M., Clarke, G. N., Seeley, J. R., & Rohde, P. (1994). Major depression in community adolescents: Age at onset, episode duration, and time to recurrence. *Journal of the American Academy of Child and Adolescent Psychiatry, 33,* 809–818.

Lewinsohn, P. M., Hops, H., Roberts, R. E., Seeley, J. R., & Andrews, J. A. (1993).

Adolescent psychopathology, I: Prevalence and incidence of depression and other DSM-III-R disorders in high school students. *Journal of Abnormal Psychology, 102*, 133–144.

Longabaugh, R., Beattie, M., Noel, N., & Stout, R. (1993). The effect of social investment on treatment outcome. *Journal of Studies on Alcohol, 54*, 465–478.

Madianos, M. G., Gefou-Madianou, D., & Stefanis, C. N. (1994). Symptoms of depression, sucidal behaviour and use of substances in Greece: A nationwide general population survey. *Acta Psychiatrica Scandinavica, 89*, 159–166.

Maggs, J.L. (1997). Alcohol use and binge drinking as goal-directed action during the transition to postsecondary education. In J. Schulenberg & J. L. Maggs (Eds.), *Health risks and developmental transitions during adolescence* (pp. 345–371). New York, NY: Cambridge University Press.

Maisto, S. A., Pollock, N. K., Lynch, K. G., Martin, C. S., & Ammerman, R. (2001). Course of functioning in adolescents 1 year after alcohol and other drug treatment. *Psychology of Addictive Behaviors, 15*, 68–76.

Marlatt, G. A. (1987). Alcohol, the magic elixir: Stress, expectancy, and the transformation of emotional states. In E. Gottheil & K. A. Druley (Eds.), *Stress and addiction* (Brunner/Mazel Psychosocial Stress Series, No. 9, pp. 302–322). Philadelphia, PA: Brunner/Mazel.

Millin, R., Halikas, J. A., Meller, J. E., & Morse, C. (1991). Psychopathology among substance abusing juvenile offenders. *Journal of the American Academy of Child and Adolescent Psychiatry, 30*, 569–574.

Moos, R. H., Finney, J. W., & Gamble, W. (1982). The process of recovery from alcoholism: II. Comparing spouses of alcoholic patients and matched community controls. *Journal of Studies on Alcohol, 43*, 888–909.

Myers, M. G., Brown, S. A., & Mott, M. A. (1993). Coping as a predictor of adolescent substance abuse treatment outcome. *Journal of Substance Abuse, 5*, 15–29.

Narrow, W. E., Regier, D. A., Rae, D. S., & Manderscheid, R. W. (1993). Use of services by persons with mental and addictive disorders: Findings from the National Institute of Mental Health Epidemiologic Catchment Area Program. *Archives of General Psychiatry, 50*, 95–107.

Needle, R., Su, S., & Doherty, W. (1990). Divorce, remarriage, and adolescent substance use: A prospective longitudinal study. *Journal of Marriage and the Family, 52*, 157–169.

Newcomb, M. & Bentler, P. (1988). *Consequences of adolescent drug use: Impact on the lives of young adults*. Newbury Park, CA: Sage.

Newcomb, M. D. & Harlow, L. L. (1986). Life events and substance use among adolescents: Mediating effects of perceived loss of control and meaninglessness in life. *Journal of Personality and Social Psychology, 51*, 564–577.

Orvaschel, H., Lewinsohn, P. M., & Seeley, J. R. (1995). Continuity of psychopathology in a community sample of adolescents. *Journal of the Academy of Child and Adolescent Psychiatry, 34*, 1525–1535.

Pandina, R. J. & Johnson, V. (1990). Serious alcohol and drug problems among adolescents with a family history of alcoholism. *Journal of Studies on Alcohol, 51*, 278–282.

Paternoster, R. (1989). Absolute and restrictive deterrence in a panel of youth: Explaining the onset, persistence/desistence, and frequency of delinquent offenders. *Social Problems, 36*, 289–309.

Petraitis, J., Flay, B. R., & Miller, T. Q. (1995). Reviewing theories of adolescent substance use: Organizing pieces of the puzzle. *Psychological Bulletin, 117*, 67–86.

Rao, U., Ryan, N. D., Dahl, R. E., Birmaher, B., Roa, R., Williamson, D. E., & Perel, J.M. (1999). Factors associated with the development of substance use disorder in depressed adolescents. *Journal of the American Academy of Child and Adolescent Psychiatry, 38*, 1109–1117.

Ravndal, E. & Vaglum, P. (1994). Self-reported depression as a predictor of dropout in a hierarchical therapeutic community. *Journal of Substance Abuse Treatment, 11*, 471–479.

Richter, S. S., Brown, S. A., & Mott, M. A. (1991). The impact of social support and self-esteem on adolescent substance abuse treatment outcome. *Journal of Substance Abuse, 3*, 371-385.

Rohde, P., Lewinsohn, P. M., & Seeley, J. R. (1996). Psychiatric comorbidity with problematic alcohol use in high school students. *Journal of the American Academy of Child and Adolescent Psychiatry, 35*, 101–109.

Rotheram-Borus, M. J., Mahler, K. A., Koopman, C., & Langabeer, K. (1996). Sexual abuse history and associated multiple risk behavior in adolescent runaways. *American Journal of Orthopsychiatry, 66*, 390–400.

Rush, T. V. (1979). Predicting treatment outcomes for juvenile and young adult clients in the Pennsylvania substance-abuse-system. In G.M. Beschner & A.S. Friedman (Eds.), *Youth drug abuse: Problems, issues, and treatment* (pp. 629–656.). Lexington, MA: Lexington Books.

Rutter, M. (1989). Pathways from childhood to adult life. *Journal of Child Psychology and Psychiatry, 30*, 23–51.

Rutter, M. & Maughan, B. (1997). Psychosocial adversities in childhood and adult psychopathology. *Journal of Personality Disorders, 11*, 4–18.

Scheier, L. M., Botvin, G. J., Diaz, T., & Ifill-Williams, M. (1997). Ethnic identity as a moderator of psychosocial risk and adolescent alcohol and marijuana use: Concurrent and longitudinal analyses. *Journal of Child & Adolescent Substance Abuse, 6*, 21–47.

Shedler, J. & Block, J. (1990). Adolescent drug use and psychological health. *American Psychologist, 45*, 612–620.

Shoemaker, R. H. & Sherry, P. (1991). Posttreatment factors influencing of adolescent chemical dependency treatment. *Journal of Adolescent Chemical Dependency, 2*, 89–106.

Silbereisen, R. K. & Noack, P. (1988). On the constructive role of problem behavior in adolescence. In N. Bolger & A. Caspi (Ed.), *Persons in context: Developmental processes. Human development in cultural and historical contexts* (pp. 152–180). New York, NY: Cambridge University Press.

Smart, R. G. & Stoduto, G. (1997). Treatment experiences and need for treatment among students with serious alcohol and drug problems. *Journal of Child and Adolescent Substance Abuse, 7*, 63–72.

Sobell, L. C., Cunningham, J. C., Sobell, M. B., Agrawal, S., Gavin, D. R., Leo. G. I., & Singh, K. N. (1996). Fostering self-change among problem drinkers: A proactive community intervention. *Addictive Behaviours, 21*, 817–833.

Sobell, L. C., Eillingstad, T. P., & Sobell, M. B. (2000). Natural recovery from alcohol and drug problems: Methodological review of the research with suggestions for future directions. *Addiction, 95*, 749–764.

Southwick, L. L., Steele, C. M., Marlatt, G. A., & Lindell, M. K. (1981). Alcohol-related expectancies: Defined by phase of intoxication and drinking experience. *Journal of Consulting and Clinical Psychology, 49,* 713–721.
Spooner, C. (1999). Causes and correlates of adolescent drug abuse and implication for treatment. *Drug and Alcohol Review, 18,* 453–475.
Steinberg, L. & Levine, A. (1990). *You and your adolescent: A parent's guide for ages 10 to 20.* New York, NY: Harper & Row.
Stern, M., Northman, J., & Van Slyck, M. (1984). Father absent and adolescent "problem behavior": Alcohol consumption, drug use, and sexual activity. *Adolescence, 19,* 301–312.
Stice, E., Myers, M. G., & Brown, S.A. (1998). A longitudinal grouping analysis of adolescent substance use escalation and de-escalation. *Psychology of Addictive Behaviors, 1,* 12–27.
Turner, R. J. & Wheaton, B. (1994). Checklist measures of stressful life events. In L. Gordon, S. Cohen, & R. Kessler (Eds.), *Measuring stress: A guide for health and social scientists* (pp. 29–58). Oxford, UK: Oxford University Press.
Van Hasselt, V. B., Null, J. A., Kempton, T., & Bukstein, O. (1993). Social skills and depression in adolescent substance abusers. *Addictive Behaviors, 18,* 9–18.
Vega, W. A. & Gil, A. G. (1998). *Drug use and ethnicity in early adolescence.* New York, NY: Plenum Press.
Vega, W. A., Zimmerman, R. S., Gil, A. G., Warheit, G. J., & Apospori, E. (1993). Acculturation strain theory: Its application in explaining drug use behavior among Cuban and other Hispanic youth. In M. R. De La Rosa, and J. R. Adrados (Eds.), *Drug abuse among minority youth: Advances in research and methodology.* Rockville, MD: National Institute on Drug Abuse.
Vik, P. W., Grizzle, K. L., & Brown, S. A. (1992). Social resource characteristics and adolescent substance abuse relapse. *Journal of Adolescent Chemical Dependency, 2,* 59–74.
Wagner, E. F. (1996). Substance use and violent behavior in adolescence. *Aggression and Violent Behavior: A Review Journal, 1,* 375–387.
Wagner, E. F., Brown, S. A., Monti, P. M., Myers, H. G., & Waldron, H. B. (1999). Innovations in adolescent substance abuse intervention. *Alcoholism: Clinical and Experimental Research, 23,* 236–249.
Wagner, E. F. & Waldron, H. B. (2001). *Innovations in adolescent substance abuse intervention.* Oxford, UK: Elsevier Science.
Watson, A. L. & Sher, K. J. (1998). Resolution of alcohol problems without treatment: Methodological issues and future directions of natural recovery research. *Clinical Psychology: Science & Practice, 5,* 1–18.
Weinberg, N. Z., Rahdert, E., Collver, J. D., & Glantz, M. D. (1998). Adolescent substance abuse: A review of the past 10 years. *Journal of the Academy of Child and Adolescent Psychiatry, 37,* 252–261.
West, M. O. & Prinz, R. (1987). Parental alcoholism and childhood psychopathology. *Psychological Bulletin, 102,* 204–218.
Westmeyer, J., Eames, S. I., & Nugent, S. (1998). Comorbid dysthymia and substance abuse disorder: Treatment history and cost. *American Journal of Psychiatry, 155,* 1556–1560.
White, H. R. (1987). Longitudinal stability and dimensional structure of problem drinking in adolescence. *Journal of Studies on Alcohol, 48,* 541–550.

White, H. R. (1992). Early problem behavior and later drug problems. *Journal of Research in Crime & Delinquency, 29*, 412–429.

Williams, R. J., Chang, S. Y., & Addiction Centre Adolescent Reasearch Group (2000). A comprehensive and comparative review of adolescent substance abuse treatment outcome. *Clinical Psychology: Science & Practice Summary, 7*, 138–166.

Windle, M. (2000). Parental, sibling, and peer influences on adolescent substance use and alcohol problems. *Applied Developmental Science, 4*, 98–110.

Windle, M. & Tubman, J. G. (1999). Children of alcoholics. In W. K. Silverman & T. Ollendick (Eds.), *Developmental issues in the clinical treatment of children* (pp. 393–414). Needham Heights, MA: Allyn & Bacon.

Winters, K. C., Stinchfield, R. D., Opland, E., Weller, C., & Latimer, W. W. (2000). The effectiveness of the Minnesota Model approach in the treatment of adolescent drug abusers. *Addiction, 95*, 601–612.

Wolpe, P. R., Gorton, G., Serota, R., & Sanford, B. (1995). Predicting compliance of dual diagnosis inpatients with aftercare treatment. *Hospital Community Psychiatry, 44*, 45–49.

Zeitlin, H. (2000). Drug use and young people: Why is co-morbidity research so important. *Addiction, 95*, 1619–1620.

Author note

The preparation of this chapter was supported by National Institute on Alcohol Abuse and Alcoholism Grant AA10246 to the first author.

Chapter 6

Prevention

Mark R. Dadds and John McAloon

Substance use disorders (SUDs) represent a most complex and critical problem, and affect almost every developed and developing country in the world (Bukstein, 2000; World Health Organization, 1990). The purpose of the current discussion is to discuss and evaluate attempts to prevent the development of SUDs. This topic needs to be interpreted broadly. Prevention can refer to attempts to reduce the incidence of SUDs, their harm to the individual, and the impact they have on society more broadly through their association with violence, illness, and loss of productivity.

In this chapter, both direct strategies and indirect strategies will be reviewed. The former refers to attempts to directly influence people's use and abuse of drugs via controlling the supply of, and demand for, drugs. The second places emphasis on the potential of prevention and early intervention programmes for the social competence and mental health problems in young people, to reduce the incidence of SUDs in our community. This analysis is important for several reasons. First, as suggested above, SUDs represent a substantial health and community problem. Second, the efficacy of traditional prevention strategies which focus on educating people about the dangers of substance use or offer resistance skills training is not convincingly demonstrated in the literature. Third, recent developmental psychopathological research has shown that reduction in SUDs can be achieved by reducing risk factors and increasing protective factors for mental health problems. Research suggests that there is increased risk for SUDs when externalizing disorders (conduct problems, delinquency, attention deficit problems), and internalizing disorders (anxiety and depression), or their risk factors exist in young people's lives. Developmental psychopathology offers an appropriate platform to understand the interplay of associated risk and protective.

THE DEVELOPMENTAL PSYCHOPATHOLOGY PERSPECTIVE

Developmental psychopathology offers a general conceptual framework for organizing the complexity of causal processes in the development of SUDs (Thompson, 2001). Of the principles that characterize the developmental approach, the most relevant to the present discussion is the idea that the development of any given psychological disorder occurs within the context of a developing organism. This perspective emphasizes that any given child or adolescent's behaviour, pathological or not, may only be adequately understood if considered in relation to the characteristics specific to their stage of development.

A second underlying tenant of the developmental perspective is an emphasis on multi-determinism (Cicchetti and Rogosh, 1999). Essentially, it is proposed that psychopathology occurs as the result of the interaction of multiple external and internal factors that occur over time. Causal factors may be mapped generally, as they occur in relation to each other across a range of children, or specifically, as they occur for any one child. While the range of factors that influence children may be similar, the outcomes for a range of children will be diverse. The interactions between such factors are therefore conceptualized as dynamic or transactional (Vasey and Dadds, 2001), and their effects are not seen as additive but rather cumulative, with each factor influencing and being influenced by others in turn.

Causal factors are conceptualized as either risk factors or protective factors (Thompson, 2001; Sroufe and Rutter, 1984). However, the terms risk and protective are themselves fluid, and the effect of any given factor depends as much on when in the developmental picture it occurs as it does on its relationship to any number of other given factors that are present or absent. It is suggested, for instance, that risk and protective factors may emanate from the same source, a parent–child relationship may be nurturing and therefore protective and at the same time over-protective and therefore represent a risk (Vasey and Dadds, 2001). Risk and protective factors may also be understood in terms of when in the developmental picture they occur. For instance, high levels of parental protectiveness may function as a protective factor in early childhood; for the adolescent increasingly seeking autonomy it may function as a risk factor. This situation would represent the developmentally contingent nature of both risk and protective factors.

Just as no single risk or protective factor encountered in development could possibly be said to account for normative development, two further concepts from a developmental perspective are applicable. In terms of outcome, both risk and protective factors may be expected to impact in a multitude of ways on a variety of individuals, depending on the relationship those factors have to all other factors impinging on the individual. This propensity for multiple outcomes is represented by the concept of "multifinality", where any factor may lead to diverse outcomes depending both on the relationship it bears to other factors operating in the developmental system, and on where in the course of development it occurs. In a similar fashion, the concept of "equifinality" accounts for the propensity for a range of different risk and/or protective factors to result in the same or similar outcomes depending on when and how it/they are introduced into the developmental systems (Vasey and Dadds, 2001). Finally, the developmental perspective proposes that it is essential to emphasize a broad-based range of intrinsic and contextual influences on both typical and atypical development (Thompson, 2001).

Epidemiological data on SUDs

Excellent data about the prevalence rates of both substance use and substance abuse disorders come from the Monitoring the Future Survey (MTF: Johnston *et al.*, 2000), and the National Comorbidity Survey (NCS: Kessler *et al.*, 1994). The MTF was first undertaken in 1975. With funding from the National Institute on Drug Abuse, and conducted by the University of Michigan's Institute for Social Research, the MTF survey originally set out to collect data on lifetime, past year, and past month drug use by students in the 12th grade. In 1991 the MTF survey included 8th and 10th graders in its sample and has since reported prevalence rates for lifetime, past year, and past month drug use for all three grade year groups by drawing on a nationally representative sample of both private and public secondary schools drawn from mainland United States (Johnston *et al.*, 2000).

The MTF data suggest that while substance use peaked in the late 1970s and early 1980s, and then proceeded to fall across the remainder of the 1980s, use is again generally increasing. The authors report that in 1975, 55% of American adolescents had used an illicit drug by the time they left high school (Johnston *et al.*, 2000). Additional evidence suggests that an estimated 25 million Americans were reported to be current users of illicit substances in 1979 (Substance Abuse and Mental Health Services Administration, 1999). In 1981, the number of American adolescents who had used an illicit drug by the time they left school had risen to 66%, a figure which declined significantly during the remainder of the 1980s. Forty-one per cent of American adolescents had used an illicit drug by the time they left school in 1992 (Johnston *et al.*, 2000). Prevalence rates began to increase again in the 1990s with 11.7 million Americans being described as current users of illicit substances in 1993 and 14.8 million or 5.3% being described as current users of illicit substances in 1999 (Substance Abuse and Mental Health Services Administration, 1999). Other prevalence statistics include some 80% of 12th grade American adolescents and 52% of 8th grade American adolescents having consumed alcohol at some point in their lifetime, and some 54% of American 12th grade adolescents and 27% of American 8th grade adolescents having used illicit drugs at some point in their lifetime (Johnston *et al.*, 2000).

Another important aspect of the MTF survey is that it offers insights into both changes in patterns of substance use among American adolescents over time, and some, albeit limited, insight into patterns of misuse of substances by American adolescents. For instance, the data suggest that while the lifetime use of alcohol by 12th grade adolescents peaked in 1991 at 88%, it has remained relatively consistent over the mid- and late-1990s at around 80%. Similar lifetime patterns of alcohol use are evident for both 8th and 10th grade adolescents, with high points in 1991 of 70.1% for 8th graders and 83.8% for 10th graders, followed by declines in use over the mid- and late-1990s until 2000 when 51.7% of 8th graders and 71.4% of 10th graders reported some lifetime use (Johnston *et al.*, 2000).

Comparative trends in the use of substances may also be drawn from the MTF data. For instance, on the basis of their data, Johnston and colleagues determined that after two years of a general decline in prevalence, drug use among 8th, 10th, and 12th graders remained steady in 2000. This finding is supported by the levels of use of individual drugs. For instance, the use of marijuana has gradually declined over the second half of the 1990s. This pattern is in contrast to that of the so-called club drugs (MDMA—ecstasy) which have generally increased in prevalence over the same period, as have the use of heroin and steroids. However, inhalants, LSD and amphetamines have all generally declined in prevalence over the second half of the 1990s. These trends, it is hypothesized, illustrate the need to consider that the determinants associated with choice and use of any given drug or drugs are, at least in part, a function of those drugs themselves. Such a conclusion has important implications for the development of prevention strategies.

It is also interesting to note that no displacement effect appears evident between substances or groups of substances. The "club drugs" demonstrate patterns consistent with their currently fashionable status, patterns that are in contrast to cigarettes and inhalants which are both relatively less fashionable and, according to the MTF data, in decline in terms of use. Johnston and colleagues (2000) also note that no displacement effect appears evident between alcohol and marijuana. Rather, it appears that these two drugs have moved more in parallel over the course of the decade, contrary to popular wisdom that specifies an either/or relationship between them.

In addition to the importance of generating accurate information about levels of the use of substances, both in overall, individual, and comparative terms, it is also essential to generate accurate data which account for levels of problems associated with the consumption of those substances. The NCS (Kessler *et al.*, 1994) sought to generate data about the lifetime and 12-month prevalence of DSM-III-R psychiatric disorders. As such, the NCS represents one of the first assessments of a nationally representative sample that returned data pertinent to the prevalence of SUDs. In terms of overall population, the NCS reported that 35.4% of men and 17.9% of women develop abuse or dependence for any substance at some point in their lifetime. When these data are broken down they reveal, amongst other things, that 20.1% of men in the United States are alcohol-dependent, and 9.2% of men in the United States are drug-dependent. These figures are interesting when compared with the similar figures for women, for whom 8.2% are alcohol-dependent and 5.9% are drug-dependent (Kessler *et al.*, 1994). When further broken down, this time in terms of age, the data suggest that 9.1% of males and 5.6% of females between the ages of 15 and 24 display a lifetime prevalence of dependence on drugs other than alcohol (Hawkins *et al.*, 1997).

Risk and protective factors for SUDs

Consistent with the developmental psychopathology perspective (discussed above), it is possible to account for a range of factors that act to increase the risk for the development of SUDs, or act to protect against the development of SUDs. Different risk and protective factors will become evident at different times during any given individual's development, will (inter)act in a manner consistent with the notion of multi-determinism, and will be subject to the principles of multifinality and equifinality (Vasey and Dadds, 2001). It is also possible to classify risk and protective factors that influence later substance use as either contextual or individual-interpersonal (Hawkins *et al.*, 1992). This section will present the findings of research that has sought to identify risk factors that operate to influence the development of later substance use, thereby influencing the later development of SUDs.

Comprehensive discussion of SUD risk and protective factor research has been provided by a number of writers (Cicchetti and Rogosch, 1999; Hawkins *et al.*, 1992; Weinberg and Glantz, 1999). Risk and protective factors that operate with regard to SUDs may operate in more general or broad developmental terms, and equally, they may operate specifically in relation to the development of SUDs (Cicchetti and Rogosch, 1999). Contextual risk factors are generally those that operate within a societal context. As such they operate as a function of current laws and legislation, of current moral or societal norms, and as a function of current economic wellbeing. Individual-interpersonal risk factors pertain more to personal, interpersonal, and environmental characteristics. Table 6.1 presents a summary of the findings of risk factor research conducted with regard to SUDs. The content of this table is drawn from a variety of sources (Botvin, 1999; Bukstein, 2000; Cicchetti and Rogosch, 1999; Hawkins *et al.*, 1992; Hawkins *et al.*, 1997; Glantz and Hartel, 1999; Weinberg and Glantz, 1999).

Table 6.2 shows that many of the risk and protective factors for the development of SUDs are the same risk and protective factors for mental health problems and resiliency in young people. Thus, a common pathway to SUDs is through conduct problems and delinquency with their associated features

Table 6.1 Risk and protective factors in the development of SUDs

Contextual/societal factors	
	Risk factor
Laws and norms:	Decreased purchase cost
	Decreased drinking age
	No restrictions on sale
Availability	Increased availability
Extreme economic deprivation	Poverty (not social class)
Neighbourhood disorganization	High population density
	High residential mobility
	Physical deterioration
	Low levels of attachment to neighbourhood

Individual/interpersonal factors	
	Risk Factor
Physiological factors	Genetic risk for addictive behaviour
Psychological factors	Comorbidity with other psychological disorders (bipolar disorder, depression anxiety disorders, PTSD, conduct and antisocial problems)
	High sensation seeking; low harm avoidance
Family drug behaviour	Parental/sibling alcoholism
	Parental use of illicit drugs
	High drug salience in family
	Modelling by older brother
	Father's substance use and emotional stability
	Perceived parental permissiveness
Family management practices	Inconsistent child management practices
	Low parental education
	Low aspirations for child
	Parental nondirectiveness/permissiveness
	Negative communication patterns
	Inconsistent, unclear behaviour limits
	Unrealistic parental expectations
	Perceptions of father as hostile
	Parental interactions and psychological instability
Family environment	Marital discord
	High family conflict
	Low parent–child closeness
	Low maternal involvement
	Low family bonding
	Low family involvement and attachment
Academic	Intellectual ability
	Poor school performance
	Lack of commitment to school
	Failure in school
	Truancy
Peer	Low peer acceptance
	Early aggression
	Low inhibition
	Peer substance use
Onset of drug use	Early onset predicts level of use and range of substances

Table 6.2 Developmental risk factors for externalizing disorders and associated intervention opportunities

Developmental phase		Risk factors	Potential interventions
Prenatal infancy:	Child:	Environmental toxicity Temperamental difficulties	Environmental safety, e.g., lead minimization Early identification of children at risk through temperamental and behavioural problems, and families at high-risk through socioeconomic adversity and psychopathology
	Family:	Poverty/low SES/social isolation Family violence/conflict/separation Parental psychopathology Poor health/nutrition	Provision of adequate healthcare/parental and infant support programmes, home visiting programmes. Promotion of social equality/support/community connectedness. Provision of family support, education and therapy services, premarital and pre-parenting education programmes
	Social:	Economic hardship/unemployment Family breakdown/isolation Cultures of violence	Promotion of non-violent cultures and communities
Toddler – late childhood:	Child:	Learning and language difficulties Impulsivity	Early remediation of learning and language difficulties Provision of parent training and broader family interventions
	Family:	Coercive family processes/violence Low care and nurturance Inadequate monitoring of child	Family and marital support programmes After-school care and monitoring of children Peer social skills programmes
	Social:	Inadequate child care and parental support Lack of educational opportunities Negative parent–school relationship	Provision of positive school environments and educational opportunities Promotion of quality parent–school relationships
Adolescence:	Child:	School – employment failure Cognitive bias to threat/hostility Peer rejection/deviant peer group Substance abuse/depression	Cognitive behavioural skills programmes for teenagers Academic and work transition skills programmes Crisis support for family/youth individuation problems, breakdown and homelessness
	Family:	Conflict/individuation problems Rejection/homelessness	Family–adolescent therapy services Substance abuse prevention programmes
	Social:	Lack of education/employment Culture of violence	Cultures of community respect and connectedness

of social adversity, school failure, and family conflict and breakdown. Increasing evidence shows that there is a related but diverse pathway to SUDs associated with internalizing problems, that is, anxiety and depression, as well. Thus, patterns of comorbidity are critical to our understanding of developmental aspects of SUDs. Comorbidity can be defined as the co-occurrence of one or more disorders in the same child or adolescent either at the same time or in some causal sequence (Kessler, 1995; Ollendick and King, 1994). The issue of comorbidity has significant implications for the development of preventive interventions for a range of psychological disorders. This is particularly true of both childhood and adolescent internalizing disorders (IDs) and externalizing disorders (EDs), especially given the pervasive nature of comorbidity between these two disorders and SUDs (Ollendick et al., 1999; Glantz et al., 1999).

Data from clinical samples point to a high overlap between SUDs and IDs, independent of whether the referred problem is an SUD (Reiger et al., 1990) or ID (Bibb and Chambless, 1986) disorders. However, the frequency and nature of this comorbidity can be highly variable in SUD groups, ranging from acute IDs at referral that appear secondary to the SUD and quickly remit in treatment, leaving the "pure" SUD problem to run its course, to longstanding IDs that may underlie the SUD. Contamination by referral issues thus makes clinical studies unsuitable for obtaining community estimates of the comorbidity between SUDs and IDs and researchers must turn to epidemiological studies. Two of the most up-to-date and comprehensive of these were the ECA and NCS surveys in the US (see Kessler, 1995). These were consistent in showing that the lifetime comorbidity odds-ratio of having both an ID and SUD ranged from approximately 2.5 to 3.5. Thus, one has approximately three times the chance of suffering an SUD if one has an ID, and vice versa, compared to a disorder-free person. These odds-ratios are means collapsed across specific IDs and SUDs. They would be considerably higher if calculated according to the presence of any type of ID, and may be higher for social phobia and panic/depression in particular. There thus exists, depending on the nature of the causal links between them, an opportunity for joint preventive efforts. Possible linkages are discussed next.

Comorbidity is also common in EDs. Kazdin and colleagues (1992) found that 70% of youth aged 7 to 13 referred for conduct problems met criteria for more than one disorder, and the mean number of diagnoses per case was slightly over two. EDs have been demonstrated to be strongly and consistently associated with SUDs (Glantz et al., 1999). For instance, results from the National Comorbidity Survey (NCS) (Kessler et al., 1996) indicate that nearly 60% of those with a lifetime diagnosis of conduct disorder also had at least one lifetime diagnosis of an addictive disorder. The same study estimates that comorbidity between antisocial personality disorder and SUDs is even higher (83.6%), while accounts of the rates of comorbidity between attention deficit disorders (ADD) and SUDs is less clear, possibly due to the complex relationship between ADD and a range of conduct disorder cluster behaviours.

Recent research has shown that reduction in SUDs can be achieved by reducing risk factors and increasing general mental health and resiliency in young people. Such interventions typically focus on the pathway to SUDs through conduct problems and delinquency, and, more recently, on the pathway to SUDs associated with internalizing problems, that is, anxiety and depression. In the next section, attempts to prevent SUDs will be addressed: first, through direct approaches to modifying substance use, and then via indirect pathways that focus on their comorbidty with mental health problems and their shared risk and protective factors.

RECENT TRENDS IN THE PREVENTION OF SUDS

The marked and global increase in substance use which characterized the last four decades of the twentieth century, and which peaked in the late 1970s and early 1980s, was of sufficient proportion to result in declarations of war on drugs by policy makers, especially in the USA (Botvin, 1999). As a result, a number of efforts directed at prevention of the substance use and abuse were undertaken and, directly or indirectly, may be argued as having been responsible for the decline in substance use in the 1980s. However, given that the period of the 1990s saw a return to increased consumption of a range of substances, and an associated rise in SUDs, it may be argued that initial efforts directed at better understanding the etiology of SUDs, and at developing demonstrably effective strategies of prevention of SUDs, were not altogether successful.

Approaches that have been adopted to reduce substance use generally fall into two categories; those termed "supply reduction strategies", and those termed "demand reduction strategies". In addition, it is also pertinent to describe different models of prevention based on how the targeted population is selected. Traditional models of preventive intervention have drawn heavily from the public health classification model of disease prevention. Within this model, prevention is classified along a continuum of intensity (Mrazek and Haggerty, 1994; National Institute on Drug Abuse, 1997; Windle, 1999), and ranges from targeting the entire population to targeting individuals for whom intervention is considered to be of high priority.

Universal preventive intervention strategies target a broad a spectrum of the population. Within this strategy all groups within the population are considered to be at some degree of risk regardless of their group or individual degree of risk, and therefore capable of benefiting in some way from intervention. In contrast, selective preventive intervention strategies target people who demonstrate a greater degree of risk by virtue of social, physical, economic, or environmental characteristics than the community or society as a whole. Indicated preventive intervention strategies target individuals who have been identified as being at high risk for the development of some problem, for instance, an anxiety disorder or a substance use disorder, or individuals who are already exhibiting behaviours consistent with those disorders.

Supply reduction strategies

As the name suggests, supply reduction strategies seek to reduce the availability of substances thereby curtailing the potential for the development of SUDs. The most common strategies adopted to reduce the availability of illicit drugs include the use of law enforcement agencies to control the sale, supply or use of them, controlling their importation and traffic, and inhibiting their production or means of production. In terms of legalized substances, supply reduction strategies seek to control availability by placing restrictions on sale or supply, or limiting the availability of the substances by means of age restriction.

Numerous supply reduction strategies apply to the sale and supply of alcohol. For instance, age restrictions, restrictions on hours of sale, and restrictions on place, time, and amount of sale and consumption are common in the sale of alcohol. There is some evidence to suggest that the availability of alcohol directly affects levels of consumption (Gorsuch and Butler, 1976). For instance, some authors cite the co-occurrence of reductions in the incidence of cirrhosis of the liver (Cook and Touchen, 1982) and alcohol-related traffic fatalities (Saffer and Grossman, 1987) and increases in the controls exerted over alcohol as evidence in support of increasing restrictions to regulate supply, thereby reducing the potential for alcohol use disorders. It is interesting to note that increases in the levels of tax applied to alcohol seem more effective in reducing alcohol-related illness, injury and death than do placing restrictions on the age of the purchaser or amount that may be sold or consumed (Windle, 1999). It was demonstrated in one study that increasing the tax on alcohol by 1% led to a 0.5% reduction in consumption.

The supply of illicit drugs does not, however, seem to follow this trend. Funding directed at supply reduction strategies by the United States Congress rose from $1.5 billion in 1981 to $13.8 billion in 1996 (National Institute on Drug Abuse, 1997). However, neither the availability nor the price of illicit drugs seem to have been affected. Between 1986 and 1989, federal spending on supply reduction more than doubled. In the same period, the average price of purchase of a gram of cocaine decreased by 25% from $US100 per gram to $US75 per gram (Hawkins *et al.*, 1992). On the basis of the evidence available it seems that traditional supply reduction strategies are ineffectual in reducing demand for illicit substances, in raising the price of illicit substances, or in eliminating illicit substance abuse (Botvin, 1999; Bukstein, 1995; Hawkins *et al.*, 1992).

Demand reduction strategies

The second general class of prevention strategies are commonly centred on reducing the demand by any given population to indulge in substances that may result in SUDs. In their most recent and arguably most effective form, these include engaging risk and protective factors from the developmental psychological perspective. It is, however, first worth noting two other interesting and influential developments in the history of demand reduction strategies. The first sought to instil prevention by means conveying cultural, religious, and other societal norms. The social and cultural norms were generally religiously motivated, were disseminated in churches and schools, and were bound in appeals to religious belief, scripture, threats of eternal damnation, and other appeals to moral and civic righteousness (Bukstein, 1995). In more recent times, the moral was replaced with a desire to deliver potentially wayward citizens with prevention simply by means of instilling fear. A classic example of this attempt at fear can be found in the 1936 film *Reefer Madness*, a film that sought to document the madness that can befall even those who use illicit substances only occasionally. There is some evidence to suggest that the promotion of fear or negative attitudes toward substance use and users is effective. Black (1989, cited in Hawkins *et al.*, 1992) studied anti-drug saturation advertising and found increased negativity toward drugs, drug users, and drug-taking behaviour, and increases in communication on the subject of drugs as a result of the activity.

A second and more recent example of demand reduction strategies can be found in the range of school-based education programmes that operate on the assumption that social influences (i.e., peers, media) are instrumental in the development of substance use. The programmes therefore seek to teach adolescents skills that allow them to resist this pressure and avoid the onset of substance use (Hansen and Graham, 1991; Windle, 1999). Generally, the skills taught within school-based education programmes are resistance skills training, or social skills training. Social skills training credits a greater range of social influences as being instrumental in the development of substance use, and programmes generally seek to assist adolescents by enhancing a broad range of skills, both specific to substance use and more general social ability skills (for instance, Project DARE –Drug Abuse Resistance Programme). Resistance training programmes focus more on skills related to the identification and resistance of pressure to engage in substance use (for instance, "Just Say 'NO!'") (Norman and Turner, 1993; Windle, 1999).

Despite the large amount of research carried out into school-based intervention programmes, it is hard to draw clear conclusions regarding their efficacy. Evaluation of such programmes, it should be noted, is enormously difficult (Lorion and Ross, 1992); however, some general conclusions may be drawn. Programmes that simply teach refusal skills to adolescents, or that teach refusal skills with limited additional social skills training, rarely produce the desired effect (Ennett *et al.*, 1994; Hansen and Graham, 1991). Second, reduction in use as a result of programmes like project DARE tend to be short-lived suggesting the need for booster sessions (Windle, 1999). Finally the effects that are achieved in school-based education programmes tend to vary by substance (Johnston *et al.*, 2000; Windle, 1999), a finding which has implications for the idea of more general prevention of SUDs.

Prevention of SUDs via mental health programmes

Externalizing Disorders (EDs) is a generic term which collectively refers to a range of psychological disorders that are characterized by a cluster of problem behaviours which are generally outwardly directed, or have overt or external consequences or expression. Diagnostically, EDs include childhood and adolescent Oppositional Defiant Disorder (ODD), which is distinguished by hostile and defiant behaviour (American Psychological Association, 1994), Conduct Disorder (CD), which includes serious breaches of the basic rights of others or major age-appropriate societal norms or rules in addition to ODD features (American Psychological Association, 1994), and Attention Deficit-Hyperactivity Disorder (ADHD), which is characterized by persistent inattention and impulsivity (American Psychological Association, 1994). A range of other childhood and adolescent behavioural problems may also be included under the term EDs. Generally these refer to historical variations in terminology or diagnosis, or themselves contain other variants on the above. For example, EDs would also include antisocial behaviour, delinquency, aggressive behaviour, which are currently of more value descriptively than they are diagnostically.

Adhering to formal diagnostic categories (for instance, those cited in the DSM-IV) is beneficial in that it allows clinicians and researchers a common language and definitional system. On this basis, interpretations and generalizations may be made of clinical studies of children given these diagnoses. However, such definitions are problematic, especially for prevention science. Numerous children are referred for treatment of disruptive behaviour problems who do not meet formal diagnostic criteria. The cut-off point between those who attract a formal diagnosis and those whose behaviour problems are "sub-clinical" is largely arbitrary, and often inconsistent. Many studies have used broad samples of children referred for disruptive behaviour problems, or children selected from non-referred samples who are found to have disruptive behaviour problems on the basis of a screening measure. Only a subset of recent studies has used formally diagnosed children. A review limited to these latter studies would lose much of the richness of accumulated evidence about the characteristics of disruptive children.

EDs are the most common disorders referred to child mental health clinics and rates are much higher in boys than girls and in families and geographical areas marked by low socio-economic status (West, 1982).

Recent research has begun to map a clear developmental trajectory of EDs from birth to adulthood although, consistent with the tenants of developmental psychopathology, it is not possible to attribute the development of EDs to any one single causal factor. Rather, a range of risk factors interact from individual, family and social contexts to contribute to a range of possible outcomes. Low SES has been established as a marker for many possible risk factors including genetics, environmental toxicity, poor educational opportunities, poverty, social isolation, lack of employment, and modelling of violence (Dadds, 1996). Age of onset is also important in this regard given the evidence to suggest that early onset is associated with a poorer prognosis (Loeber, 1990) with regard to EDs in boys. Similarly, the extent to which problem behaviour is expressed across multiple settings (i.e. home, school, and community) is also a predictor of severity and durability of conduct problems (Kazdin, 1993; Loeber, 1990). Table 6.3 presents a summary of the findings of risk factor research conducted with regard to EDs (Dadds, 1996).

In comparison to the understanding which has already been gained on the developmental trajectories of EDs, relatively little is known about risk and protective factors associated with Internalizing Disorders (IDs) and the developmental trajectories of IDs in young people. IDs is a generic term which refers to a range of psychological disorders that are characterized by internal expression or consequence. Diagnostically, and for the purposes of the present discussion, IDs include childhood and adolescent anxieties and depressive disorders.

Despite the clinical and social salience of childhood externalizing problems, epidemiological studies using child reports indicate that anxiety disorders are the most common behavioural/emotional disorder through childhood and adolescence (Bernstein and Borchardt, 1991; Kashani and Orvaschel, 1990). A recent school-based recruitment study showed that anxiety problems exceeded externalizing problems in 7 to 14-year-olds using either self-report or teacher nomination measures (Dadds *et al.*, 1997). The modal onset of most anxiety disorders is in middle childhood to adolescence (panic and agoraphobic states generally begin later); however, recent research has confirmed that early temperamental characteristics can be identified in infancy that are predictive of later anxiety problems. Although many children appear to "grow out of" their anxiety problems, others maintain some anxiety diagnosis into adolescence or adulthood. Anxiety problems are more common in females irrespective of age. Generally, the prevalence of anxiety disorders is similar in children, adolescents, and adults, although their presentation may change with age (Costello and Angold, 1995, for review).

Prospective studies of DSM-IV defined anxiety or depressive disorders in

156　Substance Abuse and Dependence in Adolescence

Table 6.3 Developmental risk factors for anxiety disorders and associated intervention strategies

Developmental phase	Risk factors		Potential mechanisms of prevention
Infancy:	Child:	Shy temperament; behavioural inhibition	Early identification of high risk children and anxious parents
	Family:	Neglect or overprotection Parental psychopathology especially anxiety	Parental support and parent training to foster responsive parenting, secure attachment, and positive parental coping strategies
	Society:	Environmental stress	
Childhood:	Child:	Reticence/behavioural inhibition/shyness Social isolation	Social problem-solving training encouraging proactive solutions. Increasing focus on cognitive strategies as child matures. Exposure programmes to overcome fears.
	Family:	Parental psychopathology Overprotection of child in face of challenges, selective attention to threat, and avoidant solutions Parental overcontrol or criticism	Enhancement of social skills and opportunities for peer interaction Training parents to model effective cognitive and behavioural coping Positive parental strategies to manage child avoidance. Responsive parenting
	Society:	Social isolation, insularity	Family connections to school and community
Adolescence:	Child:	As above. Possibility of comorbid disorders, especially depression and substance use	As above. Cognitive-behavioural training with increasing focus on adolescent and related issues (depression, substance use)
	Parent:	As above	Increasing focus on issues of autonomy for family
	Society:	Peer pressure. Regarding comorbidity: Prevalence of substance use	Parental training in balancing autonomy and independence with family support

adolescents noted that most adult disorders were preceded by adolescent disorders (Pine *et al.*, 1998). Typically the evidence converges to show that anxious children are of higher risk for other affective disorders, especially depression (Beidel and Turner, 1997; Cole *et al.*, 1998). Interestingly, the reverse of childhood depression leading to later anxiety was not found. These research findings indicate that early childhood through to adolescence is perhaps the most promising time for the targeting of prevention programmes for anxiety problems and IDs in general.

The most salient factors emerging in the literature are temperamental predispositions to be shy and fearful of novel people, objects, or situations (behaviour inhibition or reticence), the existence of parental anxiety or depressive problems, and exposure to traumatic environmental events. Secure attachment, an easy temperament, and social skills stand out as ongoing protective mechanisms. From a public health perspective, many factors converge to influence the trajectory of anxiety disorders. Prevention could target any or all of these variables, leading to multifactorial models of programme development. However, a more parsimonious and ultimately efficacious perspective may highlight specific mechanisms associated with the onset and maintenance of IDs that switch in and out at various points in the life of the person. Models of prevention need to focus on such windows of opportunity.

PREVENTION OF SUDS VIA INTERNALIZING AND EXTERNALIZING DISORDERS

It is likely that alternative developmental pathways to SUDs exist both through IDs and EDs. In addition, it is likely that, given the survey of risk factor research already presented, that these pathways are in fact interweaving and represent a myriad of developmental trajectories (Greenberg *et al.*, 1999). Recent research has shown that anxiety and depression may feature in externalizing problems in young people far more significantly than has been traditionally acknowledged (Bukstein, 2000). Measures of attention deficit, for example, are highly confounded by the presence of anxiety problems (Perrin and Last, 1992), and internalizing problems can enhance externalizing problems through adolescence (Loeber *et al.*, 1994). Unfortunately, longitudinal studies that simultaneously consider early IDs and EDs problems as predictors of later SUDs are not available, and should be a research priority. It is possible, however, to review a number of preventive intervention strategies that have been developed and that have met with some success. In this manner, it may be possible to further demonstrate the potential for developing preventive strategies that address the development of SUDs by focusing on their comorbidity with IDs and/or EDs, and their shared risk factors.

From a developmental perspective, there are likely to be optimal times and optimal methods for taking preventive action for a range of disorders.

Considerable overlap exists in the risk factors that pertain to a range of psychological outcomes throughout development. Consistent with the principles of multifinality and equifinality (discussed above), numerous outcomes may be identified to result from the inclusion of any one risk factor throughout development. There is therefore considerable overlap in the risk factors that are implicit in the development of both IDs and EDs and substance use disorders. As multiple risk factors interact throughout development (Thompson, 2001), and as their interplay is both transactional and cumulative (Bukstein, 1995; Vasey and Dadds, 2001), the process of prevention may also be conceptualized within a developmental framework. Hawkins and colleagues (1997) suggest that there are five principles which might best guide preventive interventions undertaken from within the developmental perspective. These are the reduction of risk factors, the enhancement of protective factors, addressing these factors at a developmentally appropriate level, intervening before the behaviour appears or stabilizes, and addressing multiple risk factors with multiple strategies.

There is evidence to support the contention that interventions for both internalizing disorders and externalizing disorders, both of which share numerous risk factors, will act to reduce the prevalence of SUDs if directed at the appropriate windows of opportunity (Dadds, 2000).

Early childhood

If risk factors do operate in a cumulative fashion, early exposure to risk factors will increase the likelihood of continued exposure to additional risk factors, and the earlier interventions should have the greatest effect in altering developmental trajectories (Reid and Eddy, 1997). Evidence in support of such interventions comes from research that considered prevention within the context of a broader environment as opposed to a more discrete intervention. For instance, in an article which reviewed research into antisocial and delinquent behaviours, both were substantially reduced in a range of studies which sought to promote overall development and wellbeing of children (Zeigler *et al.*, 1992). It was suggested by the authors that the success of these preventive efforts was due to the fact that all the studies in question sought to improve family interactive behaviour, both internally and in a broader social context, thereby improving social competency in a range of social situations. The development of social competencies is listed as a protective factor for the development of internalizing disorders (Dadds, 2000), particularly anxiety disorders. In addition, the development of appropriate strategies to deal with family conflict as well as family attachment and family bonding have been identified as factors which act to protect against the development of SUDs (Hawkins *et al.*, 1992).

In the realm of family and temperament risk factors, infancy and early childhood are ideal points of prevention. Home visiting programmes focus on improving the capacity of at-risk parents to provide a nurturing healthy environment for their children in the early years of life. Parents are usually selected into such programmes via the neonatal health care systems on the basis of multiple risk factors such as poverty, teenage mother, low birth-weight child, and history of abuse. Models of intervention generally revolve around the formation of a trusting, empathic relationship with the home visitor (usually a nurse) hypothesized to promote parenting efficacy, and thus, an increase in healthy parenting behaviours and secure attachment with the infant. These programmes have been implemented throughout the world for many years. However, only recently have controlled designs been used to evaluate their effectiveness. The most comprehensive evaluation of such a programme has been reported by Olds and colleagues who now have data up to 15 years follow-up from their original intervention.

In the original trial, 400 women with either low income, single-parent status, unmarried, or teenage pregnancy were recruited during pregnancy and randomized to standard well-child infant care or two levels of home visiting by a trained nurse. In the most intense condition, the visiting continued until the child's second birthday. While a range of positive outcomes have been shown to be associated with the intensive visiting, perhaps the most impressive are the recent data showing reductions in delinquency, substance use, and numbers of sexual partners for the children at 15 years of age (Olds et al., 1998). Olds and Kitzman (1993) reviewed similar well-designed studies and concluded that there exists substantial evidence to support the effectiveness of these home visiting EI programmes in promoting a range of healthy outcomes for children at risk due to social disadvantage and sub-optimal parenting. Further, sufficient research has been reported in this area to allow for analyses of factors moderating intervention outcomes (e.g., Cole et al., 1998).

Given the effects attributable to interventions in most other EI research, however, it is difficult to understand how a non-specific, intervention in the first two years of life can lead to such powerful effects 15 years later. Replications and results from other communities are needed as most of the evidence supporting home visitations comes from the one study. A recent trial of a similar programme for at-risk mothers in Australia was also successful in producing immediate gains for mothers and infants (Armstrong et al., 1999); however, the results were not impressive in terms of differences from the control group at two-year follow-up (Fraser et al., 2000).

Nevertheless, these results are overall impressive. They are also consistent with the previous literature reviewed on EDs showing that the most impressive findings come from programmes that target children early in the first few years of life via parenting and family life seen with a broad ecological framework. Waiting till the school years, and especially adolescence, may be too late with regard to delinquency and violence.

The most common forms of internalizing problems are shyness, inhibition, and anxiety problems such as specific phobias and separation anxiety disorder. There is a vast literature showing that brief cognitive-behavioural treatments implemented through the parents are successful in reducing these problems (see Dadds et al., 1997, for review), and in a general developmental sense, these therefore offer potential as preventive interventions for SUDs. However, the evidence for the use of primary, secondary, indicated or selected interventions for IDs in this age group is scarce.

LaFreniere and Capuano (1997) implemented a six-month intensive home-based indicated prevention programme for mothers and preschoolers. Children receiving high teacher ratings on the anxious-withdrawn behaviour scale were invited to be in the programme. The project offered information on child development, including booklets on "Development", "Behaviour", "Security", "The Body", and "Parental Needs". Additional sessions were provided to address core skills in parenting, as well as any additional personal or parental concerns in order to alleviate stress within the parent–child relationship. Finally, parents were assisted to build a social support network. At the conclusion of the programme, anxious-withdrawn preschoolers as assessed by teachers showed significant gains in social competence, but reduction in anxious-withdrawn behaviour only approached significance. Parenting stress in the intervention group did not show a significant reduction relative to controls, although a subjective positive bias was noted in mothers who participated in the intervention.

A parent–teacher universal prevention programme for children aged 4 to 5 years, aimed at reducing the incidence of internalizing disorders later in childhood was recently evaluated in Brisbane, Australia (Roth and Dadds, 1999). The project was a large-scale community project that attempted to identify children at risk in this young age group, and determine the short- and long-term effects of a prevention programme through a controlled trial. Entitled REACH for Resilience, the programme aims to teach parents and teachers strategies and ways of thinking that can increase children's ability to cope with challenges, especially through adult modelling of these strategies and encouragement of children's efforts. Analysis of recruitment and retention patterns showed that, in the intervention group, the most stressed parents agreed to participate and attended the treatment sessions. In the comparison group, the most stressed parents self-selected out. At post-treatment and follow-up, the groups were not different on any of the parent and child adjustment or diagnostic measures. Thus, while the results are encouraging in terms of reaching the most needy parents, this confounds results and makes conclusions about intervention effects dubious.

Thus, the empirical evidence is inconclusive regarding optimal prevention of internalizing disorders in early childhood and it would be drawing a very long bow to argue at this stage that such interventions could potentially reduce incidence of SUD in later life. However, drawing from the literature on resilience (Cowen et al., 1997, 1996), the experience of a positive and continuing relationship with a caregiver seems to be a major factor influencing resilient versus non-resilient children (Werner, 1993). Secondly, children's temperament (easily soothed, low emotionality, sociable) tends to elicit positive responses from adults as well as children, thereby assisting with the development of social competence (Fox and Calkins, 1993). Thirdly, an internal locus of control (having a sense of influence over life's events) was more evident in resilient children, and can be supported by age-appropriate problem-solving strategies (Shure, 1997; Wyman *et al.*, 1993). And, fourthly, an optimistic outlook predicted socio-emotional adjustment and a stronger internal locus of control (Wyman *et al.*, 1993). Thus, prevention initiatives in early childhood should focus on developing secure attachments, modelling of appropriate coping strategies, such as optimism, problem-solving, seeking social support, and ultimately taking action. Longitudinal studies are necessary to (a) develop efficacious and effective programmes, (b) discover the specific factors necessary and sufficient to prevent the onset of anxiety disorder and build resilience, and (c) track the effectiveness of these strategies over time.

The EDs that most commonly appear within early childhood are generally characterized by disruptive behaviour in the home and preschool (Tremblay *et al.*, 1995). Research shows that disruptive behaviour in early childhood represents a most salient risk factor for the continued expression of behavioural disorders (Dadds, 1996; Hawkins *et al.*, 1992; Tremblay *et al.*, 1995) and SUDs (Cicchetti and Rogosch, 1999; Hawkins *et al.*, 1992). Research further suggests that brief behavioural treatments implemented with multiple points of focus, for instance, via parenting skills in the home and via social skills training in schools, can prove more effective components of preventive intervention strategies than programmes of single focus which only target discrete domains (Kazdin, 1987, 1993). It is in a similar manner that efforts that seek to alter behaviour that occurs as a result of development must themselves address the components of that development. In this manner, both parent- and child-focused components can be seen as essential within the context of preventive intervention strategies (Coie and Jacobs, 1993; Dodge, 1993).

Considerable work has been done on the development and evaluation of tertiary treatments for EDs. The most successful are parent training and family interventions, and for older children, individual or group social-cognitive work with the child. Research has supported the efficacy of behavioural family interventions in the short term and over follow-up periods of years after the termination of treatment (Miller and Prinz, 1990). The last few decades have witnessed continuous refinement of the BFI approach. Empirical evidence and clinical experience suggested that not all parents or families benefit to the same extent from treatment (Miller and Prinz, 1990), and difficulties are commonly encountered when there are concurrent family problems, parental psychopathology, and economic hardship. Several authors have made various proposals to improve the outcome of treatment by expanding the focus of treatment to the multiple systems that provide the context for family life (Henggeler *et al.*, 1997; Miller and Prinz, 1990). Of particular interest to EI is the Triple P approach (Sanders, 1999) which offers various levels of intervention intensity, from simple provision of information through to a full multisystemic, individually tailored intervention. Of the different approaches encompassed by behavioural family intervention, parent training for the treatment of younger ODD children has the most accumulated evidence regarding its therapeutic effectiveness. There is less evidence to suggest that behavioural family intervention is effective in altering the course of the more severe end conduct problem children, especially beyond the years of early childhood.

One example of an effective multi-focused preventive intervention administered to a select sample comes from Tremblay and colleagues (1995). In this study, disruptive kindergarten boys were randomly allocated to a dual-focused preventive intervention condition or to a control condition. All the participants were from inner-city low socio-economic neighbourhoods. The components of the dual-focused intervention programme included home-based parent training in effective child-rearing practice, and appropriate social skills training for child participants. The child participants were compared with controls at the programme's end, prior to puberty, at puberty, and during adolescence. Based on these comparisons the programme was judged successful for the following reasons: a significantly larger number of boys who undertook the intervention than controls remained in regular and age-appropriate classrooms until the end of elementary school, the boys who participated in the treatment programme also showed significantly less delinquent behaviour when yearly assessments were carried out between the ages of 10 and 15 years. The demonstrable reduction in disruptive behaviour that resulted from this intervention may be taken as evidence for the potential to curtail the later development of SUDs by addressing developmentally common risk and protective factors.

Middle childhood

Middle childhood appears to be an especially advantageous time for anxiety prevention and early intervention. Developmentally, this is the time when most anxiety disorders emerge, and these have been shown to be predictive of adolescent depression (Cole *et al.*, 1998). As children's cognitive abilities mature, cognitive restructuring techniques (CBT) are able to be utilized in helping at-risk children change the meaning of aversive events and experiences (Kazdin *et al.*, 1992). This is especially important because the impact of stressful events appears to be largely mediated by that individual's evaluation of the event in relation to their wellbeing. Dadds and colleagues (1998) suggest that intervention with parents is especially important with younger age groups of children, whereas for older children the cognitive work and exposure may be sufficient. A further advantage for this age group is that self-report measures are reliable and valid tools of assessment, although it is still imperative to seek information from multiple sources given the potential for report to exist. For instance, in the case of anxiety problems, using teacher nominations in conjunction with children's self-reports seems most efficacious, as each method taps different types of anxiety problems, yet structured interviews support the validity of each method (Dadds *et al.*, 1997).

Only recently have controlled clinical trials with children diagnosed with anxiety disorders been reported. The programmes included individual cognitive work to reduce threat appraisal, exposure, and enhancement of parental communication and child-rearing skills. The results are impressive with improvement maintained in 60% to 90% overall in the controlled trials. Although these studies were treatment not prevention studies, they are worth considering in some detail due to their important implications for design and implementation of anxiety prevention and early intervention.

Two controlled treatment studies for children with a primary anxiety disorder diagnosis were conducted by Kendall and his colleagues (Kendall, 1994; Kendall *et al.*, 1997), consisting of 16 to 20 CBT sessions for the children. In the first controlled trial ($N = 47$) over 60% of the treatment group no longer met criteria for an anxiety disorder, and these gains were maintained at one-year follow-up. Kendall's second randomized clinical trial ($N = 94$) replicated his earlier study with very similar results. Over 50% of children no longer retained their primary anxiety disorder post-treatment (with significant reduction in severity for others), compared to only 6% ($n = 2$) in the waitlisted group. Effects were not modified by comorbidity, gender, or ethnicity. Periodic assessments of treatment gains suggested that psycho-education (eight weeks) alone was not sufficient treatment, but when followed by active exposure (eight weeks), these two segments together created significant reductions in anxiety disorders.

Barrett (1998) showed that similar success rates could be achieved by presenting the combined CBT–family treatment in a group format to anxious children and their parents, thereby significantly reducing costs of intervention, and Barrett and colleagues (2001) showed durable treatment effects up to six years following treatment. Mendlowitz and colleagues (1999) also examined the effect of parental involvement in CBT group intervention on anxiety, depression, and coping strategies in school-age children. Similar to Barrett and colleagues (1996), all treatment groups showed positive change, and concurrent parental involvement enhanced the treatment effects. Cobham *et al.* (1999) used the same group intervention to assess the role of parental anxiety in treatment outcome, and the extent to which the second component of Barrett and colleagues (1996) family treatment (parent skills for managing their own anxiety) could alleviate putative poorer treatment outcomes associated with high parental anxiety. Results indicated that high parental anxiety was a risk factor for poorer treatment outcomes for anxious children, and that specifically targeting parental anxiety for intervention could overcome this risk factor in the context of a cognitive-behavioural programme for the child.

In addition, Hayward and colleagues (2000) examined the efficacy of CBT group therapy for adolescents (CBGT-A) in females with social phobia and the effect of this treatment on the risk for major depression. At one-year follow-up there were no significant differences by treatment condition. There was also suggestive evidence that treatment of social phobia lowers the risk for relapse of major depression among those with a history of major depression. Combining social phobia and major depression as the outcome produced more robust treatment effects in the one-year follow-up and it was concluded that treatment of social phobia may result in a reduction of major depression.

A selected prevention project targeted children ($N = 1786$) aged 7 to 14 in Brisbane, Australia (Dadds *et al.*, 1997). Inclusion in the project ranged from children who were exhibiting mild anxious features, but remained disorder-free, to those who were in the less severe range of a DSM-IV anxiety disorder. An intensive screening process incorporated parent, child and teacher reports, telephone calls and face-to-face interviews. Children with (a) disruptive behaviours (impulsive, aggressive, hyperactive, non-compliant), (b) lack of English as a first language in the home, (c) developmental delay or other problem, (d) no anxiety problem according to teacher reports, and (e) invalid child reports (ticked 'yes' to all items) were excluded from the sample. The final sample consisted of 128 children. Any child with severe symptoms or whose parents requested individual help for their child's anxiety were referred for individual treatment and no longer included in follow-up assessments.

The intervention was based upon an adaptation of Kendall's Coping Cat Workbook, a 10-session programme presented in group format for teaching children strategies to cope with anxiety. The sessions were conducted weekly for one hour at the child's school, in groups of 5 to 12 children. In addition, parents periodically attended three sessions covering: (a) child management skills, (b) modelling and encouraging the strategies children were learning through the Coping Koala Prevention Programme, and (c) how to use Kendall's FEAR plan to manage their own anxiety. The monitoring group received no intervention, but were contacted at planned intervals for follow-up assessments.

Interestingly, at post-intervention no significant differences were found between the monitoring and the intervention groups. Yet, at six-month follow-up, the intervention group showed a significant reduction in the onset of disorder (16% onset), relative to the monitored group (54% onset). Most importantly, the success of their programme in reducing the existing rate of anxiety disorder and preventing the onset of new anxiety disorders was successfully maintained at a two-year follow-up (Dadds *et al.*, 1999). These results are very promising. Given that over half of the at-risk children in the monitoring group progressed from mild anxious symptoms into a full-blown anxiety disorder, middle childhood and early adolescence appear to provide an important "window of opportunity" for prevention initiatives.

There is also evidence that programmes that build social skills in primary school children without necessarily focusing on IDs can reduce ID symptoms. Such effects have been shown in the PATHS programme, for example, using a range of well-designed studies using universal, deaf, and behaviourally at-risk students (Greenberg et al., in press).

One interesting study that sought to assess the impact of a universal preventive intervention at first grade level was undertaken by Ialongo and colleagues (1999). The programme assessed the immediate effects of the intervention on poor achievement, concentration problems, aggression, and shy behaviours. These factors have all been identified, either individually or in combination, as risk factors for later development of SUDs, IDs (for instance, social phobia, affective disorder, anxieties) and EDs. The intervention was based on Patterson's (1986) model of antisocial behaviour development which suggests that a distinctive developmental trajectory can be mapped between parental practice with regard to social compliance and aversive behaviour and the later onset of SUDs and antisocial behaviour (Patterson, 1982). In attempting to address the risk factors described above, it was the intention of the study to reduce the risk for the development of more serious forms of antisocial behaviour and substance use in adolescence and adulthood (Ialongo et al., 1999).

The authors reported that, over the first and second grade measurement period, the classroom-centred intervention (CC) displayed the greatest effect in reducing the target behaviours. This intervention was specifically directed at enhancing teachers' behavioural management skills and instructional practices. The second intervention (FSP) was designed to improve communication between parents and teachers, and to offer parents insight into child behaviour management practices. It is interesting to note that this strategy was reported as being less successful in curtailing the target behaviours. However, as expected, the intervention was influenced by gender and by pre-intervention level of risk (Ialongo et al., 1999). No follow-up evaluation was documented in this study.

The evidence with regard to treatment and prevention of externalizing disorders is also strong in middle childhood. There are a number of prevention programmes that aim to reduce aggression and promote social skills in children via universal curriculum-based programmes in schools. These may have some impact on EDs but are outside the scope of this review (see Greenberg et al., 2001). Greenberg and colleagues (2001) located ten EI programmes that have shown success in reducing EDs or their risk factors. Similar to tertiary models, the majority of these utilize child-cognitive skills training, parent training, or both. Only the most recent and well-evaluated will be reviewed here.

As an example of a child-focused programme, Lochman and colleagues

(1993) evaluated a 26-session social skills training programme focusing on peer-relations, problem-solving, and anger management, with a sample ($n = 52$) of 9- to 11-year-old aggressive–rejected children. Compared to controls, the programme children were rated as significantly less aggressive by teachers and more socially accepted by peers at post-treatment and at one-year follow-up. By contrast, in Lochman's (1985) programme, children who had received an anger coping programme were, three years after the intervention, not different from controls in terms of parent-ratings of aggression and observations of disruptive-aggressive behaviour, or in terms of self-reported delinquency. Tierney and colleagues (Big Brother/Big Sister Programme; 1995) randomly assigned 959 10- to 16-year-old adolescents to a mentor or a wait-list control condition. Those with a mentor reported they engaged in significantly less fighting, were less likely to initiate the use of drugs and alcohol, and perceived their family relationships more positively. However, there were no significant differences between groups in terms of self-reported delinquency. While encouraging, these data are based solely on self-report.

One problem with the use of group interventions for indicated ED youth is that iatrogenic effects have been found in programmes where antisocial youth were grouped together (Dishion et al., 1996). In contrast, studies have found that ED youth benefit from being in groups with non-problem children. For example, Hudley and Graham (1993, 1995) paired aggressive 10- to 12-year-old boys with non-aggressive peers in a 12-lesson school-based intervention focusing on improving the accuracy of children's perceptions and interpretations of others' actions. Compared to controls, teacher ratings indicated that the programme successfully reduced aggressive behaviour immediately following the intervention. There has been no follow-up data to date. A similar 22-session integration programme by Prinz and colleagues (1994) was evaluated up to six months following the intervention. Children in the programme were rated by teachers as significantly less aggressive than controls at post-test and follow-up. Significant improvements were also noted in the intervention children's prosocial coping and teacher-rated social skills.

Overall, the evidence is not strong that child-focused EI interventions are effective with EDs. In general, their results are modest and not durable, the sample sizes are small and, due to the nature of the interventions, they are limited to older children and adolescents. However, child-focused interventions remain a component of more comprehensive programmes that are showing more impressive results.

Parent-focused interventions generally have produced more clinically significant outcomes. As noted earlier, there have been numerous demonstrations of the effectiveness of social-learning-based parent-training programmes for families of children with EDs. Numerous independent replications in community settings have produced significant results (Sanders, 1999). While most of these programmes developed as tertiary treatments and have been evaluated on clinical populations, a number of authors have argued they are excellent EI strategies in that they effectively reduce EDs early in their growth to later delinquency (e.g., Sanders, 1999). As we saw earlier, however, one limitation of a referral-based approach is that it leaves initiatives for intervention in the hands of parents who, as we saw earlier, may not seek help even in extreme situations.

Parent interventions have also been recently applied in both universal prevention and EI formats. Webster-Stratton has recently used a parent-training model with young Head Start children (Webster-Stratton and Hammond, 1998). The programme can thus be regarded as *selected* and the entry procedure is not dependent on parent referrals. Parents of Head Start children were randomly assigned to receive the intervention or serve as a control by only receiving the usual services. The nine-week intervention consisted of parent-training groups and a teacher-training programme. Results at post-test and 12–18 months' follow-up indicate significant improvements in parent behaviour, parental involvement in school, child conduct problems, and school-based behaviour.

Recently, a number of EI programmes have been evaluated that adopt developmental models of EDs and, as such, utilize multiple interventions across settings and time. This is consistent with a general view that a more comprehensive approach is necessary to alter the developmental trajectories of children who live in high-risk environments and are showing early signs of EDs (CPRG, 1992; Reid and Eddy, 1997).

One recent study entitled the LIFT (Linking the Interests of Families and Teachers) Intervention examined the efficacy of a universal preventive intervention in the reduction of conduct problems (Reid *et al.*, 1999). LIFT was ten weeks in duration, and targeted three distinct domains that had been identified by a developmental model of the development of conduct problems. A sample of 671 first and fifth graders was drawn from 12 elementary schools, the participants and their families both participated in the study. The intervention condition consisted of a parent-training component in the BFI tradition, together with a playground behavioural programme and a teacher–parent communication programme. It was hypothesized that the intervention would have significant effects on three specific areas: levels of child physical aggression in the playground, mother aversive behaviour that was displayed during interactions with their children, and teacher ratings of child peer positive behaviour over the year following the intervention. The results indicated that the intervention had significant results on child physical aggression in the playground, and on mother aversive behaviour in mother–child interactions. In addition, the results for children's behaviour in the classroom were in the expected direction. All results were immediate and applied to both first and fifth grade participants.

Kazdin and Wassell (2000) evaluated a preventive intervention involving cognitive problem-solving skills training (PSST) and child/parent management training (PMT). Child functioning at school was incorporated into the therapy for school-aged children, and over the course of the intervention, parents were brought into their children's sessions, and vice versa, children visited their parents' sessions in order to participate in the development and discussion of treatment. The children, aged between 2 and 14 years, their parents, and their families in general, all responded to treatment. In general, the children's functioning, as well as parent and family functioning, all improved over the course of the intervention. This improvement was demonstrated within a range of child behavioural symptoms, parental symptoms and levels of stress, and family functioning, relationships and support (Kazdin and Wassell, 2000). Generally, larger effects were demonstrated on children's outcome measures, and effects of less magnitude were demonstrated on parent and family outcome measures. While the authors note that the children in this study were all under referral for conduct problems, and that similar experimental results have not been demonstrated for populations exhibiting IDs, support for the generalizability of therapy based on demonstration of risk factors is warranted. For instance, it is noteworthy that improvements in both parental functioning and stress, as well as family functioning, relationships and support, have been demonstrated as important for children with both internalizing and externalizing disorders (Cobham *et al.*, 1999; Kazdin and Wassell, 2000). In addition, changes in family and parent functioning may be expected to contribute to beneficial outcomes as far as long-term treatment effects for children are concerned.

In the Montreal Prevention Experiment, Tremblay and colleagues (McCord *et al.*, 1994; Tremblay *et al.*, 1992, 1996; Vitaro and Tremblay, 1994) combined parent training and child skill training. Primary school boys rated high on aggressive and disruptive behaviour ($n = 166$) were randomly assigned to a two-year intervention or placebo control condition. Children worked with normative peers to develop more prosocial and adaptive social behaviour, while parents worked with family consultants approximately twice a month for two years to learn positive discipline techniques and how to support their child's positive behaviour. Initial results did not reveal clear group differences. At the three-year follow-up when the boys were age 12, the treatment group was significantly less likely than control boys to engage in fighting, be classified as having serious adjustment difficulties, and to engage in aggression or delinquent activity. These results came from a variety of self-, teacher-, peer-, and parent-report measures. Effects of the treatment on other forms of antisocial behaviour (e.g., self-reported stealing) and substance use continued into early adolescence. Other EI programmes have found durable effects which did not emerge until follow-up assessments (see Dadds *et al.*, 1997). It should also be noted that intervention effects were reported by multiple informants across multiple domains of adjustment (i.e. behavioural, social, school/academic).

The First Steps Programme (Walker *et al.*, 1998a,b) also intervenes with both parents and children, the latter having been identified at kindergarten for exhibiting elevated levels of antisocial behaviour. Families with an at-risk child receive a six-week home intervention and children participate in a classroom-based, skill-building and reinforcement programme that lasts two months. The programme has been evaluated with 42 subjects in two cohorts using a randomized–controlled design. Positive treatment effects were found for both adaptive and academic behaviour at post-intervention and at follow-up into early primary school. A replication (Golly et al., 1998) with a new sample of 20 kindergarten students has produced similar results. Similar positive results have been found for a programme for students aged 6 to 12 exhibiting aggressive and disruptive behaviour, that targets the child, the parents, and the classroom (Pepler et al., 1991, 1995). In this programme, the parent training is optional and it is important to note that significant group differences were found only on teacher ratings. Parents failed to see significant behaviour changes in the intervention children.

The Conduct Problems Prevention Research Group (CPRG, 1992) implemented Fast Track, a school-wide programme that integrates universal, selective, and indicated models of prevention into a comprehensive longitudinal model for the prevention of conduct disorders and associated adolescent problem behaviours. A randomized-control trial of 50 elementary schools in four US urban and rural locations is still underway. The universal intervention includes teacher consultation in the use of a series of grade level versions of the PATHS Curriculum throughout the elementary years. The targeted intervention package includes a series of family (e.g., home visiting, parenting skills, case management), child (e.g., academic tutoring, social skills training), school, peer group, and community interventions. Targeted children were identified by multi-gate screening for externalizing behaviour problems during kindergarten and consisted of children with the most extreme behaviour problems in schools (10%) in neighbourhoods with high crime and poverty rates (selected aspect). At present, evaluations are available for the first three years (CPRG, 1999a, 1999b). There have been significant reductions in special education referrals and aggression both at home and at school for the targeted children. The initial results provide evidence for improved social and academic development, including lower sociometric reports of peer aggression, and improved observers' ratings of the classroom atmosphere in the intervention sample. Evaluations will continue through middle school as Fast Track adopts an ecological–developmental model that assumes that, for high-risk groups, prevention of antisocial behaviour will be achieved by enhancing and linking protective factors within the child, family, school, and community.

It can be seen that recent community trials have been conducted that use randomized–controlled designs to evaluate multi-component programmes based on comprehensive ecological and developmental models of EDs. There are a number of characteristics that appear to be associated with successful

EI for externalizing problems in children. These include: (1) early identification and intervention, beginning not later than preschool or early primary school years; (2) incorporation of family-based intervention as a core target for change; (3) adoption of a comprehensive model that emphasizes a broad ecology (child, family, school, community); (4) adoption of a longitudinal/developmental approach to risk and protective factors and windows of opportunity for intervention; and (5) use of a comprehensive mix of selected (e.g., poor neighbourhoods), indicated (identification of aggressive children), and universal (e.g., classroom programme) strategies.

Thus, successful prevention/early intervention and treatment in middle childhood has been achieved with regard to both IDs and EDs. Some of the studies cited have been able to demonstrate long-term improvements for children up to two years post-intervention. The long-term success of these interventions has clear implications for a concomitant reduction in community costs and family distress. None of the above studies took measures of SUDs at follow-up. However, it is reasonable to speculate that these interventions have some potential for reducing the incidence of depression and SUDs in the adolescent years.

Adolescence

Prevention of anxiety disorders in adolescence has received limited attention, although it should be noted that the treatment and prevention studies by Barrett, Dadds, and Kendall reviewed above all included children up to 14 years in their successful reductions in anxiety disorders. Stress Inoculation Training Programmes, which use a similar intervention to the anxiety treatments, have been shown to reduce anxious symtomology in universal adolescent samples as well as children evaluated to be at risk due to family breakdown (Pedro-Carroll et al., 1992).

However, in later adolescence, the pressing nature of such life-threatening issues as depression, suicide, drug and alcohol abuse, or safe sex practices come to the fore. With respect to internalizing problems, the prevention of depression has gained prominence in research investigations. To date, one of the most successful programmes for reduction of depressive symptoms in young people has been the Pennsylvania Depression Programme for adolescents aged 10 to 13 years (Jaycox et al., 1994). The study included three separate programmes focusing on teaching (a) cognitive skills, (b) social problem-solving skills, and (c) a combination of cognitive and social problem-solving skills. Training in assertiveness, negotiation and coping skills were also included. After finding no significant difference between the three intervention modalities, the groups were combined, resulting in a treatment sample of 69 participants and a wait-list control group of 74 participants. Significant improvements in depressive symptoms were obtained for the intervention group compared to controls at post-testing, six-month follow-up, and two-year follow-up (Gillham *et al.*, 1995). This innovative study indicates that psycho-educational prevention efforts to build resilience to depression seem promising during early adolescence. A limitation of the study was the possible biasing effect of a self-selected sample in conjunction with the low initial recruitment rate (between 13% and 19%) and high attrition rate (30%).

Also of note with regard to IDs are studies by Lewinson and colleagues (1990) and Clarke and colleagues (1995), who reported a significant improvement in depression for an indicated intervention group compared to wait-list for 14- to 15-year-old adolescents. In another indicated trial, Hains and Ellmann (1994) reported positive results for their programme which consisted of problem-solving, cognitive restructuring, and anxiety management, reducing depression scores in volunteer adolescents who had been classified as having high arousal levels. These authors also experienced difficulty with possible self-selection bias.

The above studies provide evidence for the usefulness of selective and indicated prevention programmes. They also highlight the well-known difficulties associated with recruitment and retention of adolescents. To adolescents, such programmes could be seen to put them at risk of being singled out from the peer group at an age when peer group acceptance is especially important. This problem might be substantially reduced if intervention programmes for adolescent depression could be implemented routinely as part of the school curriculum, as either an alternative or complement to indicated programmes.

The Resourceful Adolescent Programme (RAP; Shochet *et al.*, 1997) was developed to meet this need. It consists of components for adolescents (RAP-A) and their families (RAP-F). The RAP-A is a fully manualized ten-week group treatment run in groups of approximately eight to ten participants per group that focuses on building resilience in adolescence as a way of preventing depression. Given its universal delivery, participation rates approach 100% for the adolescents, although recruitment of families has remained a problem. Early results from controlled trials indicate it is associated with reductions in self-reported depression, especially for adolescents with pre-existing depression at pretreatment (Shochet *et al.*, in press).

Thus, the evidence from adolescent groups is consistent with that from younger groups, supporting the efficacy of psychological skills-building programmes to reduce the incidence of IDs in young people. It should be noted that the content of the anxiety prevention and depression prevention programmes tend to be very similar, and include core foci on cognitive skills, emotion regulation, dealing with challenges, and social problem-solving skills. However, none of the above studies has specifically measured SUDs as outcomes and so their effect in that regard remains unknown.

The picture is somewhat different for EDs, since adolescents who display various disorders consistent with EDs represent a population of high risk for the development of SUDs and therefore a population for whom intervention may well be beneficial. If such interventions are effective, reductions may not only be expected in recurrent prevalence of EDs, but also in the incidence, prevalence and severity of SUDs (Bukstein, 2000). Of the preventive interventions for EDs, particularly conduct problems, research indicates that Behavioural Family Intervention (BFI) has a high degree of efficacy, both in the short term and after long-term follow-up (Miller and Prinz, 1990). Typically, BFI will target parental interaction skills and parenting practice skills. In addition, a range of additional family risk factors will be addressed where warranted, for instance, the psychological state of the parents (depression, anxiety, irritability), the presence of other identifiable marital problems, social support training, and the presence of SUDs.

The majority of SUD prevention studies for adolescents have focused on externalizing and social adversity risk factors. Several programmes of research have now shown that reductions in externalizing disorders can be effectively produced by the provision of skills-building programmes for the child, his or her family, and the school environment, through the primary school years (see Greenberg et al., in press). Several of these studies have shown effective reductions in SUDs following from the targeting of externalizing behaviour (e.g., The Anger Coping Programme: Lochman, 1992; Big Brother/Sister: Tierney et al., 1995).

There are several studies in which the promotion of general resilience in primary school children has been shown to reduce substance use into adolescence. For example, Schinke and Tepavac (1995) showed that a universal school-based intervention that focuses on personal and social decision-making and assertive skills reduced actual and potential substance use in 8- to 11-year-olds. The Seattle Social Development Project is a universal programme that combines parent and teacher training throughout the primary school years. Controlled trials have compared early versus late scheduling of the intervention in large samples. Secondary school intervention was not effective, however, the early intervention model (i.e., targeting social competence in the primary school years and continuing across developmental phases) has been shown to effectively reduce SUDs at 18 years of age (Hawkins et al., in press). Similarly, a number of well-designed studies that have targeted improved parent–child relationships have shown positive long-term benefits in terms of reductions or delays in drug-taking (e.g., Kosterman et al., 1997).

Several programmes that aim to build skills and general resilience have been presented as selective programmes. For example, Short (1998) reports on a preventive intervention for 10- to 13-year-old children from divorced homes based on the rationale that coping skills mediate the effects of family stress on adolescent mental health and substance use. The intervention has been associated with improved coping and reductions in externalizing, internalizing, and substance use problems. The overlap in skills focus between these programmes is notable. That is, the focus on improving coping skills, problem-solving skills, and interpersonal relationships is common to most of the interventions. Also similar is their demonstrable positive outcomes, encouraging some optimism that the utilization of school-based programmes that increase resilience and reduce social and personal problems have the potential to reduce the development of SUDs.

INTERVENTION AND COMMUNITY HEALTH ISSUES IN THE PREVENTION OF SUDS

The extent to which intervention technologies can actually make a difference in the community is influenced by a number of pragmatic public health issues. Most of the intervention studies reviewed were a combination of effectiveness with efficacy trials. That is, while they were conducted in "real world" settings, they evaluated the intervention under optimal delivery conditions, e.g., within the context of a funded research programme, using careful experimental designs and measures, and implemented by highly trained and motivated staff. The question remains as to the community effectiveness of such interventions when implemented in the not-so-optimal conditions of existing mental health and educational systems. Many interventions are evaluated up to the efficacy trial stage and the community effectiveness remains unknown. In the area of prevention, effectiveness trials are essential and therefore more work is needed to evaluate these interventions when implemented in community settings by non-specialist, non-research-motivated staff.

Recruitment of participants is one of the major obstacles for preventive interventions, regardless of type of prevention. Because participants have not self-referred for treatment and may not even feel they have any problems, especially in early childhood, the sense of urgency and motivation that drives clinical interventions is often absent. With childhood anxiety problems, parents and teachers often have not even noticed anxiety problems or often assume that children will "grow out of it". In the LaFreniere and Capuano (1997) study of selected children less than one-third of identified participants were successfully recruited. The Roth and Dadds (1999) trial of a parenting intervention applied universally to preschool children has maintained contact with approximately half of those invited to participate. Indicated prevention projects in middle childhood show similar rates of recruitment. Although no adolescent studies were found specifically targeting adolescent anxiety problems, selected and indicated programmes for depression in adolescents have typically achieved very low participation rates. The Shochet and colleagues (in press) school-based universal prevention of depression programme received parental consent for 86% of potential students. However, when an additional parental component was added to the programme, attendance by parents at three evening sessions was very low, with 36% attending one session and only 10% attending all three sessions.

With regard to SUDs, there may be more precise ways to use indicated and selected programmes. The preventive and early intervention studies reviewed above either used universal interventions or targeted children already showing signs of IDs or at risk due to the presence of risk factors such as family conflict or psychopathology. While there are many similarities in the risk factors for IDs and SUDs, there may be risk factors that are more relevant to identifying children particularly at risk for SUDs. Children of parents with existing SUDs is an obvious one. There is clear evidence that these children are at risk for SUDs themselves, as well as a range of other social and health problems (Chassin *et al.*, 1999). The mechanisms of transmission appear to be a combination of specific biological risk for addiction as well as social adversity (O'Connor *et al.*, 2000). Pragmatically, however, this is a difficult group to recruit effectively. While numerous programmes have reported working with such children, the numbers are small and the ratio of participants to those offered participation is often not made clear. In contrast, studies that have deliberately measured the success rates of recruiting of children of parents with SUDs into intervention programmes, the data are not encouraging (Gensheimer *et al.*, 1990; Michaels *et al.*, 1992). Understandably, identifying oneself as such is not appealing to young people and few do. Thus, identification of young people at risk via direct family experience with SUDs may be a useful tertiary clinical strategy but is unlikely to offer much power as a larger community strategy. One solution to this is to offer such programmes universally in schools with particular attention paid to the needs of children with SUD parents (e.g., Nastasi and DeZolt, 1994). Studies reviewed above indicate that recruiting young people via universal strategies, and indicated and selected strategies for IDs, have done well in reaching children potentially at risk for SUDs and this augurs well for increasing attention to such programmes.

Third, caution must be used when findings on parent–child relationships are generalized to substance-using families. Positive relationships with peers and family are a common target in programmes that aim to build resilience and reduce mental health problems in young people. As would be expected, these also form a central focus for many preventive programmes for SUDs. However, it should be noted that the situation may be a little more complex with regard to SUDs than simply conceiving of positive interpersonal relationships as a protective factor. Modelling of substance-use habits via close relationships is a key factor in the development of many forms of substance use and longitudinal studies show that adolescents are more likely to imitate substance use if they have a close relationship with the substance user (Andrews *et al.*, 1997). Further, studies on families with opiate addiction show that positive family management practices have minimal protective influence on child development compared to that typically found in addiction-free families (Gainey *et al.*, 1997).

A fourth issue concerns the administrative systems that control the resource allocations and structures for mental health services. As we have seen, the most evidence to date that anxiety and depression problems can be prevented comes from school-based intervention trials. However, the responsibility for mental health promotion is typically within statutory health rather than education departments, and programme designers may find their efforts frustrated by a lack of communication between the two groups. Intersectorial issues, concerned with the overlapping structure and functions of the various agencies that have responsibility for health and education of young people, are a major issue for the science and practice of prevention, particularly for SUDs where statutory responsibilities may span several agencies.

CONCLUSIONS AND IMPLICATIONS

Substance use disorders are a substantial health and community problem. Attempts to prevent their development and impact have utilized direct and indirect methods. Direct methods typically try to reduce supply and demand through policy changes, policing of drug trades, education about the dangers of drugs, and skills training programmes emphasizing resisting pressure to indulge. The evidence supporting the effectiveness of these direct strategies is mixed. Attempts to influence supply are difficult to evaluate and highly loaded issues that mix science with moral and political arguments. Traditional prevention strategies that focus on educating people about the dangers of substance use are largely unsuccessful. The evidence for the effectiveness of social skills progammes is more positive but effects appear to be short-lived and of dubious value for people at high risk for substance problems.

In contrast, more convincing evidence exists to show that reductions in SUDs can be achieved by reducing risk factors and increasing general mental health and resilience in young people. Such interventions typically focus on the pathway to SUDs through conduct problems and delinquency with their associated features of social adversity, school failure, and family conflict and breakdown. However, increasing evidence shows that there is a related but diverse pathway to SUDs associated with internalizing problems, that is, anxiety and depression. Given that strong evidence shows the incidence of both externalizing and internalizing problems can be reduced via tertiary and preventive interventions targeted at pre-adolescents, these strategies have enormous potential. An attempt was made to present a developmental map of the risk and protective factors that influence the persistence versus transience of IDs in young people. These switch in and out at various developmental points of the lifespan, and thus a series of windows of opportunity for intervention were identified.

REFERENCES

Abikoff, H. & Klein, R. G. (1992). Attention-deficit, hyperactivity and conduct disorder: Comorbidity and implications for treatment. *Journal of Consulting and Clinical Psychology*, 60, 881–892.

American Psychological Association (1994). *Diagnostic and Statistical Manual of Mental Disorders (4th edn DSM-IV)*. Washington, DC: American Psychiatric Press.

Ammerman, R. T. and Hersen, M. (1997). Prevention and treatment with children and adolescents in the real world context. In R.T. Ammerman and M. Hersen (Eds.), *Handbook of prevention and treatment with children and adolescents*. New York: John Wiley.

Andrews, J. A., Hops, H., & Duncan, S. C. (1997). Adolescent modeling of parent substance use: The moderating effect of the relationship with the parent. *Journal of Family Psychology*, 11, 259–270.

Armstrong, K. L. Fraser, J. A. Dadds, M.R., & Morris, J. (1999). A randomised controlled trial of nurse home visiting to vulnerable families with newborns. Journal of Pediatrics and Child Health, 35, 237–244.

Barrett, P. M. (1998). Evaluation of cognitive-behavioral group treatments for childhood anxiety disorders. *Journal of Clinical Child Psychology*, 27, 459–468.

Barrett, P. M., Dadds, M. R., & Rapee, R. M. (1996). Family treatment of childhood anxiety: A controlled trial. *Journal of Consulting and Clinical Psychology*, 64, 333–342.

Barrett, P. M., Duffy, A. L. Dadds, M. . & Rapee, R. M. (2001). Cognitive-behavioral treatment of anxiety disorders in children: Long-term (6-year) follow-up. *Journal of Consulting and Clinical Psychology*, 69, 135–141.

Barrett, P. M., Duffy, A. L., Dadds, M. R., & Rapee, R. M. (in press). Cognitive-behavioural treatment of anxiety disorders in children: Long-term (6-Year) follow-up. *Journal of Consulting and Clinical Psychology*.

Beidel, D. C. & Turner, S. M. (1997). At risk for anxiety: I. Psychopathology in the offspring of anxious parents. *Journal of the American Academy of Child and Adolescent Psychiatry*, 36, 918–924.

Bernstein, G. A. & Borchardt, C. M. (1991). Anxiety disorders of childhood and adolescence: A critical review. *Journal of the American Academy of Child and Adolescent Psychiatry*, 30, 519–532.

Bernstein, G. A. & Borchardt, C. M. (1996). Anxiety disorders in children and adolescents: A review of the past 10 years. *Journal of the American Academy of Child and Adolescent Psychiatry*, 35, 1110–1119.

Bibb, J. L. & Chambless, D. L. (1986). Alcohol use and abuse among diagnosed agoraphobics. *Behavior Research and Therapy*, 24, 49–58.

Biederman, J., Wilens, T., Mick, E., & Faraone, S. V. (1997). Is ADHD a risk factor for psychoactive substance use disorders: Findings from a four year prospective follow up study. *Journal of the American Academy of Child and Adolescent Psychiatry*, 36, 21–29.

Botvin, G. L. (1999) Adolescent drug abuse prevention: Current findings and future directions. In M.D. Glantz & C. R. Hartel (Eds.), *Drug abuse: Origins and interventions*. Washington, DC: American Psychological Association.

Brown, D. & Peterson, L. (1997). Unintentional injury and child abuse and neglect. In R. T. Ammerman & M. Hersen (Eds.), *Handbook of prevention and treatment with children and adolescents.* New York: John Wiley.

Bukstein, O. G. (1995). *Adolescent substance abuse: Assessment, treatment and prevention.* New York: Wiley.

Bukstein, O. G. (2000). Disruptive behaviour disorders and substance use disorders in adolescents. *Journal of Psychoactive Drugs, 32,* 67–70.

Chassin, L., Pitts, S. C., DeLucia, C., & Todd, M. (1999). A longitudinal study of children of alcoholics: Predicting young adult substance use disorders, anxiety, and depression. *Journal of Abnormal Psychology, 108,* 106–119.

Cicchetti, D. & Rogosch, F. A. (1999). Psychopathology as risk for adolescent substance use disorders: A developmental psychopathology perspective. *Journal of Clinical Child Psychology, 28,* 355–365.

Clarke, G. N., Hawkins, W., Murphy, M., Sheeber, L. B., Lewinson, P. M, & Seeley, J. R. (1995). Targeted prevention of unipolar depressive disorder in an at-risk sample of high school adolescents: A randomised trial of a group cognitive intervention. *Journal of the American Academy of Child Adolescent Psychiatry, 34,* 312–321.

Cobham, V. E., Dadds, M. R., & Spence, S. H. (1999). The role of parental anxiety in the treatment of childhood anxiety. *Journal of Consulting and Clinical Psychology, 66,* 893–905.

Coie, J. D. & Jacobs, M. R. (1993). The role of social context in the prevention of conduct disorder. *Development and Psychopathology, 5,* 263–275.

Cole, D. A., Peeke, L. G., Martin, J. M., Truglia, R., & Seroczynski, A. D., (1998). A longitudinal look at the relation between depression and anxiety in children and adolescents. *Journal of Consulting and Clinical Psychology, 66,* 451–460.

Cook, P. J. & Touchen, G. (1982). The effect of minimum drinking age on youthful auto fatalities, 1970–1977. *Journal of Legal Studies, 13,* 169–190.

Costello, E. J. & Angold, A. (1995). Developmental epidemiology. In D. Cicchetti, E. L. Cowen, A. D. Hightower, J. L. Pedro-Carroll, W. C. Work, P .A. Wyman, & W. G. Haffrey (Eds.), *School-based prevention of children at-risk: The Primary Mental Health Project.* Washington, DC: APA.

Cowen, E. L., Wyman, P. A., & Work, W. C. (1996). Resilience in highly stressed urban children: Concepts and findings. *Bulletin of the New York Academy of Medicine, 73,* 267–284.

Cowen, E. L., Wyman, P. A., Work, W. C., Kim, J. Y., Fagen, D. B., & Magnus, K. B. (1997). Follow-up study of young stress-affected and stress-resilient urban children. *Development and Psychopathology, 9,* 565–577.

CPRG. (Conduct Problems Prevention Research Group) (1992). A developmental and clinical model for the prevention of conduct disorder: The FAST Track Program. *Development and Psychopathology, 4,* 509–527.

CPRG. (Conduct Problems Prevention Research Group) (1999a). Initial impact of the FastTrack Prevention trial for conduct problems: The high risk sample. *Journal of Consulting and Clinical Psychology.*

CPRG. (Conduct Problems Prevention Research Group) (1999b). Initial impact of the FastTrack Prevention trial for conduct problems: Classroom effects. *Journal of Consulting and Clinical Psychology.*

Dadds, M. R., Barrett, P. M., & Cobham, V. E. (1998). Anxiety disorders. In T. H.

Ollendick (ed.), *Comprehensive clinical psychology: Vol. 4: Children and adolescents: Clinical formulation and treatment.* Oxford, UK: Elsevier Science.

Dadds, M. R., Holland, D. E., Laurens, K. R., Mullins, M., Barrett, P. M., & Spence, S. H. (1999). Early intervention and prevention of anxiety disorders in children: Results at two-year follow-up. *Journal of Consulting and Clinical Psychology*, 67, 145–150

Dadds, M. R. (1996). Conduct disorder. In R.T. Ammerman & M. Hersen (Eds.), *Handbook of prevention and treatment with children and adolescents.* New York: John Wiley.

Dadds, M. R. (2000).The comorbidity of substance use and emotional disorders: Potential for innovative prevention strategies. *Paper prepared for the National Comorbidity Project Workshop.* [Available from the author]

Dadds, M. R., Schwartz, S., & Sanders, M. R. (1987). Marital discord and treatment outcome in the treatment of childhood conduct disorders. *Journal of Consulting and Clinical Psychology*, 55, 396–403.

Dadds, M. R., Spence, S. H., Holland, D. E., Barrett, P. M., & Laurens, K.R. (1997). Prevention and early intervention for anxiety disorders: A controlled trial. *Journal of Consulting and Clinical Psychology*, 65, 627–635.

Dishion, T. Spracklen, K .M., Andrews, D. W., & Patterson, G. R. (1996). Deviancy training in male adolescent's friendships. *Behavior Therapy*, 27, 373–390.

Dodge, K. A. (1993). The future of research on the treatment of conduct disorder. *Developmental Psychopathology*, 5, 311–319.

Ennett, S. T., Tobler, N. S., Ringwalt, C. L., & Flewelling, R. L. (1994). How effective is drug abuse resistance education? A meta-analysis of project DARE outcome evaluations. *American Journal of Public Health*, 84, 1394–1401.

Fox, N. A. & Calkins, S. D. (1993). Social withdrawal: Interactions among temperament, attachment, and regulation. In K. H. Rubin & J. B. Asendorph (Eds.), *Social withdrawal, inhibition and shyness in childhood.* Hillsdale, NJ: Lawrence Erlbaum.

Fraser, J. A., Armstrong, K. L., Morris, J., & Dadds, M. R. (20010). Home visiting intervention for vulnerable families with newborns: Follow-up results of a randomised controlled trial. *Child Abuse and Neglect*, 24, 1399–1429.

Gainey, R. R., Catalano, R. F., Haggerty, K. P., & Hoppe, M. J., (1997). Deviance among the children of heroin addicts in treatment: Impact of parents and peers. *Deviant Behaviour*, 18, 143–159.

Gensheimer, L. K., Roosa, M. W., & Ayers, T. S. (1990). Children's self-selection into prevention programs: Evaluation of an innovative recruitment strategy for children of alcoholics. *American Journal of Community Psychology*, 18, 707–723.

Gillham, J. E., Reivich, K. J., Jaycox, L. H., & Seligman, M. E. (1994). Prevention of depressive symptoms in school children: Two-year follow-up. *Psychological Science*, 6, 343–350.

Glantz, M. D. & Pickens, R. W. (1992). Vulnerability to drug abuse: Introduction and overview. In M. D. Glantz & R. W. Pickens (Eds.), *Vulnerability to drug abuse.* Washington, DC: American Psychological Association.

Glantz, M. D., Weinberg, N. Z., Miner, L. L., & Colliver, J. D. (1999). The etiology of drug abuse: Mapping the paths. In M. D. Glantz & C. R. Hartel (Eds.), *Drug abuse: Origins and interventions.* Washington, DC: American Psychological Association.

Golly, A., Stiller, B., & Walker, H. M. (1998). First step to success: Replication and social validation of an early intervention program. *Journal of Emotional and Behavioral Disorders, 6,* 243–250.

Gorman, D. M. (1996). Do school-based social skills programs prevent alcohol use among young people? *Addiction Research, 4,* 191–210.

Gorsuch R. L. & Butler, M. C. (1976). Initial drug abuse: A review of predisposing social psychological factors. *Psychological Bulletin, 83,* 120–137.

Greenberg, M., Zins, J. E., Elias, M. J., & Weissberg, R. P. (in press). School-based prevention: Promoting positive youth development through social and emotional learning. *American Psychologist.*

Greenberg, M. T., Domitrovich, C., & Bambarger, B. (1999). *Preventing mental disorders in school age children: A review of the effectiveness of prevention programmes.* College of Health and Human Development. Pennsylvania State University.

Greenberg, M. R., Domitrovich, C., & Bambarger, B. (2001). The prevention of mental disorders in school-age children: Current state of the field. *Prevention and Treatment, 4,* Article 1. Retrieved August 34, 2001, from http://journals.apa.org/prevention/volume4/pre0040001a.htm.

Hains, A. A. & Ellman, S. W. (1994). Stress inoculation training as a preventative intervention for high school youths. *Journal of Cognitive Psychotherapy, 8,* 219–232.

Hansen, W. B. & Graham, J. W. (1991). Preventing alcohol, marijuana, and cigarette use among adolescents: Peer pressure resistance training versus establishing conservative norms. *Preventive Medicine, 20,* 414–430.

Hawkins, J. D. Catalano, R. F. & Miller, J. Y. (1992). Risk and protective factors for alcohol and other drug problems in adolescence and early adulthood: Implications for substance abuse prevention. *Psychological Bulletin, 112,* 64–105.

Hawkins, J. D., Kosterman, R., Maguin, E., Catalano, R. F., & Arthur, M. W. (1997) Substance use and abuse. In R. T Ammerman & M. Hersen (Eds.), *Handbook of prevention and treatment with children and adolescents.* New York.

Hawkins, J., Catalano, R., Kosterman, R., Abbott, R., & Hill, K. (in press). Preventing adolescent health risk behaviors by strengthening protection during childhood. *Archives of Pediatrics and Adolescent Medicine.*

Hayward, C., Varady, S., Albano, A. M., Thienemann, M., Henderson, L., & Schatzberg, A.F. (2000). Cognitive-behavioral group therapy for social phobia in female adolescents: Results of a pilot study. *Journal of the American Academy of Child and Adolescent Psychiatry, 39,* 721–726.

Henggeler, S. W., Melton, G. B., Brondino, M. J. Schere, D G., & Hanley, J. H. (1997). Multisystemic therapy with violent and chronic juvenile offenders and their families. *Journal of Consulting and Clinical Psychology,* 65, 821–833.

Hudley, C. & Graham, S. (1993). An attributional intervention to reduce peer-directed aggression among African-American boys. *Child Development, 64,* 124–138.

Hudley, C. & Graham, S. (1995). School-based interventions for aggressive African-American boys. *Applied and Preventive Psychology,* 4, 185–195.

Ialongo, N. S., Werthamer, L., Kellam, S. G., Brown, C. H., Wang, S., & Lin, Y. (1999). Proximal impact of two first grade preventive interventions on the early risk behaviours for later substance abuse, depression, and antisocial behaviour. *American Journal of Community Psychology, 27,* 599–641.

Jaycox, L. H., Reivich, K. J., Gillham, J., & Seligman, M. E. P. (1994). Prevention of depressive symptoms in school children. *Behaviour Research Therapy, 32,* 801–816.

Johnston, L. D., O'Malley, P. M., & Bachman, J. G. (2000). *The monitoring the future national survey results on adolescent drug use: Overview of key findings, 2000* (NIH Publication No.01–4923). Rockville, MD: National Institute on Drug Abuse.

Kann, R. T. & Hanna, F. J. (2000). Disruptive behaviour disorders in children and adolescents: How do girls differ from boys? *Journal of Counselling and Development. Summer 2000*, Vol 8.

Kashani, J. H. & Orvaschel, H. (1990). A community study of anxiety in children and adolescents. *American Journal of Psychiatry, 147*, 313–318.

Kazdin, A. E. (1995). *Conduct disorders in childhood and adolescence* (2nd edn). Thousand Oaks, CA: Sage.

Kazdin, A. E. (1993). Adolescent mental health, prevention and treatment programmes. *American Psychologist, 48*, 127–141.

Kazdin, A. E. (1987). *Conduct disorders in childhood and adolescence*: Vol. 9, *Developmental clinical psychology and psychiatry*, CA: Thousand Oaks.

Kazdin, A. E., Siegal, T. C., & Bass, D. (1992). Cognitive problem solving skills training and parent management training in the treatment of antisocial behaviour in children. *Journal of Consulting and Clinical Psychology, 60*, 733–747.

Kazdin, A. E. & Wassell, G. (2000). Therapeutic changes in children, parents and families resulting from treatment of children with conduct problems. *Journal of the American Academy of Child and Adolescent Psychiatry, 39*, 414–420.

Kendall, P. C. (1994). Treating anxiety disorders in children: Results of a randomized clinical trial. *Journal of Consulting and Clinical Psychology, 62*, 100–110.

Kendall, P. C., Flannery-Schoeder, E., Paanichelli-Mindel, S. M., Southam-Gerow, M., Henin, A., & Warman, M. (1997). Therapy for youths with anxiety disorders: A second randomized clinical trial. *Journal of Consulting and Clinical Psychology, 65*, 366–380.

Kessler, R. C. (1995). Epidemiology of psychiatric comorbidity. In Tsuang, Tohen & Zahner (eds.), *Textbook in psychiatric comorbidity*. Wiley-Liss Inc.

Kessler, R. C., McGonagle, K. A., Zhao, S., Nelson, C. B., Hughs, M., Eshleman, S., Wittchen, H-U, & Kendler, K. S. (1994). Lifetime and 12-month prevalence of DSM-III-R psychiatric disorders among persons aged 15–54 in the United States: Results form the National Comorbidity Survey. *Archives of General Psychiatry, 51*, 8–19.

Kessler, R. C., Nelson, C. B., McGonagle, K. A., Edlund, M. J., Frank, R. G., & Leaf, P. J. (1996). The epidemiology of co-occurring addictive and mental disorders: Implications for prevention and service utilisation. *American Journal of Orthopsychiatry, 66*, 17–31.

Kiselica, M. S. (2001). Overcoming barriers to the practice of primary prevention: An agenda for the mental health professions. *Prevention and Treatment, 4*, Commentary. Retrieved 2001, from http://journals apa.org/prevention/volume4.htm.

Kosterman, R., Hawkins, J., Spoth, R., Haggerty, K. P., & Zhu, K. (1997). Effetcs of a preventive parent-training intervention on observed family interactions: Proximal outcomes from Preparing for the Drug Free Years. *Journal of Community Psychology, 25*, 337–352.

LaFreniere, P. J. & Capuano, F. (1997). Preventive intervention as means of clarifying direction of effects in socialization: Anxious-withdrawn preschoolers case. *Development and Psychopathology, 9*, 551–564.

Lerner, J. V. & Vicary, J. R. (1984). Difficult temperament and drug use:Analysis from the New York longitudinal study. *Journal of Drug Education, 14,* 1–8.

Lewinsohn, P. M., Clarke, G. N., Hops, H., & Andrews, J. (1990). Cognitive-behavioural treatment for depressed adolescents. *Behaviour Therapy, 21,* 385–401.

Loeber, R. (1990). Development and risk factors of juvenile antisocial behaviour and delinquency. *Clinical Psychological Review, 10,* 1–42.

Loeber, R., Russo, M. F., Stouthamer-Loeber, M., & Lahey, B. B. (1994). Internalizing problems and their relation to the development of disruptive behaviours in adolescence. *Journal of Research on Adolescence, 4,* 615–637.

Lochman, J. E. (1985). Effects of different length treatments in cognitive-behavioral interventions with aggressive boys. *Child Psychiatry and Human Development, 16,* 45–56.

Lochman, J. E. (1992). Cognitive-behavioral intervention with aggressive boys: Three year follow-up and preventative efforts. *Journal of Consulting and Clinical Psychology, 60,* 426–432.

Lochman, J. E. Coie, J. D., Underwood, M. K., & Terry, R. (1993). Effectiveness of a social relations intervention for aggressive and nonaggressive, rejected children. *Journal of Consulting and Clinical Psychology, 61,* 1053–1058

Lonigan, C. J. & Phillips, B. M. (2001). Temperamental influences on the development of anxiety disorders. In M. W. Vasey & M. R. Dadds (Eds.), *The Developmental Psychopathology of Anxiety*. Oxford, UK: Oxford University Press.

Lorion, R. P. & Ross, J. G. (1992). Programmes for change: A realistic look at the nation's potential for preventing substance involvement among high-risk youth. *Journal of Community Psychology* [Special Issue], 3–9.

McCord, J., Tremblay, R. E., Vitaro, F., & Desmarais-Gervais, L. (1994). Boys' disruptive behavior, school adjustment, and delinquency: The Montreal Prevention Experiment. *International Journal of Behavioral Development, 17,* 739–752.

Mendlowitz, S. L., Manassis, K., Bradley, S., Scapillato, D., Miezitis, S., & Shaw, B. F. (1999). Cognitive-behavioral group treatments in childhood anxiety disorders: The role of parental involvement. *Journal of the American Academy of Child and Adolescent Psychiatry, 38,* 1223–1229.

Michaels, M. L., Rossa, M. W., & Gensheimer, L. K. (1992). Family characteristics of children who self-select into a preventive program for children of alcoholics. *American Journal of Community Psychology, 20,* 663–672.

Miller, G. E. & Prinz, R. J. (1990). Enhancement of social learning family interventions for childhood conduct disorder. *Psychological Bulletin, 108,* 291–307.

Mrazek, P. J. & Haggerty, R. J. (1994). *Reducing risks for mental disorders: Frontiers for preventive intervention research*. Washington, DC: National Academy Press.

Nastasi, B. K. & DeZolt, D. M. (1994). *School interventions for children of alcoholics*. New York: Guilford Press.

National Institute on Drug Abuse (1997). *Drug abuse prevention: What works?* National Institute on Drug Abuse, Office of Science Policy and Communications. Public Information Branch, 4500 Fishers Lane, Rockville MD 20587.

Newcomb, M. D. & Harlow, L. L. (1986). Life events and substance use among adolescents: Mediating effects of perceived loss of control and meaningless in life. *Journal of Personality and Social Psychology, 51,* 564–577.

Norman, E. & Turner, S. (1993). Adolescent substance use prevention programmes: Theories, models and research in the encouraging 80's. *The Journal of Primary Prevention, 14,* 3–20.

O'Connor, T. G., Caspi, A., DeFries, J. C., & Plomin, R. (2000). Are associations between parental divorce and children's adjustment genetically mediated? An adoption study. *Developmental Psychology, 36,* 429–437.

Olds, D. L., Henderson, C. R., Talelbaum, R., & Chamberlain, R. (1986a). Improving the delivery of prenatal care and outcomes of pregnancy: A randomised trial of nurse home visitation. *Paediatrics, 77,* 16–28.

Olds, D. L., Henderson, C. R., Chamberlain, R., & Talelbaum, R. (1986b). Preventing child abuse and neglect: A randomised trial of nurse home visitation. *Paediatrics, 78,* 65–78.

Olds, D. L., Henderson, C. R., & Talelbaum, R. (1994). Prevention of intellectual impairment in children of women who smoke cigarettes during pregnancy. *Paediatrics, 93,* 228–233.

Olds, D. L. & Kitzman, J. (1993). Review of research on home visiting for pregnant women and parents of young children. *Future of Children, 3,* 53–92.

Ollendick, T. H. & King, N. J. (1994). Diagnosis, assessment, and treatment of internalising problems in children: The role of longitudinal data. *Journal of Consulting and Clinical Child Psychology, 62,* 918–927.

Ollendick, T. H., Seligman, L. D., & Butcher A. T. (1999). Does anxiety mitigate the behavioural expression of severe conduct disorder in delinquent youths? *Journal of Anxiety Disorders, 13,* 565–574.

Patterson, G. R. (1982). *Coercive family process.* Eugene, OR: Castalia Press.

Patterson G. R. (1986). Performance models for antisocial boys. *American Pshychologist, 41,* 432–444.

Pedro-Carroll, J. L., Alper-Gillis, L. J., & Cowen, E. L. (1992). An evaluation of the efficacy of preventive intervention for 4th-6th grade urban children in divorce. *Journal of Primary Prevention, 13,* 115–130.

Pepler, D. J., King, G., & Byrd, W. (1991) A social-cognitively based social skill training program for aggressive children. In D. Pepler & K. Rubin (Eds.), *The development and treatment of childhood aggression* (pp. 361–379). Hillsdale, NJ: Lawrence Erlbaum.

Pepler, D. J., King, G., Craig, W., Byrd, W., & Bream, L. (1995) The development and evaluation of a social skills group training program for aggressive children. *Child and Youth Care Forum, 24,* 297–313

Perrin, S. & Last, C. G. (1992). Do childhood anxiety measures measure anxiety? *Journal of Abnormal Child Psychology, 20,* 567–578.

Pine, D. S., Cohen, P., Gurley, D., Brook, J., & Ma, Y. J.(1998). The risk for early-adulthood anxiety and depressive disorders in adolescents with anxiety and depressive disorders. *Archives of General Psychiatry, 55,* 56–64.

Prinz, R. J., Blechman, E. A., & Dumas, J. E. (1994). An evaluation of peer coping-skills training for childhood aggression. *Journal of Clinical Child Psychology, 23,* 193–203.

Prinz, R. J. & Miller, G. E. (1994). Family based treatment for childhood antisocial behaviour: Experimental influences on dropout and engagement. *Journal of Consulting and Clinical Psychology, 62,* 645–650.

Reid, J. B. & Eddy, J. M. (1997). The prevention of antisocial behaviour: Some considerations in the search of effective interventions. In D. M. Stoff, J. Breiling, & J. D. Maser (Eds.), *Handbook of antisocial behaviour.* New York: John Wiley.

Reid, J. B., Eddy, J. M., Fetrow, R. A. & Stoolmiller, M. (1999) Description and

immediate impacts of a preventive intervention for conduct problems. *American Journal of Community Psychology, 27*, 483–517.
Reiger, D. A., Farmer, M. E., Rae, D. S., Locke, B. Z., Keith, B. J., Judd, L. L., & Goodwin, F. K. (1990). Comorbidity of mental health disorders with alcohol and other drug abuse. *Journal of the American Medical Association, 264*, 2511–2518.
Roth, J. & Dadds, M. R. (1999). Reach for resilience: Evaluation of a universal program for the prevention of internalizing problems in young children. *Griffith Early Intervention Project.* School of Applied Psychology, Griffith University.
Saffer, H. & Grossman, M. (1987). Beer taxes, the legal drinking age, and motor vehicle fatalities. *Journal of Legal Studies, 16*, 351–374.
Sanders, M. R. (1999). Triple P-Positive Parenting Program: Towards an empirically validated multilevel parenting and family support strategy for the prevention of behavior and emotional problems in children. *Clinical Child and Family Psychological Review, 2*(2), 71–90.
Schinke, S. P. & Tepavac, L. (1995). Substance abuse prevention among elementary school students. *Drugs and Society, 8*, 15–27.
Sher, K. J., Walitzer, K. S., Wood, P. K., & Brent, E. E. (1991). Characteristics of children of alcoholics: Putative risk factors, substance use and abuse, and psychopathy. *Journal of Abnormal Psychology, 100*, 427–448.
Shochet, I., Holland, D., & Whitefield, K. (1997). *The Griffith Early Intervention Depression Project: Group Leader's Manual.* Brisbane: Griffith Early Intervention Project.
Shochet, I. M., Dadds, M. R., Holland, D., Whitefield, K., Harnett, P., & Osgarby, S. M. (in press). Short-term effects of a universal school-based program to prevent adolescent depression: A controlled trial. *Journal of Consulting and Clinical Psychology.*
Short, J. L. (1998). Evaluation of a substance abuse prevention and mental health promotion program for children of divorce. *Journal of Divorce and Remarriage, 28*, 139–155.
Shure, M. B. (1997). Interpersonal cognitive problem solving: Primary prevention of early high-risk behaviors in the preschool and primary years. In G.W. Albee & T. P. Gullota (Eds.). *Primary prevention works.* London: Sage.
Sroufe, L. A. & Rutter, M. (1984). The domain of developmental psychopathology. *Child Development, 55*, 17–29.
Substance Abuse and Mental Health Services Administration (1999). *National Household Survey on Drug Abuse.* Office of Applied Studies, Substance Abuse and Mental Health Statistics.
Thompson, R. A. (2001). Childhood anxiety disorders from the perspective of emotional regulation and attachment. In M. W. Vasey & M. R. Dadds (Eds.), *The developmental psychopathology of anxiety.* Oxford: Oxford University Press.
Tierney, J. P., Grossman, J. B., & Resch, N. L. (1995). *Making a difference: The impact study of Big Brother/Sister.* Philadelphia, PA: Public/Private Ventures.
Tremblay, R. E. Masse, L. C., Pagani, L., & Vitaro, F. (1996). From childhood physical aggression to adolescent maladjustment: The Montreal Prevention Experiment. In R. DeV. Peters & R. J. McMahon (Eds.), *Preventing childhood disorders, substance abuse, and delinquency* (pp. 268–298). Thousand Oaks, CA: Sage.
Tremblay, R. E., Pagani-Kurtz, L, Masse, L. C., Vitaro, F., & Pihl, R. O. (1995). A bimodal preventive intervention for disruptive kindergarten boys: Its impact

through mid-adolescence. *Journal of Consulting and Clinical Psychology, 63,* 560–568.
Tremblay, R. E. Vitaro, F., Bertrand, L., LeBlanc, M., Bearschesne, H., Boileau, H., & David, L. (1992). Parent and child training to prevent early onset delinquency: The Montreal Longitudinal Eperimental Study. In J. McCord & R. E. Tremblay, Eds.), *Preventing antisocial behavior* (pp. 117–138). New York: Guildford Press.
Tuma, J. M. (1989). Mental health services for children: The state of the art. *American Psychologist, 44,* 188–198.
Vasey, M. W. & Dadds, M. R. (2001). An introduction to the developmental psychopathology of anxiety. In M. W. Vasey & M. R. Dadds (Eds.), *The developmental psychopathology of anxiety.* Oxford: Oxford University Press.
Vitaro, F. & Tremblay, R. E. (1994). Impact of a prevention program on aggressive children's friendships and social adjustment. *Journal of Abnormal Child Pshchology, 22,* 457–475.
Walker, H., Kavanagh, K., Stiller, B., Golly, A., Severson, H., & Feil, E. (1998a). First step to success: An early intervention approach for preventing school antisocial behavior. *Journal of Emotional and Behavioral Disorders, 6,* 66–80.
Walker, H. M. Stiller, B. S., Severson, H. H., Feil, E. G., & Golly, A. (1998b). First step to success: Intervening at the point of school entry to prevent antisocial patterns. *Psychology in the Schools, 35,* 259–269.
Webster-Stratton, C. & Hammond, M. (1998). Conduct problems and level of social competence in head start children: Prevalence, pervasiveness, and associated risk factors. *Clinical Child and Family Psychology Review,* 1, 101–124.
Weinberg, N. Z. & Glantz, M. D. (1999). Child psychopathology risk factors for drug abuse: Overview. *Journal of Clinical Child Psychology, 28,* 290–297.
Werner, E. E. (1993). Risk, resilience, and recovery: Perspectives from the Kauai longitudinal study. *Development and Psychopathology,* 5, 503–515.
West, D. J. (1982). *Delinquency: Its roots, careers and prospects.* Cambridge, MA: Harvard University Press.
Westermeyer, J. (1997) Substance-related disorders. In R.T. Ammerman & M. Hersen (Eds.), *Handbook of prevention and treatment with children and adolescents.* John Wiley and Son. New York: John Wiley.
Windle, M. (1999). *Alcohol use among adolescents.* Vol. 42, *Developmental clinical psychology and Psychiatry.* Thousand Oaks, CA: Sage.
World Health Organization (1990). *Preventing and controlling drug abuse.* In M. Gossop & M. Grant (Eds). Geneva: WHO.
Wyman, P. A., Cowen, E. L., Work, W. C., & Kerley, J. H. (1993). The role of children's future expectations in self-system functioning and adjustment to life stress: A prospective study of urban at-risk children. *Development and Psychopathology,* 5, 649–661.
Zeigler, E., Taussig, C. & Black, K. (1992). Early childhood intervention: A promising preventative for juvenile delinquency. *American Psychologist, 47,* 997–1006.

Chapter 7
Psychological intervention
Robert J. Williams

Most adolescent substance abusers neither seek out nor receive formal treatment for their substance abuse. Despite this, most adolescent substance abusers eventually curb their substance use by their mid- to late-20s (Fillmore, 1988; Kandel and Raveis, 1989; Labouvie, 1996; Pape and Hammer, 1996). One explanation for this concerns the nature of the teenage years that encourages experimentation with a wide variety of behaviours, including substance use. This need for rebellion and experimentation is not as strong for someone in their late 20s. Another explanation concerns the process of "natural recovery", where individuals simply identify and rectify their problems themselves (Burman, 1997; Granfield and Cloud, 1999).

Sometimes overlooked are the "interventions" contributing to this phenomenon. Environmental pressures are usually involved when people decide to make important changes in their life. There are pervasive influences operating in the environments of almost all adolescent substance abusers discouraging substance use. Anti-drug messages are prevalent in the media, in school, and often in family and peer contexts. The problems that sometimes occur because of substance use (parental conflict, peer conflict, school problems, physical sequelae, employment consequences) provide further inducement for change. The new roles that develop in the mid- to late-20s (jobs, marriage, parenting) are other things that tend to conflict with continued substance use (Kandel and Raveis, 1989; Labouvie, 1996).

Thus, it is important to recognize that "interventions" for adolescent substance abuse are pervasive. And, for the most part, they can be said to be effective. It is a continuum between these types of environmental pressures and formal treatment programmes. Somewhat intermediate are meetings an adolescent may have with his/her school counsellor or family physician, or attendance at drop-in group counselling sessions provided in many high schools for substance use and abuse (Wagner *et al.*, 1999).

FORMAL TREATMENT PROGRAMS

Formal treatment programmes come in many forms. The main dimensions upon which they vary are their location (hospital or substance abuse treatment facility), their intensity (residential, day treatment, outpatient), their duration (few sessions to over a year), and their comprehensiveness. Comprehensiveness is reflected in whether the programme is theoretically focused (e.g., 12-step, outward bound) or eclectic; whether it provides a limited or broad range of services (i.e., just substance abuse treatment or substance abuse treatment and recreational, occupational, educational, psychiatric services); and the number of modalities by which treatment is provided (e.g., group therapy or individual, group and family therapy). See Figure 7.1.

Treatment programmes can be roughly grouped into four main types, although there is considerable (and increasing) overlap between these programmes. One type of treatment is outpatient treatment. The focus is usually individual counselling, although sometimes family therapy and group treatment are also used. Alternatively, group therapy may be the primary treatment modality when self-help groups such as Alcoholics Anonymous (AA) and Narcotics Anonymous (NA) are provided as the first line of treatment. Outpatient treatment tends to be less intensive than hospital treatment

	LOCATION	
Hospital	←——————→	Substance abuse treatment facility
	INTENSITY	
Outpatient	←——————→	Residential
	Day treatment	
	DURATION	
Few sessions	←——————→	> 1 year
	COMPREHENSIVENESS	
Theroetically focused (e.g. 12-step, outward bound)	←——————→	Eclectic
Limited range of services (just substance abuse treatment)	←——————→	Broad range of services (recreational, occupational educational, psychiatric)
Single modality (e.g., individual)	←——————→	Multiple modalities (individual, gorup, family)

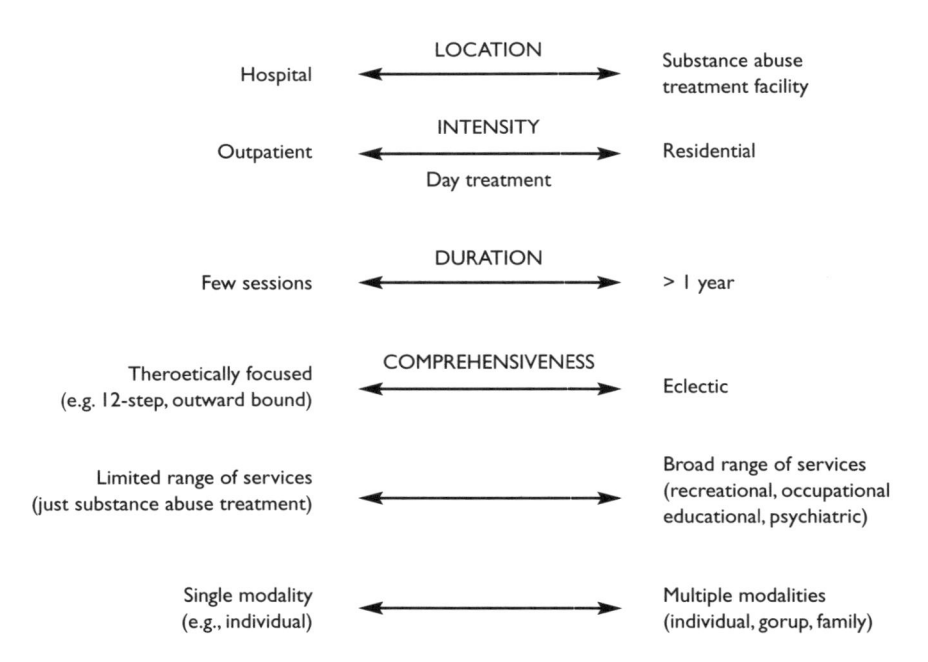

Figure 7.1 Dimensions upon which formal treatment programmes vary.

Psychological intervention 187

(e.g., One to two sessions per week), but longer in duration. Treatment usually has no set length, varying anywhere from one session to years, with a modal length of perhaps three months. Outpatient programmes are the most common form of substance abuse treatment for adolescents in North America (US Department of Health and Human Services, 1997a).

Another type of treatment is the "Minnesota model". This is a short (four- to six week) hospital inpatient programme typically offering a comprehensive range of treatment (individual counselling, group therapy, medication for comorbid psychiatric conditions, family therapy, schooling, and recreational programming). This type of programme sometimes also has an AA/NA 12-step orientation and is often followed by outpatient treatment. Most of the large multi-site, multi-programme treatment outcome studies such as the Treatment Outcome Prospective Study (TOPS) and the Chemical Abuse Treatment Outcome Registry (CATOR) have studied this type of programme.

A third, less common type of treatment is a lengthy (six- month to two-year) "therapeutic community" type programme based in a specialized substance abuse treatment facility (Jainchill et al., 1995; Pompi, 1994). These tend to be highly regimented residential settings with treatment facilitated by paraprofessionals, but run by the residents themselves. Members progress through a hierarchy of responsibilities within this community of former substance abusers. In the older, traditional therapeutic communities, adolescents comprise only a small minority of the treatment population. However, there are newer forms of this treatment that provide services exclusively to adolescents. These programmes retain the indoctrinational and highly structured nature of traditional therapeutic communities. They are often day programmes where the recovering adolescent lives in the home of an adolescent further progressed in treatment. Because of their structured nature and length, these types of programmes tend to have very high drop-out rates.

A fourth type of programme is the "outward bound"/lifeskills training type programme (e.g., McPeake et al., 1991; Richardson, 1996). This type of programme is occasionally provided as the primary treatment, and sometimes as a supplement to other treatment types. It is typically an intensive three- or four-week outing that exposes adolescents to a non-drug lifestyle and presents them with challenges intended to facilitate personal development and resistance to drugs.

PROBLEMS IN MEASURING THE EFFECTIVENESS OF FORMAL TREATMENT PROGRAMMES

There are several difficulties in establishing the effectiveness of treatment programmes. The first concerns how to measure success. A common measure in the adolescent literature is abstinence rates. However, for adolescents, reduction in substance use is probably a better measure. Abstinence is an appropriate goal for an adult with many years of drug dependence and a history of relapse. However, abstinence is probably a less realistic or clinically essential goal for a 15- or 16-year old, at least with respect to substances such as alcohol. Problems in other life areas (employment/school, social, legal, family, psychological, medical) must also be considered in evaluating success. The usual motivation for treatment is not the substance use itself, but the impact that substance abuse is having on the person's life.

Another problem concerns how long to wait after discharge to evaluate treatment effectiveness. Evaluations done at the end of treatment, or shortly thereafter, tend to overestimate the enduring effects of treatment (Miller and Sanchez-Craig, 1996). However, very long follow-up periods may also distort the effects of treatment because of the natural trend for substance use to peak in the late teens to early 20s and diminish thereafter. Studies that have done follow-up in the late teens or early 20s show very low rates of substance reduction or even increases (e.g., Marzen, 1990; Sells and Simpson, 1979; US Department of Health and Human Services, 1998). By comparison, studies providing follow-up in the mid-20s tend to show fairly high rates of abstinence and substance reduction (e.g., Richardson, 1996; Vaglum and Fossheim, 1980).

A final problem concerns ascertainment of substance use. Most studies rely on self-report of either the parent or adolescent. This is problematic, as parental awareness of adolescent substance use tends to be quite poor (Friedman *et al.*, 1990; Williams *et al.*, 2002). Although adolescent self-report is much better, it is influenced by the demand characteristics and memory requirements of the situation. Under-reporting is characteristic of recent arrestees (Fendrich and Xu, 1994; Harrison, 1995; Magura and Kang, 1996); for less socially acceptable drugs (e.g., cocaine) (Lundy *et al.*, 1997; Wish *et al.*, 1997); when parents are present (Aquilino, 1997); and when answers are given verbally (Aquilino, 1997; Turner *et al.*, 1992). Similarly, individuals tend to be less honest about substance use after treatment than before treatment (Wish *et al.*, 1997), with repeated assessments being associated with progressively less honest reporting (Fendrich *et al.*, 1997). Retrospective reports are influenced by current substance use status, with higher reports of retrospective use being associated with higher current use and vice versa (Collins *et al.*, 1985; Czarnecki *et al.*, 1990).

In some cases these problems may not apply, and in other cases the magnitude of these influences may not be that large. Nonetheless, corroboration is always preferable. Relying exclusively on biochemical drug testing does not necessarily improve validity because of problems with false negatives. Some substances are present in such minute quantities (e.g., LSD) they are virtually impossible to detect. Unless done frequently, urinalysis is poor at detecting substances that are quickly metabolized (e.g., alcohol, cocaine). Hair assays are expensive, do not screen for all substances, and are unable to detect drug use for the three days prior to the test (Kintz, 1996; Magura *et al.*, 1995). Sweat analysis is unable to detect some substances (e.g., alcohol), is insensitive for other substances (e.g., marijuana), and requires compliance in wearing a sweat-absorbing patch for a period of time (Kintz *et al.*, 1996; Sunshine and Sutliff, 1997). Thus, it would appear that the most valid procedure for establishing substance use is by means of a positive report by the adolescent *or* a positive result from biochemical testing. In the absence of biochemical testing, a positive report by *either* the adolescent or parent may suffice.

TREATMENT EFFECTIVENESS

A comprehensive review of the literature on the effectiveness of adolescent substance abuse treatment has recently been completed by Williams and Chang (2000). These investigators identified eight multi-programme, multi-site studies (CATOR, DATOS, TOPS, UDCS, DARP, NTIES, SROS, Friedman & Glickman, 1986) and 45 single-programme studies. The methodology in these studies tended to be weak. The most common problems were poor follow-up rates, lack of control groups, failure to include dropouts in the results, reliance exclusively on parental report, and follow-up periods that were either too short (at discharge) or too long (>3 years). The following is their summary of treatment effectiveness from the 21 methodologically stronger studies that included dropouts in the results, had follow-up rates greater than 75%, did not rely exclusively on parental report, and where the average age of the treatment group was < 21 at time of follow-up (see Williams and Chang, 2000, for details).

Sustained abstinence

Eight studies reported abstinence rates at discharge or post-discharge, with four of them assessing abstinence at more than one time period. Figure 7.2 is a graphic presentation of these results. The one multi-site, multi-programme study is identified (NTIES), as are studies with repeated measures. The only time periods with more than two data points are 6 months and 12 months. *Average sustained abstinence at 6 months is 38% (range 30–55) and 32% at 12 months (range 14–47).*

Although there appears to be some tendency for abstinence rates to decrease with time since discharge, the amount of decrease is fairly small. Richter and colleagues' (1991) repeated measures study actually obtained a slight increase due to sampling differences between the two time periods. The one study reporting abstinence at discharge (Lewis *et al.*, 1990) found only 39–40% of adolescents receiving outpatient family therapy or family education were abstinent by the end of treatment. Brown and colleagues (1989, 1990) have reported that two-thirds of adolescent relapse occurs in the first

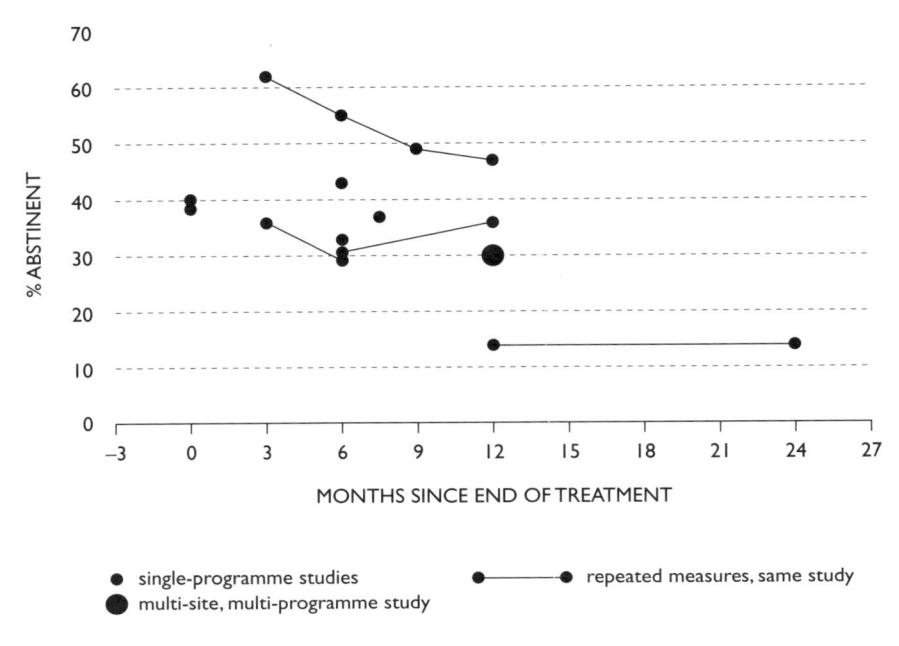

Figure 7.2 Percentage of adolescents with sustained abstinence as a function of time since discharge. Each data point represents a different study. Connected data points represent repeated measures in the same study.

three months post-treatment (see also Brown, 1993). While this might be true for the short inpatient programmes Brown and her colleagues have studied, it does not appear to be the case for outpatient programmes, where only a minority of adolescents actually *achieve* abstinence by the end of treatment.

Reduced substance use

Thirteen studies reported the percentage of adolescents with decreased substance use following treatment or the average group decrease in substance use. *In 12 out of 13 studies there was a reduction in substance use following treatment.* Braukmann and colleagues (1985) did not find group homes or teaching family group homes to reduce substance use in conduct-disordered males. Most studies did not quantify the extent to which substance use had been reduced. Friedman and Glickman (1986), in their examination of 30 outpatient programmes (sample of 5,603), reported that average drug usage at discharge decreased to approximately 50% of pretreatment levels. Friedman (1989) reported a 50% reduction in average drug usage at nine months post-treatment for adolescents in family therapy groups as well as adolescents whose parents attended parent support groups. In Lewis and colleagues (1990), 38% of adolescents receiving outpatient family education reported reduced substance use at discharge and 55% receiving family therapy reported reduced substance use. At six months post-discharge 57% of adolescents reported reduced substance use in the inpatient programmes studied by Brown and colleagues (1990) and by Richter and colleagues (1991). At 12 months post-discharge 51–55% of adolescents reported reduced marijuana use in the multi-site, multi-programme DATOS-A study (Hser *et al.*, 1999) and 62% reported reduced substance use in Richter and colleagues (1991).

Functioning in other life areas

Eight studies evaluated the effect of treatment on other aspects of the adolescent's life. Most of these studies simply reported whether there were group improvements as a result of treatment and did not indicate the degree of improvement. Four out of the five studies that examined illegal behaviour found decreases following treatment, with Braukmann *et al.* (1985) being the exception. Sixteen to 30% fewer adolescents committed an illegal act in the previous year compared to the year before treatment in the multi-site, multi-programme DATOS-A study (Hser *et al.*, 1999). Forty-one to 48% fewer adolescents committed an illegal act in the previous year compared to the year before treatment in the multi-site, multi-programme NTIES study (US Department of Health and Human Services, 1997b). The four studies that examined change in mental health all found improvements following treatment. The three studies examining change in family problems all found improvement following treatment. Two of the three studies examining school functioning reported improvements. Friedman *et al.* (1986) did not find improved school functioning in their study of 30 different outpatient programmes but did find improvements in employment following treatment.

Effectiveness compared to no treatment

The evidence presented thus far indicates that the majority of adolescents who enter into substance abuse treatment have significantly reduced substance usage and significant improvements in life functioning in the year subsequent to treatment. However, in the absence of no-treatment control groups, the extent to which this improvement is due to treatment, as opposed to natural recovery, regression to the mean, or a placebo effect, is uncertain. Surprisingly, there are only two studies that provide evidence on this issue. Braukmann *et al.* (1985) found that teaching-family group homes produced superior drug reductions among conduct-disordered youth during treatment, but at three-month follow-up there was no significant difference between the treatment and no-treatment group. Grenier (1985) compared a wait control group to a random sample of former patients in a hospital inpatient programme. At nine months post-treatment, 66% of the treatment group was not currently using drugs versus only 20% of the control group.

Although more direct comparisons with no treatment are required, there is other evidence that bears on this issue. First, a treatment effect above and beyond natural recovery, placebo response, or regression to the mean is implied by the fact that for the 15 studies that compared treatments, 9 found an advantage for one type of treatment over another (9 out of 12 if eliminating the three studies comparing variants of family therapy) (see Williams and Chang, 2000). Secondly, the related, but better researched areas of adult substance abuse treatment and treatment for adolescent emotional/behavioural problems have clearly established that treatment is superior to no treatment (Agosti, 1995; Hoag and Burlingame, 1997; Kazdin, 1990; Mann and Borduin, 1991; Miller *et al.*, 1995; Target and Fonagy, 1996; U.S. Department of Health and Human Services, 1995; Weisz *et al.*, 1995). It would be surprising if this was not also the case for adolescent substance abuse treatment.

Client variables related to better outcome

Client variables predictive of outcome tend to be the same ones found in most treatment literatures: i.e., success increases when treating milder problems in clients with higher levels of functioning. The client variable with the most consistent relationship to positive outcome in Williams and Chang's (2000) review was lower pretreatment substance use, found in six out of seven studies. Better school attendance and functioning at pretreatment was related to success in three out of four studies. Other variables with some evidence of a relationship to success are less conduct disorder, being employed, having fewer prior substance abuse treatments, and less psychopathology. Greater motivation for treatment was found to predict success in the two studies that measured this. Studies examining demographic variables such as race/ethnicity, gender, socioeconomic status, religion, and age have not found these variables to be consistently related to outcome.

Environmental variables related to better outcome

The adolescent's family has an important influence on successful treatment as illustrated by family therapy's superior efficacy relative to other forms of outpatient treatment (see below). The nature and quality of the parent–adolescent relationship can either promote or deter substance use depending on the amount of conflict that occurs, the degree of parental control and monitoring, and the amount of support provided. Parental social support, particularly in their own non-use of substances, is related to successful outcome in studies that have examined this (e.g., Brown *et al.*, 1996; Friedman *et al.*, 1995; Richter *et al.*, 1991). Lower levels of family pathology/higher levels of family functioning is also predictive (Friedman *et al.*, 1995; Shoemaker and Sherry, 1991). On the other hand, a family history of substance abuse has not been shown to influence outcome (Hser *et al.*, 1999 [DATOS-A]; Richter *et al.*, 1991).

The adolescent's peer group is equally, if not more, important. Having a non-using peer group has been shown to be a significant predictor of success (Hser *et al.*, 1999 [DATOS-A]; Brown *et al.*, 1996; Richter *et al.*, 1991; Shoemaker and Sherry, 1991). Adolescents are usually much more resistant to changing their peer group than their substance use. However, experience suggests that a long-term change to substance use inevitably requires changes to the adolescent's social environment making drugs less available and acceptable. Creation of new non-using peers through involvement in aftercare or new recreational activities is often an easier way of accomplishing this than directly requiring the adolescent to abandon his/her old peers. This is undoubtedly one of the reasons that attendance in aftercare (e.g., AA/NA) is predictive of success (Alford *et al.*, 1991; Kennedy and Minami, 1993; Shoemaker and Sherry, 1991). This may also be one of the reasons that provision of comprehensive services is helpful (see below), as adolescents with associated psychological, school, and/or legal problems tend to gravitate to substance-using peer groups.

Treatment variables related to better outcome

Only some aspects of treatment have been studied. There are some studies comparing types of outpatient therapy, providing preliminary evidence that behavioural or cognitive-behavioural therapy may be superior to supportive counselling (Azrin *et al.*, 1994) or interactional group therapy (Kaminer *et al.*, 1998). Similarly, other studies have shown evidence that providing material incentives (e.g., vouchers) contingent upon abstinence improves outcome over standard therapy (Hudney *et al.*, 2000; Kaminer, 2000).

There is *good* evidence that family therapy is superior to other types of outpatient therapy. Family therapy was more effective than other forms of non-family outpatient therapy (individual counselling, adolescent group therapy, family drug education, meetings with probation officer) in five out of six studies (Henggeler *et al.*, 1991; Joanning *et al.*, 1992; Lewis et al., 1990) Liddle *et al*, 1993 (cited in Stanton and Shadish, 1997). Friedman (1989) did not find family therapy to be superior to parent support groups. The superiority of family therapy in substance abuse treatment has also been identified in a couple of recent reviews of the general family therapy literature (Stanton and Shadish, 1997; Waldron, 1997).

Treatment completion is another variable that several studies have found to have a very strong relationship to positive outcome (Alford *et al.*, 1991; Cady *et al.*, 1996; Friedman *et al.*, 1986; Rush, 1979 [UDCS]; Sells and Simpson, 1979 [DARP]). This same finding has been consistently found in the adult substance abuse treatment literature. However, it is unclear whether this reflects the impact of treatment or whether treatment completion is simply an indicator of motivation. The latter seems more likely considering that duration of treatment is largely unrelated to outcome in the adult substance abuse and psychotherapy literature (Bien *et al.*, 1993; Johnstone and Zolese, 1999; Pfeiffer *et al.*, 1996; Steenbarger, 1994).

A comprehensive analysis of 30 treatment programmes (sample of 5,603 adolescents) by Friedman and Glickman (1986) merits special attention. These investigators found that programmes with therapists having more than two years of experience had better outcomes. Another important finding was that programmes that provided a comprehensive range of services (i.e., provision of schooling, vocational counselling, recreational activities, birth control, etc.) had better success. Number of different services received has also been shown to be robustly associated with outcome for adults (McLellan *et al.*, 1994). It is interesting to note, however, that "dual-diagnosis programmes" offering integrated services for individuals with both mental health problems and substance abuse have not shown an advantage over standard programmes (Ley *et al.*, 2001).

There are no well-designed studies comparing the comparative efficacy of the main treatment types (outpatient, short-term inpatient, long-term residential, outward bound). Duration of treatment and intensity of treatment have also not been investigated. However, the related areas of adult substance abuse treatment and treatment for adolescent emotional/behavioural problems may provide some guidance on these issues. With regard to treatment setting (outpatient, residential, inpatient), adult substance abuse research has found a slight advantage for inpatient over outpatient treatment in some circumstances (Annis, 1996; Finney *et al.*, 1996; Longabaugh, 1996). The impact of treatment setting on adolescent emotional/behavioural problems is less well researched, but evidence to date has not found any differential impact on outcome (Bates *et al.*, 1997; Curry, 1991).

Duration of treatment also has a weak effect on outcome. A review of brief interventions for alcohol problems has found them often to be as effective as more extensive treatment (Bien *et al.*, 1993). It also appears that short hospital stays and time-limited therapy do not adversely affect mental health outcome for most people (Johnston and Zolese, 1999; Pfeiffer *et al.*, 1996; Steenbarger, 1994).

Type of therapy is important. Therapies with better success rates in the treatment of alcoholism are the community reinforcement approach (because of its environmental pervasiveness and behavioural orientation?), behavioural contracting, social skills training and motivational enhancement (Miller *et al.*, 1995). However, there is very little evidence that certain types of alcoholics are best matched with certain types of therapy (at least with respect to outpatients receiving either cognitive-behavioural therapy, motivational enhancement therapy, or 12-step therapy) (Project MATCH Research Group,

1997a, 1997b). Behavioural therapy is also superior to nonbehavioural therapy for adolescent emotional/behavioural problems (Target and Fonagy, 1996; Weisz *et al.*, 1995). Family therapy appears particularly effective for conduct-disordered youth (Mann and Borduin, 1991; Target and Fonagy, 1996).

In general, therapist experience, training and professional discipline have a very weak relationship to mental health treatment outcome (Roth and Fonagy, 1996; Smith *et al.*, 1980; Weisz *et al.*, 1995), although experience may enhance client retention and improve outcome for more severely disturbed patients (Roth and Fonagy, 1996). Much more important than training or experience is the quality of the therapeutic relationship between therapist and client (Horvath and Symonds, 1991; Morris and Nicholson, 1993; Roth and Fonagy, 1996). This is believed to be fostered through therapist qualities of flexible/intelligent thinking, good interpersonal skills, and genuine empathy (Lazarus, 1993; Miller, 1993; Miller *et al.*, 1995; Mohr, 1995; Najavits and Weiss, 1994).

SUMMARY AND RECOMMENDATIONS

There are pervasive environmental pressures discouraging adolescent substance abuse. For most adolescent substance abusers these are the only "interventions" they will receive. But for most, this will be sufficient. Formal treatment programmes are uncommon types of intervention provided to a small minority of substance abusers. Individuals who enter into these programmes are individuals where less formal intervention has been unsuccessful, there is typically an adult caregiver strongly motivated to change the adolescent's behaviour (as treatment entry is usually not initiated by the adolescent themselves), and there are adults in the adolescent's life who are able to exert some degree of control over him or her. All of these characteristics have implications for successful treatment.

Formal treatment programmes come in many forms. The main dimensions upon which they vary are their location, their intensity, their duration; and their comprehensiveness. The main types are short-term hospital inpatient programmes, outpatient therapy, and long-term therapeutic community programmes. Methodologically stronger studies examining the effectiveness of treatment programmes have usually found most adolescents receiving treatment to have significant reductions in substance use and problems in other life areas in the year following treatment. Sustained abstinence averages 38% (range 30–55) at six months post-treatment and 32% at 12 months (range 14–47). Success rates are lower for adolescents with more severe substance abuse problems, lower levels of functioning, and higher levels of associated individual and family pathology.

There are several things that parents, clinicians and programmes can do to better ensure treatment success:

- Motivation is very important. If the adolescent lacks motivation to change then it is necessary to cultivate this motivation, either through counselling or provision of incentives.
- Having a behavioural orientation with clear behavioural goals and some form of reward for achieving these goals would appear to be important.
- Comprehensive services should be provided in areas other than just substance abuse (i.e., schooling, psychological, vocational, recreational, medical, family, legal). Problems in these other areas contribute both to the development and the maintenance of substance abuse.
- The adolescent's social environment has to be addressed. The impact of individual skill development is limited unless accompanied by environmental changes that decrease the opportunities and acceptability of substance use. Family therapy is a necessary part of treatment. Parental and peer group non-use of substances is also very important.
- Choosing a good therapist is likely to have more importance than where, how long, or how intensive the treatment is.
- Given the general equivalencies of treatment types, it makes sense to initially seek out the least expensive, least intrusive, most readily accessible type of treatment that offers the elements mentioned above. Progressively more intrusive and intensive treatment will have to be provided for individuals unsuccessful in less structured settings.

REFERENCES

Agosti, V. (1995). The efficacy of treatments in reducing alcohol consumption: A meta-analysis. *The International Journal of the Addictions, 30,* 1067–1077.

Alford, G. S., Koehler, R. A., & Leonard, J. (1991). Alcoholics Anonymous–Narcotics Anonymous model inpatient treatment of chemically dependent adolescents: A 2-year outcome study. *Journal of Studies on Alcohol, 52,* 118–126.

Annis, H. M. (1996). Inpatient versus outpatient setting effects in alcoholism treatment: Revisiting the evidence. *Addiction, 91,* 1804–1807.

Aquilino, W. S. (1997). Privacy effects on self-reported drug use: Interactions with survey mode and respondent characteristics. In L. Harrison & A. Hughes (Eds.), *The validity of self-reported drug use: Improving the accuracy of survey estimates* (NIDA Research Monograph 167). Rockville, MD: US Department of Health and Human Services.

Azrin, N. H., Donohue, B., Besalel, V. A., Kogan, E. S., & Acierno, R. (1994). Youth drug abuse treatment: A controlled outcome study. *Journal of Child & Adolescent Substance Abuse, 3,* 1–16.

Bates, B. C., English, D. J., & Kouidou-Giles, S. (1997). Residential treatment and its alternatives: A review of the literature. *Child & Youth Care Forum, 26,* 7–51.

Bien, T. H., Miller, W. R., & Tonigan, J. S. (1993). Brief interventions for alcohol problems: A review. *Addiction, 88,* 315–335.

Braukmann, C. J., Bedlington, M. M., Belden, B. D., Braukmann, B. P. D., Husted, J. J., Ramp, K. K., & Wolf, M. M. (1985). Effects of a community-based group-home treatment program on male juvenile offenders use and abuse of drugs and alcohol. *American Journal of Drug and Alcohol Abuse*, *11*, 249–278.

Brown, S. A. (1993). Recovery patterns in adolescent substance abuse. In J. S. Baer, G. A. Marlatt, & R. J. McMahon (Eds.), *Addictive behaviours across the lifespan: Prevention, treatment and policy issues* (pp. 161–183). London: Sage.

Brown, S. A., Gleghorn, A., Schuckit, M. A., Myers, M. G., & Mott, M. A. (1996). Conduct disorder among adolescent alcohol and drug abusers. *Journal of Studies in Alcohol*, *57*, 314–324.

Brown, S. A., Mott, M. A., & Myers, M. G. (1990). Adolescent alcohol and drug treatment outcome. In R. R. Watson (Ed.), *Drug and alcohol abuse prevention* (pp. 373–403). New York, NY: Humana Press.

Brown, S. A., Vik, P. W., & Creamer, V. A. (1989). Characteristics of relapse following adolescent substance abuse treatment. *Addictive Behaviours*, *14*, 291–300.

Burman, S. (1997). The challenge of sobriety: Natural recovery without treatment and self-help groups. *Journal of Substance Abuse*, *9*, 41–61.

Cady, M. E., Winters, K. C., Jordan, D. A., Solberg, K. B., & Stinchfield, R. D. (1996). Motivation to change as a predictor of treatment outcome for adolescent substance abusers. *Journal of Child & Adolescent Substance Abuse*, *5*, 73–91.

Collins, L. M., Graham, J. W., Hansen, W. B., & Johnson, C. A. (1985). Agreement between retrospective accounts of substance use and earlier reported substance use. *Applied Psychological Measurement*, *9*, 301–309.

Curry, J. F. (1991). Outcome research on residential treatment: Implications and suggested directions. *American Journal of Orthopsychiatry*, *61*, 348–357.

Czarnecki, D. M., Russell, M., Cooper, M. L., & Salter, D. (1990). Five-year reliability of self-reported alcohol consumption. *Journal of Studies on Alcohol*, *51*, 68–76.

Fendrich, M., Mackesy-Amiti, M. E., Wislar, J. S., & Goldstein, P. (1997). The reliability and consistency of drug reporting in ethnographic samples. In L. Harrison & A. Hughes (Eds.), *The validity of self-reported drug use: Improving the accuracy of survey estimates* (NIDA Research Monograph 167). Rockville, MD: US Department of Health and Human Services.

Fendrich, M. & Xu, Y. (1994). The validity of drug use reports from juvenile arrestees. *International Journal of the Addictions*, *29*, 971–985.

Fillmore, K. M. (1988). *Alcohol use across the life course: A critical review of 70 years of international longitudinal research*. Toronto, Ontario: Addiction Research Foundation.

Finney, J. W., Hahn, A. C., & Moos, R. H. (1996). Effectiveness of inpatient and outpatient treatment for alcohol abuse: The need to focus on mediators and moderators of setting effects. *Addiction*, *91*, 1773–1796.

Friedman, A. S. (1989). Family therapy vs. parent groups: Effects on adolescent drug abusers. *American Journal of Family Therapy*, *17*, 335–347.

Friedman, A. S. & Glickman, N. W. (1986). Program characteristics for successful treatment of adolescent drug abuse. *The Journal of Nervous and Mental Disease*, *174*, 669–679.

Friedman, A. S., Glickman, N. W., & Morrissey, M. R. (1986). Prediction to successful treatment outcome by client characteristics and retention in treatment in adolescent drug treatment programs: A large-scale cross validation study. *Journal of Drug Education*, *16*, 149–165.

Friedman, A. S., Glickman, N. W., & Morrissey, M. R. (1990). What mothers know about their adolescents' alcohol/drug use and problems, and how mothers react to finding out about it. In A. S. Friedman & S. Granick (Eds.), *Family therapy for adolescent drug abuse* (pp. 169–181). Lexington, MA: Lexington Books.

Friedman, A. S., Terras, A., & Kreisher, C. (1995). Family and client characteristics as predictors of outpatient treatment outcome for adolescent drug abusers. *Journal of Substance Abuse, 7,* 345–356.

Granfield, R. & Cloud, W. (1999). *Coming clean: Overcoming addiction without treatment.* New York, NY: New York University Press.

Grenier, C. (1985). Treatment effectiveness in an adolescent chemical dependency treatment program: A quasi-experimental design. *International Journal of the Addictions, 20,* 381–391.

Harrison, L. D. (1995). The validity of self-reported data on drug use. *The Journal of Drug Issues, 25,* 91–111.

Henggeler, S. W., Bourdin, C. M., Melton, G. B., Mann, B. J., Smith, L. A. et al. (1991). Effects of multisystematic therapy on drug use and abuse in serious juvenile offenders: A progress report from two outcome studies. *Family Dynamics Addiction Quarterly, 1,* 40–51.

Hoag, M. J. & Burlingame, G. M. (1997). Child and adolescent group psychotherapy: A narrative review of effectiveness and the case for meta-analysis. *Journal of Child & Adolescent Group Therapy, 7,* 51–68.

Horvath, A. O. & Symonds, B. D. (1991). Relation between working alliance and outcome in psychotherapy: A meta-analysis. *Journal of Consulting and Clinical Psychology, 38,* 139–149.

Hser, Y. I., Grella, C., Hsieh, S. C., & Anglin, M. D. (1999, June). *National evaluation of drug treatment for adolescents (DATOS-A).* Paper presented at the College on Problems of Drug Dependence, Acapulco, Mexico.

Hudney, A. J., Higgins, S. T., & Novy, P. L. (2000). Adding voucher-based incentives to coping skills and motivational enhancement improves outcomes during treatment for marijuana dependence. *Journal of Consulting and Clinical Psychology, 68,* 1051–1061.

Jainchill, N., Bhattacharya, G., & Yagelka, J. (1995). Therapeutic communities for adolescents. In E. Rahdert & D. Czechowicz (Eds.), *Adolescent drug abuse: Clinical assessment and therapeutic interventions* (NIDA Research Monograph 156). US Department of Health and Human Services.

Joanning, H., Quinn, W., Thomas, F., & Mullen, R. (1992). Treating adolescent drug abuse: A comparison of family systems therapy, group therapy, and family drug education. *Journal of Marital and Family Therapy, 18,* 345–356.

Johnstone, P. & Zolese, G. (1999). Length of hospitalisation for those with severe mental illness. *Cochrane Database of Systematic Reviews, Issue 2.*

Kaminer, Y. (2000). Contingency management reinforcement procedures for adolescent substance abuse. *Journal of the American Academy of Child & Adolescent Psychiatry, 39,* 1324–1327.

Kaminer, Y., Burleson, J. A., Blitz, C., Sussman, J., & Rounsaville, B. J. (1998). Psychotherapies for adolescent substance abusers. *Journal of Nervous and Mental Disease, 186,* 684–690.

Kandel, D. B. & Raveis, V. H. (1989). Cessation of illicit drug use in young adulthood. *Archives of General Psychiatry, 46,* 109–116.

Kazdin, A. E. (1990). Psychotherapy for children and adolescents. *Annual Review of Psychology, 41,* 21–54.

Kennedy, B. P. & Minami, M. (1993). The Beech Hill Hospital/Outward Bound Adolescent Chemical Dependency Treatment Program. *Journal of Substance Abuse and Treatment, 10,* 395–406.

Kintz, P. (1996). Drug testing in addicts: a comparison between urine, sweat, and hair. *Therapeutic Drug Monitoring, 18,* 450–455.

Kintz, P., Tracqui, A., Jamey, C., & Mangin, P. (1996). Detection of codeine and phenobarbital in sweat collected with a sweat patch. *Journal of Analytical Toxicology, 20,* 197–201.

Labouvie, E. (1996). Maturing out of substance use: Selection and self-correction. *Journal of Drug Issues, 26,* 457–476.

Lazarus, A. A. (1993). Tailoring the therapeutic relationship, or being an authentic chameleon. *Psychotherapy, 30,* 404–407.

Lewis, R. A., Piercy, F. P. Sprenkle, D. H., & Trepper, T. S. (1990). Family-based interventions for helping drug-abusing adolescents. *Journal of Adolescent Research, 5,* 82–95.

Ley, A., Jeffery, D. P., McLaren, S., & Siegfried, N. (2001). Treatment programmes for people with both severe mental illness and substance misuse (Cochrane Review). In *The Cochrane Library, 4.* Oxford: Update Software.

Longabaugh, R. (1996). Inpatient versus outpatient treatment: No one benefits. *Addiction, 91,* 1809–1810.

Lundy, A., Gottheil, E., McLellan, A. T., Weinstein, S. P., Sterling, R. C., & Serota, R. D. (1997). Under-reporting of cocaine use at post-treatment follow-up and the measurement of treatment effectiveness. *Journal of Nervous and Mental Disease, 185,* 459–462.

Magura, S. & Kang, S. Y. (1996). Validity of self-reported drug use in high risk populations: a meta-analytical review. *Substance Use and Misuse, 31,* 1131–1153.

Magura, S., Kang, S. Y., & Shapiro, J. L. (1995). Measuring cocaine use by hair analysis among criminally-involved youth. *The Journal of Drug Issues, 25,* 683–701.

Mann, B. J. & Borduin, C. M. (1991). A critical review of psychotherapy outcome studies with adolescents: 1978–1988. *Adolescence, 26,* 505–541.

Marzen, T. J. (1990). The effectiveness of an adolescent rehabilitation program for alcohol and other drug addictions in a San Francisco hospital: A 5-year follow-up study. *Dissertations Abstracts International, 51,* 2979–A.

McLellan, A. T., Alterman, A. I., Metzger, D. S., Grissom, G. R., Woody, G. E., Luborsky, L., & O'Brien, C. P. (1994). Similarity of outcome predictors across opiate, cocaine, and alcohol treatment: Role of treatment services. *Journal of Consulting and Clinical Psychology, 62,* 1141–1158.

McPeake, J. D., Kennedy, B., Grossman, J., & Beaulieu, L. (1991). Innovative adolescent chemical dependency treatment and its outcome: A model based on Outward Bound programming. *Journal of Adolescent Chemical Dependency, 2,* 29–57.

Miller, L. (1993). Who are the best psychotherapists? Qualities of the effective practitioner. *Psychotherapy in Private Practice, 12,* 1–18.

Miller, W. R., Brown, J. M., Simpson, T. L., Handmaker, N. S., Bien, T. H., Luckie, L. F., Montgomery, H. A., Hester, R. K., & Tonigan, J. S. (1995). What works? A methodological analysis of the alcohol treatment outcome literature. In R. K. Hester & W. R. Miller (Eds.), *Handbook of alcoholism treatment approaches* (2nd edn) (pp. 12–44). Needham Heights, MA: Allyn & Bacon.

Miller, W. R. & Sanchez-Craig, M. (1996). How to have a high success rate in treatment: advice for evaluators of alcoholism programs. *Addiction, 91,* 779–785.

Mohr, D. C. (1995). Negative outcome in psychotherapy: A critical review. *Clinical Psychology – Science & Practice, 2*, 1–27.

Morris, R. J. & Nicholson, J. (1993). The therapeutic relationship in child and adolescent psychotherapy: Research issues and trends. In T. R. Kratochwill & R. J. Morris (Eds.), *Handbook of psychotherapy with children and adolescents* (pp. 405–425). Boston, MA: Allyn & Bacon.

Najavits, L. M. & Weiss, R. D. (1994). Variations in therapist effectiveness in the treatment of patients with substance use disorders: An empirical review. *Addiction, 89*, 679–688.

Pape, H. & Hammer, T. (1996). How does young people's alcohol consumption change during the transition to early adulthood? A longitudinal study of changes at aggregate and individual level. *Addiction, 91*, 1345–1357.

Pfeiffer, S. I., O'Malley, D. S., & Shott, S. (1996). Factors associated with the outcome of adults treated in psychiatric hospitals: A synthesis of findings. *Psychiatric Services, 47*, 263–269.

Pompi, K. F. (1994). Adolescents in therapeutic communities: Retention and post-treatment outcome. In F. M. Tims, G. DeLeon, & N. Jainchill (Eds.), *Therapeutic community: Advances in research and application* (NIDA Research Monograph 144). Rockville, MD: US Department of Health and Human Services.

Project MATCH Research Group (1997a). Matching alcoholism treatments to client heterogeneity: Project MATCH Posttreatment drinking outcomes. *Journal of Studies on Alcohol, 58*, 7–29.

Project MATCH Research Group (1997b). Project MATCH secondary a priori hypotheses. *Addiction, 92*, 1671–1698.

Richardson, D. W. (1996). Drug rehabilitation in a treatment farm setting: The Nitawgi Farm experience, 1978–1990. *Journal of Developmental & Behavioural Pediatrics, 17*, 258–261.

Richter, S. S., Brown, S. A., & Mott, M. A. (1991). The impact of social support and self-esteem on adolescent substance abuse treatment outcome. *Journal of Substance Abuse, 3*, 371–385.

Roth, A. & Fonagy, P. (1996). The relationship between outcome and therapist training, experience, and technique. In A. Roth & P. Fonagy (Eds.), *What works for whom? A critical review of psychotherapy research* (pp. 341–357). New York, NY: Guilford Press.

Rush, T. V. (1979). Predicting treatment outcome for juvenile and young adult clients in the Pennsylvania substance abuse system. In G. M. Beschner & A. S. Friedman (Eds.), *Youth drug abuse: Problems, issues, and treatment* (pp. 629–656). Lexington, MA: Lexington Books.

Sells, S. B. & Simpson, D. D. (1979). Evaluation of treatment outcome for youths in drug abuse reporting program (DARP): A follow-up study. In G. M. Beschner & A. S. Friedman (Eds.), *Youth drug abuse: Problems, issues, and treatment* (pp. 571–628). Lexington, MA: Lexington Books.

Shoemaker, R. H. & Sherry, P. (1991). Post treatment factors influencing outcome of adolescent chemical dependency treatment. *Journal of Adolescent Chemical Dependency, 2*, 89–105.

Smith, M. L., Glass, G. V., & Miller, T. I. (1980). *The benefits of psychotherapy.* Baltimore, MD: Johns Hopkins University Press.

Stanton, M. D. & Shadish, W. R. (1997). Outcome, attrition, and family-couples treatment for drug abuse: A meta-analysis and review of the controlled, comparative studies. *Psychological Bulletin, 122*, 170–191.

Steenbarger, B. N. (1994). Duration and outcome in psychotherapy: An integrative review. *Professional Psychology – Research & Practice*, *25*, 111–119.
Sunshine, I. & Sutliff, J. P. (1997). Sweat it out. In S. H. Y. Wong & I. Sunshine (Eds.), *Handbook of analytical therapeutic drug monitoring and toxicology* (pp. 253–264). Boca Raton, FL: CRC Press.
Target, M. & Fonagy, P. (1996). The psychological treatment of child and adolescent psychiatric disorders. In A. Roth & P. Fonagy (Eds.), *What works for whom? A critical review of psychotherapy research* (pp. 263–320). New York, NY: Guilford Press.
Turner, C. F., Lessler, J. T., & Gfroerer, J. C. (1992). *Survey measurement of drug use: Methodological studies*. Rockville, MD: National Institute on Drug Abuse.
US Department of Health and Human Services (1995). *Effectiveness of substance abuse treatment, September 1995*. Substance Abuse and Mental Health Services Administration. DHHS Publication no. (SMA) 95–3067. Author.
US Department of Health and Human Services (1997a). *The prevalence and correlates of treatment for drug problems*. Substance Abuse and Mental Health Services Administration. DHHS Publication No. (SMA) 97–3135. Author.
US Department of Health and Human Services (1997b). *NTIES: The National Treatment Improvement Evaluation Study final report*. Substance Abuse and Mental Health Services Administration, Center for Substance Abuse Treatment, National Opinion Research Center at the University of Chicago, March 1997.
US Department of Health and Human Services (1998). *Services Research Outcomes Study*. Substance Abuse and Mental Health Services Administration, Office of Applied Studies (OAS), September 1998.
Vaglum, P. & Fossheim, I. (1980). Differential treatment of young abusers: A quasi-experimental study of a therapeutic community in a psychiatric hospital. *Journal of Drug Issues*, *10*, 505–516.
Wagner, E. F., Brown, S. A., Monti, P. M., Myers, M. G., & Waldron, H. B. (1999). Innovations in adolescent substance abuse intervention. *Alcoholism: Clinical and Experimental Research*, *23*, 236–249.
Waldron, H. B. (1997). Adolescent substance abuse and family therapy outcome: A review of randomized trials. *Advances in Clinical Child Psychology*, *19*, 199–234.
Weisz, J. R., Weiss, B., Han, S. S., Granger, D. A., & Morton, T. (1995). Effects of psychotherapy with children and adolescents revisited: A meta-analysis of treatment outcome studies. *Psychological Bulletin*, *117*, 450–468.
Williams, R. J. & Chang, S. (2000). A comprehensive and comparative review of adolescent substance abuse treatment outcome. *Clinical Psychology: Science & Practice*, *7*, 138–166.
Williams, R. J., McDermitt, D., & Bertrand, L., & Davis, R. M. (2002). Parental awareness of adolescent substance use. *Addictive Behaviors*, *27*, 1–8.
Wish, E. D., Hoffman, J. A. & Nemes, S. (1997). The validity of self-reports of drug use at treatment admission and at follow-up: comparisons with urinalysis and hair assays. In L. Harrison & A. Hughes (Eds.), *The validity of self-reported drug use: Improving the accuracy of survey estimates* (NIDA Research Monograph 167). Rockville, MD: US Department of Health and Human Services.

Chapter 8

Family-based therapy

Timothy J. Ozechowski and Howard A. Liddle

In a recent address to members of the American Psychological Association, Ellen Berscheid (1999) acclaimed "the greening of relationship science" (p. 206), or the emergence of a multidisciplinary science of the study of human relationships and their connection to a wide range of conditions encountered by researchers and practitioners in the psychological and behavioural sciences. Particularly compelling was Berscheid's observation of the potential for relationship science to reshape the landscape of the field of psychology. Part of this reshaping has taken the form of a new subspecialty within psychology: family psychology intervention science (Liddle *et al.*, 2002). This new subspecialty is concerned with using basic and applied research to understand the relational and systemic nature of human problems, and with developing and testing theory- and reseach-based interventions.

By virtue of its focus on the inherently social and contextual nature of human functioning, and its applied research orientation, family psychology intervention science entails a new kind of synergy between the domains of research and clinical practice. In family psychology intervention science there is a unique convergence between the objects of empirical study and the units of clinical intervention, namely, individuals acting and interacting in a relational context. This convergence of focus between research and clinical practice has helped relax the boundaries between other historically separate roles and functions in clinical psychology including researcher/practitioner, research subject/clinical case, experimental procedure/clinical intervention, laboratory/clinic, and more recently, clinical research setting/naturalistic ecological setting. The integration of research and practice in family psychology intervention science creates new avenues and opportunities for the development, testing, and dissemination of science-based, clinically valid, empirically supported treatments.

Berscheid's laudatory observations about the greening of relationship science, and the emergence of family psychology intervention science, both are exemplified by the current status of family-based therapy for adolescent drug abuse. Family-based therapy is firmly established as a bona fide clinical and research specialty within the adolescent drug abuse treatment field. The developmental progress which has taken place in this specialty is impressive. Family-based interventions are widely utilized across a variety of adolescent drug abuse treatment settings both as a stand-alone approach and in combination with other clinical services (e.g., Hamilton *et al.*, 2000; Stage, 1999). Moreover, a broad base of federal government support exists for research on family-based therapy for adolescent drug abuse and related problems. Funding mechanisms from US government agencies such as the National Institute on Drug Abuse (NIDA), the National Institute on Alcohol Abuse and Alcoholism (NIAAA), and the Center for Substance Abuse Treatment (CSAT), provide support for groundbreaking multisite research projects (e.g., The Cannabis Youth Treatment Study [www.chestunt.org]), as well as a research centre and training programme specializing in the development and testing of family-based treatments (Liddle and Hogue, 2001). Prominent research reviews attest to the efficacy of family-based therapy relative to other established treatments for adolescent drug abuse (Cormack and Carr, 2000; Gilvarry, 2000; Liddle and Dakof, 1995a,b; Ozechowski and Liddle, 2000; Stanton and Shadish, 1997; Waldron, 1997; Weinberg *et al.*, 1998; Winters *et al.*, 1999). Furthermore, family-based interventions are recognized as core components of the continuum of care for adolescent drug abuse as established by leading organizations such as the American Academy of Child and Adolescent Psychiatry (AACAP, 1997) and CSAT (1999).

In the remainder of this chapter, we provide an account of the evolution and current status of family-based therapy as an empirically supported treatment modality for adolescent drug abuse and co-occurring behaviour problems. Specifically, this chapter highlights developmental milestones and areas of progress including theory development, treatment specification, studies of the impact of family-based interventions on a range of clinical outcomes, identification of core components and mechanisms of effective treatment, and studies of in-session processes associated with treatment outcome. In addition, current challenges and new frontiers for ongoing treatment development research efforts are highlighted.

EVOLUTION OF FAMILY-BASED THERAPY FOR ADOLESCENT DRUG ABUSE

From family therapy to family-based therapy

Interventions with drug-abusing adolescents and their families have been in formal stages of development and testing for over 20 years. First-generation treatment models in this area were "family therapy" approaches in the traditional sense in that they espoused a pure family systems orientation and regarded the family as the primary unit of assessment and intervention (see

Hoffman, 1981; Nichols and Schwartz, 1998). Early models of family therapy for adolescent drug abuse viewed adolescent functioning as reciprocally connected to parent, sibling, and extended family functioning, and to patterns of communication and interaction within and between various subsystems within the family (e.g., parent–adolescent, parent–parent, adolescent–sibling, etc.). Techniques derived from classic structural and strategic family therapy (Haley, 1976; Minuchin, 1974) such as "reframing" and "enactment" (Minuchin and Fishman, 1981), figured prominently in early family therapy intervention strategies. These techniques are highly therapist-directed in-session activities designed to promote functional shifts in lines of authority, communication, emotional connection, and interaction within families of adolescent drug abusers. The central hypothesis in early family therapy approaches for adolescent drug abuse is that improvements in family functioning will promote improvements in individual adolescent functioning and make drug use and other problem behaviours less likely (Diamond and Liddle, 1999).

Current treatment models have evolved beyond a classic family systems orientation and a pure family therapy approach to treatment. Contemporary models are "family-based" in that they focus on individuals and systems besides the family and are grounded in orientations beyond family systems theory. In addition to family systems concepts, family-based therapy approaches are informed by principles of cognitive-behaviour theory (Alexander and Parsons, 1973, 1982; Turner, 1993), attachment theory (Allen et al., 1996), adolescent developmental theory (Baumrind and Moselle, 1985), and social ecological theory (Bronfenbrenner, 1979). This expansion of family-based therapy's theoretical foundation is consistent with a wealth of basic research which has revealed a complex and interconnected network of risk and protective factors for adolescent drug abuse spanning the multiple social and ecological spheres in which teens live (Brook et al., 1989; Hawkins et al., 1992; Jessor et al., 1995; Kilpatrick et al., 2000; Petraitis et al., 1998; Resnick et al., 1997). Risk factors include high levels of family conflict and stress, low levels of family bonding and cohesion, poor parental monitoring and behaviour management skills, exposure to substance using and delinquent peers, low bonding to school and other prosocial environments, etc. Family-based clinical approaches view drug abuse and related problem behaviours as symptomatic of the disruptive effects of multiple ecological risk factors on normal adolescent development (see Baumrind and Moselle, 1985; Lerner and Galambos, 1998). Clinical procedures and techniques in family-based therapy are crafted according to research-based guidelines and are intended to facilitate normal adolescent development across ecological systems (Dishion et al., 1988; Liddle et al., 1998, 2000).

Contemporary family-based therapy approaches for adolescent drug use and related behavioural problems, such as Multidimensional Family Therapy (MDFT) (Liddle, 1999, 2000) and Multisystemic Therapy (MST) (Henggeler *et al.*, 1998), are hinged upon detailed and ongoing assessment of risk and protective factors for adolescent drug abuse within a nexus of interconnected and nested social systems including the individual, family, peer, school, neighbourhood, community, and culture. The format and methods of contemporary family-based therapy mirror the scope and complexity with which adolescent problem behaviours are understood. For instance, "sessions" may occur in the home, school, or other appropriate setting within the adolescent's social context rather than a therapist's office. Therapy sessions may involve individual and multi-person meetings with the adolescent, parents, siblings, extended family, and key individuals outside the family including school teachers, probation officers, vocational specialists, ministers, etc. Members of the adolescent's peer group may be involved in treatment as well. Family-based treatment delivery is typically more frequent and intensive than the traditional outpatient regimen of one-hour sessions once per week. Therapists as well as other clinical support staff may maintain daily contact with cases during the initial stages of treatment and may be on-call to respond in crisis situations. Intervention strategies in family-based therapy are tailored to work within each adolescent's and family's unique profile of risk and protection. The underlying hypothesis in family-based therapy is that adolescent drug abuse and problem behaviours will subside when therapists work in close connection with the adolescent, his or her family, and significant members of other systems to orchestrate and implement meaningful, practical, and developmentally facilitative lifestyle changes.

METHODOLOGICAL ADVANCES IN FAMILY-BASED TREATMENT RESEARCH

The favourable status of family-based therapy as a bona fide intervention modality for adolescent drug abuse and related behavioural problems is largely attributable to a solid and rich tradition of clinical research. Empirical studies in this area date back to the early 1980s and were among the first controlled investigations ever conducted in the field of adolescent drug abuse treatment or in family therapy (Friedman, 1989; Joanning *et al.*, 1992; Lewis *et al.*, 1990; Liddle and Dakof, 1995a; Szapocznik *et al.*, 1983, 1986, 1988). The first generation of research on family-based therapy for adolescent drug abuse exemplified cutting-edge clinical research according to standards in place at the time. Novel and distinguishing features of the first wave of research include well-defined treatment and comparison conditions, availability of documented clinical guidelines and treatment procedures (early versions of treatment manuals), ongoing supervision of therapists implementing the treatments, standardized measures of drug use and other key outcomes, and multiple waves of data collection before, during, and after treatment. Furthermore, some early studies were conducted in community-based clinics which were adapted to support high-quality science. Research conducted during this early historical period firmly established family-based therapy as a safe, acceptable, viable, and promising treatment approach for adolescent drug abuse (Liddle and Dakof, 1995a).

Current research on family-based therapy for adolescent drug abuse has become more advanced in many ways, although it is driven by the same pioneering spirit of a generation ago. Contemporary family-based treatment research is guided by new ideas and sensibilities about the science of developing effective treatments. Guidelines and frameworks for research-based treatment development have been articulated in numerous areas including clinical psychology (Chambliss and Holon, 1998; Kazdin, 1997), psychotherapy research (Docherty, 1984; Kazdin, 1994a), drug abuse treatment (Carroll and Rounsaville, 1990; Onken et al., 1997), child and adolescent treatment (Kazdin 1994b; Kazdin and Kendall, 1998), and services research (Wagner et al., 2000). Although not identical, collectively these frameworks specify standards, criteria, and procedures for conducting programmatic research that would establish the components, processes, and mechanisms of theory- and research-based interventions, as well as the effects of those interventions when implemented in various clinical settings with specific patient populations.

Contemporary family-based treatment development research has become more rigorous and sophisticated under the influence of these new clinical research guidelines. Advances include the specification of complex clinical procedures in highly detailed and comprehensive treatment manuals (Henggeler et al., 1998; Liddle, 2000), more systematic and comprehensive methods of assessment (Leccese and Waldron, 1994; Liddle and Rowe, 1998), development of procedures for monitoring therapist adherence and its effects on treatment outcome (Hogue et al., 1996, 1998; Schoenwald et al., 2000), closer attention to internal validity threats (e.g., therapist effects, pretreatment group equivalence, differential attrition, etc.), clearly specified inclusion and exclusion criteria for clinical research cases, and the use of larger-sized samples. In addition, there is greater diversity in the types of designs employed in family-based treatment development research including studies of mediators and mechanisms of treatment effects (Huey et al., 2000; Schmidt et al., 1996), in-session process-outcome studies (Diamond and Liddle, 1996, 1999; Diamond et al., 1999; Jackson-Gilfort et al., in press), studies of treatment costs and cost effectiveness (Dennis et al., in press; Schoenwald et al., 1996), and studies of the transportability of family-based treatments into community-based clinical settings (Dennis et al., in press; Henggeler et al., 1999). Altogether, these advances in research design and implementation have enhanced what is known about ingredients of effective family-based therapy and the breadth and depth of its impact on drug use and related adolescent and family problems (Ozechowski and Liddle, 2000).

Milestones along the pathway toward empirically supported family-based treatment

As indicated previously, family-based therapy has grown and matured impressively over the past several decades as a science-based clinical modality and research specialty in the adolescent drug abuse treatment field. The expansion of family-based therapy into a broad-based ecological intervention modality is neither accidental nor random. The scope and complexity of family-based interventions is consistent with new knowledge of the many factors related to the onset and trajectory of adolescent drug abuse. Parallel advances in developmental psychopathology research (Kazdin and Kagan, 1994) and adolescent treatment research (Carr, 2000; Kazdin, 1994b; Miller and Prinz, 1990), as well as the results of first-generation family therapy studies (Liddle and Dakof, 1995a) have shaped the evolution of contemporary family-based therapy. Family-based interventions have become highly sophisticated, are multifaceted, and attempt to orchestrate change simultaneously within and across multiple social systems. Clinical procedures are now specified with unprecedented levels of precision. Technological advances in research design and implementation have helped investigators illuminate the range of family-based therapy's effects as well as the mechanisms and processes related to those effects. Moreover, innovative cutting-edge research projects are currently underway which promise to further sharpen knowledge of the "nuts and bolts" of family-based therapy and to reveal the possibilities and challenges of adapting and transferring effective family-based interventions to non-research settings. These advances are steps along the pathway toward the development of empirically supported family-based treatment for adolescent drug abuse. In the following section of this chapter we highlight specific developmental markers and milestones along this pathway, and provide an overview of the current state of the science of family-based therapy for adolescent drug abuse.

THE EFFECTS OF FAMILY-BASED THERAPY ON ADOLESCENT FUNCTIONING

Drug use

Family-based therapy has been tested in numerous controlled clinical trials against a variety of other established adolescent drug treatments. In every clinical trial conducted to date, family-based therapy has been shown to significantly reduce levels of adolescent drug use from pre- to post-treatment as measured primarily by adolescent self-reports (see Ozechowski and Liddle, 2000). The effects of family-based therapy appear to generalize to a variety of different substances including alcohol, marijuana, cocaine, and other illicit drugs (see Azrin *et al.*, 1994; Friedman, 1989; Henggeler *et al.*, 1999; Lewis *et al.*, 1990; Liddle, 2002; Liddle *et al.*, 2001). Family-based therapy has been shown to have superior pre- to post-treatment effects on drug use compared to individual therapy (Henggeler *et al.*, 1991; Liddle, 2002; Waldron *et al.*, 2001), adolescent group therapy (Azrin *et al.*, 1994; Joanning *et al.*, 1992; Liddle *et al.*, 2001) and family psychoeducational drug counseling (Joanning *et al.*, 1992; Lewis *et al.*, 1990; Liddle *et al.*, 2001). Family-based therapy has been shown to be equally effective compared to a parent training group intervention (Friedman, 1989) and "one person" family therapy (Szapocznik *et al.*, 1983, 1986). Moreover, the effects of family-based therapy appear to endure at least six to twelve months beyond the termination of treatment (Friedman, 1989; Henggeler *et al.*, 1991; Liddle, 2002; Liddle *et al.*, 2001; Szapocznik *et al.*, 1983, 1986).

Behaviour problems associated with drug use

Numerous clinical trials have examined the effects of family-based therapy on behavioural problems known to be concomitant with drug use. Most studies in this category have assessed adolescent behaviour problems using parent reports on comprehensive behaviour problem checklists and inventories. Externalizing behaviour such as delinquency and aggression and internalizing behavioural symptoms such as depression have been studied. As is the case regarding drug use, family-based therapy has demonstrated efficacy in every clinical trial examining behavioural problems in addition to drug use. Most studies have shown family-based therapy to be equally effective compared to alternative treatments in reducing problem behaviour (Friedman, 1989; Liddle *et al.*, 2001; Szapocznik *et al.*, 1983, 1986, 1988). A few studies suggest the effects of family-based therapy may be superior to those of alternative treatment conditions including individual cognitive-behavioural therapy (Liddle, 2002), supportive group counseling (Azrin *et al.*, 1994), and a generic "treatment as usual" condition coordinated through the juvenile justice system (Henggeler *et al.*, 1991).

Psychiatric comorbidity

Adolescent drug abuse is often accompanied by psychiatric symptoms such as conduct disorder, attention-deficit hyperactivity disorder, anxiety, and depression (Brook *et al.*, 1998; Bukstein, 2000; Weinberg and Glantz, 1999). Accordingly, contemporary adolescent drug treatments address psychiatric symptoms in addition to drug use behaviour (AACAP, 1997). A limited number of studies has examined the effects of family-based therapy on comorbid psychiatric symptoms based on adolescent self-report questionnaires. Again, across all studies family-based therapy has exhibited significant effects in reducing psychiatric symptoms (Azrin *et al.*, 1994; Friedman, 1989;

Szapocznik et al., 1983, 1986, 1988). Based on existing studies, the family-based therapy appears to be equally as effective as other established adolescent drug treatments. Enhanced versions of family-based therapy which incorporate psychiatric evaluations and adjunctive pharmacological treatments are currently being evaluated (see Henggeler et al., 1999; Liddle, 2000). Results of these studies should greatly expand knowledge of the ways family-based therapy can impact on comorbid psychiatric symptomatology.

FACTORS OR MECHANISMS ASSOCIATED WITH TREATMENT EFFICACY

Therapist adherence

Issues related to the integrity of treatment delivery, especially the assessment of therapist adherence and competence, have received much recent attention in the psychotherapy research literature (Elkin, 1999; Kazdin, 1994a; Waltz et al., 1993). Efforts to ensure high-quality treatment delivery have always been central features of family-based treatment research. Historically, treatment integrity has been monitored and maintained through intensive clinical supervision of therapists in both family-based and alternative treatment conditions (Azrin et al., 1994; Friedman, 1989; Joanning et al., 1992; Liddle et al., 2001; Waldron et al., 2001). Recently, formal methods of rating and documenting therapist adherence have been developed and integrated in family-based treatment research. For instance, Szapocznik and colleagues (Szapocznik et al., 1988; Santisteban et al., 1996) developed a therapist-report rating form to assess adherence to a set of specialized family-based procedures for engaging adolescents and families in treatment. Additionally, Henggeler and colleagues (Henggeler et al., 1997; Schoenwald et al., 2000) developed a rating form to assess adherence to principles of MST from the adolescent, caregiver, and therapist perspectives. Finally, Liddle and colleagues (Hogue et al., 1996, 1998) have developed an observational rating procedure for assessing therapist adherence to prescribed MDFT procedures.

The development of therapist adherence measures has enabled researchers to begin exploring the link between therapist adherence and clinical outcomes in family-based therapy. For example, Henggeler and colleagues (1999) found that post-treatment levels of adolescent drug use, criminal activity, and out-of-home placements were related to ratings of therapist adherence to MST. Further analyses showed therapist adherence may also predict improvements in family cohesion and parental monitoring skills (Huey et al., 2000). These findings begin to flesh out the manner in which successful family-based treatment hinges on faithful implementation of prescribed procedures. Additional research is needed to delineate links between adherence to specific aspects of manualized treatments and a range of adolescent, family, and extra-familial outcomes. Furthermore, methods of assessing other aspects of treatment integrity, such as therapist competence and treatment differentiation, need to be developed and incorporated in family-based treatment research.

Engagement and retention in treatment

Length of time in treatment has been shown to be a strong and consistent predictor of drug abuse treatment outcome for adults (Goldstein *et al.*, 2000; Simpson *et al.*, 1999) and adolescents (Latimer *et al.*, 2000a; Latimer *et al.*, 2000b). Thus, engaging and retaining adolescents and families is likely to be a key ingredient of success in adolescent drug abuse treatment. Although multi-problem adolescents and their families are often difficult to involve and maintain in treatment (Armbruster and Kazdin, 1994; Morissey-Kane and Prinz, 1999; Prinz and Miller, 1996), family-based therapies have consistently exhibited impressive rates of treatment engagement and retention (Stanton and Shadish, 1997). For instance, the use of specialized family-based pretreatment engagement interventions has been shown to enhance likelihood of adolescents and families attending the first session of treatment (Donohue *et al.*, 1998; Santisteban *et al.*, 1996; Szapocznik *et al.*, 1988). Family-based engagement interventions include multiple pretreatment contacts with parents and adolescents to establish rapport, encourage first session attendance, address questions and concerns about treatment, gather information about the case, and in some cases to begin implementing therapeutic interventions that would facilitate first session attendance.

Family-based therapy has been shown to retain cases in treatment at a very high level. Studies suggest rates of retention in family-based therapy are typically between 70% and 90% (Ozechowski and Liddle, 2000). Particularly impressive results were obtained by Henggeler and colleagues (1996) in which 57 out of 58 cases (98%) assigned to MST completed a full course of treatment lasting 130 days. In addition, Waldron and colleagues (2001) reported 56 out of 59 cases (95%) receiving family-based therapy were retained in treatment. Rates of retention in family-based therapy have been shown to be dramatically higher than in "treatment as usual" provided through the juvenile justice system (Henggeler *et al.*, 1991, 1996). Retention in family-based therapy also is generally higher than in other established adolescent drug treatments (Azrin *et al.*, 1994; Henggeler *et al.*, 1991; Joanning *et al.*, 1992; Liddle *et al.*, 2001; Stanton and Shadish, 1997).

Family functioning

Improvement in core dimensions of family functioning (e.g., communication, cohesion, conflict, parenting practices) is hypothesized to be a central mechanism by which family-based therapy achieves its effects on drug use and other areas of adolescent functioning. The effects of family-based therapy on both self-reported and observed family functioning have been studied in a number of clinical trials. Across all studies, family functioning has been shown to improve in family-based therapy (Azrin *et al.*, 1994; Friedman, 1989; Huey *et al.*, 2000; Joanning *et al.*, 1992; Liddle *et al.*, 2001; Waldron *et al.*, 2001), although it remains unclear whether family functioning improves more so in family-based therapy than in other established forms of treatment.

There is evidence linking improvements in family functioning to reductions in drug use and delinquent behaviour in family-based therapy. Specifically, Schmidt and colleagues (1996) conducted observational ratings of the quality of parenting behaviour exhibited during the first three and last three sessions for 29 adolescents completing 14 to 16 sessions of MDFT. Schmidt and colleagues (1996) found the quality of parenting behaviour improved in 20 out of 29 cases. Furthermore, improvements in parenting quality were accompanied by reductions in drug use in 59% of cases and by improvements in delinquency in 50% of cases. Along the same lines, Huey and colleagues (2000) found that levels of both family cohesion and parental monitoring improved in MST, and that these improvements were related to reductions in delinquent behaviour. Moreover, using a path analytic strategy Huey and colleagues (2000) found the effects of MST on delinquent behaviour were mediated by improvements in family functioning, thereby supporting the hypothesis that improved family functioning is a mechanism for reducing adolescent delinquency in MST.

Involvement in school

Academic failure and disconnection from school are commonly associated with adolescent drug abuse (Ary *et al.*, 1999; Hawkins *et al.*, 1992). Moreover, a strong attachment to school is a known buffer against teens' involvement with drugs (Jessor *et al.*, 1995; Resnick *et al.*, 1997). Accordingly, school bonding and academic functioning are areas in which family-based therapy attempts to promote change. School teachers and other personnel are often involved in ecologically oriented family-based treatment approaches. Additionally, attendance and performance at school are often the focus of interventions between parents and teens in family-based therapy.

The effects of family-based therapy on adolescent school attendance and academic performance have been examined in a few studies. Across all studies, these aspects of school functioning have shown greater improvement in family-based therapy than in alternative treatments. For instance, Liddle and colleagues (2001) found adolescents in MDFT improved their grades (generally from failing to passing) from intake to one-year post-treatment whereas no such improvements were observed for adolescent group therapy or multi-family education group treatment. Moreover, Azrin *et al.* (1994) and Brown and colleagues (1999) both reported greater increases in school attendance in family-based therapy compared to alternative conditions. Finally, Friedman (1989) found that mothers' reports of adolescents' problems in school decreased somewhat more so in family-based therapy than in a parent-training group treatment.

In-session process associated with change mechanisms

The techniques and processes during treatment which activate certain change mechanisms in family-based therapy have been studied using observational process research methods (Diamond and Diamond, 2002; Robbins *et al.*, 1996, 2000). Observational process-outcome studies are critical components of a comprehensive treatment development research agenda in family-based therapy. Clinical process-outcome studies can provide rich clues about the proper timing and sequencing of specific treatment techniques, about nuances in therapist behaviour that help certain interventions to work, and about therapist–family interactions associated with intervention success. Clinical process information is invaluable for informing manual development and the training and supervision of therapists.

Several process studies have examined therapist behaviours associated with engagement and alliance building in family-based therapy with drug-abusing adolescents. First, Diamond and colleagues (1999) studied videotapes of the first three therapy sessions from five cases exhibiting improved therapist–adolescent alliances and five cases in which initially poor alliances did not improve. Diamond and colleagues (1999) found that therapists more extensively implemented prescribed MDFT alliance-building interventions in cases showing improved therapist–adolescent alliances compared to unimproved alliance cases. These interventions include attending to the adolescent's experience, presenting the therapist as an ally, and helping the adolescent formulate personally meaningful goals for treatment. In a related process study, Jackson-Gilfort *et al.* (in press) examined the process of engaging African-American males into family-based therapy. Using observational coding of videotaped therapy sessions, Jackson-Gilfort *et al.* (in press) found that African-American males are more likely to become engaged in treatment when therapists discuss prescribed culturally relevant themes including a sense of alienation, anger and rage, and the journey from boyhood to manhood.

Process research methods have also been used to examine therapist interventions connected to improved family functioning. Specifically, Diamond and Liddle (1996, 1999) examined the process of "impasse resolution" between parents and adolescents in family-based therapy. Diamond and Liddle (1996, 1999) coded five videotaped therapy sessions containing successful impasse resolutions and five sessions in which impasses were not resolved. Diamond and Liddle (1996, 1999) found that successful impasse resolution is characterized by therapists' implementation of manualized interventions including (a) blocking, diverting, or working through negative affect, (b) amplifying feelings of sadness, regret, and loss, (c) soliciting the adolescent's thoughts and feelings, (d) focusing the conversation on parent–adolescent interaction, (e) fostering parents' empathy for the adolescent, and (f) supporting parents' efforts to manage the adolescent's behaviour.

Summary

The current state of the science of family-based therapy for adolescent drug abuse is encouraging. Empirical evidence shows family-based therapy can have clinically significant effects on levels of adolescent drug use, externalizing and internalizing behaviour problems, and symptoms of psychiatric comorbidity, and these effects endure at least 12 months beyond the termination of treatment. Family-based therapy is equally effective as, and perhaps more effective than, other forms of adolescent drug treatment. Factors related to successful outcomes in family-based therapy include high rates of engagement and retention in treatment, improvements in core dimensions of family functioning, and increased attendance and performance in school. Research has begun to reveal the connection between successful treatment outcomes and therapist adherence to prescribed manualized interventions. Process-outcome studies have helped explicate the link between the implementation of manual-based interventions and key treatment mechanisms such as engagement and alliance building, and parent–adolescent impasse resolution.

Existing research provides a solid foundation for the current status of family-based therapy as a science-based empirically supported treatment for adolescent drug abuse. Key elements underlying the effectiveness of ecological family-based treatment models such as MDFT and MST include a broad-based and developmentally focused approach to treatment, the design of well-targeted and intensive interventions, and ecologically valid methods of service delivery. Despite these advances, much has yet to be learned about the effects of family-based therapy as well as the methods, mechanisms, and processes by which family-based interventions work. Family-based therapy will continue to evolve and improve as treatment development research charts new territory in unexplored areas.

NEW FRONTIERS FOR FAMILY-BASED TREATMENT DEVELOPMENT RESEARCH

As this chapter has attempted to show, "the greening of relationship science" (Berscheid, 1999) is an apt metaphor to describe the developmental status of family-based therapy as a clinical and research specialty in the adolescent drug abuse treatment field and as a branch of family psychology intervention science (Liddle et al., 2002). Tremendous strides have been made over the past two decades in defining the components and parameters of this specialty. Family-based therapy for adolescent drug abuse has formed its own identity and has a distinct history. Its developmental course has been charted by a rich and vibrant tradition of theory-driven cutting-edge clinical research.

The family-based therapy for adolescent drug abuse specialty is now poised to enter a new stage of development. Federal support for family-based treatment research is at an all-time high and numerous groundbreaking research projects are underway. Over the next decade, a wealth of new data will shed additional light on the inner workings of effective family-based therapy and its transferability to a variety of community-based clinical settings. A framework for synthesizing collective findings and informing new waves of research would help to consolidate and streamline knowledge within this specialty. More specifically, the adoption of a *treatment development* perspective within the family-based treatment research community could facilitate more coordinated and systematic progress (Liddle and Hogue, 2001). As mentioned previously, different but connected sets of treatment development research guidelines have been articulated in clinical psychology and related areas (Carroll and Rounsaville, 1990; Docherty, 1984; Kazdin, 1994a; Kazdin, 1997; Kazdin and Kendall, 1998; Onken et al., 1997; Wagner et al., 2000). This chapter highlights family-based treatment development activity and progress that has already taken place in accordance with existing guidelines. We conclude this chapter by discussing important next steps for more fully implementing a treatment development research agenda in family-based therapy for adolescent drug abuse.

Additional research is needed to broaden and refine knowledge of the effects of family-based therapy on adolescent functioning. In particular, very little is known about the impact of family-based therapy on teens' association with drug-using peers. It is well known that peer influences play a powerful role in the onset and maintenance of adolescent drug use (Bailey and Hubbard, 1990; Dishion et al., 1995; Duncan et al., 1998; Farrell and White, 1998; Wills and Cleary, 1999) as well as in relapse from adolescent drug treatment (Brown et al., 1994, 1989; Latimer et al, 2000a,b). Thus, peer relationships are a critical domain of assessment and intervention in family-based treatment development research.

Some existing evidence suggests family-based therapy reduces teens' affiliation with drug-using peers by virtue of improved parental monitoring and family functioning (Huey et al., 2000). Moreover, reductions in externalizing behaviour problems in family-based therapy would suggest an impact on peer-related functioning given the inherently social nature of these types of behaviours (Friedman, 1989; Henggeler et al., 1991, 1999; Liddle, 2002; Liddle et al., 2001; Szapocznik et al., 1983, 1986, 1988). Future family-based treatment development research should include more comprehensive and detailed assessments of adolescents' peer relationships. The development and testing of family-based interventions which more directly involve and impact upon peer functioning is also needed.

Understanding mechanisms of change is another important frontier for family-based treatment development research. Studies are needed which establish causal connections between changes in adolescent drug use outcomes and improvement in hypothesized mechanisms of change such as parental monitoring, family bonding, connection to school and other prosocial environments, reduced affiliation with drug-using peers, etc. Investigating mechanisms of change requires long-term measurement of multiple domains of functioning in family-based treatment research. Researchers should also begin to utilize data analytic techniques capable of modelling direct and indirect relationships among changes in multiple domains. Techniques such as latent growth curve modelling (Willett and Sayer, 1994) and longitudinal structural equation modelling (Farrell, 1994) are well suited for studying mechanisms of change.

Little is known about moderators of the effects of family-based therapy for adolescent drug abuse. Adolescent, parent, family, therapist, and other contextual factors that may differentially impact on clinical outcomes in family-based therapy have been virtually unstudied. For instance, only one study has examined gender differences in the impact of family-based therapy on adolescent drug problems (Henggeler *et al.*, 1999). This study found the benefits of family-based therapy may deteriorate substantially by six months post-treatment among female adolescents compared to their male counterparts. Further studies are needed to understand differences in the clinical needs and profiles of male and female adolescent drug abusers (Dakof, 2000). The manner in which family-based interventions should be specially tailored in gender-sensitive ways should also be studied. Other important moderators of treatment effectiveness in need of study include race and ethnicity, psychiatric comorbidity, levels of parental and sibling substance use, and differences in adolescent pretreatment motivation (Ozechowski and Liddle, 2000).

More research is needed on the long-term effects of family-based therapy for adolescent drug use and related areas of functioning. A few studies have found significant effects up to one year post-treatment in family-based therapy (Friedman, 1989; Henggeler *et al.*, 1991; Liddle, 2002; Liddle *et al.*, 2001; Szapocznik *et al.*, 1983, 1986). Longitudinal studies extending beyond one year post-treatment are needed. Moreover, research is needed on the optimal length of family-based therapy to achieve lasting change in drug use and behavioural functioning. In addition, it is unknown whether follow-up or booster sessions improve the long-term durability of treatment outcomes (see Bry and Krinsley, 1992). Along these same lines, studies of the environmental and contextual correlates of long-term post-treatment success and relapse have yet to be conducted.

The ingredients and parameters of effective family-based therapy represent another important treatment development frontier. Investigating these dimensions of treatment requires expanding the repertoire of research designs which have been employed in this area. For instance, dose–response studies have yet to be conducted in family-based treatment research. Other types of parametric design strategies (see Kazdin, 1994a, 1998) are needed to identify the amount, frequency, duration, and intensity of family-based therapy necessary for producing particular outcomes. Dismantling and constructive research designs are needed to isolate the effects of specific treatment components, to test different combinations and sequences of interventions, and to study different versions of family-based therapy. In addition, process-outcome studies are needed in all phases and stages of treatment to sharpen understanding of how manualized interventions should be implemented and how therapist behaviour is linked to immediate and long-term changes in adolescent and family functioning. Using process research methods to study therapist adherence and competence is a particularly critical need (Hogue *et al.*, 1996, 1998).

The effectiveness of family-based therapy when transported and integrated into non-research clinical settings is another extremely important research frontier. Studies of the transportability of family-based therapy have just begun to emerge. Existing findings suggest that transferring empirically supported family-based treatment into non-research clinical settings results in markedly diminished levels of therapist adherence which in turn may dampen treatment effectiveness (Henggeler *et al.*, 1999). Additional research is needed on the many factors involved in disseminating empirically supported family-based therapy. In particular, research is needed on the manner in which established family-based treatment models should be "packaged" or tailored to fit the clinical and administrative contingencies of different treatment systems (see Strosahl, 1998). Moreover, effectiveness researchers should assess organizational levels of readiness, receptivity, and capacity to adopt and support the integration of family-based procedures into existing services (Backer, 1995; Brown, 1995; Corrigan *et al.*, 1998). Methods of teaching and training community-based clinicians and supervisors to faithfully implement manualized family-based interventions also need to be developed and tested (see Keller and Galanter, 1999; Sorensen *et al.*, 1988).

Finally, the costs and cost-effectiveness of family-based therapy is another area in need of further exploration. Few estimates exist of the costs of providing family-based therapy for adolescent drug abuse (Dennis *et al.*, in press). One study by Schoenwald and colleagues (1996) suggests the direct costs of providing family-based therapy for adolescent drug abuse may be substantially offset by reductions in post-treatment incarcerations and other out-of-home placements. Further cost–benefit and cost-effectiveness studies are needed to investigate whether (a) the costs of providing family-based therapy are worth the outcomes and (b) whether family-based therapy is more cost-effective than other forms of treatment (see French, 1995; Yates, 1997; Zarkin et al., 1994). The costs and benefits associated with integrating family-based therapy into existing adolescent drug treatment services is a particularly critical area for future cost research.

Profound changes lie ahead for the manner in which family-based treatment development research will be conducted. Calls and mandates from policy makers, funding agencies, health care administrators, practitioners, and other professionals in the adolescent drug treatment community to "bridge the gap" between research and practice require extensive expansion in treatment research methods and practices (Backer et al., 1995; Institute of Medicine, 1998). In particular, family-based treatment development research will require unprecedented levels of collaboration among researchers, administrators, and providers within local clinical service delivery systems (Altman, 1995; Backer et al., 1995; Institute of Medicine, 1998; Sobell, 1996). Family-based treatment development research will take place in naturalistic treatment settings and treatment systems themselves will become part of the focus of study (Wagner et al., 2000). Family-based treatment development research will combine traditional experimental research methods with those of applied services research (Hendrick et al.,1993; Schoenwald and Henggeler, 2002). Qualitative interviews, needs assessments, ethnographic field observations, and focus groups are examples of services research strategies that will become instrumental components of family-based treatment development research.

The changing face of family-based treatment development research bodes well for continued growth and maturation within this specialty. We hope this review helps to crystallize an emerging treatment development orientation in family-based therapy for adolescent drug abuse.

REFERENCES

AAACP (American Academy of Child and Adolescent Psychiatry) (1997). Practice parameters for the assessment and treatment of children and adolescents with substance use disorders. *Journal of the American Academy of Child and Adolescent Psychiatry, 36*, 140S-156S.

Alexander, J. F. & Parsons, B. V. (1973). Short-term behavioral intervention with delinquent families: Impact on family process and recidivism. *Journal of Consulting and Clinical Psychology, 81*, 219–225.

Alexander, J. F. & Parsons, B. V. (1982). *Functional family therapy: Principles and procedures.* Carmel, CA: Brooks/Cole.

Allen, J. P., Hauser, S. T., & Borman-Spurrell, E. (1996). Attachment theory as a framework for understanding sequelae of severe adolescent psychopathology: An 11-year follow-up study. *Journal of Consulting and Clinical Psychology, 64*, 254–263.

Altman, D. G. (1995). Sustaining interventions in community systems: On the relationship between researchers and communities. *Health Psychology, 14*, 526–536.

Armbruster, P. & Kazdin, A. (1994). Attrition in child psychotherapy. In T. H. Ollendick and R.J. Prinz (Eds.), *Advances in clinical child psychology* (Vol. 16, pp. 81–108). New York, NY: Plenum Press.

Ary, D. V., Duncan, T. E., Biglan, A., Metzler, C. W., Noell, J. W., & Smolkowski, K. (1999). Development of adolescent problem behavior. *Journal of Abnormal Child Psychology, 27*, 141–150.

Azrin, N. H., Donohue, B., Besalel, V. A., Kogan, E. S., & Acierno, R. (1994). Youth drug abuse treatment: A controlled outcome study. *Journal of Child and Adolescent Substance Abuse, 3*, 1–16.

Backer, T. E. (1995). Assessing and enhancing readiness for change: Implications for technology transfer. In. T. E. Backer, S. L. David, & G. Soucy (Eds.), *Reviewing the behavioral science knowledge base on technology transfer.* NIDA Research Monograph No. 155. Rockville, MD: National Institute on Drug Abuse.

Backer, T. E., David, S. L., & Soucy, G. (Eds.) (1995). *Reviewing the behavioral science knowledge base on technology transfer.* NIDA Research Monograph No. 155. Rockville, MD: National Institute on Drug Abuse.

Bailey, S. L. & Hubbard, R. L. (1990). Developmental variation in the context of marijuana initiation among adolescents. *Journal of Health and Social Behavior, 31*, 58–70.

Baumrind, D. & Moselle, K. A. (1985). A developmental perspective on adolescent drug abuse. *Advances in Alcohol and Substance Abuse, 4*, 41–67.

Berscheid, E. (1999). The greening of relationship science. *American Psychologist, 54*, 260–266.

Bronfenbrenner, U. (1979). *The ecology of human development: Experiments by nature and design.* Cambridge, MA: Harvard University Press.

Brook, J. S., Cohen, P., & Brook, D. W. (1998). Longitudinal study of co-occurring psychiatric disorders and substance use. *Journal of the American Academy of Child and Adolescent Psychiatry, 37*, 322–330.

Brook, J. S., Nomura, C., & Cohen, P. (1989). A network of influences on adolescent drug involvement: Neighborhood, school, peer, and family. *Genetic, Social, and General Psychology Monographs, 115*, 123–145.

Brown, B. S. (1995). Reducing impediments to technology transfer in drug abuse programming. In T. E. Backer, S. L. David, & G. Soucy (Eds.), *Reviewing the behavioral science knowledge base on technology transfer.* NIDA Research Monograph No. 155. Rockville, MD: National Institute on Drug Abuse.

Brown, S. A., Myers, M. G., Mott, M. A., & Vik, P. W. (1994). Correlates of success following treatment for adolescent substance abuse. *Applied and Preventative Psychology, 3*, 61–73.

Brown, S. A., Vik, P. W., & Creamer, V. A. (1989). Characteristics of relapse following adolescent substance abuse treatment. *Addictive Behaviors, 14*, 291–300.

Brown, T. L., Henggeler, S. W., Schoenwald, S. K., Brondino, M. J., & Pickrel, S. G. (1999). Multisystemic treatment of substance abusing and dependent juvenile offenders: Effects on school attendance at posttreatment and 6-month follow-up. *Children's Services: Social Policy, Research, and Practice, 2*, 81–93.

Bry, B. H. & Krinsley, K. E. (1992). Booster sessions and long-term effects of behavioral family therapy on adolescent substance abuse and school performance. *Journal of Behavior Therapy and Experimental Psychiatry, 23*, 183–189.

Bukstein, O. G. (2000). Disruptive behavior disorder and substance abuse disorders in adolescents. *Journal of Psychoactive Drugs, 32*, 67–79.

Carr, A. (Ed.) (2000). *What works with children and adolescents?: A critical review of psychological interventions with children, adolescents, and their families.* New York, NY: Routledge.

Carroll, K. M. & Rounsaville, B. J. (1990). Can a technology model of psychotherapy research be applied to cocaine abuse treatment? In L. S. Onken and J. B. Blaine (Eds.), *Psychotherapy and counseling in the treatment of drug abuse.* NIDA Research Monograph 104. Rockville, MD: National Institute on Drug Abuse.

Chambliss, D. L. & Hollon, S. D. (1998). Defining empirically supported therapies. *Journal of Consulting and Clinical Psychology, 66,* 7–18.

Cormack, C. & Carr, A. (2000). Drug abuse. In A. Carr (ed), *What works with children and adolescents?: A critical review of psychological interventions with children, adolescents, and their families* (pp. 155–177). New York, NY: Routledge.

Corrigan, P. W., Williams, O. B., McCracken, S. G., Kommana, S., Edwards, M., & Brunner, J. (1998). Staff attitudes that impede the implementation of behavioral treatment programs. *Behavior Modification, 22,* 548–562.

CSAT (Center for Substance Abuse Treatment) (1999). *Treatment of adolescents with substance use disorders. Treatment Improvement Protocol (TIP) Series 32.* Rockville, MD: US Department of Health and Human Services.

Dakof, G. A. (2000). Understanding gender differences in adolescent drug abuse: Issues of comorbidity and family functioning. *Journal of Psychoactive Drugs, 32,* 1–24.

Dennis, M. L., Titus, J. C., Diamond, G., Donaldson, J., Godley, S. H., Tims, F., Webb, C., Kaminer, Y., Babor, T., French, M., Godley, M. D., Hamilton, N., Liddle, H., & Scott, C. (in press). The Cannabis Youth Treatment (CYT) experiment: A multi-site study of five approaches to outpatient treatment for adolescents. *Journal of Substance Abuse Treatment.*

Diamond, G. S. & Diamond, G. M. (2002). Studying core mechanisms of change: An agenda for family-based process research. In H. Liddle, H. Santisteban, D. Levant, J. Bray, (Eds.), *Family psychology science-based interventions.* Washington, DC: American Psychological Association Press.

Diamond, G. S. & Liddle, H. A. (1996). Resolving a therapeutic impasse between parents and adolescents in Multidimensional Family Therapy. *Journal of Consulting and Clinical Psychology, 64,* 481–488.

Diamond, G. S. & Liddle, H. A. (1999). Transforming negative parent–adolescent interactions: From impasse to dialogue. *Family Process, 38,* 5–26.

Diamond, G. M., Liddle, H. A., Hogue, A., & Dakof, G. A. (1999). Alliance building interventions with adolescents in family therapy: A process study. *Psychotherapy: Theory, Research, Practice, and Training, 36,* 355–368.

Dishion, T. J., Capaldi, D., Spracklen, K. M., & Li, F. (1995). Peer ecology of male adolescent drug use. *Developmental Psychopathology, 7,* 803–824.

Dishion, T. J., Reid, J. B., & Patterson, G. R. (1988). Empirical guidelines for a family intervention for adolescent drug use. *Journal of Chemical Dependency Treatment, 1,* 189–224.

Docherty, J. P. (1984). Implications of the technology model of psychotherapy. In J. B. W. Williams and R. L. Spitzer (Eds.), *Psychotherapy research: Where are we and where should we go?* New York, NY: Guilford Press.

Donohue, B., Azrin, N., Lawson, H., Friedlander, J., Teicher, G., & Rindsberg, J. (1998). Improving initial session attendance of substance abusing and conduct disordered adolescents: A controlled study. *Journal of Child and Adolescent Substance Abuse, 8*, 1–13.

Duncan, S. C., Duncan, T. E., Biglan, A., & Ary, D. (1998). Contribution of the social context to the development of adolescent substance use: A multivariate latent growth modeling approach. *Drug and Alcohol Dependence, 50*, 57–71.

Elkin, I. (1999). A major dilemma in psychotherapy outcome research: Disentangling therapists from therapies. *Clinical Psychology Science and Practice, 6*, 10–32.

Farrell, A. D. (1994). Structural equation modeling with longitudinal data: Strategies for examining group differences and reciprocal relationships. *Journal of Consulting and Clinical Psychology, 62*, 477–487.

Farrell, A. D. & White, K. S. (1998). Peer influences and drug use among urban adolescents: Family structure and parent–adolescent relationship as protective factors. *Journal of Consulting and Clinical Psychology, 66*, 248–258.

French, M. T. (1995). Economic evaluation of drug abuse treatment programs: Methodology and findings. *American Journal of Drug and Alcohol Abuse, 21*, 111–135.

Friedman, A. S. (1989). Family therapy vs. parent groups: Effects on adolescent drug abusers. *The American Journal of Family Therapy, 17*, 335–347.

Gilvarry, E. (2000). Substance abuse in young people. *Journal of Child Psychology and Psychiatry and Allied Disciplines, 41*, 55–80.

Goldstein, M. F., Deren, S., Magura, S., Kayman, D. J., Beardsley, M., & Tortu, S. (2000). Cessation of drug use: Impact of time in treatment. *Journal of Psychoactive Drugs, 32*, 305–310.

Haley, J. (1976). *Problem solving therapy*. San Francisco, CA: Jossey-Bass.

Hamilton, N., Brantley, L., Tims, F., Angelovich, N., & McDougall, B. (2000). *Family Support Network (FSN) for adolescent cannabis users* [Vol. 3 of the Cannabis Youth Treatment (CYT) manual series]. Rockville, MD: Center for Substance Abuse Treatment. Substance Abuse and Mental Health Services Administration [Online: http://www.samhsa.gov/csat/csat.htm].

Hawkins, J. D., Catalano, R. F., & Miller, J. Y. (1992). Risk and protective factors for alcohol and other drug problems in adolescence and early adulthood: Implications for substance abuse prevention. *Psychological Bulletin, 112*, 64–105.

Hendrick, T. E., Bickaman, L., & Rog, D. J. (1993). *Applied research design: A practical guide*. Newbury Park, CA: Sage.

Henggeler, S. W., Borduin, C. M., Melton, G. B., Mann, B. J., Smith, L. A., Hall, J. A., Cone, L., & Fucci, B. R. (1991). Effects of multisystemic therapy on drug use and abuse in serious juvenile offenders: A progress report from two outcome studies. *Family Dynamics of Addiction Quarterly, 1*, 40–51.

Henggeler, S. W., Melton, G. B., Brondino, M. J., Scherer, D. G., & Hanley, J. H. (1997). Multisystemic therapy with violent and chronic juvenile offenders and their families: The role of treatment fidelity in successful dissemination. *Journal of Consulting and Clinical Psychology, 65*, 821–833.

Henggeler, S. W., Pickrel, S. G., & Brondino, M. J. (1999). Multisystemic treatment of substance abusing and dependent delinquents: Outcomes, treatment fidelity, and transportability. *Mental Health Services Research, 1*, 171–184.

Henggeler, S. W., Pickrel, S. G., Brondino, M. J., & Crouch, J. L. (1996). Eliminating (almost) treatment dropout of substance abusing or dependent delinquents through home-based multisystemic therapy. *American Journal of Psychiatry, 153*, 427–428.

Henggeler, S. W., Schoenwald, S. K., Borduin, C. M., Rowland, M. D., & Cunningham, P. B. (1998). *Multisystemic treatment of antisocial behavior in children and adolescents.* New York, NY: Guilford Press.

Hoffman, L. (1981). *Foundations of family therapy.* New York: Basic Books.

Hogue, A., Liddle, H. A., & Rowe, C. (1996). Treatment adherence process research in family therapy: A rationale and some practical guidelines. *Psychotherapy, 33,* 332–345.

Hogue, A., Liddle. H. A., Rowe, C., Turner, R. M., Dakof, G., & LaPann, K. (1998). Treatment adherence and differentiation in individual versus family therapy for adolescent substance abuse. *Journal of Consulting and Clinical Psychology, 45,* 104–114.

Huey, S. J., Henggeler, S. W., Brondino, M. J., & Pickrel, S. G. (2000). Mechanisms of change in Multisystemic Therapy: Reducing delinquent behavior through therapist adherence and improved family and peer functioning. *Journal of Consulting and Clinical Psychology, 68,* 451–467.

Institute of Medicine (1998). *Bridging the gap between practice and research: Forging partnerships with community-based drugs and alcohol treatment.* Washington, DC: National Academy Press.

Jackson-Gilfort, A., Liddle, H. A., & Dakof, G. (in press). Using culturally specific themes to enhance engagement of African-American males in family therapy: A process study. *Journal of Black Psychology.*

Jessor, R., Van Den Bos, J., Vanderryn, J., Costa, F. M., & Turbin, M. S. (1995). Protective factors in adolescent problem behavior: Moderator effects and developmental change. *Developmental Psychology, 31,* 923–933.

Joanning, H., Quinn, Q., Thomas, F., & Mullen, R. (1992). Treating adolescent drug abuse: A comparison of family systems therapy, group therapy, and family drug education. *Journal of Marital and Family Therapy, 18,* 345–356.

Kazdin, A. E. (1994a). Methodology, design, and evaluation in psychotherapy research. In A. E. Bergin & S. L. Garfield (Eds.), *Handbook of psychotherapy and behaviour change* (4th ed., pp. 19–71). New York, NY: John Wiley.

Kazdin, A. E. (1994b). Psychotherapy for children and adolescents. In A. E. Bergin & S. L. Garfield (Eds.), *Handbook of psychotherapy and behavior change* (4th edn, pp. 543–594). New York, NY: John Wiley.

Kazdin, A. E. (1997). A model for developing effective treatment: Progression and interplay of theory, research, and practice. *Journal of Consulting and Clinical Psychology, 26,* 114–129.

Kazdin, A. E. (1998). *Research design in clinical psychology* (3rd edn). Needham Heights, MA: Allyn & Bacon.

Kazdin, A. E. & Kagan, J. (1994). Models of dysfunction in developmental psychopathology. *Clinical Psychology: Science and Practice, 1,* 35–52.

Kazdin, A. E. & Kendall, P. C. (1998). Current progress and future plans for developing effective treatments: Comments and perspectives. *Journal of Clinical Child Psychology, 27,* 217–226.

Keller, D. S. & Galanter, M. (1999). Technology transfer of network therapy to community-based addictions counselors. *Journal of Substance Abuse Treatment, 16,* 183–189.

Kilpatrick, D. G., Acierno, R., Schnurr, P. P., Saunders, B., Resnick, H. S., & Best, C. L. (2000). Risk factors for adolescent substance abuse and dependence: Data from a national sample. *Journal of Consulting and Clinical Psychology, 68,* 19–30.

Latimer, W. W., Newcomb, M., Winters, K. C., & Stinchfield, R. D. (2000a). Adolescent substance abuse treatment outcome: The role of substance abuse problems severity, psychosocial, and treatment factors. *Journal of Consulting and Clinical Psychology, 68*, 684–696.

Latimer, W. W., Winters, K. C., Stinchfield, R., & Traver, R. E. (2000b). Demographic, individual, and interpersonal predictors of adolescent alcohol and marijuana use following treatment. *Psychology of Addictive Behaviors, 14*, 162–173.

Leccese, M. & Waldron, H. B. (1994). Assessing adolescent substance use: A critique of current measurement instruments. *Journal of Substance Abuse Treatment, 11*, 553–563.

Lerner, R. M. & Galambos, N. L. (1998). Adolescent development: Challenges and opportunities for research, programs, and policies. *Annual Review of Psychology, 49*, 413–446.

Lewis, R. A., Piercy, F. P., Sprenkle, D. H., & Trepper, T. S. (1989). The Purdue brief family therapy model for adolescent substance abusers. In T. Todd & M. Selekman (Eds.), *Family approaches with adolescent substance abusers*. New York, NY: Gardner.

Lewis, R. A., Piercy, F. P., Sprenkle, D. H., & Trepper, T. S. (1990). Family-based interventions for helping drug abusing adolescents. *Journal of Adolescent Research, 5*, 82–95.

Liddle, H. A. (1999). Theory development in family-based therapy for adolescent drug abuse. *Journal of Clinical Child Psychology, 28*, 521–532.

Liddle, H. A. (2000). *Multidimensional family therapy treatment manual for the Cannabis Youth Treatment Multisite Collaborative Project*. Rockville, MD: Center for Substance Abuse Treatment.

Liddle, H. A. (2002). Multidimensional family therapy vs. cognitive behavior therapy for adolescent substance abusers. *National Institute on Drug Abuse Monograph: Proceedings of the College on Problems of Drug Dependence*. Rockville, MD: National Institutes of Health.

Liddle, H. A. & Dakof, G. A. (1995a). Efficacy of family therapy for drug abuse: Promising but not definitive. *Journal of Marital and Family Therapy, 21*, 511–544.

Liddle, H. A. & Dakof, G. A. (1995b). Family-based treatments for adolescent drug abuse: State of the science. In E. Rahdert & D. Czechowicz (Eds.), *Adolescent drug abuse: Clinical assessment and therapeutic interventions* (NIDA Research Monograph No. 156, pp. 218–254). Rockville, MD: National Institute on Drug Abuse.

Liddle, H. A., Dakof, G. A., Parker, K., Diamond, G. S., Barrett, K., & Tejeda, M. (2001). Multidimensional family therapy for adolescent drug abuse: Results of a controlled clinical trial. *American Journal of Drug and Alcohol Abuse, 27*(4), 651–687.

Liddle, H. A. & Hogue, A. (2001). Multidimensional family therapy: Pursuing empirical support through planned treatment development. In E. Wagner and H. Waldron (Eds.), *Adolescent substance abuse*. Needham Heights, MA: Allyn & Bacon.

Liddle, H. A. & Rowe, C. L. (1998). Family measures in drug abuse prevention research. In R. Ashery (Ed.), *Drug abuse prevention through family interventions* (NIDA Research Monograph 177, pp. 324–372) Rockville, MD: National Institute on Drug Abuse.

Liddle, H. A., Rowe, C., Diamond, G. M., Sessa, F., Schmidt, S., & Ettinger, D. (2000). Towards a developmental family therapy: The clinical utility of adolescent development research. *Journal of Marital and Family Therapy, 26,* 491–506.

Liddle, H. A., Rowe, C., Dakof, G., & Lyke, J. (1998). Translating parenting research into clinical interventions for families of adolescents. *Clinical Child Psychology and Psychiatry, 3,* 419–443.

Liddle, H. A., Santisteban, D., Levant, R., & Bray, J. (Eds.) (2002). *Family psychology: Science-based interventions.* Washington, DC, American Psychological Association.

Miller, G. E. & Prinz, R. J. (1990). Enhancement of social learning interventions for childhood conduct disorder. *Psychological Bulletin, 108,* 291–307.

Minuchin, S. (1974). *Families and family therapy.* Cambridge, MA: Harvard University Press.

Minuchin, S. & Fishman, H. C. (1981). *Family therapy techniques.* Cambridge, MA: Harvard University Press.

Morrissey-Kane, E. & Prinz, R. J. (1999). Engagement in child and adolescent treatment: The role of parental cognitions and attributions. *Clinical Child and Family Psychology Review, 2,* 183–198.

Nichols, M. P. & Schwartz, R. C. (1998). *Family therapy: Concepts and methods* (4th edn). Needham Heights, MA: Allyn & Bacon.

Onken, L. S., Blaine, J. D., & Battjes, R. J. (1997). Behavioral therapy research: A conceptualization of a process. In S. W. Henggeler & S. B. Santos (Eds.), *Innovative approaches for difficult-to-treat populations* (pp. 477–485). Washington, DC: American Psychiatric Press.

Ozechowski, T. J. & Liddle, H. A. (2000). Family-based therapy for adolescent drug abuse: Knowns and unknowns. *Clinical Child and Family Psychology Review, 3,* 269–298.

Petraitis, J., Flay, B. R., Miller, T. Q., Torpy, E. J., & Greiner, B. (1998). Illicit substance use among adolescents: A matrix of prospective predictors. *Substance Use and Misuse, 33,* 2561–2604.

Prinz, R. J. & Miller, G. E. (1996). Parental engagement interventions for children at risk for conduct disorder. In R. D. Peters & R. J. McMahon (Eds.), *Preventing disorders, substance abuse, and delinquency.* Thousand Oaks, CA: Sage.

Resnick, M. D., Bearman, P. S., Blum, R. W., Bauman, K. E., Harris, K. M., Jones, J., Tabor, J., Beuhring, T., Sieving, R. E., Shew, M., Ireland, M., Bearinger, L. H., & Udry, J. R. (1997). Protecting adolescents from harm: Findings from the National Longitudinal Study on Adolescent Health. *Journal of the American Medical Association, 278,* 823–831.

Robbins, M. S., Alexander, J. F., Newell, R. M., & Turner, C. W. (1996). The immediate effect of reframing on client attitude in family therapy. *Journal of Family Psychology, 10,* 28–34.

Robbins, M. S., Alexander, J. F., & Turner, C.W. (2000). Disrupting defensive family interactions in family therapy with delinquent adolescents. *Journal of Family Psychology, 14,* 688–701.

Santisteban, D. A., Szapocznik, J., Perez-Vidal, A., Kurtines, W. M., Murray, E. J., & LaPerriere, A. (1996). Efficacy of intervention for engaging youth and families into treatment and some variables that may contribute to differential effectiveness. *Journal of Family Psychology, 10,* 35–44.

Schmidt, S. E., Liddle, H. A., & Dakof, G. A. (1996). Changes in parental practices and adolescent drug abuse during multidimensional family therapy. *Journal of Family Psychology, 10,* 12–27.

Schoenwald, S. K. & Henggeler, S.W. (2002). Services research and family based treatment. In H. A. Liddle, D. Santisteban, R. Lavant, & J. Bray (Eds.), *Family psychology: Science-based interventions.* Washington, DC American Psychological Association.

Schoenwald, S. K., Henggeler, S. W., Brondino, M. J., & Rowland, M. D. (2000). Multisystemic Therapy: Monitoring treatment fidelity. *Family Process, 39,* 83–103.

Schoenwald, S. K., Ward, D. M., Henggeler, S. W., Pickrel, S. G., & Patel, H. (1996). Multisystemic therapy treatment of substance abusing or dependent adolescent offenders: Costs of reducing incarceration, inpatient, and residential placement. *Journal of Child and Family Studies, 5,* 431–444.

Simpson, D. D., Joe, G. W., Fletcher, B. W., Hubbard, R. L., & Anglin, M.D. (1999). A national evaluation of treatment outcomes for cocaine dependence. *Archives of General Psychiatry, 56,* 507–514.

Sobell, L. C. (1996). Bridging the gap between scientists and practitioners: The challenge before us. *Behavior Therapy, 27,* 297–320.

Sorensen, J. L., Hall, S. M., Loeb, P., & Allen, T. (1988). Dissemination of a job seekers' workshop to drug treatment programs. *Behavior Therapy, 19,* 143–155.

Stage, S. A. (1999). Predicting adolescents' discharge status following residential treatment. *Residential Treatment for Children and Youth, 16,* 37–56.

Stanton, M. D. & Shadish, W. R. (1997). Outcome, attrition, and family-couples treatment for drug abuse: A meta-analysis and review of the controlled, comparative studies. *Psychological Bulletin, 122,* 170–191.

Strosahl, K. (1998). The dissemination of manual-based psychotherapies in managed care: Promises, problems, and prospects. *Clinical Psychology: Science and Practice, 5,* 382–386.

Szapocznik, J., Kurtines, W. M., Foote, F. H., Perez-Vidal, A., & Hervis, O. (1983). Conjoint versus one-person family therapy: Some evidence for the effectiveness of conducting family therapy through one person. *Journal of Consulting and Clinical Psychology, 51,* 889–899.

Szapocznik, J., Kurtines, W. M., Foote, F., Perez-Vidal, A., & Hervis, O. (1986). Conjoint versus one-person family therapy: Further evidence for the effectiveness of conducting family therapy through one person with drug-abusing adolescents. *Journal of Consulting and Clinical Psychology, 54,* 395–397.

Szapocznik, J., Perez-Vidal, A., Brickman, A. L., Foote, F. H., Santisteban, D., Hervis, O., & Kurtines, W. M. (1988). Engaging adolescent drug abusers and their families in treatment: A strategic structural systems approach. *Journal of Consulting and Clinical Psychology, 56,* 552–557.

Turner, R. M. (1993). Dynamic cognitive-behavior therapy. In T. Giles (Ed.), *Handbook of effective psychotherapy* (pp. 437–454). New York, NY: Plenum Press.

Wagner, E. F., Swenson, C. C., & Henggeler, S. W. (2000). Practical and methodological challenges in validating community-based interventions. *Children's Services: Social Policy, Research, and Practice, 3,* 211–231.

Waldron, H. B. (1997). Adolescent substance abuse and family therapy outcome: A review of randomized trials. In T. H. Ollendick & R. J. Prinz (Eds.), *Advances in clinical child psychology* (Vol. 19, pp. 199–234). New York, NY: Plenum Press.

Waldron, H. B., Slesnick, N., & Brody, J. L., Turner, C., & Peterson, T. (2001).

Four- and seven-month treatment outcomes for substance abusing youth. *Journal of Consulting and Clinical Psychology, 69*, 802–813.

Waltz, J., Addis, M., Koerner, K., & Jacobson, N. (1993). Testing the integrity of a psychotherapy protocol: Assessment of adherence and competence. *Journal of Consulting and Clinical Psychology, 61*, 620–630.

Weinberg, N. Z. & Glantz, M. D. (1999). Child psychopathology risk factors for drug abuse: Overview. *Journal of Clinical Child Psychology, 28*, 290–297.

Weinberg, N. Z., Rahdert, E., Colliver, J. D., & Glantz, M. D. (1998). Adolescent substance abuse: A review of the past 10 years. *Journal of the American Academy of Child and Adolescent Psychiatry, 37*, 252–261.

Willett, J. B. & Sayer, A. G. (1994). Using covariance structure analysis to detect correlates and predictors of individual change over time. *Psychological Bulletin, 116*, 363–381.

Williams, R. J. & Chang, S. Y. (2000). A comprehensive and comparative review of adolescent substance abuse treatment outcome. *Clinical Psychology: Science and Practice, 7*, 138–166.

Wills, T. A. & Cleary, S. D. (1999). Peer and adolescent substance use among 6th–9th graders: Latent growth analyses of influence versus selection mechanisms. *Health Psychology, 18*, 453–463.

Winters, K., Latimer, W., & Stinchfield, R. (1999). Adolescent treatment. In P. J. Ott, R. E. Tartar, & R. T. Ammerman (Eds.), *Sourcebook on substance abuse: Etiology, epidemiology, assessment, and treatment* (pp. 350–361). Boston, MA: Allyn & Bacon.

Yates, B. T. (1997). From psychotherapy research to cost-outcome research: What resources are necessary to implement which therapy procedures that change what processes to yield which outcomes? *Psychotherapy Research, 7*, 345–364.

Zarkin, G. A., French, M. T., Anderson, D. W., & Bradley, C. J. (1994). A conceptual framework for the economic evaluation of substance abuse interventions. *Evaluation and Program Planning, 17*, 409–418.

Chapter 9

Concluding remarks

Cecilia A. Essau, Paula Barrett, and Kerry A. Marsh

For adolescents to experiment with all things forbidden seems almost a "rite of passage". What they often do not anticipate are the negative outcomes or consequences that their actions may bring about. According to Elkind (1974) adolescents have a mistaken belief in their own invincibility. Known as the invincibility fable, this notion suggests that adolescents are falsely secure in their beliefs that they will not get sick or killed as they are immune to the laws of mortality and probability, and as such may participate in risky behaviours. Adolescents are faced with new relationships, situations and environments, and are secure in the belief that experimenting with licit or illicit substances will not lead to addiction, crime or worse (Elkind, 1974). They may turn to the use of licit and illicit drugs as a means of coping or to alleviate the stress (Beman, 1995).

The overwhelmingly negative impact of drug and alcohol use is becoming increasingly more apparent. For example, according to the Australian Institute of Health and Welfare report into substance usage in Australia (Higgins *et al.*, 2000) an estimated 22,000 deaths and more than a quarter of a million hospital episodes were drug-related in 1997 alone. The estimated direct health care cost of drug dependence and harmful use in Australia is enormous with figures in the hundreds of millions (Collins and Lapsley, 1996, cited in Higgins *et al.*, 2000). This increase in prevalence and associated health costs has resulted in a plethora of studies conducted to identify etiological and resilience factors, and gold standards for prevention and treatment of substance abuse and dependence in adults. In contrast, a search of the literature produced only 437 articles relating to substance use disorders (SUD) in adolescence.

Although these studies have increased our knowledge on substance use disorders in adolescents, their data should be interpreted with caution due to some methodological problems. In this chapter, we will discuss some progress and unresolved issues related to research into substance use and into SUD in adolescents. Our focus will be categorized into four main areas: classification systems, assessment, epidemiology and comorbidity; risk and protective factors; course and outcome; and prevention and intervention.

CLASSIFICATION SYSTEMS

The International Classification of Diseases (ICD; World Health Organization, 1993), now in its tenth edition, and the *Diagnostic and Statistical Manual of Mental Disorders* (American Psychiatric Association, 1994), now in its fourth edition, have been considered the diagnostic standard for substance-related disorders (see Chapter 2 in this volume). In ICD-10, the type of psychoactive substance is first identified, followed by the subsequent classification of the behaviour as hazardous, harmful or including dependence symptoms. DSM-IV separates abuse and dependence based on the consequences of substance use, including tolerance and withdrawal. Abuse is considered to be prodromal to dependence, and therefore may be considered as a less maladaptive disorder. Some authors argued that its residual category status may hinder the availability of treatment for adolescents with substance abuse since it implies that the disorder is not severe enough to warrant professional treatment (Martin *et al.*, 1996).

In both classification systems, the same criteria can be applied to adults and adolescents, and without distinguishing adult and adolescent features of SUD (Martin *et al.*, 1995). However, their appropriateness for use in adolescents has been questioned (Martin *et al.*, 1995; Stewart and Brown, 1995) since little is known about the validity or the reliability of these criteria when applied to adolescents. Age distinction is important when considering legal and social consequences of substance consumption needed to diagnose substance abuse. The same behaviour that may cause legal consequences for adolescents such as purchase of alcohol is not subjected to legal sanctions for an adult. Drinking may also cause problems in interpersonal relationships (with parents) for adolescents because alcohol consumption is prohibited. Therefore, the threshold for negative consequences associated with substance use may be lower for adolescents than for adults, even if the amount of alcohol consumed were similar (Harrison *et al.*, 1998).

Adolescent substance users may not have the type of consequences associated with chronic consumption found in adults, such as medical complications of the disorder (Brown *et al.*, 1992). Furthermore, criteria related to tolerance and negative psychosocial consequences generally take place after prolonged drug exposure, and as such may be inappropriate when applied to adolescents (Kaminer and Tarter, 1999). As reported by Martin *et al.* (1995), only 23% of adolescents with alcohol dependence met the withdrawal criteria which is substantially lower than rates reported by adults (Robins and Regier, 1991). Also, the number of adolescents with substance abuse who reported blackouts and symptoms related to withdrawal were lower than those reported for adults (Martin *et al.*, 1995); thus, withdrawal symptoms are less likely to be manifested when not accompanied by prolonged heavy drinking. Most adolescents with substance abuse and dependence reported problems at home/family and, to a lesser extent, at school and work (Martin et al., 1995). In the 1995 Minnesota Student Survey (Harrison et al., 1998), physical health problems associated with substance use were found to be infrequent in adolescents. Giving up activities in order to use substances was also relatively rare. In this study, older compared to younger students had a higher prevalence of physically hazardous use (specifically driving after use). In both grades, abuse diagnosis outnumbered dependence diagnosis, with greater difference found in the older than the younger adolescents. Giving up activities because of substance use has the most positive predictive value for a diagnosis of dependence, followed by use despite health problems, all-day use/recovery, and using more than intended. Tolerance, all-day use/recovery, and more use than intended were the criterion items with the highest sensitivity for a dependence diagnosis. Since their finding (Harrison et al., 1998) failed to support the abuse/dependence structure, they suggested combining the abuse and dependence criteria into a single set of profiles.

Some criteria may be difficult to operationalize, and are subjected to different interpretations (Grant and Towle, 1991; Harrison et al., 1998). Examples of these terms included "larger amount", "longer periods", "persistent desire", "recurrent use", and "important activities". Second, tolerance is a complex phenomenon, with individual variations in the amounts of a substance needed to produce intoxication (Harrison et al., 1998). The criteria associated with impaired control may also be problematic because the most common reason for consuming substances among adolescents was related to "out-of-control use" (i.e., to get high or smashed) (Harrison et al., 1997).

Some authors (Winters et al., 1993) have argued that the criterion threshold has been set too low for adolescents. As reported by Harrison and colleagues (1998), of the ten criterion symptoms included in the 1995 Minnesota Student Survey, four most frequently occurred alone or in combination with only one or two others, three occurred most often in combination with one or two others, three occurred most often in combination with one to four others, and the remaining three occurred most often in combination with four to six others. These authors stress the importance of retaining this range because restricting the criterion set to items with high specificity for the diagnosis may comprise rather than enhance construct validity. Furthermore, the threshold of fewer than five criterion symptoms may be too low to define a SUD because they could be those with the lowest rates of positive predictive value and specificity relative to dependence.

An unresolved issue is whether there are subclusters of abuse and dependence symptoms that are specific to individuals in different age groups. Like other psychiatric disorders, the criteria for delineating SUD from "problematic" substance consuming are difficult to justify. It could be that adolescents who fail to meet diagnostic criteria for substance use disorders still may have some impairments in their daily functioning and are at risk for negative outcomes in adulthood.

ASSESSMENT

Most instruments for assessing substance use have been developed in adult populations and may be inappropriate for use in adolescents (see Chapter 2 in this volume). The reliability and validity of most measures of substance use and SUD among adolescents has not been well established. Most studies have used checklists or self-report questionnaires to assess substance use and SUD because they are easy and less expensive to administer. However, they can be problematic when used for clinical assessment. The lack of opportunity for rapport building during questionnaire administration (Weber *et al.*, 1994) and adolescents' lack of motivation, lack of interest and/or reading difficulties may limit the reporting of sensitive information (McLellan *et al.*, 1992). Since substance use is illegal, social desirability may also influence the reporting of substance use and associated problems. Therefore, response bias may play a large role in the type of information obtained. An unresolved issue is how to collect sensitive information. According to some authors, the questionnaire is better suited for gathering socially disapproved behaviours among non-clinical samples (Turner *et al.*, 1998); other recommended the use of clinical interviewing (Morrison *et al.*, 1995).

Another complication is the heterogeneous nature of adolescent substance use problems (Farrell and Strang, 1991). Not only do the types of substances used by adolescents vary, but the frequency with which use occurs, the beliefs about the effects and consequences from use, the motivations underlying use, and factors precipitating substance use also differ (Henly and Winters, 1989). Furthermore, substance misuse is embedded within the developmental context of adolescence. Developmental changes during adolescence are accompanied by normative increases in negative affect, substance use, and other problem behaviours. Puberty and its associated biological changes may precipitate behavioural and emotional changes which make it difficult to separate from the effects of alcohol and drug use (Brown *et al.*, 1990).

In order to produce a comprehensive picture of the adolescent's substance problem, the adolescent's developmental stage needs to be considered. Adolescents of different ages may differ in their ability to report their behaviours and emotions. To evaluate similar characteristics across the age groups may require not only different measures, but may also include changes to the same measures. A major problem is that any changes of assessment procedures may influence the results and conclusions, since the same items may be interpreted differently by youths at different developmental stages. Furthermore, in assessing age-appropriateness versus clinical relevance of adolescents' behaviour, we need to have knowledge about the age-appropriateness of the behaviour and about how to operationalize them.

Vik, Brown and Myers (1997) argued that assessment of substance use should be conceptualized from the perspective of an interaction between biological, psychological, and social factors in the development and maintenance of substance use. This could involve the evaluation of the following areas: (i) substance involvement characteristics such as use context and consequences; (ii) intrapersonal characteristics (e.g., coping/social skills); (iii) environmental factors (e.g., family functioning, social support); and (iv) functioning in major life domains (e.g., academics, interpersonal relations). Others recommended having a broad-spectrum assessment (Donovan, 1988) that ideally includes information from adolescents themselves (e.g., clinical interview, self-administered structured questionnaires), from significant others (e.g., parents), and objective measures (e.g., neuropsychological, toxicology screens). While the latter are useful to confirm self-reports, such investigation may be expensive and need to be conducted by trained personnel. Meyers *et al.* (2000) recently recommended that since SUD is associated with various life domains, assessment procedure should include the assessment of risk and protective factors (Table 9.1).

Table 9.1 Assessment of risk and protective factors in substance use disorders

Domains	Information to be assessed
Substance use	Duration of use, date of last use, longest period of abstinence, route of administration, severity indicators, history of substance use treatment
Mental health functioning	Type and severity of comorbid disorders
Family member	Parental psychiatric and alcohol/drug problems
Educational status	Educational problems, future educational and employment plans
Peer relationship	Peer group composition, gang involvement, peer rejection
Stressful life events	Personal, family- and community-related stressors
Legal status	Type, consequences, and delinquent and offending behaviour
Sexual behaviour	Use of barrier and non-barrier contraceptive
Use of free time	Types and pattern of employment and leisure-time activities;
Health status	Presence of allergies, infectious disease, other medical problems

Source: Slightly modified from Meyers *et al.* (2000).

EPIDEMIOLOGY

With the development of highly structured diagnostic instruments which can be administered by lay interviewers, numerous epidemiological studies on substance use and SUD in adolescents have been conducted in recent years.

As discussed by Essau and colleagues (see Chapter 3 in this volume), substance use is very common in adolescents. However, most of these data are based on studies conducted in various industrialized countries: in the United States, in some European countries (e.g., United Kingdom, Germany, Switzerland), and in Australia. Therefore, these data cannot be regarded as representative of the worldwide pattern of substance consumption and substance use disorders on account of the differences in societal views and laws regarding alcohol and drugs. Studies that give information on cross-cultural patterns of substance use and abuse are needed. However, studies differ as to how a case with a SUD is defined, and in the way in which they combine information from different sources, in the timeframe covered, and in the sampling frame.

A major problem in comparing the prevalence of alcohol use is related to measures of alcohol use and in the lack of uniform definitions used. Further, the alcohol content of a standard drink varies across studies and countries, and there are no clear criteria on how to define "moderate drinking", problem drinking, heavy drinking, or hazardous drinking. Thus, different rates of substance used and substance use disorders may reflect true differences, or difference in the methodology used.

Most studies were conducted in either schools or clinical settings. Since school dropouts and absentees are at higher risk for substance use than those who remain in school, the prevalence of substance use among a sample recruited in schools may be underestimated. Adolescents from clinical settings are typically involved with multiple drugs, so that the patterns of their withdrawal and dependence symptoms may be complex (Stewart and Brown, 1995).

COMORBIDITY

Recent studies have consistently shown high comorbidity rates between SUD and other disorders such as conduct disorder, depression, and anxiety disorders (Weinberg et al., 1998). Kilpatrick and colleagues (2000) also found that substance abuse was common in adolescents who had been physically or sexually assaulted, or who witnessed violence. Other studies have shown comorbidity between substance abuse and anorexia or bulimia nervosa in girls (Wiederman and Pryor, 1997), and post-traumatic stress disorder (Kilpatrick et al., 2000). In addition to comorbid psychiatric disorders, substance abuse has also been linked to several antisocial behaviours (i.e. impulsivity, aggression, and violence) in adolescent males, that combined with the substance abuse may lead to a diagnosis of antisocial personality disorder (Matykiewiecz et al., 1997).

Despite this high comorbidity rate, its meaning for etiological and classification issues remain unclear (Caron and Rutter, 1991; Nottelmann and

Jensen, 1999). It is unclear (i) whether comorbidity arises from the overlapping diagnostic criteria or artificial subdivision of syndromes; or (ii) whether the disorders have the same etiological or risk factors; (iii) or whether one disorder may be an early manifestation of another disorder. Perspective longitudinal studies that examine the temporal sequences of disorders may shed some light.

Although the meaning of comorbidity remains unresolved, comorbidity seems to be associated with an earlier onset, a more chronic course, and lifestyle factors such as less social stability that may lead to resistance to treatment (Newman *et al.*, 1998). Accordingly, as the rates of substance use increase in adolescents, so does concern for a highly vulnerable group of young people who are at higher risk of early onset of substance use and the development of SUD, and subsequent comorbid psychiatric disorders (Nelson *et al.*, 1998). According to Crome (1999) comorbidity contributes significantly to problems of non-compliance and relapse faced by "hard to engage populations" such as the homeless, the unemployed, those engaged in illegal activities, and those showing antisocial or aggressive behaviours.

Course and outcome

Most research on substance use disorders in youth are cross-sectional in nature. While these studies have been a useful way to demonstrate correlates of substance use, they have been unable to establish causal relations among those variables, and therefore cannot lead to a clear developmental understanding of substance use and misuse (see Chapter 5 in this volume). As reported by Kandel (1975), substance use generally take place in a social context, initially by using gateway substances such as alcohol and cigarettes, which are legal for adults and are readily available to adolescents. Initial use may occur because of curiosity or easy access to a substance.

Only prospective longitudinal studies will help to clarify the "gateway model", and to identify developmental continuities that precede and cause progression toward a substance use disorder. Longitudinal data can be used to explore how chains of experiences could influence the course and outcome of substance use disorders. Despite these advantages, longitudinal studies are uncommon, possibly due to their cost, logistical difficulty, and potential problems with attrition (Rutter, 1994). Additionally, there are numerous issues which present challenges for longitudinal research, including the time interval between the index and the follow-up investigations. Theoretically, the time span should not be so long that the developmental changes will be missed; but neither should it not be so short as to reduce "practice effects".

Finally, there is no general consensus as to the indices of course and outcome for SUD, which may hinder direct comparison of findings across studies. However, in accordance with the DSM-IV definition for psychiatric disorders, the indicators of course and outcome of the presence of SUD should include the presence of substance consumption, SUD, the presence of other disorders, the presence of psychosocial impairment, and health services utilization.

ETIOLOGICAL MECHANISMS AND RISK FACTORS

Whereas research abounds on the etiological basis of substance abuse amongst adolescents, it is now widely recognized that multiple risk factors may contribute to the presence and continuation of substance use by adolescents. These factors operate simultaneously and often interact in complex ways. As it appears that adolescents are experimenting with substances at an early age (Warren *et al.*, 1997), identifying potential risk factors that may lead to initial use or continued use has become paramount. A review by Beman (1995; see also Chapter 4 in this volume) identified that risk factors could be organized into four main categories of risk:

- demographic (e.g., age and gender)
- social (e.g., family factors that include poor parenting practices, especially those that encompass coercion or inadequate supervision or attention; chronic parent/child conflict; pervasive expression of negative emotion; or quality of parent/child relationship; as well as peer influence)
- behavioural (e.g., use of legal substances such as tobacco and alcohol)
- individual risk factors (e.g., early temperament characteristics, early conduct problems, a risk-taking orientation, stressful life events, poor academic performance)

On the one hand, this information has been useful, not only for generating hypotheses about possible mechanisms involved in the onset of substance use and misuse, but also more importantly, for prevention and intervention purposes. On the other hand, it should be stated that most of these factors are also correlates of many other psychiatric disorders. An important unresolved issue is specificity: do these factors impose specific vulnerability or risk for substance use disorders or increased vulnerability for any disorder – not just substance abuse or dependence?

In contrast to the number of studies on risk factors, only very few studies have examined protective factors of substance use disorders. It would be most useful to identify factors that protect high-risk adolescents against having depression.

TREATMENT

What is known from past and current research is that a large number of adolescents with substance abuse disorders also have comorbid conditions such as conduct disorder, depression, and anxiety. Comorbidity itself poses difficulties for therapy for several reasons. Firstly, most treatments are targeted at specific symptomatology and may well have been developed and validated on pure diagnostic groups. Secondly, the extent of comorbidity and the range of disorders make treatment more diversified, with a need to target both the substance abuse and the specific comorbid disorder. As this issue is only beginning to be addressed for adolescent substance use disorders, further research is necessary. As indicated by Nelson and colleagues (1998), rates of comorbidity increase with early onset substance abuse, which is an alarming indication of what is in store for future generations as the rates of substance abuse increase during adolescence. Further, although bipolar disorder has been problematic for the treatment of adult substance abuse for decades, its existence in adolescence is only just beginning to be recognized. Accordingly, a growing body of research suggests that early onset bipolar disorder may also be problematic during adolescence. This trend may also be evident in other psychological disorders that have been found to be comorbid in adult substance abuse, but not yet explored in adolescents. For example, schizophrenia is recognized as having its roots in late adolescence, and has been linked with adult substance abuse. It may well be that substance initiation may have occurred at around the same point in time, possibly as a means of self-medication.

Moreover, it seems that the relationship of substance abuse and deviant behaviours are well researched, both in adolescence and adulthood. However, the substance abuse literature appears not to have focused on bullying. Whilst Berthold and Hoover (2000) found that substance abuse was a serious outcome for those who bully, it appears not to be have been linked to the victim. Considering that the victim is usually depressed, anxious, and isolated, and that bullying is often a relational act, it makes sense that bullied adolescents are at an increased risk of substance abuse. So further research into substance abuse as an outcome of relational bullying is needed.

In an effort to curb this growing trend, governments all over the world are channelling vast amounts of funding into research and intervention programmes (Table 9.2). We have seen substantial changes over the past thirty years or more in terms of treatment and interventions, such as the move to a theoretical basis for interventions, and also the move toward harm-minimization rather than abstinence. However, several problems still exist in respect to current research and interventions. Firstly, most of the current research addresses substance use and abuse collectively. Since most adolescents who use a substance do not go on to develop a substance use disorder, future research needs to differentiate between these two groups. Further, while there are different trajectories for different types of drugs, most research and interventions aimed at adolescent substance abuse attempt to address substances collectively, when different modalities may be more effective for different types of substances.

Table 9.2 Trends in the prevention and intervention of substance use disorders

Years	Type of prevention/intervention
1960s	• Information deficit model: Aims to provide knowledge of the adverse health effects of drug use (Blanton et al., 1997; Johnson et al., 2000). • Peer education approach: Providing information and raising awareness of the dangers of substance use, whilst empowering adolescents to say no. Examples of this style of approach include the Crew 2000 Peer Education Project (McDermott and McBride, 1993), the Youth Awareness Programme (Shiner and Newburn, 1996), and the Drug Prevention in Youth Programme (Foas, 1995).
1970s and early 1980s	• Personality deficit model: Aimed at educating about personality characteristics that may be precursors to substance use, and at increasing self-esteem and personal development through school-based programs (Rowling, 1995). • Psychosocial model of substance use: Highlights the influence of family, peers, and mass media. Advocates the development of social skills, decision-making skills, communication and assertiveness skills, as well as information (McDonald, 1999). • Social-cognitive model: Inclusion of problem-solving and coping strategies, self-instructional techniques for behavioural self-control, and relaxation techniques. This style of intervention was followed by a close derivative, "Life Skills Programs" (Botvin et al., 1984).
1980s	• National Campaign Against Drug Abuse adopted the concept of "harm minimization": Provides skills and knowledge to say no or seek alternatives during the crucial stage of experimentation, as well as information on the effects of drugs, legal issues, risk reduction, and where to get help if needed (Riley, 1993). • "Peer-led" interventions: Adolescents are more likely to adopt a modelled behaviour if it results in an outcome they value, if the model is someone they admire and is similar to themselves (Bandura, 1999). The "Alcohol and Other Drugs Program", a New Zealand peer-led intervention, was also based on this premise (Elliott and Lambourn, 2000).

The majority of interventions are universal programmes aimed at being delivered within the school curriculum, with the notion of educating adolescents about drugs (see Chapter 6 in this volume). This method has been found to be effective as an avoidance strategy with non-using adolescents, but has had little influence on the discontinuation of substance use for adolescents who are already using substances. One of the major problems identified with this group is that many adolescents may see substance use as a means of escape or a means of coping. In addition, adolescents who have experienced no visible ill-effects or deem their experience to be pleasant are unlikely to change their behaviours. Interventions need to focus on alternative coping methods and on a variety of styles of problem-solving skills to avoid the use of drugs as a method of escaping daily problems, such as those used in social cognitive theory. In addition to utilizing the already existing social support network that surrounds young people, in terms of both family and peers, interventions need to focus on teaching adolescents how to access support in their naturally occurring support systems. These support systems can then be supplemented by school-based as well as community support networks, thus creating a holistic support system rather than a contextual one.

Also problematic in past and current interventions is the tendency to focus on one or two of the risk factors, even though it is widely recognized that substance use and abuse is multi-determined. As a result, reduction in substance use may be encapsulated within the context in which it is learned. For example, school-based programmes aimed at peer influence may ignore family or behavioural and individual factors, and therefore may not be generalizable to other social contexts. Future research and intervention programmes need to take more of a community focus, to enable the generalizing of skills and education to other settings. Whilst the schools and the broader education system are doing ground-breaking work in an attempt to reduce the progression from substance use to dependency and abuse, a broader community focus would add support and more opportunity to engender the harm-minimization message.

Whilst research and interventions appear to have targeted peer aspects of substance abuse well, a focus on the family is what seems to be lacking in most approaches to adolescent substance abuse. There is no doubt that, at this stage in a child's life, the peer group are more influential in substance use; however, it seems that familial factors may be more influential in actual dependence and abuse factors. Whilst it is recognized that experimentation is part of normal adolescence, dependence and abuse arise from different psychosocial aspects of the young person's life; therefore parents need to be more aware of the reasons why adolescents may go on to be regular users of substances. It is these aspects too that need to be addressed through more community- and family-focused interventions.

It is important to remember that the majority of adolescents do not go on to develop substance abuse disorders, suggesting that, even without intervention, some teenagers have skills and strengths that help them through what is probably one of the most turbulent periods of any human being's life. Accordingly, a focus of the skills and resources of our youth is perhaps the best way of approaching the reducing of substance abuse in adolescence. As espoused by Kim and colleagues (1998) promoting adolescents' positive attributes rather than focusing on their deficits can only enhance their self-efficacy and abilities, and overall self-esteem, while promoting the opportunity for problem solving and skills building. Thus, by recognizing their worth and promoting their existing knowledge and skill bases, and giving them the opportunity to develop self-regulatory agency, our youth can make informed choices that may turn the tide of substance abuse in adolescence.

REFERENCES

American Psychiatric Association (1994). *Diagnostic and Statistical Manual of Mental Disorders* (4th edn), Washington, DC: American Psychiatric Association.

Bandura, A. (1999). Sociocognitive analysis of substance abuse: An agentic perspective. *Psychological Science, 10*, 214–217.

Beman, D. S. (1995). Risk factors leading to adolescent substance abuse. *Adolescence, 30*, 201–208.

Berthold, K. A. & Hoover, J. H. (2000). Correlates of bullying and victimization among intermediate students in the Midwestern USA. *School Psychology International, 21*, 65–78.

Blanton, H., Gibbons, F. X., Gerard, M., Conger, K. J., & Smith, G. E. (1997). Role of family and peers in the development of prototypes associated with substance use. *Journal of Family Psychology, 11*, 271–288.

Botvin, G. J., Baker, E., Renick, N. L., Filazzola, A. D. & Botvin, E. M. (1984). A cognitive-behavioural approach to substance abuse prevention. *Addictive Behaviours, 9*, 137–147.

Brown, S. A., Mott, M. A., & Myers, M. G. (1990). Adolescent alcohol and drug treatment outcome. In R. R. Watson (Ed.), *Drug and alcohol abuse prevention* (pp. 373–403). Clifton, NJ: Humana Press.

Brown, S. A., Mott, M. A., & Stewart, M. A. (1992). Adolescent alcohol and drug abuse. In C. E. Walker & M. C. Roberts (Eds.), *Handbook of clinical child psychology* (2nd edn, pp. 677–693). New York, NY: Wiley.

Caron, C. & Rutter, M. (1991). Comorbidity in child psychopathology: Concepts, issues, and research strategies. *Journal Child Psychology and Psychiatry, 32*, 1063–1080.

Collins, D. & Lapsley, H. (1996). The social costs of drug abuse in Australia in 1998 and 1992. *National campaign against drug abuse: Monograph No. 30*. Canberra, Australia: Australian Government Printers.

Crome, H. B. (1999). Overview: Psychiatric comorbidity and substance misuse: What are the issues? *Drugs, Education, Prevention and Policy, 6*, 149–150.

Donovan, D. M. (1988). Assessment of addictive behaviors: Implications of an emerging biopsychosocial model. In D. M. Donovan & G. A. Marlatt (Eds.), *Assessment of addictive behaviors* (pp. 3–48). New York, NY: Guilford Press.

Elkind, O. (1974). *Children and adolescents: Interpretive essays on Jean Piaget.* York: Oxford University Press, *22*, 503–513.

Elliott, K. J. & Lambourn, A. J. (2000). Sex, drugs and alcohol: Two peer-led approaches in Tamaki Makaurau/Auckland, Aotearoa/New Zealand. *Journal of Adolescence, 22*, 503–513.

Farrell, M. & Strang, J. (1991). Substance use and misuse in childhood and adolescence. *Journal of Child Psychology and Psychiatry, 32*, 109–128.

Foas, S. W. (1995). Evaluation of a peer led drug abuse/risk reduction project for runaway/homeless youths. *Journal of Drug Education*, *25*, 321–333.

Grant, B. F. & Towle, L. H. (1991). A comparison of diagnostic criteria: DSM-III-R, proposed DSM-IV, and proposed ICD-10. *Alcohol Health Research World*, *15*, 284–292.

Harrison, P. A., Fulkerson, J. A., & Beebe, T. J. (1997). Multiple substance use among adolescent physical and sexual abuse victims. *Child Abuse and Neglect*, *21*, 529–539.

Harrison, P. A., Fulkerson, J. A., & Beebe, T. J. (1998). DSM-IV substance use disorder criteria for adolescents: A critical examination based on a Statewide School Survey. *American Journal of Psychiatry*, *155*, 486–492.

Henly, G. A. & Winters, K. C. (1989). Development of psychosocial scales for the assessment of adolescents involved with alcohol and drugs. *International Journal of the Addictions*, *24*, 973–1001.

Higgins, K., Cooper-Stanbury, M., & Williams, P. (2000). *Statistics on drug use in Australia 1998*. Canberra: Australian Institute of Health & Welfare (Drug Statistics Series). www.aihw.gov.au.

Johnson, L. D., O'Malley, P. M., & Bachman, J. G. (2000). *Monitoring the future national results on adolescent drug use: Overview of key findings, 1999*. Bathesda, MA: National Institute on Drug Abuse.

Kaminer, Y. (1999). Addictive disorders in adolescents. *Psychiatric Clinics of North America*, *22*, 275–288.

Kandel, D. (1975). Stages in adolescent involvement in drug use. *Science*, *190*, 912–914.

Kilpatrick, D. G., Acierno, R., Saunders, B., Resnick, H. S., Best, C. L., & Schnurr, P. P. (2000). Risk factors for adolescent substance abuse and dependence: Data from a national sample. *Journal of Consulting and Clinical Psychology*, *68*, 19.

Kim, S., Crutchfield, C., Williams, C., & Hepler, N. (1998). Toward a new paradigm in substance abuse and other problem behaviour prevention for youth: Youth development and empowerment approach. *Drug Education*, *28*, 1–17.

Liddle, H. A. & Dakof, G. A. (1995). Family-based treatment for adolescent drug use: State of the science. In *Adolescent drug abuse: Clinical assessment and therapeutic interventions*. NIDA Monograph 156. Rockville, MD: National Institute on Drug Abuse.

Martin, C. S., Kaczynski, N. A., Maisto, S. A., Bukstein, O. M., & Moss, H. B. (1995). Patterns of DSM-IV alcohol abuse and dependence symptoms in adolescent drinkers. *Journal of Studies on Alcohol*, *56*, 672–680.

Martin, C. S., Langenbucher, J. W., Kaczynski, N., & Chung, T. (1996). Staging in the onset of DSM-IV alcohol symptoms in adolescents: survival/hazard analysis. *Journal of Studies on Alcohol*, *57*, 549–558.

Matykiewicz, L., La Grange, L., Reyes, E., Vance, P., & Wang, M. (1997). Adolescent males, impulsive/aggressive behaviour, and alcohol abuse: Biological correlates. *Journal of Child and Adolescent Substance Abuse*, *6*, 27–37.

McDermott, P. & McBride, W. (1993). Crew 2000: Peer coalition in action. *Druglink*, *Nov/Dec*, 13–15.

McDonald, J. (1999). Drug education: Past approaches and future possibilities. *Youth Studies Australia*, *18*, 11–15.

McLellan, A. T., Kuschner, H., Metzger, D. S., Peters, R., Smith, I., Grissom, G., Pettinati, H. M., & Argeriou, M. (1992). The fifth edition of the Addition Severity

Index: Historical critique and normative data. *Journal of Substance Abuse and Treatment, 9*, 199–213.

Meyers, K., Hagan, T. A., Zanis, D., Webb, A., Franz, J., Ring-Kurtz, S., Rutherford, M., & McLellan, A. T. (2000). Critical issues in adolescent substance use assessment. *Drug and Alcohol Dependence, 55*, 235–246.

Morrison, C. S., McCusker, J., Stoddard, A. M., & Bigelow, C. (1995). The validity of behavioral data reported by injection drug users on a clinical risk assessment. *International Journal of Addiction, 30*, 889–899.

Nelson, C. B., Heath, A. C., & Kessler, R. C. (1998). Temporal progression of alcohol dependence symptoms in the US household population: Results from the National Comorbidity Survey. *Journal of Consulting and Clinical Psychology, 66*, 474–483.

Newman, D. L., Moffitt, T. E., Caspi, A., & Silva, P. A. (1998). Comorbid mental disorders: Implications for treatment and sample selection. *Journal of Abnormal Psychology, 107*, 305–311.

Nottelmann, E. D. & Jensen, P. S. (1999). Comorbidity of depressive disorders in children and adolescents: Rates, temporal sequencing, course and outcome. In C. A. Essau & F. Petermann (Eds.), *Depressive disorders in children and adolescents: Epidemiology, risk factors, and treatment*. Northvale, NJ: Jason Aronson.

Riley, D. (1993). *Pragmatic approaches to drug use from the area between intolerance and neglect.* Ontario: Canadian Centre for Substance Abuse.

Robins, L. N. & Regier, D. A. (Eds.) (1991). *Psychiatric disorders in America.* New York, NY: Free Press.

Rowling, L. (1995). *Philosophical frameworks and models of drug education.* Paper presented at National Initiatives in Drug Education Conference, Canberra.

Rutter, M. (1994). Comorbidity: Meanings and mechanisms. *Clinical Psychology: Science and Practice, 1*, 100–103.

Shiner, M. & Newburn, T. (1996). *Young people, drugs and peer education: An evaluation of the youth awareness programme (YAP).* Paper 13, Drugs Prevention Initiative. London: Home Office.

Stewart, D. G. & Brown, S. A. (1995). Withdrawal and dependency symptoms among adolescent alcohol and drug abusers. *Addiction, 90*, 627–635.

Turner, C. F., Ku, L., Rogers, S. M., Lindberg, L. D., Pleck, J. H., & Sonenstein, F. L. (1998). Adolescent sexual behavior, drug use, and violence: Increased reporting with computer survey technology. *Science, 280*, 867–873.

Vik, P. W., Brown, S. A., & Myers, M. G. (1997). Assessment of adolescent substance use problems. In E. J. Mash & L. G. Terdal (Eds.), *Assessment of Childhood Disorders*, 3rd ed., pp 717–748. New York: Guilford Press.

Warren, C., Kann, L., Small, M., Santelli, J., Collins, J., & Kolbe, L. (1997). Age of initiating selected health-risk behaviours among high school students in the United States. *Journal of Adolescent Health, 21*, 225–231.

Weber, L. R., Miracle, A., & Skehan, T. (1994). Interviewing early adolescents: Some methodological considerations. *Journal of Social and Applied Anthropology, 53*, 42–47.

Weinberg, N. Z., Rahdert, E., Collier, J. D., & Glantz, M. D. (1998). Adolescent substance abuse: A review of the past 10 years. *Journal of the American Academy of Child and Adolescent Psychiatry, 37*, 252–262.

Wiederman, M. W. & Pryor, T. (1996). Substance abuse among women with eating disorders. *Addictive Behavior, 21*, 269–272

Winters, K. C., Weller, C. L., & Meland, J. A. (1993). Extent of drug abuse among juvenile offenders. *Journal of Drug Issues, 23*, 515–524.

World Health Organization (1993). *International classification of mental and behavioral disorders.* Geneva: World Health Organization.

Index

Abstinence, 23, 235
Abuse, 27, 48, 101
Academic functioning, 80
Adolescence, 1, 4, 7, 10, 91, 227, 229
Adverse consequences, 30
Age-appropriateness, 230
Age of initiation, 8
Agreement estimates, 33
Alcohol, 24, 42–43, 47, 63, 77, 92, 97, 99, 123; abuse, 49, 75, 80, 170; consumption, 1; Dependence Syndrome, 35; dependent, 147; expectancies, 127; use, 6, 7
Alcoholics Anonymous, 123; -based substance abuse treatment, 122
American Psychiatric Association, 27
American Psychological Association, 201
Amphetamines, 34, 43, 63, 65, 70
Anger Coping Programme, 172
Annual prevalence, 64
Anticholinergic drugs, 71
Anti-drug messages, 185
Anti-drug saturation, 153
Antisocial behaviour, 80
Anxiety, 80
Anxiolytics, 63
Assessment, 36, 230–231
Assessment instrument, 36
Assessment of Liability and Exposure to Substance Use and Antisocial Behavior, 50–51
Australia, 71
Austria, 67

Barbiturates, 71
Behaviour genetics, 102
Behavioural dysregulation, 93

Behavioural Family Intervention, 172
Behavioural inhibition, 156

Cannabis, 43, 47, 63, 65, 78
Cannabis Youth Treatment Study, 202
CATEGO, 44
Chemical Abuse Treatment Outcome Registry (CATOR), 187
Child-rearing practice, 162
Children's Interview for Psychiatric Syndromes, 49
Cigarettes, 68, 92, 98–99
Classification, 21
Classification criteria for adolescents, 33
Classification systems, 21, 228
Client variables, 192
Clinical populations, 88
Clinical sample, 150
Clinical setting, 63
Club drug, 9, 64, 146
Cocaine, 8, 34, 43, 63, 70, 72
Codeine, 71
Cognitive problem solving skills training, 167
Cognitive restructuring techniques, 162
Community-based populations, 88
Community-dwelling adolescents, 127
Community reinforcement approach, 194
Comorbid, 5
Comorbid disorders, 78, 80
Comorbidity, 63, 77–78, 80, 127, 148, 150, 209, 227, 232
Conduct problem, 93, 150
Conduct Problems Prevention Research Group, 169
Coping Cat Workbook, 164
Coping Koala Prevention Programme, 164

Course and outcome, 119–134
Crack, 8
Craving, 30
Crime, 227
Criteria for intoxication, 30
Cross-cultural acceptability, 38, 44
Cross-cultural differences, 36
Cross-sectional studies, 89, 94, 231
Cut-off point, 154

Dance drug, 66
Delinquency, 209
Delinquent act, 13
Dependence, 23-24, 27, 30, 101; Diagnosis, 27
Depression, 170
Developmental phase, 156
Developmental psychopathology, 143–144, 147
Developmental stage, 230
Developmental trajectory, 155
Developmentally inappropriate, 144
Diagnostic agreement, 32; Classification scheme, 36
Diagnostic and Statistical Manual of Mental Disorders, 2, 27, 77; DSM-III, 22, 77; DSM-III-R, 34, 74; DSM-IV, 2–5, 22, 24–25, 34, 42, 43, 45–46, 155, 228
Diagnostic criteria, 22
Diagnostic instrument, 231
Diagnostic interview, 36; Adolescent Diagnostic Interview (ADI), 49; Alcohol Use Disorder and Associated Disabilities Interview Schedule-Alcohol/Drug-Revised (AUDADIS-ADR), 32, 38, 42–43, 45; Composite International Diagnostic Interview, 31, 38, 46; Diagnostic Interview for Children and Adolescents (DICA), 47–48; Diagnostic Interview Schedule, 73; Diagnostic Interview Schedule for Children, 73, 74; Diagnostic Interview Survey for Children (DISC), 48; Munich-Composite International Diagnostic Interview, 70; Schedules for Clinical Assessment in Neuropsychiatry (SCAN), 31, 38, 43–45, 74; Structured Clinical Interview for the DSM (SCID), 34, 46
Diagnostic orphan, 26

Diagnostic reliability, 37
Difficult temperament syndrome, 92
Direct modelling, 96
Discrepancy Interview Protocol, 38
Dual-diagnosis programmes, 192
Dyzygotic twin, 102

Ecstasy, 68
Edwards and Gross Alcohol Dependence Syndrome, 23
Empathy, 14
Enactment, 205
Environmental pressures, 185, 195
Environmental stress, 156
Epidemiologic surveys, 63; Bremen Adolescent Study, 70, 75, 78, 80; Christchurch Health and Developmental Study, 74; Dunedin Multidisciplinary Health and Developmental Study, 73–74; Early Development Stages of Psychopathology (EDSP), 70; Epidemiological Catchment Area study, 4, 39; Methods for the Epidemiology of Child and Adolescent Mental Disorders study, 48, 73; National Comorbidity Survey, 145, 150; Oregon Adolescent Depression Project, 72
Epidemiology, 231
Experience Sampling Method, 15
Externalizing disorder, 79, 93, 143, 150, 155, 157–158, 165

Familial aggregation, 91
Family-based therapy, 203–206, 208–210, 212, 214–217; cost-effectiveness, 217; Multidimensional Family Therapy (MDFT), 205, 210, 212–213; Multisystematic Therapy (MST), 205, 210–211
Family bonding, 205
Family cohesion, 210
Family drug behaviour, 148
Family environment, 148
Family functioning, 211
Family history of alcohol and drug problems, 97
Family management practices, 148
Family-related factor, 95
Family structure, 96
Feighner criteria, 39

First Step Programme, 168
Formal treatment programs, 186–187
France, 66

Gateway model, 233
Genetic markers, 91
Germany, 68-69, 75
Greece, 65

Hallucinogens, 34, 40, 43, 47, 78
"Hard" alcoholic drug, 69
Hard drugs, 67, 97
Harmful use, 30, 33, 35
Harmful use diagnoses, 30
Health-comprising behaviours, 16
Health-related problems, 9–10
Health Survey of England, 67
Helpfulness Rating Scale, 131
High-risk, 88–89
Hypnotics, 63

Illicit drug, 6, 7, 101, 227
Illicit substance, 66, 73
Infancy, 156
Information deficit model, 234
Inhalants, 34, 43, 47, 63–64; use, 8
Initiation, 7, 88
Intergenerational transmission of alcohol and drug use disorders, 91
Internalizing disorder, 79, 143, 150, 155, 157–158
International Classification of Diseases, 27, 228; ICD-10, 24–25, 34, 42, 43, 44, 228
International Statistical Classification of Diseases and Related Health Problems, 2
Interrater reliability, 47, 48
Intervention, 236 See also Treatment
Interview, 37
Israel, 66

Juvenile delinquency, 2
Juvenile justice programmes, 97

Kappa, 37, 48; estimates, 32, 49; reliability coefficients, 47

Lifetime prevalence, 6, 8
Longitudinal data, 16, 231
Longitudinal designs, 16, 89
Longitudinal studies, 89, 101, 121, 130

Maladaptive relationship patterns, 95
Marijuana, 7–8, 64–65, 68, 73, 92, 101, 146
Mental health functioning, 231
Mental health problems, 143, 194
Mental health promotion, 175
Michigan's Institute for Social Research, 145
Minnesota model, 187
Monozygotic twin, 102
Monitoring the Future Study, 6, 63–64, 145
Montreal Prevention Experiment, 168
Motivational enhancement, 194
Multi-determinism, 144, 147
Multi-focus preventive intervention, 162
Multiple indicators, 104
Multiple risk factor model, 104
Multi-site, multi-programme study, 189, 191

National Campaign Against Drug Abuse, 236
National Drug Strategy Survey, 71, 77
National Household Study on Drug Abuse, 6
National Institute on Alcoholism and Alcohol Abuse, 38, 42
National Parents' Resource Institute for Drug Education, 64
National Secondary School Students Drug Use Survey, 72
Natural recovery, 129
Netherlands, the, 74
New Zealand, 71–73
Nicotine, 63
Nomenclature, 21, 23, 26, 30, 33, 36, 41, 46, 51
No-treatment group, 191

Occasional use, 5
Opiate, 34
Opioids, 63; use, 70
Outcome, 123
Over-protective, 144

Painkillers, 72
Parent–child attachment, 95–96
Parent–child relationships, 144, 174
Parental model, 96

Parenting practices, 95
Peer: attitudes, 88, education approach, 234; influences, 94; models, 88; relationships, 5
Pennsylvania Depression Programme, 170
Perceived community support, 97
Personality deficit model, 236
Phencyclidine, 63
Physical assault, 97
Physiological criteria, 24
Physiological dependence, 24
Physiological symptoms, 34
Pictorial Instrument for Children and Adolescents, 50
Poor academic achievement, 97
Positive outcome, 132
Post-treatment, 121–122, 125–126, 190, 192, 195; outcome, 122
Prenatal infancy, 149
Prescription psychoactive medications, 40, 44
Present State Exam, 43–44
Pre-treatment, 190, 192
Prevalence, 5, 39, 63, 72, 74, 146
Prevalences of dependence diagnoses, 45
Prevention, 13, 143, 151, 154, 157, 158, 236; Demand reduction strategies, 151, 153; intervention, 162; programmes, 14; Supply reduction strategies, 151–152
Problem Behaviour Theory, 10, 80, 104, 107
Protective factors, 11, 103–104, 105, 110, 129, 143–144, 147, 148, 227, 231; index (PFI), 105–108
Psychiatric disorders, 47–49, 51, 74, 127; Agoraphobia, 78; Alcohol use disorder, 42–43, 79–80, 102; Amphetamines dependence, 45; Amphetamine disorders, 78; Antisocial personality disorder, 150; Anorexia nervosa, 232; Anxiety disorder, 170; Attention-Deficit/hyperactivity Disorder, 79, 154; Bulimia nervosa, 232; Cannabis dependence, 45; Cocaine dependence, 45; Conduct disorder, 93, 154; Conversion disorders, 78; Depressive disorders, 78; Disruptive behaviour disorder, 79; Dysthymia, 80; Dysthymic disorders, 78; Major depression, 78, 80; Obsessive-compulsive disorder, 78; Oppositional defiant disorder, 93, 154; Panic disorder, 78; Post-traumatic stress disorder, 78, 98; Social phobia, 78; Specific phobia, 78; Substance abuse, 2, 5, 72, 87–88, 120-121, 129, 235; Substance dependence, 26–27, 63, 72, 87, 101, 109, 119; Substance-related disorders, 72; Substance use dependence, 42; Substance use disorders, 2, 4, 21, 36, 48, 76–79, 101, 103, 143, 175, 233; Substance use-related disorder, 2, 21, 31; Undifferentiated somatoform disorder, 78
Psychoactive substances, dependence diagnosis, 27
Psychiatric symptoms, 50, 52
Psychological functioning, 105
Psychological traits, 10
Psychometric properties, 42
Psychosocial impairment, 80
Psychosocial model of substance use, 236
Psychosocial stressors, 49
Puberty, 1, 230

Questionnaires, 230

Raves/house parties, 66
Reckless behaviours, 1; driving, 1
Reduced substance use, 190
Reframing, 205
Reliability, 42–43, 226; estimates, 48
Research Diagnostic Criteria, 24
Resistance skills training, 143
Resourceful Adolescent Programme, 171
Risk factors, 10, 87–88, 90, 101, 105, 109, 144, 147–148, 205, 227, 231, 234; Biological-based, 90; Biological-genetic, 88; Contextual/societal factors, 148; Developmental risk factors, 149; Environmental factors, 5; Genetic-biological factors, 91; Individual risk factors, 88; Negative life events, 97, 98, 108; Peer-related factors, 94; Physiological factors, 148; Psychological factors, 92, 148; School- and community-related factors, 96; Stressful life events, 231
Risk factor index (RFI), 99–100, 106–108

Index

Risk-taking, 1, 9–11, 15–16, 93
Rutter Child Scales, 73

School-based: education programmes, 153; programmes, 173; support networks, 237; universal prevention of depression programme, 173
School curriculum, 236
Seattle Social Development Project, 172
Sedative, 43, 46, 63
Selective programmes, 172
Self-control, 93
Self-efficacy, 14
Self-report, 231
Semi-structured interview, 49
Sensation seeking, 93
Sense of compulsion, 30
Sexual abuse, 97
Social competence, 143
Social ecological theory, 205
Social functioning, 52
Social skill training, 14, 143, 153, 165–166, 175, 194
"Soft" alcoholic drug, 69
Soft drugs, 67
Spain, 65, 74
Stress Inoculation Training Programmes, 170
Subthreshold, 26
Suicide, 2, 170
Substance, 63
Substance Abuse and Mental Health Services Administration, 6–8
Substance Abuse Module (SAM), 39–42
Substance abusers, 185
Substance-abusing adolescents, 128
Substance intoxication, 30
Substance misuse, 2, 34, 50, 63
Substance-related problems, 27
Substance-specific intoxication diagnoses, 27
Substance-specific syndrome, 30
Substance-specific withdrawal criteria, 27
Substance use, 2, 4, 9, 11–12, 63, 90, 93, 98, 126, 143, 185, 233; classification, 36
Substance withdrawal, 29
Sustained abstinence, 187

Temperament, 92, 93; predisposition, 157
Temporal sequence of disorders, 77
Test–retest, 47; reliability, 48
Therapist adherence, 210
Tobacco, 92
Toddler – late childhood, 149
Tolerance, 24, 29
Tranquillizers, 42, 65
Treatment, 234; Classroom-centred intervention, 165; Cognitive-behavioural therapy, 193–194; Family therapy, 14, 193; Group therapy, 14; Hospital-based treatment, 97; Individual therapy, 14; Parent-focused interventions, 166; Parent interventions, 167; Parent training, 167; Parental involvement, 163; Parental monitoring skills, 210; Peer-led intervention, 236; Psychoeducational drug counseling, 209; Psychological intervention, 185
Treatment effectiveness, 188–189
Treatment outcome, 36
Treatment Outcome Prospective Study (TOPS), 187
Treatment samples, 120

United Kingdom, 66
United States, 63, 72, 147
Universal prevention intervention, 165
Universal prevention programme, 160

Validity, 49, 226
Violent victimization, 97
Vulnerability, 101, 103, 234

Wait control, 191
Wait-list control, 170
Withdrawal criterion, 24–25
"Withdrawal-gate" dependence, 25
Withdrawal symptoms, 35
Withdrawal syndrome, 51
World Health Organization, 27, 31, 38, 143

Youth Risk Behavior Survey, 64